AF841809
054998

Cognitive Science

Series Editors:
Marc M. Sebrechts
Gerhard Fischer
Peter M. Fischer

David S. Gorfein
Editor

Resolving Semantic Ambiguity

With 26 Illustrations

Springer-Verlag
New York Berlin Heidelberg
London Paris Tokyo

David S. Gorfein
Department of Psychology
Adelphi University
Garden City, NY 11530
USA

Library of Congress Cataloging-in-Publication Data
Resolving semantic ambiguity / David S. Gorfein, editor.
p. cm. — (Cognitive science)
Bibliography: p.
Includes index.
ISBN 0-387-96906-3 (alk. paper)
1. Ambiguity. 2. Semantics. I. Gorfein, David S. II. Series:
Cognitive science (New York, N.Y.)
P325.5.A46R47 1989
415—dc19 88-39483

Printed on acid-free paper.

© 1989 by Springer-Verlag New York Inc.
All rights reserved. This work may not be translated or copied in whole or in part without the written permission of the publisher (Springer-Verlag, 175 Fifth Avenue, New York, NY 10010, USA), except for brief excerpts in connection with reviews or scholarly analysis. Use in connection with any form of information storage and retrieval, electronic adaptation, computer software, or by similar or dissimilar methodology now known or hereafter developed is forbidden.
The use of general descriptive names, trade names, trademarks, etc. in this publication, even if the former are not especially identified, is not to be taken as a sign that such names, as understood by the Trade Marks and Merchandise Marks Act, may accordingly be used freely by anyone.

Typeset by Digitype, Inc., Blue Ridge Summit, Pennsylvania
Printed and bound by Edwards Brothers, Inc., Ann Arbor, Michigan.
Printed in the United States of America.

9 8 7 6 5 4 3 2 1

ISBN 0-387-96906-3 Springer-Verlag New York Berlin Heidelberg
ISBN 3-540-96906-3 Springer-Verlag Berlin Heidelberg New York

Preface

In any finite period of time, research workers hotly pursue the answers to important questions and design new studies which they believe will elucidate the processes in question. Too often, the current research lends the investigation in new directions and to new problems sometimes at a microscopic level. At such times, it is helpful to pause in the process to reflect on the goals of the research and to seek the wisdom of one's peers. The opportunity for such reflection is limited. Only at meetings of national scope can we hope to find a number of those whose work has immediate implications for our problems and who can speak from a background of similar experience. Even then our time is often limited by our need to hear the latest in the paper sessions and often to communicate our own ideas. Our opportunity to interact is often limited by the nature of the meeting in that professional meetings are often disciplinary and our research topic may be interdisciplinary. Therefore, we at Adelphi University decided several years ago that our faculty and graduate students as well as the research community would be well served if we periodically hosted focused research conferences in the areas of faculty specialization. This book represents the third such effort on our part following a broad conference on memory and a more focused conference on subjective contours (cf. Gorfein & Hoffman, 1987; Petry & Meyer, 1987).

The purpose of the conference on the resolution of semantic ambiguity held in April of 1988 was twofold. One was to bring together a cross section of senior and younger investigators of ambiguity to provide the pause to reflect and examine the scope of the enterprise. A second purpose was to put down in one place a sample of the current thought in the field to allow new investigators a basic foundation on which to build their research enterprise. Thus, from the beginning, it was agreed there would be a book from the conference and that the book would reflect both the ideas of the individual researchers and through colloquy the sense of their interactions.

Some History

The editor of this volume came to the problem of semantic ambiguity and its resolution by an indirect path. In an attempt to understand the problem of proactive interference in short-term memory (STM), the question was raised as to the adaptive nature of forgetting in such a brief period (6–30 seconds). Intuitively, this seemed maladaptive. When we noticed the parallel between the trial-by-trial nature of STM and the conditions of priming in semantic memory, we developed an idea, the "set principle" (Gorfein, 1987; Gorfein & Viviani, 1981), which suggested that proactive interference in STM was the negative side of a coin (a mechanism) that promoted communication in conversation and text. In an attempt to test those ideas, homographs became a material of convenience. Once we got into these materials as a tool, the rest followed. In early December of 1986, I decided that my work would benefit by an airing of my ideas with a group devoted to the problems of ambiguity resolution. I had been very impressed by a review article by Greg Simpson that had appeared in 1984 (Simpson, 1984). Other researchers had impressed me in my readings. I wrote to a number of the principal investigators, inviting them to participate in a conference to be held at Adelphi in the spring of 1988 and asked them to nominate other participants. The group that assembled at Adelphi for the conference was the product of that advice, my choices, and the circumstances that make some people available and others unavailable. The conference was a mixture of formal paper presentations and colloquia (topical discussions). Extended versions of the papers appear in this book, as well as attempts to reflect the flavor of the colloquia. The participants report that they were stimulated. It is hoped that this book will stimulate others.

References

Gorfein, D. S., & Hoffman, R. R. (Eds.) (1987). *Memory and Learning: The Ebbinghaus Centennial Conference.* Hillsdale, NJ: Erlbaum.

Petry, S., & Meyer, G. E. (Eds.) (1987). *The perception of illusory contours.* New York: Springer-Verlag.

Acknowledgments

In my planning the conference and in preparing this book, I benefited from the help of a number of people. The conference participant choice was improved a great deal by the advice of Dr. Michael Tanenhaus. Dr. Kenneth Forster called my attention to Graeme Hirst, whose wisdom and perspective is reflected in his chapter as well as in the colloquy. All of the participants argued well and long. Tram Neill of my own department helped raise many of the questions addressed. Robert Hoffman was drafted to moderate a session and took over many of the onerous chores (audiovisual, etc.) associated with a conference. He also helped clarify the issues (see Chapter 11).

The research and the ideas expressed in my part of this volume are the outcome of much hard work by my students. The single strongest influence came from Andrea Bubka, who has tirelessly debated every issue with me. Her insatiable appetite for more data is thoroughly congenial to mine, and together we have produced much more data than can be reported in a single chapter (or volume). Chapter 7 is filled with her studies and studies she influenced.

Each of the chapters in this volume has been thoroughly discussed by members of our graduate seminar on the resolution of separate ambiguity. Tram Neill co-led this seminar, whose participants in alphabetical order included Jean Beck, Stephanie Berger, Andrea Bubka, Dr. Marjorie Caplan, Elizabeth-Anne Cooper, David Griese, Scott Lissner, Ruth McShane, Reuben Molloy, Steve Siegel, Andrea Spata, Claire Virgile, and Jeanne Viviani. They all make excellent sounding boards for the ideas expressed, and it is not at all unlikely that some of them will contribute to the forthcoming literature on ambiguity.

Organizing a conference requires a fair amount of work. The secretaries in the Department of Psychology: Eleanor Shaw and Pat Carey, did a major part of this work. They, together with Angela Mavaro, handled this manuscript. Without them there would be no book. A number of students served as gofers in bringing participants to and from the airport. I wish to acknowledge Stephanie Berger, Andrea Bubka, Elizabeth-Anne Cooper, David Griese, and Ruth McShane for their help in this regard.

A conference of this scope is not possible without funds. Our experience with federal agencies is that conferences are particularly subject to the whims of individual reviewers, and despite their modest cost, are unlikely to be funded. (This may be "sour grapes," but a comparison of reviews suggests that the word *whim* is not a bad choice.) That this conference happened at all then is through the generosity of Adelphi University. In particular, the funds for this conference were made available by Adelphi President, Dr. Peter Diamandopoulos, who truly believes that the purpose of a university is to promote knowledge. Dr. Diamandopoulos's contribution was not limited to money. He made possible the use of the Adelphi University's Alumni House as a conference center; assigned his assistant Dr. Carl Rhines to smoothe things; and allowed his secretary, Ruth McShane, herself a Ph.D. candidate in psychology, the time to do the things only a President's office can do and only a person as capable as Ms. McShane does seemingly easily. Dr. Diamanadopoulos is clearly a good friend of psychology.

David S. Gorfein

Contents

Contributors

(Affiliations are those at time of conference. Current addresses are cited where they have changed).

LAWRENCE W. BARSALOU, Department of Psychology, Georgia Institute of Technology, Alanta, Georgia 30332, USA

DORRIT BILLMAN, Department of Psychology, University of Pennsylvania, Philadelphia, Pennsylvania 19104, Current: Department of Psychology, Georgia Institute of Technology, Atlanta, Georgia 30332, USA

ANDREA BUBKA, Department of Psychology, Adelphi University, Garden City, New York 11530, Current: Department of Psychology, Vassar College, Poughkeepsie, New York 12601, USA

MATTHEW B. CLARK, Department of Psychology, Washington State University, Pullman, Washington 99164, USA

KENNETH I. FORSTER, Department of Psychology, University of Arizona, Tucson, Arizona 85721, USA

DAVID S. GORFEIN, Department of Psychology, Adelphi University, Garden City, New York 11530, USA

GRAEME HIRST, Department of Computer Science, University of Toronto, Toronto, Ontario, Canada M5S 1A5

ROBERT R. HOFFMAN, Department of Psychology, Adelphi University, Garden City, New York 11530, USA

GEORGE KELLAS, Child Language Program, University of Kansas, Lawrence, Kansas 66045, USA

RICHARD M. KLEIN, Department of Psychology, Adelphi University, Garden City, New York 11530, USA

PENNY PRATHER, Boston V. A. Medical Center, and Boston University School of Medicine, Boston, Massachusetts 02115, USA

GREG B. SIMPSON, Department of Psychology, University of Nebraska at Omaha, Omaha, Nebraska 68182, USA

MARILYN CHAPNIK SMITH, Department of Psychology, Scarborough College, University of Toronto, Toronto, Ontario, Canada M5S 1A5

DAVID SWINNEY, The Graduate Center, City University of New York, New York, New York 10036, USA

PATRIZIA TABOSSI, Department of Psychology, University of Bologna, Bologna, Italy

W. TRAMMELL NEILL, Department of Psychology, Adelphi University, Garden City, New York 11530, USA

MARIANNE F. WALTERS, Department of Psychology, Adelphi University, Garden City, New York 11530, USA

PAUL WHITNEY, Department of Psychology, Washington State University, Pullman, Washington 99164, USA

Part I Introduction

Chapter 1 sets a historical context for the problems addressed in the book and features a critique of the data base on which we build our theories. This chapter also gives an overview of the book.

In Chapter 2, Simpson addresses the question of where in "real life" one deals with semantic ambiguity. He points to the ubiquity of ambiguity and presents the case for studying ambiguity, whether of words or sentences.

1

Resolving Semantic Ambiguity: An Introduction

ANDREA BUBKA AND DAVID S. GORFEIN

What processes allow a person to know that the statement "I'm blue" usually means that a person is feeling sad rather than the person is the color blue? Or that on the sports page the headline "All tied up" refers to the same number of games or points achieved by some sport's teams, rather than someone being entwined in rope? Or that in a gambling casino, the request "Hit me" is a request for cards and not violence? Or that the question "What would you say to an omelet?" does not usually warrant the reply "Bonjour, omelet"?

In each of these examples, only one conscious interpretation comes to mind. The interesting problem of investigation for the study of ambiguity processing is how does a person arrive at the intended meaning for an ambiguity?

As these few examples have shown, ambiguity is everywhere. Whether resolving the meaning of a homograph or of a few words which when arranged together produce ambiguity, the disambiguating process occurs rapidly and usually results in little confusion. By understanding the principles involved in resolving ambiguity, we can further develop an understanding of achieving meaning in general in word recognition and ultimately understand the mechanisms embodied in the organization of memory itself. (See also Chapter 2 by Simpson.)

Since ambiguities are comprehended in such a way that the intended meaning is chosen, it would seem that under the appropriate circumstances, there is no ambiguity. However, several investigators have in fact found ambiguity to affect comprehension processing, even in constrained contexts. By including an ambiguous word in a sentence, processing of that sentence is slowed (MacKay, 1966). Using the phoneme monitoring task, in which a subject presses a key when a particular phoneme is detected, sentence processing again requires longer processing when an ambiguous word is included in the sentence (e.g., Cairns & Kamerman, 1975; Foss, 1970; Foss & Jenkins, 1973). These results were not attributed to slower lexical access for ambiguous words; rather in the investigators' view, in the presence of an ambiguous word, both meanings are unconsciously accessed and one of the meanings is then selected for consciousness. Swinney and Hakes (1976) did find, however, that under strongly biased contextual conditions, an ambiguous word acted like an unambiguous word. These results suggest that context is an important influence in ambiguity processing, but does not determine completely how a person arrives at the intended meaning of an ambiguity.

The study of semantic ambiguity involves analyzing the states and processes that occur before, during, and after an ambiguous word or sentence is experienced. The states that we refer to are those in which a meaning has been achieved. The processes by which meaning is achieved have been elaborated by a number of theorists. These ambiguity resolution processes are investigated by measuring performance on a task in which the state (achievement of meaning) is examined.

Before an ambiguous word or sentence is experienced, a contextual situation may affect the states and processes that occur. The states and processes involved in a primed and unprimed experience may or may not be the same, depending on your theoretical beliefs. Many theorists believe that context is an important influence in resolving ambiguities, so much so that the ambiguity in a situation goes unrecognized, consciously and unconsciously.

Theorists have not agreed upon the processes that occur during and after the experience of a homograph. Simpson (1984) reviewed three process models which will be briefly discussed here, along with two other models which were proposed subsequent to that review.

Lexical-Access Models

The major lexical-access models reviewed by Simpson are the exhaustive-access, context-dependent, and ordered-access models. The frequency-ordered search model and the activation-suppression model also will be considered. The models differ in the roles that context and polarity play in access, and also in the number of meanings that are achieved as a result of the access process. Each model has received experimental support. Therefore, interpretation of the data as well as analysis of experimental designs shall be examined in order to understand the literature. In Table 1.1, a brief description of the five lexical-access models for ambiguity processing is presented.

The exhaustive or multiple-access theorists (e.g., Onifer & Swinney, 1981) postulate that when a homograph is encountered, all meanings are accessed. After all the meanings have been retrieved, the appropriate meaning is selected, based on context, and the inappropriate meanings are no longer available. Variations on the model have the context-inappropriate meaning suppressed or simply dissipate passively over time. For the meaning achieved the outcome is the same; the inappropriate meaning is not available.

TABLE. 1.1. Lexical-access models.

Model	Context effect
Exhaustive or multiple access (Onifer & Swinney, 1981; Seidenberg, Tanenhaus, Leiman, & Bienkowski, 1982) When an ambiguous word is encountered, all meanings are accessed.	There is no effect of context initially. Postaccess process: After all meanings have been retrieved, the appropriate meaning is selected, based on context, and the inappropriate meaning is no longer available.
Context-dependent (Glucksberg, Kreuz, & Rho, 1986; Schvaneveldt, Meyer, & Becker, 1976; Simpson, 1981)	Context directs access completely. In the absence of context, the primary meaning will be accessed.
Ordered access (Forster & Bednall, 1976; Hogaboam & Perfetti, 1975) Since most ambiguous words have meanings that are not equal in frequency, the most dominant meaning is accessed first. It is a serial, self-terminating search.	The order of access is not influenced by context. If the primary meaning does not fit the context, the secondary meaning will be accessed after the primary meaning.
Context-sensitive frequency (Bubka, 1988; Gorfein & Bubka, 1985) Meanings are sought in parallel, but frequency of meanings affects which meaning is achieved. The primary meaning usually achieves meaning, and the secondary meaning is not available. This process is task-dependent. In order to complete some tasks, the secondary meaning will have to be accessed.	Context facilitates the process. Presenting a secondary context can alter the access to the secondary meaning, making it more similar to the primary meaning.
Activation-suppression (Neill, this volume; Neill, Hilliard, & Cooper, 1988) Multiple meanings may be activated in parallel by an ambiguous word. Access is determined by strength of association to the ambiguous word and strength of association to its context.	Retrieval is not completely determined by context. Rather, it is context-sensitive so that context can facilitate lexical access. The context-inappropriate meanings are suppressed. In the absence of context, the secondary meanings are suppressed.

Reaction time has been measured in the lexical-decision task, among others, in order to analyze which meanings of a homograph have been accessed. In a lexical decision, the task is to decide if a string of letters is a word or a nonword. Employing the cross-modal task, a visual letter string is presented following the occurrence of a homograph in an aurally presented sentence. A number of investigators (Onifer & Swinney, 1981; Swinney, 1979; Tanenhaus & Donnenwerth-Nolan, 1984) have found that a homograph in a sentence context, followed by a long stimulus onset asynchrony (SOA), primes lexical decision only when the target word is related to the context. The unprimed meaning is not available. Under short

SOA conditions, investigators have found that both meanings are about equally available, in that primary- and secondary-meaning lexical-decision items are responded to equally fast. Such results support the exhaustive-access model.

According to the context-dependent theory (Glucksberg, Kreuz, & Rho, 1986; Schvaneveldt, Meyer, & Becker, 1976; Simpson, 1981), context directs access completely. In the absence of context, Schvaneveldt et al. (1976) found that access is frequency-sensitive; the primary meaning is the most probable meaning to be accessed. Glucksberg and colleagues (Gildea & Glucksberg, 1984; Glucksberg et al., 1986) report that a sentence context intended to bias a meaning of a homograph created expectancy effects, since nonword targets in a lexical decision showed inhibition effects (i.e., longer reaction times) due to the similarity of the nonwords to the expected targets (nonwords were the target words used in the experiment with a single letter changed). (However, see Swinney and Prather, Chapter 12, in this volume.) Results of this type have led the context-dependent theorists to believe that context not only facilitates lexical access, but is the driving process of such access.

While the context-dependent process depends on context entirely, and the exhaustive-access process is influenced by context upon the completion of retrieving all meanings, the ordered-access theorists hypothesize that initial access is not influenced by context at all. Instead, they hypothesize that the most dominant meaning is accessed first. According to the ordered-access theorists (Forster & Bednall, 1976; Hogaboam & Perfetti, 1975), lexical access occurs in a serial, self-terminating process. The order of access is not affected by context, but the context will affect termination of the process of meaning access. If the primary meaning does not fit the context, the secondary meaning will be accessed after the primary meaning.

Data support of some form of the ordered-access model comes from investigations (Cooper, Gorfein, & Bubka, 1988; Forster & Bednall, 1976; Hogaboam & Perfetti, 1975) employing the ambiguity detection task, in which participants indicate whether a letter string is ambiguous. In effect, participants are forced to seek out more than one meaning. Detection decisions are shortest when the context (in the form of a sentence or single word) is biased toward the secondary meaning. When a primary-meaning context is presented, the longer reaction times (with respect to control reaction times in which the context is unrelated to the target word) indicate that it is difficult to access the secondary meaning. The high error rate for the primary primed items suggests that participants are not accessing any other meaning. However, when homographs are balanced, there are no differences in decisions when preceded by primary- and secondary-meaning contexts. There should not be any differences at this level since the labels *primary* and *secondary* are arbitrary when homographs are balanced.

Onifer and Swinney (1981) claim that ambiguity detection is a postperceptual task. They assert that all meanings are activated immediately, but by the time the ambiguity decision is being processed, the inappropriate meaning has already been suppressed. Their argument is that since processing time occurs rapidly, the ambiguity decision results may not reflect the initial activation of both meanings; rather only post-access processing may be detected.

This question of preaccess and postaccess processing has been a main obstacle to understanding ambiguity processing. There have been interpretation problems, in that lexical access may occur in a series of steps according to one set of theorists (i.e., exhaustive access), in which all meanings are first accessed and then context allows the selection of a meaning; or it may occur in only one step according to other sets of theorists (i.e., context-dependent), in which only one meaning is accessed, although the final outcome may be the same. Unfortunately, many of the experimental tasks used in the investigation of ambiguity processing, such as ambiguity detection, have been considered inappropriate by the exhaustive-access theorists since the preaccess processing cannot be easily measured. That is, by the time an ambiguity decision is measured, the exhaustive access of meanings has already come and gone, with the context-appropriate meaning remaining. This result may give the false impression that only one meaning was ever accessed initially.

The frequency-ordered search theory (Bubka, 1988; Gorfein & Bubka, 1985) postulates that the polarity of a homograph and context determine which meaning is achieved during lexical access. The meanings of a homograph are sought in parallel with the most frequent meaning being achieved for an unbalanced homograph, in the absence of a context. For balanced homographs, either meaning may be achieved. In both cases, after a meaning is reached, the search is terminated, unless the task specifically requires that both meanings be found.

Related primes or a related context facilitates access in that view. Priming a balanced homograph may alter the achievement of meaning so that the primed meaning would be accessed. Priming an unbalanced homograph with a secondary meaning (the less frequent meaning) may affect the achievement of meaning (i.e., the secondary meaning is achieved), depending on the strength of the context and the polarity of the homograph.

For some tasks (e.g., lexical decision), only one meaning is necessary for performance, which will usually be the most frequent meaning. The primary meaning could be achieved even when a secondary-meaning prime is presented, since the achievement of either meaning produces a "yes" response. In summary, polarity determines which meaning is achieved. Depending on the task, context will facilitate the process and interact with polarity to influence the achievement of meaning.

A fifth model, the activation-suppression model (Neill, this volume; Neill, Hilliard, & Cooper, 1988), is similar to the ordered-access model and the frequency-ordered search model in that the polarity of homographs is considered to be an important variable for lexical access. The activation-suppression model is also a race model in that multiple meanings may be activated in parallel by an ambiguous word. While the frequency-ordered search model predicts that the search ends when one meaning is accessed, the activation-suppression model postulates that the other meanings may still be achieved over time. In this manner, access is exhaustive. However, unlike the exhaustive-access theorists who believe that multiple meanings are accessed before any other processing can occur, the proponents of the activation-suppression model believe in a variant of exhaustive access in that other processing can occur after a single meaning is accessed. The lexical-access process is task-dependent. A lexical decision, in which one meaning is necessary to produce a decision, can be completed after one meaning is accessed, although eventually the other meanings may be accessed. The model is context-sensitive in that context may facilitate the lexical access. The strength of association to the ambiguous word and the context work together to determine lexical access.

Difficulties in Studying Access

In reviewing the literature, a number of problems in interpretation arise. Simpson (1984) also raises a number of similar issues. We would briefly like to present the sources of our misgivings.

1. Difficulties due to signal averaging. A typical study employs a homograph as a prime (e.g., Simpson & Burgess, 1985) or a homograph embedded in text with the sentence context serving as a prime (Onifer & Swinney, 1981) and follows the homograph with a word related to one of its meanings. A word, usually matched for frequency, is employed as a comparison. If the comparison word is decided upon more slowly than the primed meaning, we say that a particular meaning has been achieved. The averaging nature of the process makes this conclusion problematic. At the extreme, all we know is that one or more individuals out of the *N* individuals on whom an item is tested, or one or more items out of the *N* items tested, have achieved a meaning sufficient to support priming. In short, in a situation in which priming is achieved, we do not know how often each meaning is achieved. It is notable that while Holley-Wilcox and Blank (1980) provided a technique for estimating the amount of priming, essentially by presenting a second control to estimate maximum priming, their significant contribution to methodology has largely been ignored (perhaps because it doubles the labor for investigators).

Even the Holley-Wilcox and Blank procedure can lead to some ambiguity of interpretation. Specifically, in their study a homograph prime, CHANGE, is followed by an alternative related to one of its meanings, COINS, which is the target for lexical decision. Two controls are used, a re-paired control like PITCHER-COINS and a highly related control like

DIMES-COINS. Thus, for some priming to be in evidence, a pair like CHANGE-COINS must be responded to faster than PITCHER-COINS. Given this event, complete priming is evidenced when the pair CHANGE-COINS produces a decision as fast as DIMES-COINS, the highly related pair. In their results, both meanings of *equiprobable* homographs were facilitated (were faster than the reprimed control) and the facilitation did not significantly differ from that of the highly related control. However, the latter result is a null hypothesis confirmation, and if we examine the appropriate means, we see that on the average the highly related pairs show 49-ms facilitation while the homograph related pair shows only 39-ms facilitation, 20% less facilitation.

2. Strategic effects. Most studies in attempting to evaluate the dual-access nature of homograph processing are susceptible to the criticism that the results are interpretable as due to a strategy in which the participant, realizing that either meaning of an ambiguous entry may occur in any context, may attempt to actively prepare for either meaning. To discourage such a strategy, a number of studies have used variations of the Stroop task (e.g., Conrad, 1974; Seidenberg, Tanenhaus, Leiman, & Bienkowski, 1982) as the priming task, as preparing both meanings in this task is potentially deleterious to one's performance. However, this approach will only work under the assumption that the participant can detect the small negative effect of the target on color naming.

A counterargument to the strategic explanation is the effect of stimulus onset asynchrony in tasks such as the cross-modal priming task (e.g., Onifer & Swinney, 1981). In those studies, the data appear to support a process in which both meanings of a homophone are available initially, but the meaning inappropriate to the context is no longer present (perhaps inhibited or suppressed) after 1.5 seconds. This conclusion needs to be more fully tested, as it is conceivable to the present authors that neither meaning is present 1.5 seconds posthomograph, but the sentence context alone may be sufficient to prime a context-appropriate meaning. In the cross-modal task, a control condition in which a white noise blip was substituted for the homograph might resolve both the strategic hypothesis and the temporal effect.

3. Conclusions often depend on the theory of the task. The presentation of an ambiguity in some task such as a lexical decision leads to a performance on the part of a participant. Unfortunately most tasks are not transparent with respect to which meaning has been achieved. Many of our conclusions are therefore based on theories of the tasks in which the materials of interest are processed. These conclusions then are susceptible to alteration as the theory of the task charges. Such a change in theory has occurred for lexical decision with a consequent change in our conclusions about lexical access (cf. Simpson, 1984). This suggests that a variety of approaches need to be taken and consistencies sought. Inconsistencies across tasks have a smaller probability of helping, as interpretations of the differences between performance access tasks then become dependent on the theories of the tasks. (See Neill's comments on word naming in Chapter 6 of this volume.)

4. Characteristics of the materials employed. Two characteristics of homographs would seem on an a priori basis to be related to access of lexical entries: frequency and polarity. By frequency, we refer to the frequency of the letter string qua letter string, not as the possessor of a particular meaning. Thus, such frequency counts as those of Thorndike-Lorge (1943) and Kucera-Francis (1967) are indifferent to meaning and reflect the occurrence of the letter string in print. By polarity of a homograph, we mean the frequency with which a particular meaning is elicited from participants in such tasks as word association (Gorfein, Viviani, & Leddo, 1982; Nelson, McEvoy, Walling, & Wheeler, 1980; Perfetti, Lindsay, & Garson, 1971). Thus, on the average, some homographs produce a relatively equal probability of one or the other association; for example, the homograph CHANGE is as likely to elicit the meaning *coins* as it is the meaning *to alter*. Other homographs have widely discrepant probabilities of producing each of their meanings; for example, in the Adelphi norms, DIAMOND produces associations as a *gem* most of the time and rarely produces associations related to *baseball infield*. A homograph where the two meanings are relatively unbalanced is said to be highly polarized, and that meaning that occurs most often is said to be the *primary*, or *dominant*, meaning. The meaning that occurs less often in associations is called the *secondary* meaning. (The word *dominance* is often substituted for the word *polarity*.)

It should be recognized that the two terms, *frequency* and *polarity*, are meant to be orthogonal in what they describe. A high-frequency homograph occurs at a specified rate, such as above 50 per million in the Kucera-Francis count, while a highly polarized homograph is one that produces unequal associations with respect to its multiple meanings. Thus, in our norms the homograph SEASON with a Kucera-Francis frequency of 105 has a polarity score of .98, while the homograph POKER with an identical polarity occurs only 6 times per million in the frequency norms.

Very few researchers have tested the range of polarity but confine their work to some limited range such as *balanced* (e.g., Holley-Wilcox, & Blank, 1980) or above 75% polarity or 85–95% polarity (Neill et al., 1988). Many studies make use of local norms that are based on a handful of individuals, such as norming populations of 25 (e.g., Onifer & Swinney, 1981), and therefore do not consider the large standard error of their scores on individual homographs. Only a few studies examine the interaction of word frequency and polarity (Forster & Bednall, 1976; Hogaboam & Perfetti, 1975). The question of how frequency and polarity interact seems to us to be a crucial question for those who intend to offer a theory of homograph processing. (See Chapter 7, by Gorfein and Bubka, in this volume for some additional evidence with respect to this point.)

The Contents of This Volume

The purpose of the Semantic Ambiguity Conference and this volume is (1) to review the major lexical-access models and models of representation, (2) to discuss the requirements of valid experimental tasks for lexical access, and (3) to analyze what we have gained from this investigation and where it is leading. This book is divided into five parts. Part I includes this chapter's introduction to the study of semantic ambiguity and Simpson's chapter on varieties of ambiguity in Chapter 2.

In Part II, Lexical Access and Post-Access Processing, the focus is on the processes that occur to resolve ambiguity when an ambiguous word is encountered. Tabossi, in Chapter 3, begins the section with an analysis of the effect of context on lexical access. She is concerned with the problem of whether lexical access occurs independently of context or whether context influences the process. Tabossi also discusses the controversy of whether the cognitive system is modular or interactive and how research on the effect of context can aid in interpreting structure.

In Chapter 4, Simpson and Kellas concentrate on the characteristics of context that determine lexical access. In a study of repetition effects of homographs under different context conditions, they argue that a postaccess process leads to a relatively long suppression of the context-inappropriate meaning.

Gorfein and Walters, in Chapter 5, present a repetition study of homophones in which an original effect of context is found. They show that the first meaning that is achieved for a homophone has persisting effects that are inconsistent with a suppression view of the repetition effect.

Neill, in Chapter 6, employs selective attention, lexical ambiguity, and visual masking studies in order to develop an activation-suppression model. The model addresses lexical access in ambiguity but emphasizes postaccess suppression effects. The model is generalized to overall human information processing.

In Chapter 7, Gorfein and Bubka provide evidence for the importance of the frequency of meanings of ambiguous words in determining meaning achievement. A general word recognition model that includes an analysis of ambiguity effects is also described. Their model can also be considered a representational theory, indicating the closeness of the issues of access and representation.

Part III, Representation, details the characteristics and structure of ambiguity in the lexicon. It begins with a chapter by Smith (Chapter 8), who employs a repetition priming paradigm to examine representation in the bilingual. She is interested in whether one lexicon—a language-free conceptual representation—exists or whether a separate independent lexicon exists for each language.

In Chapter 9, Forster describes how ambiguity could be represented in the lexicon. Investigating frequency effects in terms of a lexical search theory, Forster contemplates a separate-entries model, i.e., a separate entry for each meaning of a homograph versus a single entry for all meanings to be represented.

Barsalou and Billman complete the conference papers in this section (Chapter 10). Their paper discusses representation in terms of the systematicity that exists in long-term memory. In essence, they seek to extend an understanding of strong ambiguity, i.e., homographs and homophones, to weak semantic ambiguity, i.e., to explain how "senses" of words are achieved.

At the conference in our colloquy sections, it quickly became evident that there was much ambiguity in our theoretical and data language. Chapter 11 offers a review of the issues raised in the discussions at the conference. Hoffman, who led one of the discussions, attempts to refocus the theorizing by offering language that avoids the problems of inconsistency of terminology that tend to make theoretical issues ambiguous.

Processes that occur beyond the lexical level of ambiguity processing for individual words constitute the topic of Part IV, Ambiguity in Text. A more natural situation in which ambiguity occurs is in sentence form rather than in individual polysemous words. In Chapter 12, Swinney and Prather focus on the problem of whether modularity in lexical processing is innate or whether it is a result of a developmental process. Whitney and Clark, in Chapter 13, concentrate on how ambiguity that is broadly conceived is resolved through contextual aspects of the sentence, which the authors refer to as *cognitive control.*

Part V, the last section of the book, represents an overview. In Chapter 14, Hirst discusses the relevance of ambiguity research to the development of computer programs for understanding language processing. While linguists and psycholinguists study ambiguity processing from an overall language perspective, the cognitivists' goal is to understand the interaction between words and meanings. The role of the computational linguists is to apply the different fields' results in the form of computer programs. Through Hirst's viewpoint, we see how the study of ambiguity processing has affected the related areas of what we refer to as *cognitive science.*

Finally, in Chapter 15 we close with a review of a major issue raised in the conference and in subsequent discussions—that of connectionism and modularity. Neill and Klein attempt to show the historical roots of these issues and raise the question of how these approaches relate to the data base of the field.

2

Varieties of Ambiguity: What Are We Seeking?

GREG B. SIMPSON

For the past 20 years or so, psycholinguists and computer scientists have become increasingly interested in the problem of ambiguity in natural language processing. For psycholinguists, the work has focused largely on understanding the processes by which people arrive at a single interpretation of a message that has at least two readily discernible meanings. Sentences 1–3 give some classic examples of the kinds of sentences whose comprehension might be of interest in studies of this kind.

1. The men decided to wait by the bank.
2. Visiting relatives can be a nuisance.
3. The shooting of the hunters was terrible.

These examples, or others just like them, can be found in any psycholinguistics text. Sentence 1 illustrates lexical ambiguity: Its two meanings derive from the fact that one of the words it contains has more than one meaning (the men might be standing near a financial institution or next to a body of water). Sentence 2 represents an example of syntactic or surface-structure ambiguity. The sentence may be parsed in two ways, paraphrased roughly as "When you visit relatives, it is a nuisance," and "When relatives visit, they are a nuisance." The third sentence is also ambiguous, despite the fact that it does not contain any obviously ambiguous words and allows only a single surface-structure representation. The ambiguity in this case arises because of different possible relationships among deep-structure elements.

These are classic examples, but in isolation they do not seem very much like the kinds of sentences we expect to encounter in everyday language. This has led to the belief by some that ambiguity is an anomaly of language, a few unusual sentences that may be interesting linguistic quirks, but are not likely to tell us very much about language processing in general. However, rather than concluding that ambiguity is anomalous, I would argue instead that these sentences are anomalous examples of ambiguity. The characteristic that makes them anomalous is exactly the one that makes them excellent as textbook examples: It seems, when reading these sentences, that both meanings are available simultaneously, or very nearly so. This makes the sentences useful as pedagogical examples, but not very like the more subtle ambiguities we normally encounter in comprehension, which rarely give rise to conscious awareness of the ambiguity. However, this ease of resolution does not dismiss the problem of ambiguity. Rather, it defines the problem: When presented with a message that allows more than one possible interpretation, what are the processes by which we arrive at one of those interpretations?

I would like to argue that there are two reasons for trying to answer this question. The first was hinted above. It is becoming clear that linguistic ambiguity is a subtle but pervasive phenomenon. As will be made apparent in the coming chapters of this volume, ambiguity arises at every level of language processing, from the lexical, through syntactic and semantic, to pragmatic levels of performance. Ambiguity is a fundamental problem of language comprehension, and any attempt to understand language processing will require an explanation of the processes involved in its resolution.

The second reason for studying ambiguity is that it may shed light on questions of language that are not readily understood by other means. In this case, the more extreme forms of ambiguity that we often study provide a window to more general problems of linguistic functioning. In the remainder of this chapter, I will attempt to elaborate these claims, that ambiguity is pervasive in the language and that it can be used to good purpose as a research tool. I will first describe some examples of ambiguity that go beyond the obvious textbook varieties. Next, I will describe some recent research reflecting the use of ambiguity to explicate other aspects of language comprehension. In this section, I will focus on contributions of research in lexical ambiguity, as this area has provided very fertile ground for studying more general psycholinguistic issues.

On the Prevalence of Ambiguity in Language

Part of the reason that ambiguity may seem anomalous is that we as researchers have not always been clear about what we believe our experimental materials stand for. That is, we are usually convinced that our ambiguous words and sentences reveal characteristics about language more generally, but we have not conveyed this belief very well. It is becoming increasingly apparent, however, that most, if not all, language materials possess in varying degrees the same characteristics that we study in ambiguous materials. The stimuli we use only show these characteristics in greater relief.

Consider first the case of lexical ambiguity, as in sentence 1 above. Words such as *bank*, *spring*, and *punch* are the kinds of words commonly used in lexical ambiguity research. Each has several boldface entries in a dictionary, and each shows a variety of responses when given as a stimulus for word association (e.g., Nelson, McEvoy, Walling, & Wheeler, 1980; Perfetti, Lindsey, & Garson, 1971). If we are questioning the range of information activated in memory when a word is encountered, or the effects of context on the narrowing of activated information, these words present ideal extreme examples for studying such processes. This does not mean, however, that these same questions can't be asked of other, "unambiguous," words. Compare the word *room* to those above. This word has only a single entry in most dictionaries, and would likely yield word associations reflecting one meaning. Within this meaning, however, several different senses can be seen. Some of these are illustrated in sentences 4–7.

4. We rose when the queen entered the room.
5. The room burst into flames.
6. The room burst into applause.
7. His argument left no room for disagreement.

It is obvious that *room* is interpreted differently in these sentences. In sentence 4, it refers to a literal extent of space, the sense that is probably dominant for most people. Sentence 5 would normally be taken to refer to that space and everything in it. Sentence 6 refers only to some of the things in that space (the people), and not the space at all. In sentence 7, the extent of space is figurative. Despite these clearly distinguishable senses, most readers would probably argue that they derive from one general extent-of-space meaning, and indeed, all can be found under the same dictionary entry. This "single-meaning" word, then, presents the listener or reader with the same problem faced with more obviously ambiguous words: selecting the contextually appropriate interpretation. The metonymic use of *room* in sentence 6 is particularly interesting, as virtually any noun might serve the role of standing for another word or words with which it associated (in this case, *room* representing not the room itself, but the people in it). This illustrates the degree to which words with single dictionary entries possess the same kind of vagueness shown by multiple-entry words such as *bank*.

The problem of lexical-level ambiguity grows even more when we consider that under different circumstances, even a word that denotes a single object may be interpreted differently in different contexts, as contrasting sets of features may become activated (Barclay, Bransford, Franks, McCarrell, & Nitsch, 1974; Barsalou, 1982; Whitney, McKay, Kellas, & Emerson, 1985). This is the problem of "weak semantic ambiguity" (see Barsalou & Billman, this volume, Chapter 10), which must affect nearly every word in the lexicon. In short, it appears that all words have associated with them more information than is typically needed in a single instance. The problems that we encounter in processing words such as *bank*, therefore, surface to some degree with all words. The questions that we ask regarding the activation and selection processes associated with ambiguous words are thus no less relevant for any other word in the lexicon.

Ambiguity Beyond the Lexicon

Just as sentences such as 1 only present the most obvious type of word-level ambiguity, so too does sentence 2 only display a particularly obvious syntactic ambiguity. As with the lexical level, however, normal language routinely presents us with subtler, but more common, forms of syntactic ambiguity than the example shown in 2. A considerable amount of recent research, for example, has addressed the case of relative clause ambiguities, such as that shown in 8:

8. The realtor sold the house got a good buy.

This sentence, in its entirety, is not structurally ambiguous, but most readers and listeners experience at least a temporary "garden-path" effect at the occurrence of the main verb *got* (Clifton & Ferreira, 1987; Ferreira & Clifton, 1986; Frazier, 1987). Hirst (this volume, Chapter 14) and Tanenhaus and Carlson (1989) discuss these and other types of syntactic and thematic ambiguities, and the latter paper discusses the relationship between syntactic parsing and information in the lexicon. For now, suffice it to say that, just as in the lexical case, the syntactic ambiguities described at the outset of this chapter represent only the most blatant examples of problems that surface constantly in sentence comprehension.

Finally, there exist several types of figurative language that have rarely been considered alongside the varieties of ambiguity discussed thus far, but might profitably be treated in a similar way. We might group together such linguistic devices as indirect requests, idiomatic expressions, metaphor, sarcasm, and the like under the name of "pragmatic ambiguity." For example, a sentence such as 9,

9. He's skating on thin ice.

may be interpreted literally if the speaker is standing near a barely frozen pond, but figuratively under other circumstances describing some risky activity. Similarly, sentence 10 is usually interpreted as a request for directions, although it is literally a "yes-no" question.

10. Can you tell me where the Art Department is?

In each of these and similar cases, the context (and/or convention) will normally dictate whether the literal or figurative interpretation is to be preferred. This situation is the same as that presented by lexical and syntactic ambiguity: The comprehender, by some means, determines the single appropriate interpretation and rejects the rest.

Connections between ambiguities at the pragmatic level and those at the lexical and syntactic levels have not been made explicitly, though some tentative steps have been taken (Glucksberg, 1984; Simpson, Burgess, & Peterson, 1988). Simpson et al. have noted that some of the models that have been proposed for processing one or another kind of figurative language appear to have counterparts in the lexical ambiguity literature. For example, it has been suggested that when a pragmatically ambiguous utterance occurs, its literal meaning is derived first, and the figurative interpretation is only retrieved if the literal is found to be inappropriate (e.g., Clark & Lucy, 1975; Janus & Bever, 1985). This account bears some resemblance to the ordered-search model of lexical ambiguity resolution (Hogaboam & Perfetti, 1975), in which the most frequent meaning of an ambiguity is retrieved first, regardless of the surrounding context, and less frequent meanings are retrieved only if the dominant meaning fails to provide an acceptable interpretation. Other authors have proposed that for idiomatic expressions both the literal and the figurative meaning are derived simultaneously, and one interpretation is then selected in a subsequent stage (e.g., Estill & Kemper, 1982; Glass, 1983). Such an explanation is reminiscent of the exhaustive-access model of lexical ambiguity (Swinney, 1979). This model proposes that all meanings of an ambiguous word are activated in parallel, regardless of the context, which acts in a second stage to select among activated meanings. On the other hand, it has also been suggested that context may act immediately to bias the initial interpretation of a pragmatically ambiguous sentence. Gildea and Glucksberg (1983) have found that metaphor processing may be primed by prior information related to the metaphoric interpretation. This proposal of context sensitivity is similar to explanations of context dependence in the recognition of ambiguous words (Schvaneveldt, Meyer, & Becker, 1976; Simpson, 1981). Under such a view, the context in which an ambiguous word is encountered leads the comprehender directly to the appropriate interpretation.

The above similarities between explanations of lexical and pragmatic ambiguities suggest the possibility of a set of processes that may be common to the resolution of all types of ambiguity. Of course, such a proposal is only suggestive. There undoubtedly are factors that must be considered in the resolution of some kinds of ambiguity but not in others. For example, characteristics of verb structure (emphasized by Hirst in this volume, and by Tanenhaus and Carlson, 1989) that are relevant to the resolution of some types of syntactic ambiguity do not seem to be critical for many types of lexical ambiguity processing. It is encouraging, however (as evidenced by the present volume and the conference from which it grew), that researchers are beginning to recognize the benefit of considering ambiguity at all levels to be examples of a common problem. In every instance discussed, the comprehender is faced with the necessity of choosing among rival interpretations. It may be fruitful to consider that some mechanisms may be common to the resolution of all of these varieties of ambiguity.

Contributions of Ambiguity Research

It is clear, then, that ambiguity is extremely prevalent, and therefore worthy of study in its own right. In addition, however, it has proved to be well suited to studying a variety of other issues relevant to language processing. In the remainder of this chapter, several examples of this role of ambiguity research will be described. The emphasis here will be on the contributions of lexical ambiguity research, as this variety has been particularly prominent in the development of our thinking about the nature of word recognition processes more generally.

The most obvious contribution of this research has been to the debate concerning whether input processes are best described as a set of autonomous modules or as a less constrained set of interactive processors. Much of the research on lexical ambiguity processing in sentence context has concluded that activation for all meanings of an ambiguous word occurs regardless of the prior context (Onifer & Swinney, 1981; Seidenberg, Tanenhaus, Leiman, & Bienkowski, 1982; Swinney, 1979; Swinney & Prather, this volume; Tanenhaus, Leiman, & Seidenberg, 1979). Indeed, this research probably is cited more frequently than any other in support of the hypothesis that the lexicon represents such an autonomous input module. Some recent research proposes tempering this conclusion of lexical autonomy somewhat (including papers by Gorfein & Bubka, Simpson & Kellas, and Tabossi in the present volume), but there appears to be implicit agreement that lexical ambiguity is the ideal arena for this debate. Similarly, research on syntactic ambiguity has been used as evidence for the autonomy of syntactic processing (e.g., Clifton & Ferreira, 1987; Frazier, 1987). Clifton and Ferreira, for example, describe research in which syntactic garden-path effects are found for locally ambiguous constructions (such as in sentence 8 above) despite prior contextual information that might be used to resolve the ambiguity. This contribution of ambiguity research to issues concerning the modularity of language processing will continue to be a prominent one, as is evident from several of the papers presented in this volume. This is not its only role, however, as we have used lexical ambiguity to explore a number of very different issues in word recognition.

For the last several years, my colleagues and I have pursued a research program designed to explore the role that the frequencies of the various meanings of an ambiguous word play in that word's processing. In addition to telling us something about the role of meaning frequency, however, this research has also provided us with information concerning several other aspects of word processing. In our first series of studies (Simpson & Burgess, 1985), we found that both meanings of a homograph were activated when that homograph was presented in isolation (i.e., without biasing context), but that the speed of the activation of a meaning was commensurate with its frequency. The dominant meaning was activated immediately and remained so for several hundred milliseconds. The subordinate meaning became activated more slowly, but eventually reached a level of activation equal to that of the dominant. Subsequently, the activation for the less frequent meaning declined again. A second experiment showed that this late decline was traceable to a stage in which attentional resources were directed to the more frequent meaning. We argued that these results were compatible with a two-stage model of word recognition (e.g., Neely, 1977; Stanovich & West, 1979), in which an initial automatic activation process is followed by a focus of attention on a portion of the activated information. However, the data were also examined subsequently (Simpson & Burgess, 1988) for their compatibility with a verification account of word recognition (Becker, 1980). It was reasoned that any process that leads to activation of only one meaning should result also in a facilitation-dominant pattern of responding (relative to a neutral condition), while processes leading to multiple access should show more inhibition for unrelated stimuli than they show facilitation for related (see Simpson, 1984, for a more complete discussion of lexical ambiguity within the verification model). A subgroup of subjects did indeed show multiple access, but they displayed no inhibition for unrelated words. Subjects for whom only the dominant meaning was active, however, showed strong inhibition both for unrelated words and for words related to the subordinate meaning. The pattern obtained with ambiguous words, therefore, helped us separate more general models of word recognition.

We have also examined ambiguous word processing in second-, fourth-, and sixth-grade children (Simpson & Foster, 1986). We found that for all ages, dominant meanings again were activated more quickly, but only the oldest group showed the second stage of focusing attention on that meaning. In fact, we found in one experiment that the facilitation of responses to words related to the dominant meaning was greater for sixth graders than for fourth graders. Word recognition research with children has been extremely consistent in showing much larger facilitation effects for younger children (e.g., Schwantes, Boesl, & Ritz, 1980; Simpson & Lorsbach, 1983; Stanovich, West, & Feeman, 1981). Our results suggested that if the target information is consistent with that which is most frequently used, older children may show as much as or more advantage than younger. The results suggested to us that in addition to the quantitative differences in word recognition that occur with age (as suggested by the age-related decline that is usually seen in the amount of contextual facilitation), there are qualitative changes as well, with older children better able to use limited-capacity resources to narrow the scope of information activated during word recognition. The lexical ambiguity paradigm proved to be ideal for examining these developmental changes.

Finally, Burgess and Simpson (1988a) replicated the earlier research of Simpson and Burgess (1985), this time presenting ambiguous words foveally, but dominant and subordinate associates only to the left or right visual fields. Only right hemifield presentation replicated the results obtained in the earlier study (faster activation for the dominant meaning, followed by allocation of attention to that meaning). Left hemifield presentation showed that both meanings were still activated long after homograph presentation, indicating an asymmetry in the degree to which the cerebral hemispheres engage in the attentional narrowing of focus of activated information (see also Chiarello, 1985). Burgess has used these data in conjunction with data on language processing in brain-damaged patients to begin developing a model of the role that the two cerebral hemispheres play in resolving indeterminate messages (Burgess & Simpson, 1988b).

In a different vein, we have also used lexical ambiguity recently to explore the role of attention in the earliest stages of the extraction of meaning from a word (Kellas, Ferraro, & Simpson, 1988). This research employs a dual-task procedure, in which subjects respond to tones at the same time that they perform lexical decisions to ambiguous and unambiguous words and pseudowords. Not only are ambiguous words recognized more quickly than unambiguous (cf. Jastrzembski, 1981), but they also require less attention for their recognition than do unambiguous words. Of particular interest was a pattern that emerged from a group of elderly subjects (Kellas, Simpson, & Ferraro, in press). Overall, the elderly tended to perform both tasks more slowly. However, there was a subgroup of "expert" elderly that required less attention for word recognition than did college students, and also did not show any advantage for ambiguous words. In other words, the early extraction of meaning appeared to be more automatized for these subjects than for younger adults. Such results present a challenge to those views of cognitive aging that posit general declines either in information processing speed or in attentional capacity. Again, the use of ambiguous words, this time in direct comparison to unambiguous words, facilitated the study of some other aspect of word recognition processes.

In sum, lexical ambiguity has proved to be an excellent medium through which to study word recognition. It has allowed us to understand the distinction between word recognition models, as well as developmental changes in word processing, and hemispheric asymmetries in lexical access. Finally, and most prominently, lexical and syntactic ambiguities have served as principal domains of research concerned with the degree of autonomy that characterizes language comprehension. Simply put, the study of ambiguity has proved invaluable to our general understanding of linguistic processes.

Conclusions

The goal of this chapter has been twofold. The first purpose has been to draw some connections between the kinds of lexical and syntactic ambiguities that have been studied for years by psycholinguists and the indeterminancy of meaning that surfaces at many levels of language. We can only profit by considering ambiguity to be a general and pervasive phenomenon. I have intended to demonstrate that virtually any utterance may present a comprehender with a choice of interpretations, making an explanation of ambiguity resolution a fundamental problem of comprehension.

If our intent is a complete understanding of natural language processing (by human or machine), then explanation of the resolution of ambiguity in all of its varieties must be a primary goal. It is clear from the remainder of this volume that the importance of the role of ambiguity is now widely recognized.

A secondary purpose of this chapter has been to show that because ambiguity often presents extreme examples of some characteristics of language, it is a very useful medium by which to study those characteristics. Studies were reviewed that used lexical ambiguity as a means to exploring several issues of word recognition that, while not dependent on ambiguity per se, are more easily studied in the context of ambiguous words. In short, ambiguity serves two critical roles: as one of our most fundamental problems and as one of our most powerful tools.

Part II Lexical Access and Post-Access Processing

Most of the major theories of the processing of ambiguous words have focused on the role of context in the accessing of meaning. In this section, Tabossi in Chapter 3 reviews the nature of the evidence against a modular view, one in which the meanings of a homograph are exhaustively accessed and the meaning is selected at a higher processing level. She concludes that there is evidence for context guiding lexical access and that syntactic context may under some circumstances influence the meaning achieved.

Simpson and Kellas, in Chapter 4, present evidence that a homograph is changed by the circumstances of its initial occurrence in a repetition task in such manner as to limit the meaning achieved under subsequent occurrence. Gorfein and Walters, in Chapter 5, describe experimental evidence that both extends and limits the conclusions reached by Simpson and Kellas.

Chapters 6 and 7 contain statements of theory. Neill, in Chapter 6, extends his previous work with Strooplike phenomena to the realm of semantic memory. The section is completed in Chapter 7 by a theory and some new data offered by Gorfein and Bubka to clarify the role of frequency broadly conceived in the selection of meaning. Like many of the theories in the field, theirs cuts across the problems of access, activation, and representation.

3

What's in a Context?

PATRIZIA TABOSSI

Almost 15 years ago, when semantic networks became fashionable, William Woods (1975) raised the question of what was in their semantics. While acknowledging the attractiveness of these structures for representing knowledge, he pointed out how "the same semantic network notations could be used by different people (or even by the same person at different times for different examples) to mean different things" (p. 53). In a similar vein, in psycholinguistics the notion of context, which plays a major role, is employed in a variety of ways, and not all of them are equally well-specified.

A first, broad distinction is between the use of this notion to refer to the extralinguistic situation in which a conversation takes place, and its use to denote the discourse within which a linguistic expression occurs (Clark & Clark, 1977). But even in the latter restricted sense, context refers to different things: for instance, the letters (e.g., A,L,N,E) surrounding a character (e.g., O) in a string (e.g., ALONE) (Rumelhart & McClelland, 1982). Alternatively, in speech perception, a context can be the syllable (e.g., *big* versus *bog*) in which a sound (e.g., /b/) occurs (Liberman, 1970), whereas, in another domain, the syntactic structure *whose planet*, unlike *men planet*, is an example of an acceptable context for *planet* (Goodman, McClelland, & Gibbs, 1981).

Among these various notions, one which has become very popular is that of semantic context, often used in the study of lexical processing, in particular word recognition and lexical access. Usually, word recognition denotes the processes by means of which a written or spoken lexical item makes contact with its representation in the mental lexicon. Thus, recognizing a word is to retrieve from memory different types of information—phonological, orthographical, syntactic, and semantic—associated to that word. Within word recognition, lexical access will be employed in the present paper to refer to a more specific process—namely, the retrieval of semantic information that takes place whenever a word is recognized. Typically, research in this area is concerned with whether all or part of the semantic information relative to a word is activated when the word is encountered. In the case of an ambiguity, for instance, do we initially activate all of its meanings, regardless of the context of occurrence, or do we access only one meaning each time?

In order to investigate both word recognition and lexical access, a promising strategy, and one which is widely exploited, is that of studying how prior semantic context affects those processes. Intuitive as well as empirical reasons suggest the usefulness of this approach. Consider, for instance, the following sentences (Johnson-Laird, 1975):

1. She sat on a tomato.
2. She likes tomatoes.
3. Her face was like a tomato.

Most people would agree that different aspects of what one knows about tomatoes come to mind in the three sentences, namely, tomatoes are squashy in sentence 1, they are food in sentence 2, and they are red in sentence 3. Moreover, there is empirical evidence that the saliency of different aspects of the meaning of an unambiguous word is affected by the sentence in which it occurs (Barclay, Bransford, Franks, McCarrell, & Nitsch, 1974; Tabossi, 1982). Likewise, presented with the following sentence:

If Karpov was the chess champion that year, it was all due to the rook move in that last match,

it is most unlikely that any English speaker will think of the black bird called the rook. Indeed, lexical ambiguity resolution is a clear example of how effective context can be in determining the comprehension of a word.

The above arguments show that ultimately semantic context influences the way in which a lexical item gets interpreted, and strongly suggest the importance of investigating the effects of context on lexical processing. What these arguments do not allow one to conclude is that semantic information affects word recognition and lexical access. In fact, since these processes take place in time, it is entirely possible that lexical processing occurs independently of context effects, and only the outcome of this process is interpreted according to context.

In early phases of the research on whether lexical processing is sensitive to semantic information, single-word and sentential contexts were often considered together. According to Morton (1970), for example,

> The effect of a context on the production of a response is identical in principle to the effect of the stimulus. The context, which can be of any kind, causes what is here called the Cognitive System to send semantic information to the Logogen system. Attributes such as (noun), (animate), (male) might be produced by the sentence "He was a drunken — — —" and all logogens whose semantic sets contained these items would be incremented accordingly. These increments would effectively reduce the amount of sensory information required to produce the response, the attribute counts from the two sources simply adding without regard to source (p. 209).

Subsequently, however, it has become clear that studying the effect of these two types of semantic context can yield different conclusions and bear different theoretical consequences. Word context studies, in fact, aim to clarify how semantic information is organized and retrieved from the mental lexicon. To date, after several years of investigation and the collection of a large body of empirical evidence, most researchers agree that a word context can affect word processing. The mental lexicon is viewed as some kind of network in which the various entries have different relations. Words that are associated or semantically related are closer than words that do not share such relations. When a word is recognized (i.e., its entry becomes activated), activation automatically spreads to entries close to it (Collins & Loftus, 1975). This phenomenon, often referred to as lexical priming, is reflected in the shorter time required to identify a target (e.g., *nurse*) when it follows a word (prime) semantically related to it (e.g., *doctor*) (Meyer, Schvaneveldt, & Ruddy, 1975; Seidenberg, Waters, Sanders, & Langer, 1984).

Sentential context effects are far less understood than word context ones, to the point that there is no general agreement even on whether they exist at all. This is not a consequence of the fact that sentential context is theoretically less interesting. To the contrary, people hardly ever come across isolated words, and lexical items do not normally occur paired with their associates in the messages they understand. Moreover, investigation on sentence context effects requires a better comprehension of what kind of information various types of context render available to a listener/reader at different points in time. This, in turn, will probably contribute to improving our knowledge of how people integrate different sorts of information to reach language understanding. The final product of the comprehension system has been the object of much theoretical interest (Johnson-Laird, 1983), but the on-line construction of comprehension has only recently started to be studied.

Finally, establishing whether word recognition and lexical access can be affected by a sentential context has consequences that go beyond psycholinguistic concerns. Lexical processing, in fact, has become a crucial test for two seemingly alternative views of human cognition. According to one, the architecture of the cognitive system is made of independent modules, whose functioning is autonomous from one another and which communicate only at their outputs (Fodor, 1983; Forster, 1979). Instead, according to the other, the cognitive system is highly interactive, and is able to use at any time the available information (Rumelhart, McClelland, & the PDP Research Group, 1986). In order to gain empirical support for or against either of these hypotheses, establishing word context effects on lexical processing is not crucial. These effects, in fact, are produced within the lexical system itself and are compatible with both alternatives. On the contrary, sentential context effects, showing that processes in the lexicon can be influenced by information from outside this subsystem, would violate the modular view, whereas failure to obtain such effects would give it a strong support.

So far, the hypothesis most widely accepted among psycholinguists is that the lexicon is an autonomous subcomponent of the language comprehension system. The best-known evidence in favor of this view comes from

Swinney's studies (Onifer & Swinney, 1981; Swinney, 1979), which show the ineffectiveness of contextual biases in the access to ambiguous words. In Onifer and Swinney (1981) the subjects listened to a sentence which contained a lexical ambiguity (e.g., *ring*) and biased either its dominant (e.g., as a piece of jewelry) or its subordinate (e.g., as a sound) meaning, as in the following example:

1. The housewife's face literally lit up as the plumber extracted her lost wedding ring from the sink.
2. The office walls were so thin that they could hear the ring of their neighbor's phone whenever a call came in.

At the offset of the ambiguous item, the subjects were presented with a visual target word, on which they performed a lexical-decision task. The target was either related to the dominant meaning of the ambiguity (e.g., Finger), or was related to the subordinate meaning (e.g., Bell), or was an unrelated control (e.g., Talent, Whip). The results showed that both words related to the ambiguity were faster than their controls, irrespective of context and dominance.

A corollary of the modular view is that there is no convincing evidence of sentential context effects on lexical processing, and data that seem to support such effects either are artifacts of some sort or else have been obtained under very unusual circumstances, which cannot be taken to reflect the way in which the different components of the language system normally operate. But how well does the available evidence fit these claims? What follows is an attempt to answer this question. In order to do so, the effectiveness of various types of sentential contexts on word recognition and lexical access will be examined first. Then, some methodological issues relevant to the whole area and crucial to the interpretation of the data will be considered. Finally, the adequacy of both the interactive and the modular view will be reconsidered, and provisional conclusions drawn.

Predictive Contexts

Everybody agrees that there are occasions in which a listener can successfully anticipate what a speaker is going to say. "He sat reading a . . . ", for example, although containing no word normatively associated to *book*, strongly suggests it. Should contexts of this sort be shown to affect the processing of the word they render probable, this fact would argue against the modular view and in favor of the interactive hypothesis. Indeed, such evidence was provided in an early study by Morton and Long (1976). While listening to sentences such as the above, their subjects monitored for a word that began with a prespecified phoneme (e.g., /b/) and that was a high- or low-probable completion of the preceding context (e.g., *book* versus *bill*). The results showed that highly probable completions were responded to faster than less probable ones.

Unfortunately, these findings were obtained with the phoneme-monitoring technique, which was subsequently shown to be sensitive to a number of factors not controlled for by Morton and Long (1976) (Cutler & Norris, 1979). In particular, their results were replicated by Foss and Gernsbacher (1983), who used the same high- and low-probable words, but presented them in isolation. According to these authors, Morton and Long's results are due to the different phonetic structure of the two sets of words, the high-probable words having shorter vowels and fewer initial consonant clusters than the low-probable ones.

However, probability effects have been observed in several other studies, with different paradigms and different tasks. In Fischler and Bloom (1979), the subjects performed a lexical decision on a word presented half a second after the offset of a sentential context, which they had read for 2 seconds. The target word was a predictable, unpredictable, or anomalous completion of the sentential frame, which contained no lexical item associated to it, as in the following example:

She cleaned the dirt from her
SHOES (predictable)
HANDS (unpredictable)
TERMS (anomalous)

The results showed that the predictable targets were responded to faster than both the unpredictable and the anomalous targets.

Effects of facilitation were also found by Stanovich and West (1983), whose subjects performed a naming task on the same set of materials used by Fischler and Bloom (1979, 1980). Moreover, comparable evidence has been obtained in an eye-movement study by Balota, Pollatsek, and Rayner (1985). They found that when a sentential context renders a target word probable (e.g., "Since the wedding was today, the baker rushed the wedding *cake* to the reception"), parafoveal information visually similar to the target (e.g., *cahc*) has a much larger facilitation effect on the reading of the target than it has in the absence of a predictive context.

Predictability has also been used by Van Petten and Kutas (1987) to investigate access to lexical ambiguity. Their subjects read, one word at a time, a sentence whose last word was a homograph. The sentence biased the subordinate sense of the homograph by making its occurrence highly probable (e.g., "The gambler pulled an ace from the bottom of the *deck*"). After 200 ms from the onset of the homograph, they read out loud a target word, which was either related to the contextually appropriate meaning of the homograph (e.g., CARDS) or related to its contextually inappropriate meaning (e.g., SHIP), or was an unrelated control word (e.g., PARENT). The data showed that the inappropriate targets, which were significantly faster than the controls, were also reliably slower than the appropriate targets. Similar results were also found when, instead of naming, event-related brain potentials of the subjects silently reading were used as dependent variable.

Unfortunately, Van Petten and Kutas (1987) do not give a list of their contexts, so that one cannot exclude the possibility that words semantically associated to the subordinate meaning of the homographs occurred in the sentences. But their results are similar to those obtained in several other studies, suggesting that lexical processing can be affected by predictability, and is not therefore an entirely autonomous component of the language processing system.

This conclusion, however, is far weaker than it may sound. In fact, very rarely words are predictable, as has been shown by Gough, Alford, and Holley-Wilcox (1981), who found that the percentage of subjects' correct guesses about words in different types of context ranged between 20 and 39%. Hence, in general, predictability is a rather ineffective strategy, whose usefulness may well be shown in extreme situations such as those set up in experiments, but whose validity is certainly very limited in ordinary comprehension (Marslen-Wilson & Tyler, 1980; Stanovich & West, 1983).

With regard to context effects, highly probable words are not dissimilar from degraded stimuli, whose identification is facilitated by the prior occurrence of a semantically related context (Rueckel & Oden, 1986). As Seidenberg and Tanenhaus (1986) pointed out, "Degraded stimuli can induce subjects to use a guessing strategy that is neither required nor efficient under normal conditions" (p. 144). In this respect, evidence for sentential context effects on the processing of a subsequent congruent word would be far more challenging to a modularity view.

Congruent Contexts

It may be very risky and inefficient to guess from "She cleaned the dirt from her . . ." what the next word will be. There is no risk, however, at least in natural communicative situations, in assuming that the oncoming word will make the sentence meaningful and describe a plausible state of affairs. Hence, if effects of congruency can be demonstrated, this would be a very cogent argument in favor of the interactive hypothesis of lexical processing.

Using the gating technique in which successively increasing fragments of a word are presented to investigate spoken-word recognition, Tyler and Wessels (1983) found that the identification of a word (e.g., *benefit*) is facilitated by its occurrence in a semantic context (e.g., "The appointment with the dentist is canceled. John tries to . . ."). According to the authors, "The results . . . show that although strong syntactic constraints on form-class only marginally reduce the amount of sensory input needed, a minimal interpretative context has a substantial effect on word recognition" (p. 409). This effect, however, is unlikely to convince the skeptics. In fact, it was assessed comparing the recognition of the target word in the semantic context with its recognition in a syntactically correct but semantically anomalous sentence (e.g., "The breath with the lie shuffles only through. The terrace tries to . . ."), whose adequacy as neutral context has been questioned (Stanovich & West, 1983).

The difficulty of establishing a correct baseline is not restricted to work on spoken language (Forster, 1981; Schuberth, Spoehr, & Lane, 1981). In one of the first studies in visual-word recognition, Schuberth and Eimas (1977) asked their subjects to perform a lexical decision on a target word presented either in isolation or after a sentential frame. In the latter case, the target was a congruous or incongruous completion of the sentence. The results indicated longer reaction times after the incongruous context than after the word in isolation, which in turn produced slower responses than the congruous context. But again, even ignoring methodological questions relative to the lexical-decision task, it is unlikely that a word presented in isolation can provide a reliable neutral condition against which to measure context effects.

A more convincing approach to the neutral condition problem was taken by Stanovich and West (1983), whose subjects named a target word, after reading a sentential context, which was congruous, incongruous, or neutral. The congruous and incongruous contexts were a subset of those used by Fischler and Bloom (1979, 1980), while the neutral contexts were the three following uninformative sentential frames:

They said it was the
The next word will be
They were thinking about the

Under these experimental conditions, naming times to the target words were significantly faster following the congruent contexts than following any of the neutral contexts (Experiment 9). Comparable facilitative effects due to congruency were replicated with the whole range of Fischler and Bloom's materials (1979, 1980) in two further experiments of the same study, both with naming and with lexical decision (Experiments 10 & 11).

To what extent are the numerous findings suggesting congruency effects reconcilable with a modular view of lexical processing? Admittedly, much of the available evidence can be explained on methodological grounds with no real challenge for that hypothesis. A case in point is the study by Fischler and Bloom (1979), who, in addition to the already mentioned predictability effects, also found that the recognition of a word was inhibited by its occurrence in an incongruous context. Those results, however, were obtained with a lexical-decision task, which arguably reflects post-access, rather than access, phenomena. Indeed, when Stanovich and West reran Fischler and Bloom's (1979) experiment using the naming task, the inhibition effects observed in the earlier study disappeared. However, can the autonomy view account for the facilitation effects obtained by Stanovich and West (1983) with naming and with sentential contexts that, unlike those used in West and Stanovich (1982), contained no associations to the to-be-recognized words? These data seem to violate the modular view, and call for a reconsideration either of that hypothesis or of the reliability of the naming task (or both).

Feature Priming Contexts

Feature priming contexts, originally used to investigate the interpretation of unambiguous words, constrain the information in an upcoming word by priming its semantic features. "The man tuned the piano," for instance, makes salient a characteristic of pianos, namely, the fact that they produce sounds (Barclay et al., 1974). While intuitively clear, the notion of semantic feature, once its old formulation (Katz & Fodor, 1963) is abandoned as too determinate and inflexible (Savin, 1973), is difficult to characterize. According to Schwanenflugel and Shoben (1985), for example, "'Featural restrictions' is meant to refer to more than the traditional sense of the term 'features' and includes constraints based on general world knowledge as well" (p. 248). Although admittedly elusive, this notion has been used extensively and fruitfully in research on lexical meaning (Barsalou, 1982; Greenspan, 1986) and, more recently, on lexical access.

Whitney, McKay, Kellas, and Emerson (1985) employed a modified Stroop procedure to investigate the time course of semantic activation of unambiguous words (e.g., *trout*) in sentential contexts. The subjects listened to a sentence that either primed a high- or low-dominant property of the meaning of the last word in it (e.g., "The boy skinned the trout"; "The boy dropped his trout") or was a control (e.g., "The boy skinned his knee"; "The boy dropped his milk"). After 0, 300, or 600 ms from its end, the sentence was followed by a visual word denoting the high- or low-dominant property of the noun (e.g., *scales*, *slimy*). The subjects' task was to name the color of the ink in which the visual word was written. The interference produced by the meaning of the visual word on color naming measured the activation of the denoted property: At 0-ms delay, both properties interfered with color naming significantly more after either of the priming contexts than after the control sentences. At 300- and 600-ms delays, however, the high-dominant property was still activated following both priming contexts, but the low-dominant property interfered with color naming significantly more after the appropriate priming context than after either the inappropriate or the control context.

According to Whitney et al. (1985), these findings support the modular view on lexical access: Initially all information about a noun's meaning is accessed, regardless of context. Only subsequently context becomes effective, and those properties that neither constitute the core meaning of the noun nor are contextually relevant are dropped. But in this study contexts in which the prior sentential frames prime a property of the meaning of an upcoming word (e.g., "The lady was pricked by a rose") appear alongside with sentences that fail to do so. "The man used the oak," for instance, does emphasize the low-dominant property of oak *lumber*, and this is why at 300- and 600-ms delays selective effects of context, at least for the low-dominant properties, have been obtained. But "The man used the . . ." can hardly be considered to prime the intended property. Under these circumstances, it would be very surprising if early context effects were observed. In Whitney et al. (1985), where these two types of context are mixed, context effects may not have been obtained at a 200-ms delay, simply because, on average, their sentences did not sufficiently prime any property of the meaning of an unambiguous noun.

A different pattern of results emerges from a cross-modal lexical-decision study conducted by Tabossi (1988b). The subjects listened to sentences that either primed an aspect of the meaning of an unambiguous noun (e.g., *gold*) in the sentence or primed another aspect of its meaning, or primed no specific aspect of the noun's meaning, as in the following example:

1. In the light, the blond hair of the little girl had the luster of gold (gold is yellow).
2. At the lecture, the clever teacher spoke at length about the gold (no specific aspect of gold).
3. In the shop, the artisan shaped with ease the bar of gold (gold is malleable).

In Whitney et al.'s (1985) terminology, here the selected aspects (e.g., yellow and malleable) were both high-dominant, and comparable in their "centrality" in characterizing the word's meaning.

The findings (Experiment 1) showed that lexical decision on YELLOW presented at the offset of *gold* was fastest after context 1, next fastest after context 2, and slowest after context 3. Moreover, the same study (Experiment 2) ruled out the possibility that the results could be attributed to the facilitation produced by previous words in the sentence (e.g., *blond* or *luster*) directly priming the target YELLOW.

Effects of context were also obtained when feature priming sentences were used to bias the dominant and the subordinate meaning of an ambiguity (e.g., *port*[1]) (Tabossi, Colombo, & Job, 1987), as in the following example:

Dominant: The violent hurricane did not damage the ships which were in the port, one of the best equipped along the coast (a port is safe).

Subordinate: Deceived by the identical color, the host took a bottle of Barolo, instead of port, and offered it to his guests (port is red).

While listening to one of these sentences, the subjects performed a lexical decision on a visual word which was presented at the offset of *port*, and

[1]In this example a word in the context (*ship*) is strongly related to the ambiguity (*port*). However, this is the only sentence in which such lexical association occurs. In spite of this, the example was kept for the convenience of the English readers, since *port* is the only word in the research which maintains this ambiguity in English. In fact, all the Tabossi studies were conducted with Italian subjects and Italian materials.

which either denoted one of the features primed by the sentences or was a control (e.g., SAFE, RED, SHORT).

The results indicated that after the dominant context, SAFE was responded to faster than both RED and SHORT, which did not differ significantly from each other. After the subordinate context, however, SAFE and RED, which did not differ from each other, were both reliably faster than the control SHORT.

These findings were interpreted as evidence for effects of both dominance and context on lexical access: While the dominant meaning of an ambiguity is always activated, regardless of context, its subordinate meaning need not be accessed, unless the context biases it. Moreover, in order to reconcile their findings with Onifer and Swinney (1981), the authors suggested that the nature of the contextual bias—feature priming versus different types of biases—could explain the discrepancy.

That hypothesis was tested in Tabossi (1988), where the subjects listened to sentences that always biased the dominant meaning of the same ambiguities used in Tabossi et al. (1987). The bias, however, could be obtained either priming a "central" property of the dominant meaning of the ambiguity, as in the previous study (indeed, the same priming sentences were used), or rendering the subordinate meaning contextually incongruent. Moreover, the visual target words related to the ambiguities either denoted aspects of one of their meanings, again as in the previous study, or were semantically associated to it, as in many of Onifer and Swinney's materials (1981). The following examples illustrate the three experimental conditions:

Nonpriming context. Associated targets:
The man had to be at five o'clock at the port, for a very important meeting.
SEA; LIQUEUR; HAND.
Nonpriming context. Feature-denoting targets:
The man had to be at five o'clock at the port, for a very important meeting.
SAFE; RED; SHORT.
Priming context. Associated targets:
The violent hurricane did not damage the ships which were in the port, one of the best equipped along the coast.
SEA; LIQUEUR; HAND.

The results showed that following the nonpriming context, both the associated targets (e.g., SEA and LIQUEUR) and both the feature-denoting targets (SAFE and RED) were responded to faster than their controls (e.g., HAND and SHORT), replicating Onifer and Swinney (1981). However, following the priming context, the target words associated to the dominant meaning of the ambiguities (e.g., SEA) were faster than either the targets associated to the subordinate meaning of the ambiguities (e.g., LIQUEUR) or the controls (e.g., HAND), which did not differ from each other. Thus, irrespective of the relation between ambiguity and related visual targets (feature denoting versus association), these data replicated the selective results obtained in Tabossi et al. (1987), giving support to the hypothesis that various types of context can yield different results on lexical access.

Tabossi's research (Tabossi, 1988a, 1988b; Tabossi et al., 1987) was conducted using the cross-modal paradigm in conjunction with the lexical-decision task, and is therefore open to the criticisms concerning that task. Consider, however, the two studies on ambiguity. Here, evidence showing context effects as well as the lack of such effects has been obtained using exactly the same set of materials and the same task, which therefore cannot be responsible for the observed differences.

Feature priming contexts, unlike predictive contexts, provide semantic constraints, whose use is normally safe and cost-free. In this respect and apart from differences in strength, such contexts share one important characteristic with congruous context: Both impose semantic constraints on the information relative to an upcoming word, without making any lexical item predictable. Because it is in the nature of discourse to be informative, most contexts are likely to provide semantic constraints, and evidence that such constraints can affect lexical processing are certainly damaging for the modular view.

Methodological Considerations

It is impossible to draw conclusions from the above discussion without previously taking into account some of the methodological questions currently debated in lexical processing research. Although a number of different tasks have been employed to investigate on-line language processing (Foss, 1969; Just & Carpenter, 1980; Marslen-Wilson, 1973; Van Petten & Kutas, 1987), lexical decision and naming are by far the most popular. These two tasks, however, differ, and it is generally held that lexical decision is sensitive to strategic factors and likely to reflect post-access phenomena, whereas naming, which does not involve complex decisions, is more suitable to reflect the automatic process of accessing information from the mental lexicon. Several pieces of evidence obtained with single-word contexts (Balota & Chumbley, 1984; Lorch, Balota, & Stamm, 1986; Seidenberg et al., 1984), as well as with sentential contexts (Stanovich & West, 1983), support this conclusion.

But, carrying the difference between the two tasks to the point of accepting naming data as reliable, and rejecting lexical decision without further consideration, may be misleading. In fact, effects typically attributed to strategic post-access processes have been obtained with naming for words occurring both in sentential contexts (Forster, 1981) and in isolation (Balota & Chumbley, 1985). By contrast, there is evidence obtained with lexical decision which is difficult to interpret as reflecting post-lexical phenomena (Tabossi, 1988a).

Moreover, a similar extreme view would have to reconsider, for example, Neely's work (1976, 1977) on the automatic and strategic phenomena connected to semantic priming in visual-word recognition, whose evidence relies on lexical-decision reaction times. Also, if lexical decision necessarily reflects post-access phenomena, how do we account for Swinney's results (Onifer & Swinney, 1981; Swinney, 1979), obtained with lexical decision, and subsequently replicated with naming (Seidenberg, Tanenhaus, Leiman, & Bienkowski, 1982)? It might be claimed, perhaps, that while naming studies genuinely show no effect of context on lexical access, the lack of such effects in Swinney's work is an artifact due to backward priming (Glucksberg, Kreuz, & Rho, 1986), i.e., the phenomenon in which, given a pair of words presented one after the other, facilitation can occur not only from the first to the second, but also vice versa (Kiger & Glass, 1983; Koriat, 1981). In support of this interpretation is the fact that backward priming effects have been detected with lexical decision, but not with naming (Seidenberg et al., 1984). However, backward priming has always been shown in single-word contexts, and a recent study devoted to this issue has failed to find evidence for it in sentential contexts (Peterson, 1986).

This discrepancy between single-word and sentential context effects is neither unique nor surprising. It is well known, for instance, that the structure of the experimental sets of materials is far more effective with the former type of context than with the latter (Becker, 1980; Stanovich & West, 1981). According to Stanovich and West (1983), in fact, the processes of integration taking place during sentence understanding are probably demanding for the comprehension system, which is therefore less sensitive to some of the strategic factors effective with single-word contexts. Whether or not the explanation is correct, the fact remains that there are no grounds to claim that Swinney's results reflect backward priming and are therefore unreliable.

It may also be worth noting that, in most of the studies comparing lexical decision and naming, the time intervals between primes and targets were either long (Lorch et al., 1986; Seidenberg et al., 1984) or poorly controlled (Stanovich & West, 1983). An exception is a work by de Groot (1984), who in an associative semantic priming experiment investigated the influence on lexical-decision times of the proportion of related prime-target pairs in the materials and of the stimulus-onset asinchrony (SOA) between prime and target. But here at a short SOA (240 ms), when the proportion of related prime-target pairs was low (25%), the data showed effects of facilitation without inhibition, a pattern of results that is typically interpreted as reflecting access phenomena.

The above arguments are not meant to deny that lexical decision is more prone to post-access phenomena than naming. Rather, they aim to stress the need for a careful evaluation of the available evidence, beyond the simple distinction between data obtained using lexical decision and those obtained using naming. In fact, the interpretation of both tasks is problematic (Seidenberg et al., 1984; Stanovich & West, 1983), and as Forster (1981) has pointed out, naming and lexical decision "fall at opposite ends of a continuum. . . . The most appropriate way to cope with [their differences] is to use both types of latencies as dependent variables" (p. 472).

Conclusions

The picture that emerges from the above discussion is rather complex and fails to support unambiguously the autonomous hypothesis, according to which word recognition and lexical access are insensitive to sentential context effects. In fact, as we have seen, several pieces of evidence challenge this view. Some of these data can be disposed of on the basis of methodological arguments, and some can be taken to reflect processes that occur only under very special circumstances and are therefore not comparable with what happens during normal comprehension. Still there remain findings which belong to neither of those classes and provide evidence that appears to violate the autonomy of the lexical processing system.

Various other reasons also call for great caution before the modular hypothesis can be accepted. As Seidenberg and Tanenhaus (1986) pointed out, for example, most of the evidence in its support rely on the processing of short, morphologically simple, high-frequency words, and there is neither logical reason nor empirical ground to believe that longer and more difficult words do not allow for a larger use of contextual information. Moreover, particularly in spoken language, we do not know how discriminable words are on a strictly perceptual basis, and it is therefore very difficult to evaluate how well strictly bottom-up models of lexical processing would perform in ecologically valid conditions. It must not be forgotten, however, that studies such as that of Onifer and Swinney (1981) or Seidenberg et al. (1982) strongly argue for the insensitiveness of the lexical processing system to sentential biases. Thus, as far as the controversy between the modular and the interactive view is concerned, the available evidence on the effects that sentential contexts exert on lexical processing is contradictory.

Rather than taking the results as conflicting, the different findings can be taken to reflect various facets of the complex ways in which prior semantic information can be used by the lexical processing system. In this perspective, the internal functioning of that system is not seen as either sensitive or insensitive to whatever information is provided prior to the completion of its routines. Instead, it is conceived as variously responsive to external information, depending upon circumstances.

The need for a more flexible, and arguably more realistic, approach to lexical processing and its sensitivity to information coming from other components of the comprehension system has recently been acknowledged by Tanenhaus, Dell, and Carlson (1987), according to whom complete modularity and complete interaction can be best seen as the two extremes along a continuum. Top-down contextual information, in fact, can act at different points in time during lexical processing, producing feedback effects which can be early or late, with different consequences on the patterns of activation in the lexicon. The findings in Tabossi (1988b), for example, can be interpreted as evidence for early context effects. Context, in this case, would send early feedback to the lexical system so that the subordinate meaning of the ambiguity, which in that study is always contextually incongruous, although receiving some activation from the perceptual processing of the ambiguous word, would not reach a hypothetical access threshold. Alternatively, one might assume that the dominant meaning of the ambiguity has already received activation from context prior to its occurrence, in such a way that, as soon as the word is actually presented, its primed meaning will become available, whereas its subordinate meaning will be inhibited.

While not distinguishing between those two alternatives, Tabossi's findings (1988a) suggest that the nature of the semantic information prior to a word is decisive in determining whether and when the lexical processing system can make use of it. Until recently, this point has obtained little interest. A reason, perhaps, is that attention has been mostly focused on the architecture of the language system per se, almost as if its structure and functioning were independent from the characteristics of what has to be processed and from the conditions under which the processing takes place. Moreover, there is a genuine difficulty in specifying the semantic information provided by a sentential context and the constraints it imposes on lexical processing. An illustration of this difficulty is Onifer and Swinney's study (1981), where the sentences biased one meaning of the ambiguous items in several different ways: Some contained words associated to that meaning (e.g., "The man was surprised when he found several spiders, roaches, and other *bugs* in the corner of his room"); others rendered the occurrence of the ambiguous word, in the biased sense, very predictable (e.g., "The housewife's face literally lit up as the plumber extracted her lost wedding *ring* from the sink"); and still others made the unintended meaning implausible (e.g., "Our questions were answered by the *panel* made up by experts in the area of energy research from all over the country").

As a consequence of this state of affairs, research so far has explored the effects of the mental representation of fragments of discourse on lexical processing only sporadically (Foss, 1982; Kleiman, 1980), and although the issue seems to attract increasing interest (Kintsch & Mross, 1985; Sharkey & Sharkey, 1987), our comprehension of the constraining mechanisms of sentential context is still poor.

In the absence of better knowledge, arguments have been put forward, according to which using sentential context information would not be efficient. Forster (1981), for example, points out that in a word-context the lexical processing system can take advantage of the internal structure of the mental lexicon, in which connections among entries preexist due to the co-occurrence in the language of semantically related pairs of words. In contrast, in a sentential context the system cannot rely on such structure: "John tricked Mary into eating the . . ." should prime the class of all edible objects someone would trick someone else into eating, and it is implausible that such a class is prestructured in the lexicon. Consequently, its activation cannot be automatic, but requires complex, time-consuming inferences, whose efficiency compared with simple perceptual processes is dubious.

In my view, Forster's claim (1981) that "a sentence context effect . . . would have to involve an active, complex inferential system . . ." (p. 467) is correct, but the consequences that he draws from it are unwarranted. In particular he seems to assume that unlike the information permanently available, computed information cannot be used automatically by the comprehension system (or one of its components). But there is no reason, in principle, why it should be so. What consciously controlled strategy, in addition to "simple" understanding, is carried out by a native speaker of English in order to activate the features necessary to produce an appropriate completion to "John tricked Mary into eating the — — —"?

Indeed, the activation of those features seems to be part of the process of comprehension itself. A great amount of computation—including activating the lexicon, resolving ambiguity, drawing inferences, etc.—goes on during this process, which is nonetheless, under normal circumstances, automatic, and there is no reason, a priori, why some of the outcomes of those computations should never be available to the lexical processing system.

To sum up, granted that there are problems connected with the techniques of investigation presently at our disposal, the available evidence suggests that the lexical processing system can be affected by semantic information provided by prior sentential context in a number of different cases. Hence, there is no support for the view that it is a completely autonomous system. Several findings, however, corroborate the hypothesis that lexical processing is not sensitive to all contextual information. It follows that one crucial task for future research is to specify the nature and strength of different types of sentential contexts and to determine how they operate in order to yield various effects on the comprehension of words in discourse, ambiguous as well as unambiguous.

Acknowledgments. This research was supported by grants from the Ministry of Public Education (Fondi 40% and 60%). I would like to thank Corrado Cavallero and Carlo Umiltà for their helpful comments.

4

Dynamic Contextual Processes and Lexical Access

GREG B. SIMPSON AND GEORGE KELLAS

In the lexical ambiguity literature, the most active area of research by far has been that concerned with the effects of context on the activation and selection of the meanings of homographs. In some research (e.g., Marcel, 1980; Schvaneveldt, Meyer, & Becker, 1976), the context has taken the form of a single word that is intended to bias the interpretation of a homograph. The effects of this bias on the subsequent recognition of a target are then assessed. Most often, however, the context has consisted of one or two sentences that bias the homograph toward one of its meanings (Conrad, 1974; Glucksberg, Kreuz, & Rho, 1986; Lucas, 1987; Onifer & Swinney, 1981; Seidenberg, Tanenhaus, Leiman, & Bienkowski, 1982; Simpson, 1981; Swinney, 1979; Tabossi, Colombo, & Job, 1987; Tanenhaus, Leiman, & Seidenberg, 1979). Subjects hear the sentence containing the ambiguous word and then respond to a target (either by naming it or by performing a lexical decision) that is related to the same meaning as that suggested by the sentence (the biased meaning) or the other (unbiased) meaning. Most (though not all) of these studies have found that for a very brief period following the presentation of the homograph, responses to words related to either the biased or the unbiased meaning are facilitated in comparison to unrelated words, suggesting that both meanings of the ambiguous word are initially activated, regardless of context. Indeed, this result has become a sort of centerpiece of evidence for the hypothesis that lexical retrieval is an autonomous, encapsulated process, unaffected by contextual constraints imposed by higher levels of language processing.

Occasionally in the past, it appears to have been assumed implicitly that the processes by which single-word and sentence contexts operated were largely comparable. It has become apparent quickly, however, that "context" is not a unitary construct. Although word and sentence contexts may sometimes yield similar patterns of results, they need not, and we cannot assume that they reveal the same characteristics of language processing. Generally, a consensus has emerged that while studies employing single-word context may inform us about the nature of the internal lexicon, they may tell us very little about how that lexical structure is implemented in more natural language processing. In fact, it has become apparent recently that the same words may not have the same effect when embedded in sentences that they have when they constitute the entire context (Peterson & Simpson, 1987).

Even this division between single-word and sentence context, while important, still is not sufficient to account for different patterns of results among studies of context effects. To say that context does or does not influence lexical processing ignores a potentially large number of dimensions along which context may differ, and which may have profound influences on subsequent lexical processing.

In the remainder of this chapter, we will discuss two points that may be important in consideration of the role of context in the processing of ambiguous words. The first of these has to do with characteristics of context sentences used to bias the interpretation of an ambiguous word. The second concerns the way in which a subject processes the context, and more specifically, the effects of retrieval of one meaning of a homograph on a subsequent encounter with that word. We will describe the results of two recent experiments relevant to these points, and suggest that these results, taken together, argue for a view in which contextual effects are seen as more dynamic than has traditionally been the case—a view in which word recognition processes are sensitive not only to the structure and momentary activity within the internal lexicon, but also to the goals that a reader or listener brings to the task of comprehension.

Factors Affecting Context Effects

Strength of Sentence Context

Simpson (1981) reported an experiment in which subjects heard sentences ending in homographs and then made lexical decisions to visually presented target words and nonwords. Sentences were constructed that were ambiguous (not biased toward either meaning) or were biased either strongly or weakly toward the dominant (more frequent) or subordinate (less frequent) meaning. With the ambiguous sentences, only words related to the dominant meaning showed facilitation, relative to unrelated words (e.g., following "The men decided to wait by the bank," MONEY was responded to very rapidly, but RIVER was not). When the sentence was very strongly biased toward one meaning, only words related to that meaning were facilitated. This result is contrary to the more common finding of multiple access of ambiguous word meanings in all contexts (e.g., Conrad, 1974; Onifer & Swinney, 1981; Swinney, 1979). The only condition that showed evidence of multiple access was that in which the sentence was weakly biased in favor of the less frequent meaning (e.g., "The fishermen decided to wait by the bank"). Although words related to this meaning were facilitated, so too were those related to the dominant meaning. It was concluded that the context must be very strong in order to overcome the recognition advantage that the dominant meaning normally has over less frequent ones. This view is consistent with recent statements deriving from an interactive-activation model of language processing (McClelland, 1987).

There were two methodological points, however, on which this research was vulnerable. The first was that it is possible, particularly in the strong-context condition, that the sentences contained individual words for which the ambiguous word was a strong associate. Therefore, the effect may not have been one of selective influence of the sentence context, but simply a case of "intralexical" priming (Forster, 1981; Seidenberg, 1985) of the type seen with single-word context (Meyer & Schvaneveldt, 1971). Recently, however, several direct tests of such lexical priming effects have suggested that simple word-level spreading activation processes are not sufficient to account for context effects with sentences (Foss, 1982; O'Seaghdha, in press; Simpson, Peterson, Casteel, & Burgess, 1989). If only such a process were operating, we would expect its effects to obtain regardless of other characteristics of the sentence. However, Simpson, et al. (1989) found that when the words in sentences containing such lexical primes were scrambled, target recognition was no longer facilitated. Facilitation was lost as well with grammatical sentences that contained individual words related to the targets, but that were semantically anomalous. There is little evidence, then, that selective effects of context are attributable simply to word-level operations.

The second criticism is that in Simpson (1981), 120 ms elapsed between the offset of the auditory homograph and the onset of the visual target. Several studies have shown that this interval is critical, with very short intervals showing facilitation for both meanings, but longer ones (e.g., around 200 ms) resulting in rapid responses only to words related to the biased meaning (Onifer & Swinney, 1981; Seidenberg et al., 1982; Swinney, 1979; Tanenhaus et al., 1979). It is possible that in our earlier research, the 120-ms delay allowed the subject to use the context to select among all meanings, which were activated initially regardless of context. Another possibility, however, is that the context in this research (in the strong-bias condition) was more predictive of a single meaning than that used in other studies. In Simpson (1981), subjects rated the sentences for their degree of bias toward one meaning, and those sentences used in the strong-bias condition were rated as so strongly suggestive of one meaning that the other interpretation was meaningless or bizarre. For example, in the sentence "The vampire was disguised as a handsome count," it seems extremely unlikely that *count* could be interpreted in its mathematical sense. If some of the sentences in other studies were not as strongly biased, and if one meaning of the homograph was not much more frequent than the other, the context may have been less likely to select a single meaning initially.

A Study of Sentence Context

We conducted an experiment to test whether strongly biased sentences would show selective access of homograph meanings even at shorter context-target intervals. Subjects saw sentences ending in ambiguous words and then named word targets that either were related to the same meaning as that biased by the sentence, or were related to the other meaning, or were unrelated words. The sentences were the strongly biased sentences taken from Simpson (1981) or were very similar to them. In addition, a set of sentences not biased toward either meaning was included. Some sample sentences and targets are shown in Table 4.1. The procedure used was similar to that employed by Stanovich and West (1983). The subject read the sentence aloud, and as he or she spoke the last word (the homograph), the experimenter initiated the presentation of the target, which the subject named aloud. The experimenter's keypress presented the target either immediately (0-ms ISI) or after 300 or 700 ms.

With biased sentences, the results were very similar to those of the original study (Simpson, 1981) and were consistent with an immediate selective influence of context. Only the targets related to the same meaning as that biased by the sentence were facilitated in comparison to completely unrelated words. This pattern held equally for the dominant and subordinate meanings, and across the three ISIs. In other words, with these strongly biasing sentences, only the contextually appropriate meaning was made immediately available. Apparently, more than the 120-ms ISI used in our earlier research (Simpson, 1981) distinguishes this study from others (e.g., Onifer & Swinney, 1981; Seidenberg et al., 1982). The discrepancy also does not seem to be traceable to any difference between auditory and visual presentation of context, in light of the similarity between these results and our previous study. It might be argued that the visual presentation leads to a functionally longer ISI than auditory presentation does, allowing multiple access and the subsequent selection process to occur before target presentation even in the 0-ISI condition. However, ISI did have an effect for the unbiased sentences, and one that mirrored the effects seen when homographs are presented in isolation (Simpson & Burgess, 1985). That is, with these sentences, only the dominant meaning showed

TABLE 4.1. Sample sentences and related targets.

Sentence type	Targets: Dominant	Targets: Subordinate
Ambiguous		
I don't think this is the right key.	LOCK	TYPE
Dominant		
I couldn't get in with the wrong key.	LOCK	TYPE
Subordinate		
I made a mistake by pressing the wrong key.	LOCK	TYPE

facilitation at the shortest and longest intervals, but both meanings were activated at the 300-ms ISI.

Instead, some characteristics of the context sentences themselves appear to be responsible for the differences in results between our studies and some previous research. We cannot dismiss the problem by reiterating that our sentences were rated as very strongly biased toward one meaning, as a reading of sample sentences provided by other researchers shows that these too would likely be rated as highly biased. For example, Seidenberg et al. (1982) provide an example from an experiment that yielded an initial pattern of multiple access: "Go to the store and buy a spade." It is unlikely that subjects think consciously of a playing card in this sentence, and subject ratings would probably confirm that this sentence is quite strongly biased toward the garden implement meaning. In another way, however, this sentence differs considerably from those which we use. Compare the sentence above with "I made a mistake by pressing the wrong key," which in our research yields immediate (0-ms ISI) priming for TYPE but not for LOCK. If a cloze procedure were applied to these sentences with the homograph deleted, the latter would be likely to elicit either *key* or *button* very frequently, while the former sentence would probably generate a large number of reasonable completions (indeed, anything that could be bought in a store). So although the sentences may be equally biased toward one meaning when the ambiguous word is present, they differ in the amount of information that they provide, prior to the ambiguous word, that might be relevant for the selection of a single meaning. Therefore, in discussing "strength of context," we should be aware of two components: (1) the constraint of the context on the homograph and (2) the bias of the context once the homograph is known. Such a distinction is consistent with the results described by Tabossi in this volume (Chapter 3) and more fully elsewhere (Tabossi, 1988a). Her nonpriming contexts correspond to the kinds of stimuli that we are describing as low constraint and high bias, while her priming context exhibits both high constraint and high bias. The former stimuli led in her research to access of both meanings of the homograph, while the latter resulted in access only of contextually appropriate meanings, as in our research. In short, sentences high on both dimensions appear to be required to effect an immediate contextual influence.

How does sentence constraint exert its selective effects on homograph processing? We would argue that the prior constraining context provides information relevant to the appropriate meaning before the homograph is presented, thereby raising the activation level of that meaning. This conclusion is similar to that drawn by Seidenberg et al. (1982), who argued that the speed of retrieval of a meaning is determined by the level of activation of that meaning relative to other meanings. This activation level may be sensitive to the base frequency of the meaning (Simpson & Burgess,

1985), or certain kinds of context, which may temporarily increase the activation of one meaning. However, Seidenberg et al. attributed such contextual effects to intralexical spreading activation (i.e., activation spreading among representations of strongly associated words within the lexicon), and we do not believe that our results can be attributed solely to such a process. We attempted to avoid words within our sentences that could by themselves predict the homograph, and in any case, direct evidence for intralexical effects within sentences has been hard to find (O'Seaghdha, in press; Simpson, et al., 1989). Therefore, we do not think that our context-dependent effect is strictly an intralexical one. Rather, we would attribute it to the compatibility of features activated by the context and those associated with one of the meanings of the homograph (see also Tabossi, this volume, Chapter 3). This view is consistent with research reported by Schwanenflugel and her colleagues (Schwanenflugel & La-Count, 1988; Schwanenflugel & Shoben, 1985). Schwanenflugel and La-Count found that high-constraint sentences facilitated recognition of sentence-final target words only if those words were the most likely completions of the sentences. In low-constraint sentences, facilitation was again shown for these expected completions, but also for unexpected targets if they were related to the expected word. They propose that a sentence context leads to the generation of a set of featural restrictions. That is, a set of criteria is established that determines the features that an upcoming word should have. High-constraint sentences are those that generate a large number of such restrictions, thereby narrowing the range of potential words that will satisfy them. Facilitation, then, will only be found for the most highly expected target. Lower-constraint sentences, however, generate fewer restrictions, and more potential completions will be compatible, resulting in facilitation for a wider range of targets. Applied to the case of ambiguous words, we would argue that a high-constraint sentence will generate featural restrictions with which only one meaning of an upcoming homograph will be compatible. This compatibility will determine in part the speed with which the appropriate meaning may be retrieved.

We propose that when an ambiguous word is presented, bottom-up information from the word itself combines with the existing activation present for each of the word's meanings. If the activation levels of these meanings are equal, then all will be retrieved at the same time. However, if one meaning is already activated to a higher degree, then it will reach a recognition threshold first and will thus be selected for further processing (Seidenberg et al., 1982). Any factor that affects one meaning's activation level before the homograph is encountered will therefore have an immediate influence on the selection process. Our research has led us to propose two such factors: (1) the relative base frequencies of the meanings and (2) the featural restrictions generated by high-constraint context. Information from these sources (and perhaps others as well) converges with that provided by the ambiguous stimulus itself to determine the identity of the word and to select a single appropriate meaning (Just & Carpenter, 1987). The effects of frequency and context do not alter the bottom-up activation accruing for each meaning from the ambiguous word itself, but we nevertheless see their activity as "prelexical," in that they exert their influence on the ambiguous word before it is identified, rather than simply selecting among equally active competitors.

We believe that this account, along with our separation of sentence constraint and bias, may help reconcile some of the discrepancies in the ambiguity literature. In cases in which no sentence context is provided (Simpson & Burgess, 1985), or when very low constraint sentences are used (Seidenberg et al., 1982, or the ambiguous sentence conditions reported here and in Simpson, 1981), meaning access will be based on bottom-up information and the relative frequencies of the meanings. If the meanings are approximately equally common (Seidenberg et al., 1982), then only bottom-up information can be used, and all meanings are initially retrieved. If one meaning is more frequent than the other, however (as in our research), that meaning will be available sooner, as its resting level of activation is higher.

High-constraint sentences, on the other hand, allow the generation of featural restrictions that boost the resting level of activation of one meaning before the homograph appears. In this case, the effects of context are immediate, as in the present research and in that of Tabossi (1988a). If the restrictions are strong enough, it is even possible for the context to overcome the effects of meaning frequency. We are not claiming, of course, that only high-constraint sentences will exert contextual influence. Low-constraint sentences will still show context effects if they are highly biased toward one meaning, but these effects will be delayed. For example, Seidenberg et al. (1982) showed activation for only the contextually appropriate meaning 200 ms after the offset of the ambiguous word, although both meanings had been active earlier (see also Onifer & Swinney, 1981; Swinney, 1979; Tanenhaus et al., 1979). The point here is that high-constraint contexts provide information that is relevant to meaning selection before the ambiguous word is presented. This information may then be used immediately when the homograph occurs. Low-constraint sentences, no matter how biased they may be once the homograph is given, provide information that cannot be used for the selection until after the homograph is identified.

It is important to note, however, that in all of these cases the basis of the selection process is the same: It is based upon the level of activation of each of the homograph meanings at the time the homograph is presented. The very different patterns of results in the extant research reflect differences in the types of homographs used (in terms of relative frequencies of the meanings) and in the nature of the context that precedes them.

The Subject's Interaction with Context

Another factor that may influence the activation level of a meaning, and thereby context effects, concerns the way in which the subject is asked to process the context. This factor has been given relatively little attention in the word recognition literature, although several single-word priming studies have shown that the effects of context on subsequent target recognition depend upon how the contextual information is processed (Henik, Friedrich, & Kellogg, 1983; Smith, Theodor, & Franklin, 1983; see also Smith, this volume, Chapter 8). Generally, this research has shown that as the context is processed to a deeper level (i.e., in a way that promotes conceptual aspects of processing), context effects become more pronounced. It may be that the ability of context to select among ambiguous word meanings is also sensitive to the way in which the subject interacts with that context. That is, it is possible that "deeper" processing of context will allow immediate access to a single meaning consistent with that context, while "shallower" processing might lead to access of all meanings, regardless of how biasing that context might be.

A series of studies by Killion (1979) provided data relevant to this question. In four experiments using visual presentation of sentences ending in homographs, Killion varied the instructions to the subject concerning the task to be performed on the context. In one experiment, subjects were instructed to verify the sentence with respect to real-world knowledge. In a second, they were to read each sentence as if to comprehend it as part of a text. In the third experiment, they simply were to read the sentence, and in the final experiment, they were asked for verbatim recall of the sentence on 25% of the trials. The first two experiments resulted in facilitation only for words related to the meaning biased by the sentence, while the latter two showed access of both meanings. If we consider the first two experiments to involve more elaborated processing of the context, then the results are reminiscent of those reported by Smith et al. (1983), showing depth-of-processing effects on contextual facilitation. In this case, it appears that a task that promotes more complete comprehension of the sentences as a whole results in selective access of a homograph meaning consistent with that context. The various tasks that Killion used are common ones in psycholinguistic research, and it is not always recognized that the task selected may promote very different kinds of processing by subjects.

A Study of Repetition Context

We have recently completed another experiment that also speaks to the issue of the subject's processing of the context, albeit in a very different way. Instead of the sentences typically used to assess context effects, the experiment we describe in this section investigated the effects of multiple presentations of an ambiguous word. That is, the context in this study was not a biasing sentence, but a prior occurrence of the ambiguous word. The study was designed to assess the effects of one encounter with a homograph and one of its associates on the later processing of that homograph.

The impetus for this research was the observation that normal discourse, unlike sentences in a discrete-trials word recognition experiment, typically introduces concepts that will be activated and maintained in an active state for a relatively long period of time. That is, perhaps one of the most important differences between experimental context and more natural discourse is that the former repeatedly activates concepts for a single sentence and then dismisses them, never to activate them again. This raises questions of another kind of context: that arising from the prior activation of a concept, or in the case of lexical ambiguity, from the prior processing of one meaning of a homograph. That is, does the active processing of one meaning of a homograph have an effect on how it is processed on a subsequent encounter? We refer to this as *repetition context*, and have examined it by presenting a subject on one trial with a pair of words comprising a homograph prime and a target related to either the prime's dominant or its subordinate meaning. On a subsequent trial (separated from the first by a lag of 0, 1, 4, or 12 intervening trials), the homograph was repeated, this time paired with a target related to the same meaning as that shown on the earlier trial, or the other meaning. For example, if on one trial we showed the subject a pair such as BANK-MONEY (the latter word representing the dominant meaning), on a later trial we presented to the subject the pair BANK-SAVE (a new target also related to the dominant meaning) or BANK-RIVER (related to the subordinate meaning). On some trials, we repeated the target exactly (BANK-MONEY).

In previous research (Simpson & Burgess, 1985), we have shown that when an ambiguous word is presented in isolation, its dominant meaning becomes available immediately, while activation builds more slowly for the subordinate meaning. This less frequent meaning does not reach a level comparable to that of the more frequent until 300 ms following presentation of the ambiguous word. After both meanings have been activated, the advantage for the dominant meaning is reestablished, as activation for the subordinate meaning declines. In a second experiment, we included a neutral context condition and found that the advantage for the dominant meaning at long prime-target intervals was attributable to an active allocation of resources to information related to that meaning. This explanation was suggested by the finding that words related to the subordinate meaning, along with all unrelated words, led to slower responses than did words preceded by a neutral context.

What might we expect, then, in a study in which primes are repeated, but paired with other associates on their second presentations? One possibility is that the pattern of activation across meanings of a homograph is determined solely by the structure of lexical memory, and will obtain any time that homograph appears. Such a process might be expected on the basis of the results in one of the conditions in Simpson and Burgess (1985), in which the advantage for dominant associates was shown even when they constituted only 20% of the word targets. This pattern would be consistent with a rather pure form of lexical autonomy, in which lexical spreading activation effects are not influenced by episodic factors. In such a case, we would expect that associates of the dominant meaning will show considerable facilitation, whereas subordinate associates will display much less (a 100-ms SOA was used) on both first and second presentations. In the case of second presentations, this pattern should obtain regardless of the target shown with the prime on its first occurrence.

If, on the other hand, homograph processing is affected by prior activation of one of the meanings, then we might expect to see different results on the second presentation of a prime as a function of the meaning favored on the first. Such an influence of prior homograph processing may be to facilitate subsequent processing of targets related to the same meaning as that responded to earlier, or to inhibit targets related to the other meaning (or some combination of these). The possibility of inhibition for a new meaning is especially intriguing in light of previous suggestions that meanings may be suppressed if they are not selected by context for further processing (Seidenberg, 1985; Simpson & Burgess, 1985; Swinney, 1979; Tanenhaus et al., 1979). The evidence for suppression has been largely circumstantial to date, however. Despite our earlier finding (Simpson & Burgess, 1985) of slower responses to subordinate targets compared with those with neutral primes, we cannot conclude that such an effect rests on active suppression of the subordinate meaning. Rather, it is clear only that the response to a subordinate meaning is inhibited as attention is withdrawn from it, and must be reallocated if that meaning is required for responding. That is, such a withdrawal of attention does not necessarily constitute an active suppression of the internal representation of the unwanted meaning. Indeed, in most research (e.g., Onifer & Swinney, 1981; Seidenberg et al., 1982; Simpson, 1981; Simpson & Burgess, 1985), a meaning that is not selected for further processing, on the basis of either its dominance or the surrounding context, shows responses that are approximately equal to, but usually not slower than, those to completely unrelated targets. A stronger case for suppression could be made if it were shown that an unbiased meaning is rendered less available even than unrelated information. This study allowed a test of whether the prior processing of one meaning of an ambiguous word may facilitate the recognition of other words related to that same meaning on a subsequent presentation, or may lead instead to suppression of other meanings.

The results showed that the first time a homograph was presented, words related to the dominant meaning showed greater facilitation than did those related through the subordinate meaning. Of particular interest, however, are the naming times associated with a prime's second presentation, as a function of the prime-target relation displayed on the first. Figure 4.1

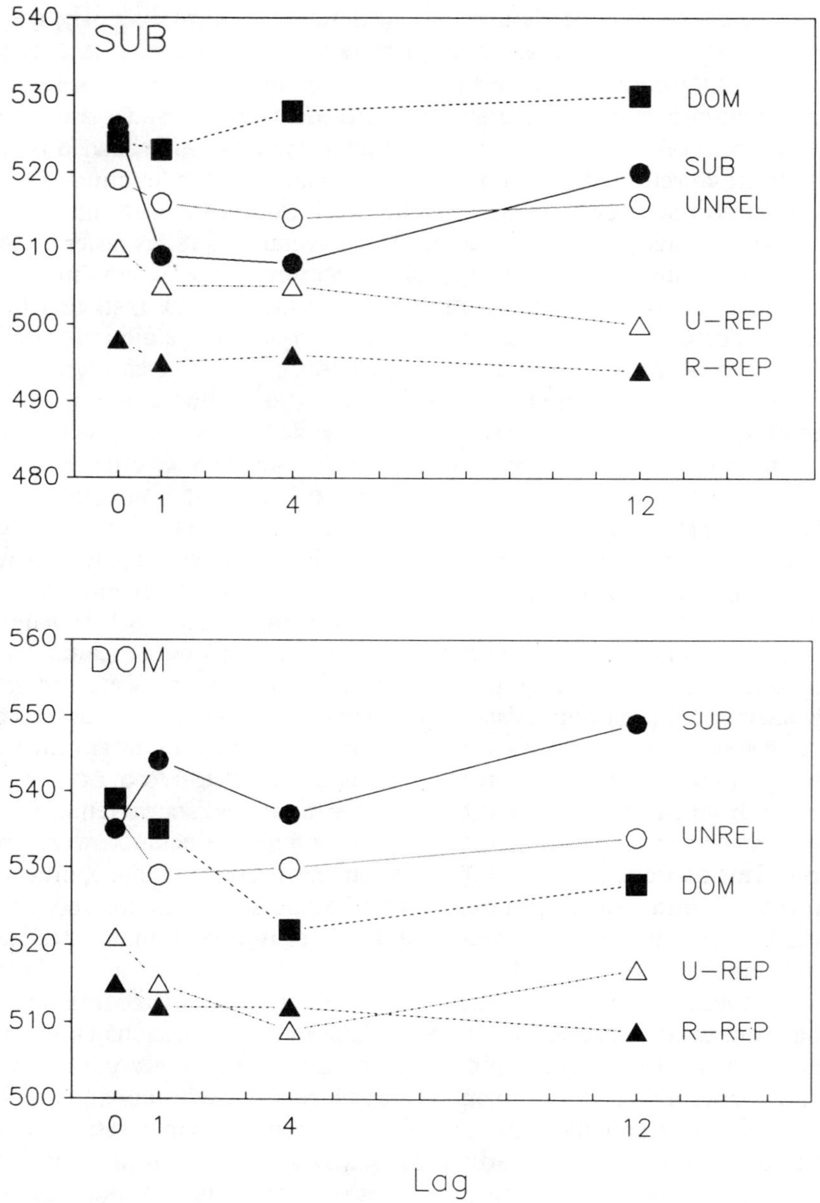

FIGURE 4.1. Mean target naming times for the second presentation of homographs. The top panel represents subjects receiving only subordinate associates on the second presentation. The bottom panel represents those receiving dominant associates on the second presentation. Within each panel, the lines represent the target type that the subject had seen on the first presentation of the homograph.

shows these results, separately for those conditions presenting subordinate and dominant associates on the second prime presentation, each line representing the meaning that had occurred on the first presentation.

The first point to note about these data is that targets repeated exactly on the second presentation were responded to much more rapidly than were any other targets. This can be seen in the two lowest lines in each panel of the figure. Even an unrelated target will lead to rapid naming if it is identical to one presented on an earlier trial. Both unrelated and related exact repetitions were also responded to an average of 18 ms faster on the second presentation than on the first. These were the only conditions to show facilitation on the second presentation relative to the first; all others yielded a pattern in which the targets on the second presentation of a prime led to equal or somewhat slower responses than did those on the first presentation. The fact that the unrelated and the related exact repetitions showed the same amount of facilitation on the second presentation (18 ms) is consistent with other recent work showing an additivity of semantic priming and word repetition (den Heyer, 1986; den Heyer, Goring, & Dannenbring, 1985).

Next, consider responses to targets that differed across the two prime presentations, taking first the trials that showed subordinate associates on the second presentation, displayed in the top panel of Figure 4.1. When the target was related to the same meaning on the second presentation as on the first (i.e., a different subordinate associate on each presentation), responses tended to be approximately the same across lags as they were when completely unrelated targets were seen on both presentations (in each of the panels of Figure 4.1, the unrelated conditions are collapsed, as they did not differ statistically). When the first presentation had shown a dominant target, however, subordinate targets on the second presentation were very slow. This appears, then, to be more an instance of an actual suppression process: A meaning different from that responded to on one occasion becomes less available for subsequent processing even than unrelated information.

The lower panel of the figure represents those conditions in which dominant targets appeared on the prime's second presentation. This panel displays a pattern that is, generally, a mirror image of that seen in the upper panel. When different dominant associates served as targets on the two presentations, responses were again approximately the same as (or slightly faster than) those to unrelated words. Naming a dominant associate was slowed, however, when a subordinate target was presented on an earlier trial. Once again, if one meaning of an ambiguous word has been processed to the level of an overt response, the other meaning appears to undergo suppression.

Two particular points may be raised about these data. First, it is clear that the suppression effect is symmetrical with respect to meaning dominance. The inhibition seen for dominant associates following subordinate is as great as that for subordinate associates following dominant. This is particularly interesting in light of the 100-ms SOA, an interval usually considered to be brief enough to reflect only automatic spreading activation processes (Neely, 1977; Posner & Snyder, 1975b). A common assumption concerning such processes is that they proceed in an obligatory manner once the prime undergoes processing. We might have expected, therefore, that although the subordinate meaning might have been suppressed fairly rapidly, the dominant meaning should not. That is, once processing of the homograph is initiated, activation should begin spreading first to those words related to the dominant meaning, as was the case on the first presentation and has so consistently been seen in our earlier research (Burgess & Simpson, 1988a; Simpson & Burgess, 1985; Simpson & Foster, 1986). These data suggest a very powerful, and very rapid, suppression process that is able to dominate the kinds of spreading activation processes that are believed to arise as a natural consequence of the structure of the internal lexicon.

A second point of interest concerns the observation that the effects found here are relatively constant across lag. The effect of responding to one meaning of an ambiguous word on the subsequent processing of that same word is as strong with 12 intervening word pairs as it is when the two encounters are on consecutive trials. Such a long-term effect is expected for exact repetitions, as a number of studies have demonstrated very robust and long-lived effects of target repetition (Ratcliff, Hockley, & McKoon, 1985; Scarborough, Cortese, & Scarborough, 1977). The pattern was also constant, however, for those conditions displaying different targets on the two presentations. In particular, those conditions that represent a change in meaning from the first presentation of a prime to the second are consistently slower than unrelated words, even at lag 12. This effect is very different from that for exact repetitions. First, of course, the effect for exact repetitions is one of facilitation relative to all other conditions. This speeding of responses is often ascribed to enhanced "perceptual fluency" occasioned by the prior presentation of a stimulus (e.g., Carroll & Kirsner, 1982; Jacoby & Dallas, 1981). The effect of a change of meaning, on the other hand, is to slow responses relative to other targets. Also, this is presumably not a perceptual effect, as the target is different on the two occasions, and therefore, a word encountered on the second presentation has not been seen earlier in the experiment. It could be argued that the prime on the second presentation, because it has been encountered recently, is recognized more quickly, leading to a functional increase in the SOA. In this case, however, we would have expected different patterns for dominant and subordinate targets. We have never found inhibition for dominant associates, regardless of SOA, so although repeating the primes undoubtedly does lead to their faster recognition, this fact cannot account fully for the pattern of target recognition times.

The pattern obtained here also argues against a process that would act after lexical access of the target to inhibit responses that were inconsistent with the word named on the earlier presentation. Under this view, a subject may have an expectancy for a repeated target on a prime's second presentation, and production of any other response is inhibited. However, the argument has recently been made that inhibitory effects are rare with target naming, as opposed to tasks (such as lexical decision) that require a binary decision (Lorch, Balota, & Stamm, 1986; West & Stanovich, 1982). Also, such an explanation cannot account for the differences seen between those conditions employing different targets on the two presentations. Rather, the repetition context effect appears to arise as a result of a temporary restructuring of the functional relationships between an ambiguous word and various associates.

Two other aspects of these data are worth special note. The first is the lack of any change in responses as a function of lag. One might expect that with intervening trials, activation of an entry presented earlier would return to its resting level. There was no evidence that such effects dissipated in the slightest even at lag 12, however. Such persistence is reminiscent of word repetition results, both in previous research (e.g., Scarborough et al., 1977) and in the exact repetition conditions of the present research. We are conducting further research to examine whether there might have been some aspect of the present procedure that obscured an effect of lag.

A second point concerns the apparent dependence of the present data on the requirement that the subject make an overt response to a meaning on an earlier trial. In the long-SOA conditions of our earlier research (Simpson & Burgess, 1985), the dominant meaning was activated before the subordinate meaning could be retrieved and responded to. Nevertheless, these responses were not slower than those to unrelated words. In the present research, on the other hand, when one meaning (either meaning) led to a response, subsequent responses to associates of the other meaning were performed more slowly than were unrelated responses. It appears, then, that it is not enough that a meaning be activated to lead to suppression of the other meaning. Rather, a response must be made on the basis of that meaning. We might consider this to be an extreme case of the task effects discussed earlier (Henik et al., 1983; Killion, 1979; Smith et al., 1983). The subject is required not simply to process the context (the earlier presentation) in some way, but to process a particular meaning to the level of a response. With this complete processing of the context, then, we would expect a pattern of selective access on the subsequent trial. Tipper (1985; Tipper & Cranston, 1985) has described a set of "negative priming" phenomena, of which the present results may be an instance (see also Neill, this volume, Chapter 6, and Neill & Westberry, 1987). An ignored stimulus, if selected against for a response on one trial in a Strooplike procedure, is more difficult to identify rapidly on a subsequent trial. For example, Tipper (1985) showed subjects a series of pairs of line drawings, the two drawings superimposed and in different colors. The subjects were to identify the picture drawn in the designated color (e.g., red) and ignore the other (green) drawing. If a picture shown in green on one trial was presented in red on the next, the naming response to this previously ignored drawing was slowed. Similar effects were shown when the picture to be named on the second trial was not identical to the ignored drawing on the first but was related to it (e.g., an ignored cat slowed the subsequent response identifying a dog). The present results appear to be an example of such negative priming, showing that the selection of one meaning of a homograph in order to respond has a detrimental effect on the subsequent processing of the other meaning. Its persistence across lag indicates that this kind of context effect is a very powerful one.

Conclusions

Over the last decade, a consensus has developed that all meanings of a lexical ambiguity are processed regardless of context, a view consistent with the hypothesis that lexical processing is an autonomous operation within the language processor (Forster, 1979; Seidenberg, 1985). Apparent violation of the multiple-access predictions have been attributed to other factors, such as intralexical priming or the critical timing of context and target presentation. Some of our recent research, however, suggests that word-level priming is a poor candidate for explaining sentence context effects (Simpson et al., 1989), and that the selective context effects shown by Simpson (1981) were not due solely to a brief delay between the context and target. With highly constraining and biasing context, only the meaning appropriate to the context may be activated under some circumstances, regardless of the context-target interval.

Recently, McClelland (1987) has challenged the view that word recognition is impervious to context. McClelland argues that an interactive-activation account (McClelland & Rumelhart, 1981) would predict that sufficiently strong context should be able to produce immediate top-down facilitative effects, and should be able to mask the effects of other variables that may, under other conditions, exert powerful influences over word recognition speed. Our sentence context research (and that of Tabossi, 1988a) is fully compatible with this view. In our recent study, we found that strong context was able immediately to overcome the effects of meaning frequency, which we have found previously to be an extremely powerful determinant of meaning activation speed when homographs are presented in isolation.

Our research involving homograph repetition shows strong effects of a very different kind of context. If one meaning is required for a response on one occasion, the other meaning appears to be suppressed, and very difficult to retrieve for a response later. The strength of this kind of context effect is shown by the fact that the dominant meaning, which is normally more accessible than the subordinate, shows this suppression as strongly as does a rare meaning.

Suppression processes have been speculated for ambiguity processing before, but rarely have responses to the supposedly suppressed meaning actually been slower than those to unrelated words. The suppression may be dependent on an earlier response to one of the homograph's meanings. That is, although the dominant meaning is typically activated first when an ambiguous word is presented (Burgess & Simpson, 1988a; Simpson & Burgess, 1985; Simpson & Foster, 1986), this activation by itself does not lead to suppression of the subordinate meaning. Similarly, although our sentence study showed context-dependent access, the responses to the unbiased meaning were no slower than those to unrelated words.

A reader or listener arrives at the task of comprehension with a set of goals that vary with the circumstances of that comprehension. A proofreader may not process text to the same level that one does when reading for a test over its contents. Research on the effects of prime task confirms that different goals have an influence on word recognition processes (Henik et al., 1983; Smith, this volume, Chapter 8; Smith et al., 1983). Killion's research (1979) indicates similarly that the same context sentences may have different effects on homograph processing as a function of the subject's task in processing the sentences. These results suggest to us the need to view context as a very dynamic construct. The processing of ambiguous word meanings is sensitive to the structure of lexical memory, in terms of the enduring relationships among ambiguous words and their various meanings, but also in terms of more transitory changes in those relationships. These changes arise from temporary alterations in the relative activation levels of the meanings. They may occur when context provides information that might be used to predict characteristics of the appropriate meaning before the homograph itself occurs, and when comprehension goals dictate further that such information should be used. In the strongest case of highly informative context and appropriate comprehension goals, a reader or listener essentially makes a "commitment" to a particular interpretation of the discourse. This commitment, in turn, becomes part of the context in which further discourse is processed. We believe that our repetition context results are an example of such a commitment. Once the subject has responded to one meaning of a homograph, that processing episode becomes part of the context in which further encounters occur. Such an episode has the effect of adjusting the activation levels of relevant concepts, and in particular, of dampening or suppressing the activation for inappropriate meanings. We see this process as closely related to that which occurs in the normal processing of extended discourse, for which it is prudent to have discourse-relevant information remain in an activated state at the expense of competing information.

In future research, we intend to explore more fully the level to which a meaning must be processed to promote the negative priming effects that we have found with repeated homograph presentations. This, along with research to investigate the relationship between repetition and sentential context, should help us understand the effects on word recognition played by contextual influences that arise repeatedly in an experiment or in natural language processing.

In any case, it appears that there are some kinds of contextual manipulations that can have immediate and powerful effects on very early stages of lexical processing. "Context" clearly is not the simple and static concept it once seemed to be. Before we either propose it as a principal determinant of lexical access or dismiss it as having no effect at all, we will need to understand it far better than we do now.

Acknowledgments. Preparation of this manuscript was supported in part by U.S. Department of Education Grant G008630072 to the Kansas Bureau of Child Research and Learning Disabilities Center of the University of Kansas. The research described herein was conducted while the first author was a Postdoctoral Trainee in the Child Language Program of the University of Kansas. We are very grateful to Kelly Lyons for her help in conducting the research.

5

When Does "Soar" Become "Sore"? Some Comments on the Chapter of Simpson and Kellas

David S. Gorfein and Marianne F. Walters

One of the problems for the field of semantic psychology and for any problem-solving effort is the "set" to employ methods and interpretations that have worked well in the past. In the field of problem solving the transfer of method or "set" to new problems was, long ago, shown to be efficient when it was appropriate but very costly when it was not (cf., e.g., Luchins, 1942). We believe that in extending the idea of inhibition to include their subject's negative transfer in the word-naming task, Simpson and Kellas may be entering a blind alley. To be sure, the authors are aware of a problem for that interpretation, since inhibition generally declines with time; but they report, "We are conducting further research to examine whether there might have been some aspect of the present procedure that obscured an effect of lag."

In this chapter we will briefly review some data that were independently arrived at as part of a doctoral dissertation conducted by Walters (1988). These data extend the time frame of the "inhibitory effects" reported by Simpson and Kellas. Further, the present work shows such effects to be insensitive to the task of the subject, thus making an inhibitory mechanism seem a good deal less tenable.

The Priority Effect

The research reported by Walters (1988) consisted of seven experiments (four pilot studies and three extensive experiments), all of which made use of an implicit memory paradigm (cf. Schachter, 1987, for a review of this literature). For our purposes we will reconfigure the results of two of those experiments to speak to the questions of lexical ambiguity although we believe that a more general conclusion is justified. We may note that while the research in these studies employed ambiguous materials (nonhomographic homophones), the aim, as Simpson suggests (Chapter 2, this volume), was to understand a more general question.

Each of the two experiments made use of what we call a three-phase design. In phase 1, the materials used were designed to bias a particular meaning of a nonhomographic homophone (from here on called *homophones*). These words had been previously normed in our laboratory for preferred spelling or meaning (Gorfein & O'Brien, 1986). In phase 2, a second biasing manipulation was introduced, with that manipulation either consistent or inconsistent with the phase 1 bias. In phase 3, a test phase, the participants were required to spell the homophone, which was presented out of context as part of a 72-item spelling test. (*Note:* In the pilot studies reported, other phase 3 tasks were employed as tests and yielded similar effects.)

Effect of Intertask Interval

Specifically, in Walters' Experiment 1, phase 1 consisted of subjects filling in the blanks in sentences such as "Like father, like s__" or "The earth revolves around the s__." One-third of the 36 homophone pairs employed in this study were presented in a sentence context designed to elicit primary meanings (spellings), one-third were designed to elicit secondary spellings, and one-third were not included in the phase 1 manipulation. These were embedded in a number of filler sentences in which the blank item was not a homophone. Phase 2 consisted of a secondary bias manipulation in which subjects were asked to remember the location of certain pictures on a page. Participants were instructed (and subsequently tested) to remember in which quadrant on the page each picture occurred. The experimenter read the names of the pictures to them in a random order, and the subject was instructed to point to the picture that best represented the name read. Thus, for the pictures in Figure 5.1, the experimenter might have read "bare, sore, knight, son." After completing the five pages of the booklet, the subject was given a sheet with four quadrants on it and told to write in *the number* of the picture that occurred in each quadrant in its appropriate place. Thus, the experimenter on the memory test for the illustrated page might now say, "1. knight, 2. sore, 3. bare, 4. son." The pictures, of course, were not present at test. Half of the items from each condition of phase 1 were pictured in phase 2 (along with two filler items, otherwise unused homophones, necessary to create five full pages of four pictures each).

The test phase was always on the same day as the phase 2 picture manipulation. For half of the subjects in this study, phase 2 commenced 10 minutes after phase 1, with a filler activity intervening. After the filler activity on day 1, the other half of the subjects were sent home and tested on the next day. All subjects were required to return for the second day to equate the two groups.

Thus, the study for our purposes can be seen as a 3 (sentence experience: primary, secondary, none) × 2 (day of phase 2 and 3) × 2 (presence or absence of secondary picture in picture phase) design. Table 5.1 reports the

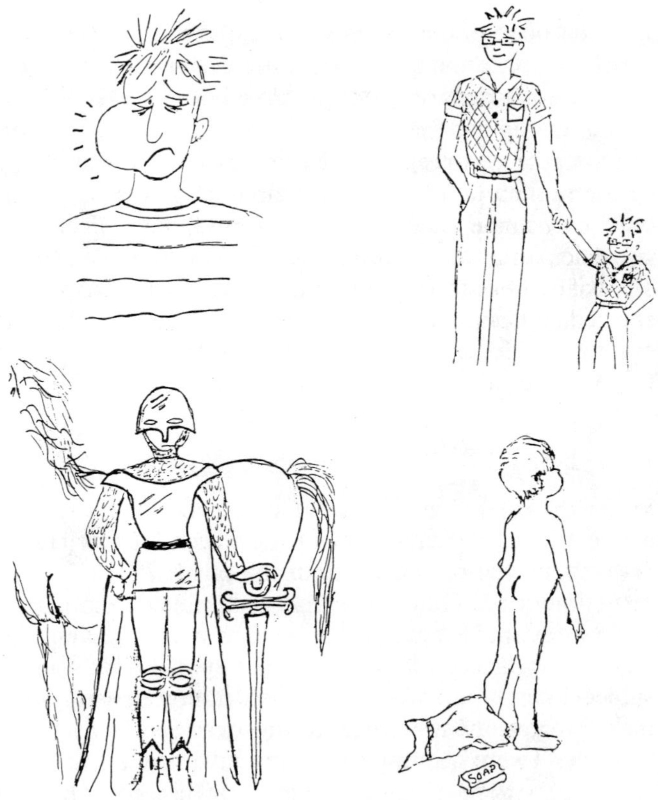

FIGURE 5.1. Typical pages of secondary priming drawings from picture memory tests. Words primed clockwise from upper left are "sore", "son", "bare", and "knight".

TABLE 5.1. Proportion of secondary spellings of homophones and rank (6 = high) as a function of sentence prime, presentation of secondary pictures, and day of presentation of pictures.[a]

Conditions		Performance			
		Pictures		Pictures	
Sentence phase material	Secondary pictures (present/ absent)	Day 1	Rank	Day 2	Rank
1. Primary	Absent	(.228)	1	(.264)	1
2. Absent	Absent	(.332)	2	(.325)	2
3. Primary	Present	(.401)	3	(.494)	4
4. Absent	Present	(.468)	4	(.506)	5
5. Secondary	Absent	(.484)	5	(.401)	3
6. Secondary	Present	(.632)	6	(.540)	6

[a]Derived from Table 6 of Walters (1988).

mean proportion of secondary spellings as a function of the experimental conditions. All comparisons within a day are within-subjects comparisons. Those across days are between-subjects manipulations.

The results, as can be seen in Table 5.1, are quite striking. While normatively (see the control or absent-absent conditions) about 33% of these words are spelled in the secondary direction, the sentence manipulation has both immediate and lasting effects, and these effects are additive with the presentation of the picture. There is a persistence of the sentence completion phase 24 hours later as shown by such comparisons as sentence alone (primary or secondary) to the control. The effect, or lack thereof, of the temporal interval is reinforced by looking at the differences in performance of the sentence plus picture conditions on day 1 and day 2.

Effects of Phase 2

In the second experiment we will examine, the conditions employed were created so that the immediate effect of the phase 1 experience could be directly observed on the performance of the phase 2 task.

In this experiment the picture-memory task used in the first study was employed in an identical manner but now as *phase 1.* Thus, 18 homophones and 2 fillers all pictured in the secondary direction was phase 1. In phase 2, subjects participated in a word association experiment in which they were asked to give the first word to come to mind for each of 92 words presented aurally. Twenty of the words were fillers, and the remaining 72 consisted of the 36 homophones immediately preceded by a word for association intended to prime the primary meaning (spelling) of the homophone, such as *glide* preceding *sôr.* Two forms of the picture test were employed to use all 36 items. Following phase 2, a spelling test, identical to that in the first experiment, was performed either immediately or after a 15-minute filled delay.

Thus, the design of this study was a 2 (presence or absence of phase 1 secondary picture) × 2 (time of spelling test—immediate or 15-minute delayed) design, with the delay of phase 3 manipulation as a between-subject treatment.

In Chapter 1 of this volume, we mentioned that most ambiguity tasks lacked transparency (i.e., we have no way of knowing what meaning state the participant has assigned to a lexical ambiguity). In this experiment, phase 2 was a primed word association task. By looking at the associations, we could determine which meaning state had been achieved by the participant. Thus, to the extent that the phase 2 (primary) manipulation has succeeded, we would expect primary word associations. On the average, we found that when the word association for an item occurred in the absence of a secondary picture in phase 1, 85.8% of the associations could be classified as primary. However, when the subject had seen the item pictured in phase 1, this effect was reliably reduced to 70.9%.

TABLE 5.2. Proportion of primary spellings as a function of time of spelling test and phase 1 experience.[a]

	Delay of spelling test		
Phase 1 picture	0 min	15 min	Mean
Present	.505	.659	.582
Absent	.790	.755	.772
Mean	.647	.707	

[a]Derived from Table 11 of Walters (1988).

More dramatic than that effect was the performance on the spelling test (see Table 5.2). As in the first experiment, the spelling test consisted of the auditory presentation of a list of 72 words embedded in which were 36 out-of-context homophones. In the control condition of the first experiment we had obtained an average of 68% primary spellings. In that study, when the subjects had been primed in the primary direction and had no experience with the secondary pictures, spelling was 75% in the primary direction. In this study (as seen in Table 5.2), in the absence of pictures, spelling performance was 77% primary. Yet, on the average, only 58.2% of the spellings of the items pictured were in the primary direction. In fact, of those items tested immediately after the word association test in which subjects had averaged 70.9% primary associations, spelling performance was only 50.5% primary. Thus, the data look as if the impact of the word association test is to temporarily suppress (or mask) the impact of the phase 1 pictures. That effect reappears in the absence of a primary context in phase 3 (spelling). The complexity of the problem is seen when looking at the delayed spelling test, which shows a larger effect of the word association of the spelling test.

Explanation

A similarity between the Simpson-Kellas results and the findings of Walters is that the first experience has a stronger effect than might otherwise be expected. Most theorists of ambiguity processing expect each experience of an ambiguity to be processed independently at least when the events are temporally separate. The strong influence of the first event has been labeled the *priority effect* (Walters, 1988).

Simpson and Kellas sought a theoretical mechanism in terms of inhibition to reconcile their results. To the degree that the processes that mediate spelling and pronunciation are similar, the temporal separation of the events (24 hours) in the first experiment we reported makes such an explanation less than problematical. The complexity of the temporal effects in Experiment 2 are even more damaging to such a position.

It is obvious that Simpson and Kellas are not alone in their theoretical problem. In a similar manner, the theory proposed by Barsalou (1987), a retrieval-based framework to account for concept stability-instability, would have equal difficulty with our results. (See Walters, 1988, p. 75–79, for the details of such an argument.) Other theories addressed to implicit memory, such as the integration-elaboration position of Mandler (1979) or the transfer-appropriate processes approach (Kolers, 1979), fail in this regard.

Nevertheless, it is obvious that lexical ambiguity must be appropriately interpretable, or ambiguous words would be useless for communication. A theory of meaning, sensitive to which meaning is established in a situation as well as which meaning is more likely, makes ecological sense. The norm for conversations, as Simpson and Kellas wisely point out, is to try to effectively communicate. Gorfein and Bubka (this volume, Chapter 7) propose a model that we believe meets these constraints by developing a stimulus-sampling-based retrieval model for meaning.

6

Lexical Ambiguity and Context: An Activation-Suppression Model

W. TRAMMELL NEILL

In 1985, *Psychological Review* published a provocative article by Jack Yates, entitled "The Content of Awareness Is a Model of the World." In this article, Yates proffers two extraordinary claims: first, that conscious awareness is a unique, independent component of cognition, with properties which differ from other components; and second, that most of our data concerning the nature of mental representations directly reflect this awareness component. The gist of Yates's argument is that the processing of information yields multiple possible interpretations of any object or event, which have different consequences for the organization and control of behavior. In order for any organized behavior to occur at all, one reasonably coherent and comprehensive interpretation must be selected. The selected interpretation (i.e., the adopted "model" of the world) is the content of awareness. In short, information processing yields ambiguity; awareness is the resolution of that ambiguity.

The ubiquity of ambiguity seems, on the surface, to be contradicted by the position of direct realism advocated by some psychologists, notably James Gibson (1979). Gibson argued that the energy flux (light, sound, pressure, etc.) impinging on the organism in its natural environment is rich in information about the world; our perceptual systems evolved to pick up this information, and so we perceive the world directly. Gibson's position has fueled intense controversy, apparently propagating a major metatheoretical schism in cognitive psychology (cf. Fodor & Pylyshyn, 1981; Turvey & Carello, 1981; Turvey, Shaw, Reed, & Mace, 1981; Ullman, 1980). However, we will here sidestep this controversy by locating ambiguity within the organism rather than in the organism's environment. That is, there is nothing in the sensory information provided by an object or event which uniquely specifies what action will be taken in regard to that object or event. Thus, while a chair may not be perceptually ambiguous, I will be aware of its perpendicular edges and surfaces if I wish to draw a picture of it; I will be aware that it affords a place to sit if I am tired of standing; I will be aware that it belongs to the category *furniture* if I am performing a semantic classification task (or perhaps am at a furniture sale). Similarly, the ambiguity of the homograph BANK is not perceptual per se; it is clearly seen to be just a pattern of black lines on a white page. Rather, it is the interpretation of which we are aware that will determine our comprehension and the course of action to be taken.

This paper attempts to integrate three research areas—selective attention, lexical ambiguity, and visual masking—into a general theory of human information processing and the representational role of conscious awareness. First, we review research indicating that selection among competing stimulus interpretations results in the specific inhibition of the unselected alternatives. This "distractor suppression effect" is construed as reflecting the second stage in a two-stage model of information processing (Keele & Neill, 1978): widespread automatic activation of associations in memory, followed by an inhibitory, attentional "narrowing-down" process. This "activation-suppression" model is then applied to the current controversy regarding how polysemous words (homographs or homophones) are processed in meaningfully related contexts. Finally, we review masking studies which indicate that stage 1 (automatic) processing occurs independently of conscious awareness.

The Suppression of Cognitive Noise

It is commonly assumed in current theories of cognition that some information processing occurs *automatically,* such that mental representations are activated in memory without attention or deliberate intention (e.g., Eriksen & Schultz, 1979; Keele, 1973; Posner & Snyder, 1975a, 1975b; Shiffrin & Schneider, 1977). A frequently cited example is the "Stroop effect", in which color naming is slowed if the colors are embedded in words which name other, incompatible colors (Dyer, 1973; Hintzman, Carre, Eskridge, Owens, & Shaff, 1972; Keele, 1972; Neill, 1978; Stroop, 1935). That the words interfere with performance indicates that their meanings are processed involuntarily. Similarly, the fact that a word such as DOCTOR is recognized more quickly following a related word such as NURSE is often attributed to an automatic "spread of activation" in memory (Anderson, 1976; Anderson & Bower, 1973; Collins & Loftus, 1975; Neely, 1976, 1977; Schvaneveldt & Meyer, 1973). These two examples illustrate that automatic activation may occur in the memory system by either of two routes: In the case of the Stroop effect, the activation is caused directly by the externally presented distractor word; in the case of the lexical "priming" effect, the activation is caused indirectly by internal association to another activated representation.

If automatic activation occurs in the memory system, then by definition it must do so regardless of appropriateness to current task demands. Consequently, irrelevant activations may lead to incompatible decisions or responses and interfere with task performance, as in the Stroop effect. In other words, automatic activation may contribute "noise" to decision processes at some point or points in the processing of information. Keele and Neill (1978) argued that the automatic activation of information in memory must be followed by some process of narrowing down the range of activated memory structures to those specifically appropriate to current task demands. It was suggested that this narrowing down may be accomplished through the inhibition of the activated, but task-inappropriate, memory structures.

Keele and Neill (1978) speculated that semantic, or "deep," dyslexia may represent an extreme failure of such a narrowing-down process. The semantic dyslexic may, for example, read the word LION as *cat* or *zoo* even though the printed word remains visible (Marshall & Newcombe, 1973; Patterson & Marcel, 1977; Shallice & Warrington, 1975). The word has been "recognized," or else the patient would not report a semantically related word. However, the patient appears unable to select which among the associated activations actually corresponds to the word to be named. As will be discussed in a later section, similar phenomena may occur with normal subjects viewing masked tachistoscopic presentations of words (Allport, 1977; Marcel & Patterson, 1978).

That distracting information may be selectively inhibited is supported by research with the Stroop color-naming task (Neill, 1977, 1982; Neill & Westberry, 1987). Suppose that the subject has received the word RED written in green. The subject now has two interpretations of the stimulus competing for control of behavior. But the subject does not sit frozen in perpetual indecision, nor does he or she respond randomly. Usually, the subject makes the correct response, *green,* albeit with some delay. What happens to the activation of *red*? If selective attention is simply a matter of facilitating the correct response, then the activation of *red* should passively dissipate over time to some pretrial baseline level. If *red* becomes the correct response on the next trial, it should then show a relative facilitation, or at worst no difference, compared with when it has not just been activated. However, Neill (1977, Experiment 1) found just the opposite: a response was especially *slowed* if it had been activated by the distractor word appearing in the preceding trial (see Table 6.1).

This "distractor suppression effect" has been replicated in several studies using the Stroop color-naming task (Lowe, 1979, 1985; Neill, 1982; Neill & Westberry, 1987; Westberry, 1983), as well as in analogous designs with other materials. Allport, Tipper, and Chmiel (1985, Experiments 1 & 2) and Tipper and Cranston (1985) required subjects to name letters written in a specified color while ignoring simultaneous letters written in another color. When a target letter to be named had appeared as a distractor on the previous trial, naming time was slowed. Allport et al. (1985, Experiments 3–9) and Tipper (1985) obtained similar effects when subjects attended to line drawings of objects while ignoring superimposed drawings in another color. A particularly interesting finding by Tipper (1985, Experiment 3) is

TABLE 6.1. Stroop color-naming times (in milliseconds) and error proportions (E) for related and unrelated conditions, with examples of stimuli.[a]

Condition		Examples: Trial n-1	Trial n	RT	E
Related	Word:	RED	BLUE		
	Color:	green	red	855	.09
Unrelated	Word:	YELLOW	BLUE		
	Color:	green	red	823	.07
Distractor suppression effect				32**	.02*

[a]From Neill (1977).
**$P < .005$.
*$P < .10$.

that the suppression effect appears to generalize to the semantic category of the ignored object. For example, having to ignore a pictured cat subsequently slows naming a pictured dog.

That the suppression effect is not strictly perceptual is evidenced by the negative transfer between physically dissimilar stimuli—e.g., between word and color in the Stroop task, or between picture and subsequent word (Tipper & Driver, 1988). This effect also does not appear to be an inhibition of the overt response. Neill and Lissner (1988) have found similar effects in a letter-matching task, in which the target pair is flanked by other distracting letters. The effects depend on similarity of letters between successive trials, independently of whether "same" or "different" responses are required. Tipper, MacQueen, and Brehaut (1988) have also found negative transfer across response modalities, such as a vocal-response trial followed by a manual-response trial. Taken together, the data indicate that the distractor suppression effect occurs at the level of a central cognitive representation of the stimulus.

Recent research has investigated the time course of the distractor suppression effect. Using the Stroop task, Neill and Westberry (1987, Experiment 2) manipulated the delay between the subject's response and presentation of the next stimulus. As shown in Figure 6.1, the suppression effect appears to persist for at least a second; by 2 seconds it has completely dissipated. In another experiment (Neill & Westberry, 1987, Experiment 1), we manipulated speed-accuracy tradeoff by instructional emphasis and feedback. If selective inhibition is an active process, then the distractor suppression effect should require time to develop. If the subjects are encouraged to respond very rapidly, at a cost to accuracy, then irrelevant memory structures may not be completely inhibited, and so a net facilitation rather than suppression may occur if such structures subsequently become task-relevant (see Figure 6.2b). Under instructions emphasizing strict accuracy, however, more time would be allowed for more complete inhibition, yielding net suppression (Figure 6.2c). As shown in Table 6.2,

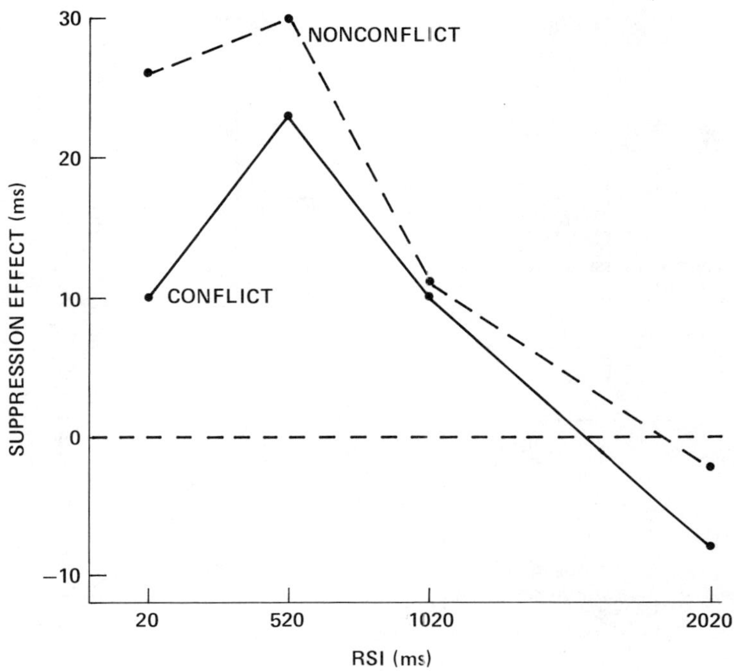

FIGURE 6.1. The distractor suppression effect for conflict and nonconflict stimuli, as a function of delay after response to preceding conflict stimulus (response-stimulus interval). (From Neill & Westberry, 1987.)

this is what occurred: Under strict accuracy instructions, the distractor suppression effect is obtained; however, under lax accuracy instructions, the effect is reversed.

In the Stroop task and related interference paradigms, there is clear evidence that selective attention involves the inhibition of information activated by an external distractor stimulus. Is there similar evidence for inhibition of information activated indirectly by association? Using a variation of the Posner and Snyder (1975a, 1975b) priming paradigm, Neill (1979) required subjects to match pairs of letters or digits as "same" or "different." On primed trials, subjects received a letter or digit warning signal which had an 80% probability of appearing in the upcoming target pair. In the 20% of trials invalidly primed, the unexpected stimuli were drawn with equal likelihood from either the same or the opposite category as the expected stimulus. Insofar as members of a category are assumed to be more highly associated to each other than to members of another category, current theories of associative activation predict that stimuli in the same category as the primed stimulus should be responded to more easily than stimuli in the opposing category. However, just the opposite

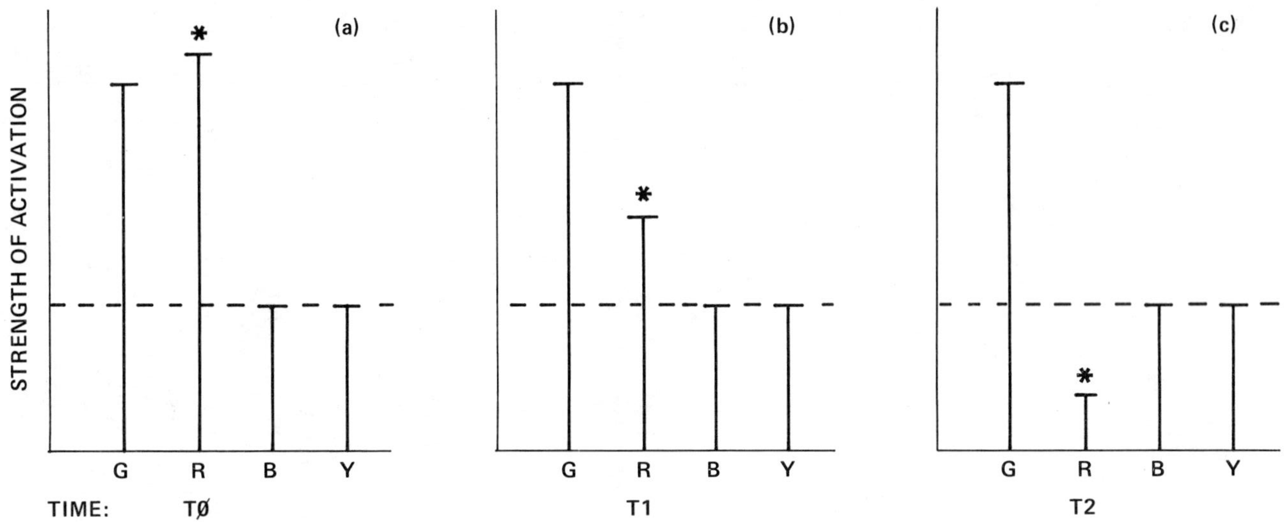

FIGURE 6.2. Hypothetical activation strengths of color-name responses after presentation of RED written in green: (a) initial activation; (b) after partial suppression; (c) after complete suppression. (From Neill & Westberry, 1987.)

TABLE 6.2. Stroop color-naming times (in milliseconds) and error proportions (*E*) as a function of stimulus type and relation to preceding conflict stimulus, under strict or lax accuracy demand.[a]

	Strict		Lax	
Stimulus	RT	*E*	RT	*E*
Conflict				
Related	882	.05	775	.11
Unrelated	851	.04	794	.10
Nonconflict				
Realted	839	.04	744	.06
Unrelated	819	.03	760	.08

[a]From Neill & Westberry (1987, Experiment 1).

result was obtained: It was easier for subjects to switch attention between categories than within a category (Table 6.3).

These result were interpreted as indicating that the activation of intracategory associates creates "cognitive noise," which may hamper either identification or matching of particular category members. For example, if A tends to activate B, then a pair such as AA might be misrecognized as AB, or AB misrecognized as BB. If, however, A is anticipated as the likely stimulus, such interference may be circumvented by suppressing the intracategory associates. On the small proportion of trials in which unexpected stimuli in that category are received, performance will be inhibited relative to stimuli in another category. The analogy to the distractor suppression effect is confirmed by an experiment in which speed-accuracy tradeoff was manipulated (Neill, 1979, Experiment 2): Under strict accuracy instructions, intracategory inhibition was obtained; when subjects were encouraged to sacrifice some accuracy for speed, intracategory facilitation was obtained instead.

A number of similar instances of intracategory inhibition can be found

TABLE 6.3. "Same" reaction times (in milliseconds) and error proportions (*E*) as a function of expectancy condition and category relation in primed letter matching.[a]

Expectancy condition and category relation	Examples			RT	*E*
Expected	A—AA,	A—Aa,	1—11	401	.04
Neutral	+—AA,	+—Aa,	+—11	468	.06
Unexpected/ similar	A—BB,	A—Bb,	1—22	517	.24
Unexpected/ opposite	A—22,	1—AA,	1—Aa	514	.19
Intracategory inhibition effect				3	.05*

[a]From Neill (1979, Experiment 1).
*$P < .02$.

in the literature, which have heretofore lacked adequate theoretical explanation. (See Roediger & Neely, 1982, for a review.) For example, Brown (1979) required subjects in several experiments to generate appropriate words in response to definitions preceded by either the correct word, a semantically related word, an orthographically related word, or an unrelated word. Contrary to expectations from the spreading activation hypothesis, subjects were slower at generating the target word when the definition was preceded by a semantically related word than when it was preceded by an unrelated word. Similar results were found when subjects were required to generate the word for a pictured object (Brown, 1979, Experiment 6). Brown proposed that the inhibition effect was due to refractoriness of associations shortly after their activation—in other words, an automatic "spread of inhibition" in semantic memory.

That Brown's results (1979) were not due to an *automatic* inhibitory mechanism was forcefully demonstrated in experiments by Roediger, Neely, and Blaxton (1983) and McEvoy (1982). Roediger et al. required subjects in one group to answer simple questions (e.g., "Who was president during the Civil War?"), preceded by one of four prime types: correct (*Abraham Lincoln*), related (*George Washington*), unrelated (*Colorado*), or neutral (*ready*). Under these conditions, subjects were slowest when given the related prime, replicating Brown's inhibition effect. However, another group of subjects only received related, unrelated, or neutral primes, never receiving a correct prime. These subjects exhibited a relative facilitation, rather than inhibition, when presented with a related prime. If a truly automatic inhibitory mechanism were involved, inhibition by related primes should not have been affected by the context of other possible prime types.

Similar results were found by McEvoy (1982), using a picture-naming task similar to that of Brown (1979, Experiment 6). Noting that other researchers have found picture naming to be facilitated by related primes (McCauley, Parmalee, Sperber, & Carr, 1980; Sperber, McCauley, Ragain, & Weil, 1979), McEvoy manipulated presence or absence of primes that correctly named the picture. Facilitation by related primes occurred when the primes never correctly named the picture, paralleling the results of Roediger et al. (1983). McEvoy concluded that the results could not be accounted for by an automatic spread of inhibition (Brown, 1979), but could be accounted for by a mechanism of strategic suppression such as proposed by Neill (1979). It appears that the possibility of correct target names as primes encourages the subject to focus attention on the prime as a possible candidate for response, then and only then resulting in the suppression of semantic associates.

It is to be emphasized that the form of inhibition exhibited in these studies differs markedly from "inhibition" as postulated in other theories of attention. In particular, Posner and Snyder (1975a, 1975b) refer to the processing of unattended signals being inhibited by the commitment of processing capacity to an attended signal (see also Neely, 1976, 1977). Inhibition in Posner's "cost-benefit" theory is de facto and nonselective, and does not reflect an operation on specific unattended information (Posner, 1982). Such nonselective inhibition cannot account for a specific bias against the response activated by a recent Stroop distractor word since less recently activated responses would also be "inhibited" in this sense. Similarly, a nonselective inhibition could not account for a disadvantage to intracategory associates relative to members of another category. In contrast, the present theory postulates a selective inhibition which operates directly on specific unattended (or more aptly, "disattended") information.

It has been convenient in the foregoing discussion to assume that the mechanism of selective inhibition serves to directly reduce the activation of task-inappropriate structures in memory (cf. Neill, 1979). However, other interpretations of selective inhibition are possible. In particular, Tipper (1985; Tipper & Cranston, 1985; see also Neill & Westberry, 1987) has suggested that what is inhibited is the activated structure's access to the mechanisms required for overt response. It is conceivable that such structures are somehow "tagged" as irrelevant, without necessarily reducing their degree of activation. Nevertheless, the specific form of the inhibition is not critical to the present discussion. What *is* important is that the ignored representations are effectively "isolated from the control of action," with the consequence that such representations are temporarily less available for the control of action even if they then become relevant to the task requirements.

The Resolution of Lexical Ambiguity

An issue of concern to many contributors to the present volume is how ambiguous (polysemous) words are processed in meaningfully related context. Does a homograph or homophone activate all of its meanings, one of which is then selected by context for further processing? Or does the context constrain the activation to only one meaning? As indicated by Simpson's comprehensive review (1984), models of ambiguity processing have generally been of three types: *context-dependent access, exhaustive access,* and *ordered access.*

According to the context-dependent (or "selective-access") model, the context in which an ambiguous word occurs determines which meaning is retrieved from memory (e.g., Perfetti & Goodman, 1970; Schvaneveldt, Meyer, & Becker, 1976; Simpson, 1981; Swinney & Hakes, 1976). In its strong form, such as proposed by Schvaneveldt et al. (1976), the model asserts that there is no processing of the context-inappropriate meanings of the word. However, as noted by Simpson (1984), many studies have found evidence that context-inappropriate meanings are activated (Conrad, 1974; Marcel, 1980; Oden & Spira, 1983; Onifer & Swinney, 1981; Seidenberg,

Tanenhaus, Leiman, & Bienkowski, 1982; Swinney, 1979; Tanenhaus, Leiman, & Seidenberg, 1979; Warren & Warren, 1976).

According to the exhaustive-access (or "context-independent") model, an ambiguous word initially activates all possible meanings in memory. Context is then used to select one of the activated meanings for further processing, such as sentence comprehension. Although somewhat counter-intuitive, this model easily accommodates the evidence for activation of context-inappropriate meanings, and has been preferred by a majority of investigators in recent years (Simpson, 1984). However, it is often found that the context-appropriate meaning is activated more rapidly or more strongly than the context-inappropriate meaning (Marcel, 1980; Oden & Spira, 1983; Schvaneveldt et al., 1976; Seidenberg et al., 1982; Swinney & Hakes, 1976; Underwood, 1980). it has been assumed, implicitly or explicitly, that exhaustive access makes all meanings equally available for post-access processing (Simpson, 1984). Perhaps most problematic for this position is that the more frequent (primary) meaning appears to be activated more strongly than a less frequent (secondary) meaning of the word (Burgess & Simpson, 1988a; Simpson, 1981; Simpson & Burgess, 1985).

A role of meaning frequency is explicitly assumed in the "ordered-access" model proposed by Hogaboam and Perfetti (1975; see also Forster & Bednall, 1976). In this model, only the primary meaning of an ambiguous word is initially retrieved, independently of context. If this meaning is consistent with the context, no further meanings are retrieved. However, if the primary meaning does not fit the context, then memory is searched again for another meaning. Since many studies of lexical ambiguity have simply averaged over primary- and secondary-sense contexts, this model accommodates the evidence for activation of context-inappropriate meanings as well as the relative advantage for context-appropriate meanings.

The ordered-access model appeared to be supported by an experiment in which subjects judged whether the last word in a sentence had more than one meaning. Hogaboam and Perfetti found ambiguity detection to be faster when the sentence was related to a secondary meaning than when it was related to the primary meaning. They interpreted this result as indicating that the mismatch between the first retrieved (primary) meaning and the secondary-sense context immediately informed the subject that the word was ambiguous. On the other hand, a match with a primary-sense context would not inform the subject whether the word was ambiguous, and so the subject would have to search memory for a secondary meaning.

While replicating the advantage of a secondary-sense context in ambiguity detection, Neill, Hilliard, and Cooper (1988) found evidence incompatible with the ordered-access interpretation. For one group of subjects, sentences like those of Hogaboam and Perfetti were intermixed with "filler" sentences which were incongruent with any meaning of the final word (see Table 6.4 for examples). For these subjects, a mismatch between an initially retrieved primary meaning and the sentence context could not

TABLE 6.4. Sample stimulus materials for ambiguity detection task.[a]

Target sentences
- A fastball is a kind of *pitch*. (homograph, primary sense)
- Every sound has a *pitch*. (homograph, secondary sense)
- To perspire is to *sweat*. (nonhomograph)

Congruent filler sentences
- To pretend is to *bluff*. (homograph, primary sense)
- A cliff is also called a *bluff*. (homograph, secondary sense)
- A person may repeat a *rumor*. (nonhomograph)

Incongruent filler sentences
- To pretend is to *bolt*. (homograph, "primary" sense)
- A cliff is also called a *bolt*. (homograph, "secondary" sense)
- A person may repeat a *mist*. (nonhomograph)

[a]From Neill, Hilliard, & Cooper (1988).

be assumed to indicate an ambiguous word. Therefore, further search for a secondary meaning would be required for both target and filler sentences, regardless of whether the sentence context was related to the primary or secondary meaning of the word. (Subjects presumably could not know whether a sentence was nonsense until the secondary meaning has been retrieved.) Accordingly, the ordered-access model predicts that the advantage of a secondary-sense context should be eliminated under these conditions. However, as shown in Table 6.5, the advantage of a secondary-sense context was preserved for homograph targets even when mixed with incongruent fillers. While the magnitude of this advantage was somewhat smaller than for another group for whom fillers were congruent, this difference was not significant (i.e., there was a main effect of context for target stimuli, but no context × condition interaction).

Neill et al. interpreted these results as evidence for "context-sensitive" parallel access of meanings. In a parallel search, the total time to retrieve

TABLE 6.5. Ambiguity detection times (in milliseconds). Error proportions are shown in parentheses.[a]

		Homograph context	
Condition	Nonhomographs	Primary	Secondary
Congruent fillers			
Targets	1749	1629	1400
	(.12)	(.24)	(.11)
Fillers	1833	1584	1413
	(.15)	(.25)	(.14)
Incongruent fillers			
Targets	1624	1500	1379
	(.18)	(.17)	(.14)
Fillers	1898	1612	1559
	(.21)	(.27)	(.23)

[a]From Neill, Hilliard, & Cooper (1988).

both meanings is limited only by the longer of the two search processes. Normally, the secondary meaning will take longer to retrieve (Figure 6.3a). Therefore, a context which facilitates the retrieval of the primary meaning will be of relatively little benefit to the time required to retrieve both meanings (Figure 6.3b). In contrast, the total retrieval time is substantially shortened by a context facilitating the retrieval of the secondary meaning (Figure 6.3c).

The present model, which is similar to the "self-terminating race" model proposed by Gorfein and Bubka (Bubka, 1988; Gorfein & Bubka, 1985; see also Simpson, 1981, 1984), is essentially a compromise between the major competing theoretical positions. As in the exhaustive-access model, it is assumed that multiple meanings may be activated in parallel by an ambiguous word. However, it is not assumed that all meanings are retrieved with equal speed or likelihood. Rather, it is assumed that the most frequent (primary) meaning will usually have a processing advantage over less frequent (secondary) meaning. But unlike the ordered-access model, this ordering is not assumed to be strictly sequential or independent of context. Like the context-dependent-access model, it is assumed that the retrieval process is influenced by context; however, retrieval is not completely determined by context (hence, "context-sensitive"). The ease with which a

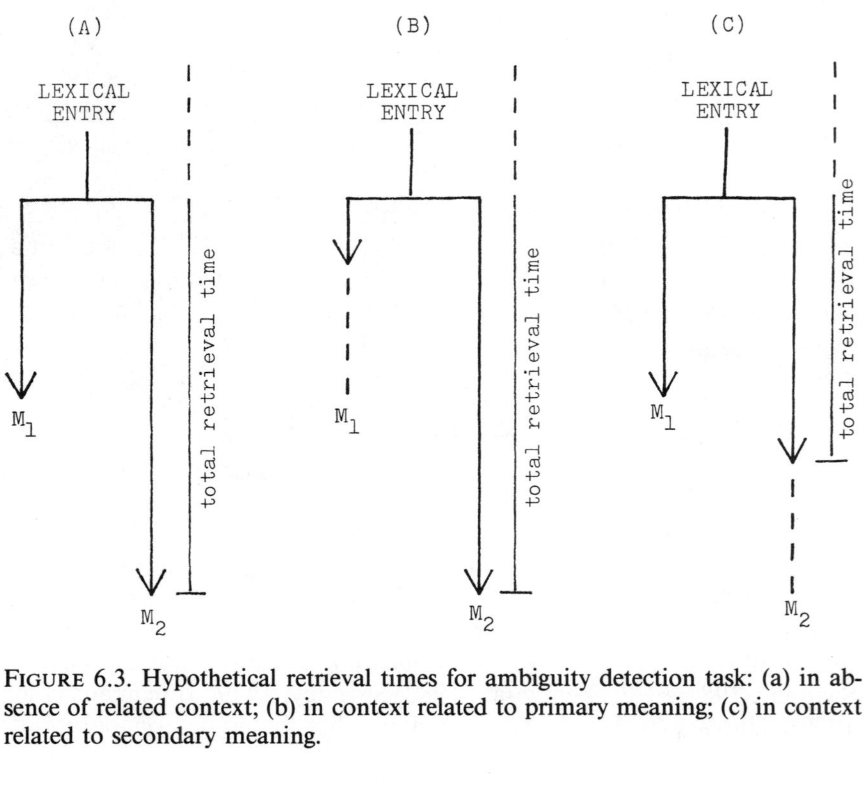

FIGURE 6.3. Hypothetical retrieval times for ambiguity detection task: (a) in absence of related context; (b) in context related to primary meaning; (c) in context related to secondary meaning.

particular meaning is retrieved will then be a joint function of strength of association to the ambiguous word and strength of association to its context.

It is the present contention that the multiple activation of meanings by a homograph or homophone creates a dilemma directly analogous to the Stroop effect. That is, multiple interpretations of the stimulus are created which compete for the control of action (construed here as whatever post-access processing is required by task demands). If this interpretation is correct, then it should be possible to demonstrate that the context-inappropriate meaning is suppressed sometime after its initial activation.

The most common paradigm for investigating the activation of meanings of a homograph or homophone has been to present the polysemous word in a context related to one of its meanings, followed by a target word related to either the context-appropriate or context-inappropriate meaning, or as a control, an unrelated word. If a homograph or homophone activates a particular meaning, then a word related to that meaning should be recognized more quickly (Meyer & Schvaneveldt, 1971; Schvaneveldt & Meyer, 1973). If the task requires such recognition, as in naming or lexical decision (word/nonword judgment), then performance will show facilitation. Alternatively, faster recognition may hamper performance if it is not compatible with task demands, such as naming the color in which the word is written (Conrad, 1974; Warren, 1972).

Schvaneveldt, Meyer, and Becker (1976) presented subjects with triplets of letter strings for lexical decision. In the conditions of present concern, the second string was a homograph preceded by a word related to one of its meanings (i.e., a "context"). In the concordant condition, the third word was related to the meaning selected by the context of the first word (e.g., SAVE-BANK-MONEY; DAY-DATE-TIME); in the discordant condition, the third word was related to an alternative meaning of the homograph (e.g., RIVER-BANK-MONEY; FIG-DATE-TIME); in the initial associates control condition, the third word was unrelated to either meaning (e.g., RIVER-BANK-TIME; FIG-DATE-MONEY). In this experiment, Schvaneveldt et al. found facilitation for the third word only in the concordant condition: there was no difference between the discordant and control conditions.

Schvaneveldt et al. interpreted this result as support for the context-dependent model, i.e., that the context-inappropriate meaning was not activated by the homograph. However, another interpretation is possible: The context-inappropriate meaning may have been activated but then quickly suppressed because of its inconsistency with the context. Several studies have, in fact, found activation of both meanings when the target is presented immediately following the homograph or homophone, but activation of only the context-appropriate meaning at longer delays (Onifer & Swinney, 1981; Seidenberg et al., 1982; Swinney, 1979; Tanenhaus et al., 1979). This result in itself does not prove that the context-inappropriate meaning has been suppressed; it is possible that its activation merely dissipates passively over time in the absence of post-access processing related to the context. On the other hand, several studies have found the context-inappropriate meaning significantly *less* available than that of a completely unrelated word. (See also Simpson, Chapter 2, this volume.)

Using materials similar to those of Schvaneveldt et al. (1976), Hekkanen (1977) required subjects to judge the physical or semantic similarity of the first two words, which were presented together for 2.4 seconds, followed by the third word requiring a lexical-decision judgment. As shown in Table 6.6, both the concordant and discordant conditions produced comparable facilitation relative to the initial associates condition, consistent with the exhaustive-access model. In a follow-up experiment, Hekkanen lengthened the duration of the initial pair to 3.0 seconds, with no other change in procedure (unpublished data, 1978; summarized in Hekkanen, 1981). Here, only the concordant condition produced significant facilitation; the discordant condition did not differ significantly from the initial associates condition, consistent with the results of Schvaneveldt et al. (1976). Finally, Hekkanen (1981), using a 3.8-second duration for the first two words, found an overt suppression effect: The discordant condition was slower than the initial associates condition. As this last study differed from the first two in some minor procedural details, any conclusion regarding the actual time course of inhibition must remain speculative. The important

TABLE 6.6. Lexical decision times to target words following homographs (in milliseconds) in studies by Hekkanen and Marcel.

	Condition		
	Concordant	Discordant	Initial associates
Examples:	MONEY BANK SAVE	MONEY BANK SHORE	MONEY BANK WRIST
Hekkanen (1979):			
SOA = 2.4 s	686	688	745
Hekkanen (1981):			
SOA = 3.0 s	598	631	640
Hekkanen (1981):			
SOA = 3.8 s	562	592	583
Marcel (1980):			
(Homographs unmasked)			
ISI = 0.6 s	499	547	545
ISI = 1.5 s	487	537	526
(Homographs masked)			
ISI = 0.6 s	511	520	548
ISI = 1.5 s	497	505	535

Note: Data from Hekkanen (1979, 1981) are from conditions requiring a semantic-relatedness judgment of the first two words.

point is that the context-inappropriate meaning may show either activation, no activation, or actual inhibition, depending on subtle differences in procedure. The finding of inhibition is particularly difficult for the context-dependent-access position, which must predict that the context-inappropriate meaning is functionally equivalent to the meaning of an unrelated word. Indeed, it is difficult to explain the inhibition of the context-inappropriate meaning unless it was activated in the first place.

Similar results were found by Marcel (1980) using procedures similar to those of Schvaneveldt et al. (1976). This study will be discussed in more detail in the next section. However, it will suffice for now to note that Marcel replicated the results of Schvaneveldt et al. using an 0.6-second interstimulus interval: Only the concordant condition produced facilitation, with no difference between the discordant and initial associates condition (Table 6.6, homographs unmasked). When a 1.5-second interval was used, the discordant condition showed significant inhibition relative to the initial associates condition, similar to the result of Hekkanen (1981).

Finally, it should be noted that evidence for selective inhibition of meaning has been found for homographs without a preceding context. Simpson and Burgess (1985) presented homographs followed at varied intervals by a related or unrelated word for lexical decision. At the very shortest interval (16 ms), only a word related to the primary meaning showed facilitation relative to an unrelated word. At longer intervals)100–500 ms), words related to either meaning showed facilitation. However, at the longest interval (750 ms), only the primary meaning again showed priming, with no difference between the secondary meaning and that of an unrelated word. Although Simpson and Burgess interpreted this as indicating inhibition of the secondary meaning after it had been activated, this really cannot be distinguished here from a passive decay in the absence of post-access processing. On the other hand, a follow-up study by Burgess and Simpson (1988a) did find significantly slower responses to a word related to the secondary meaning than to an unrelated word, at a 750-ms delay. Interestingly, this result occurred only when target words were presented to the left cerebral hemisphere (i.e., right visual field).

Taken together, the experiments on lexical ambiguity suggest that a homophone or homograph does activate both meanings, although the degree of activation is determined by both context and frequency of meaning. When multiple meanings are activated, a conflict is engendered analogous to the Stroop effect. Typically, the context-inappropriate meanings are suppressed; or in the absence of context, the secondary meanings are suppressed. In other words, one stimulus interpretation is selected for further processing, while the remaining interpretations are "isolated from the control of action."

If this analysis is correct, then caution must be applied when comparing the results of different tasks purported to measure activation. For example, Seidenberg et al. (1982, 1984) have argued that naming may provide a more "pure" measure of lexical activation than the lexical-decision task. However, it is likely to be the case that tasks also differ in the degree to which selective inhibition occurs. The results of manipulating the speed-accuracy tradeoff (Neill, 1979; Neill & Westberry, 1987) indicate that distractor suppression increases with the task demands for specificity. Naming inherently requires more specificity than lexical decision. That is, if NURSE activates *doctor*, this is likely to interfere with naming but may facilitate deciding that the string is a word. Consequently, naming tasks are likely to yield more inhibition of associates, and evidence for multiple activation will be more difficult to obtain.[1]

Masking and Conscious Awareness

The ability to report a briefly displayed visual target, such as a letter or word, can be greatly disrupted by a second stimulus, such as a pattern of random features, following the target within a quarter of a second (e.g., Averbach & Coriell, 1961; Eriksen & Hoffman, 1963; Turvey, 1973). Until recently, it has been assumed that this "backward masking" phenomenon occurs because the second stimulus either interrupts the perceptual processing of an "iconic memory" of the first stimulus or becomes "integrated" with that iconic memory such that it is difficult to selectively process the features of the first stimulus (see, for example, Eriksen & Schultz, 1978; Turvey, 1973). This phenomenon is so well-established that a masking pattern is routinely used in tachistoscopic recognition studies under the assumption that it effectively terminates the perceptual analysis of the target stimulus.

Recent work by Allport (1977; Allport et al., 1985), Marcel (1980, 1983a, 1983b; Marcel & Patterson, 1978), and others has demanded a reevaluation of the assumptions regarding masking by patterns. Allport (1977) reported that subjects often make semantically related identification errors to masked words, similar to the errors made by semantic-dyslexic patients (Patterson & Marcel, 1977; Marshall & Newcombe, 1973; Shallice & Warrington, 1975). Similarly Marcel and Patterson (1978) draw parallels between the responses of normal subjects to masked words, and semantic dyslexics to unmasked words. Marcel (1983b; see also Fowler, Wolford, Slade, & Tassinary, 1981) demonstrated that a word which is masked to below the threshold for detection still facilitates lexical decision for a subsequent semantically related word, and that the magnitude of this priming effect is comparable to that produced by an unmasked word. Marcel concludes that pattern masking does not terminate the perceptual

---

[1] I am grateful to David S. Gorfein for pointing out this implication of the theory.

processing, but rather blocks a "record" of the visual analysis from entering conscious awareness. Consequently, phonemic and semantic analysis may continue unhampered without conscious awareness of the physical stimulus.

Earlier work by Allport and Marcel has been criticized for methodological inadequacies, such as poor control for guessing probabilities (Ellis & Marshall, 1978; Fowler et al., 1981). Particularly difficult has been criticism of threshold measurement as a means of ensuring that subjects are not aware of any stimulus information (e.g., Duncan, 1985; Merikle, 1982). Indeed, signal detection theory (Green & Swets, 1966) suggests that there is no true dividing line between availability and unavailability of sensory information. Thus, it is possible that verbalizing the presence of a stimulus is simply less sensitive to weak, "subthreshold" sensory information than are other dependent measures. Such data then do not require a distinction between "conscious" and "unconscious" representations. However, more recent research indicates that masking can produce *opposite* effects on different dependent measures. Such "crossover" interactions provide strong "converging operations" (Garner, Hake, & Ericksen, 1956) for the conscious-unconscious distinction.

Smith, Haviland, Reder, Brownell, and Adams (1976) found that recognition of a brief tachistoscopic letter followed by a mask was disrupted if subjects had foreknowledge of possible letter alternatives. Subsequent research by Neill (1985; Neill & Walling, 1981) demonstrated that this "before-disruption" effect occurred when precuing biased subjects to attend to the physical appearance of the target, while more abstract processing (i.e., naming) occurred when not precued. In the course of the experiments, some subjects reported a curious subjective phenomenon: When precued, subjects were usually aware of the physical stimulus, despite difficulty of identification. In the unprecued condition, subjects sometimes experienced a "spontaneous" thought of a letter, even though the target field phenomenally appeared blank. To their surprise, this seemingly self-generated letter often turned out to be one of the alternatives displayed several seconds after the target.

The dissociation between identification and conscious awareness of the target was verified in an experiment (Neill, 1985, Experiment 3) in which subjects were required to first make a "yes-no" detection decision, followed by a forced-choice identification decision. The usual before-disruption effect was obtained: The probability of a correct target identification in the unprecued condition (.71) was significantly higher than in the precued condition (.64). In contrast, the probability of detecting a target in the precued condition (.85) was significantly higher than in the unprecued condition (.75). (False-alarm rates on blank trials were identical for both conditions.) Further, in the precued condition, subjects were at chance (.49; chance = .50) on identification if they failed to detect the target. In contrast, identification was significantly above chance in the unprecued condition (.58) in the absence of correct detection. It is not necessary here to assume that verbalized detection is either a necessary or sufficient condition for inferring conscious awareness. Conscious awareness and verbalizability should at least be positively correlated; it seems implausible that subjects were more consciously aware of the visual stimulus in the unprecued condition, yet less able to verbalize its presence.

Experiments by Allport et al. (1985, Experiments 4 & 5) demonstrate that the previously discussed distractor suppression effect is critically dependent on the ability to verbalize the presence of the stimulus. Subjects were required to name pictures drawn in red ink, ignoring superimposed pictures in green. In one condition, the "priming" stimuli were followed closely by a masking pattern, such that subjects were at chance in identifying either picture. In another condition, the masking pattern was delayed so that the target pattern was easily identified. The priming stimuli and mask were than followed by a "probe" drawing which was either identical to the priming stimulus target ("attended repetition"), categorically related to the priming stimulus target ("attended categorical"), identical to the priming stimulus distractor ("distractor repetition"), categorically related to the priming stimulus distractor ("distractor categorical"), or unrelated ("control"). As shown in Table 6.7, suppression of both the priming stimulus distractor and its categorical associates occurred when the priming stimuli were unmasked, while the priming stimulus target and its categorical associates produced facilitation. However, when the priming stimulus is masked, both the target and distractor stimuli produce facilitation. Thus, it appears that the distractor suppression effect depends on conscious awareness of the priming stimulus, while the initial activation by the distractor does not.

Similar results were obtained in a lexical ambiguity study by Marcel (1980). As described earlier, Marcel replicated the conditions of Schvaneveldt et al. (1976) using either an 0.6- or 1.5-second interstimulus interval. As shown in Table 6.6 (homographs unmasked), the discordant condition did not differ from the initial associates at the short interval, but was significantly slower at the long interval. In addition, Marcel included

TABLE 6.7. Picture-naming latencies (in milliseconds) as a function of the relation between the probe and preceding priming stimulus. Facilitation or inhibition relative to control is indicated in parentheses.[a]

	Prime unmasked	Prime masked
Attended repetition	615 (−80)	661 (−32)
Attended categorical	677 (−18)	651 (−42)
Control	695	693
Distractor categorical	726 (+31)	671 (−22)
Distractor repetition	746 (+51)	660 (−33)

[a]From Allport, Tipper, & Chmiel (1985, Experiment 5). "Perceptual integration and postcatagorical filtering." In M. I. Posner & O. S. M. Masin (eds.) *Attention and performance XI.* Copyright © 1985 by Lawrence Erlbaum Associates. Reprinted with permission.

conditions in which the second string (the homograph, in the conditions of present concern) was masked by a pattern of random features, such that subjects were unable to detect the presence of the letter string. Under these conditions, the homograph facilitated recognition of the third word if it was related to *either* meaning of the homograph (Table 6.6, homographs masked). In other words, in the absence of conscious awareness, the homograph activates both meanings; when subjects are aware of the homograph, the context-inappropriate meaning is suppressed. (Marcel also included conditions using an energy mask rather than a pattern mask. Here, the homograph yields no priming, suggesting that an energy mask *does* effectively terminate perceptual analysis.)

The relation between masking and conscious awareness remains controversial (see, for example, Holender, 1986). However, it is clear that pattern-masked stimuli produce qualitatively different results from unmasked stimuli, which cannot be explained simply by a reduction in available sensory information. To account for the data, it seems necessary to postulate two distinct states of sensory information: In one state, there is a wider range of activated information, yet the subject is unable to verbalize the presence of an external stimulus; in the other state, in which the subject can verbalize detection, some of the activated information has been suppressed. Whether we label these states *unconscious* and *conscious* may simply be an issue of terminology. Nevertheless, it is difficult to understand why one state should be associated with the suppression of information unless that state requires selection of one stimulus interpretation for the control of action. As such, Yates's (1985) assertion that "the content of awareness is a model of the world" appears to be substantiated.

Conclusions

The research on selective attention, lexical ambiguity, and visual pattern masking combines to yield the following model of human information processing, illustrated schematically in Figure 6.4: As commonly assumed in many theories, stimuli (objects or events) may be represented at a variety of "levels" of processing, on a continuum from the concrete, sensory features of the stimulus through abstract, semantic knowledge associated with it (e.g., Craik & Lockhart, 1972; Posner, 1969, 1978). The labels for these levels in Figure 6.4 are distinctions commonly made in the literature; however, no assumption is made here about the number of levels or distinctions between them. Given sufficiently strong associations between representations at different levels, and between representations within a level, multiple representations will be activated by a stimulus without attention or conscious awareness. These activated representations are "candidates" for representation in conscious awareness; as stimulus interpretations, they include not only information about stimulus identity,

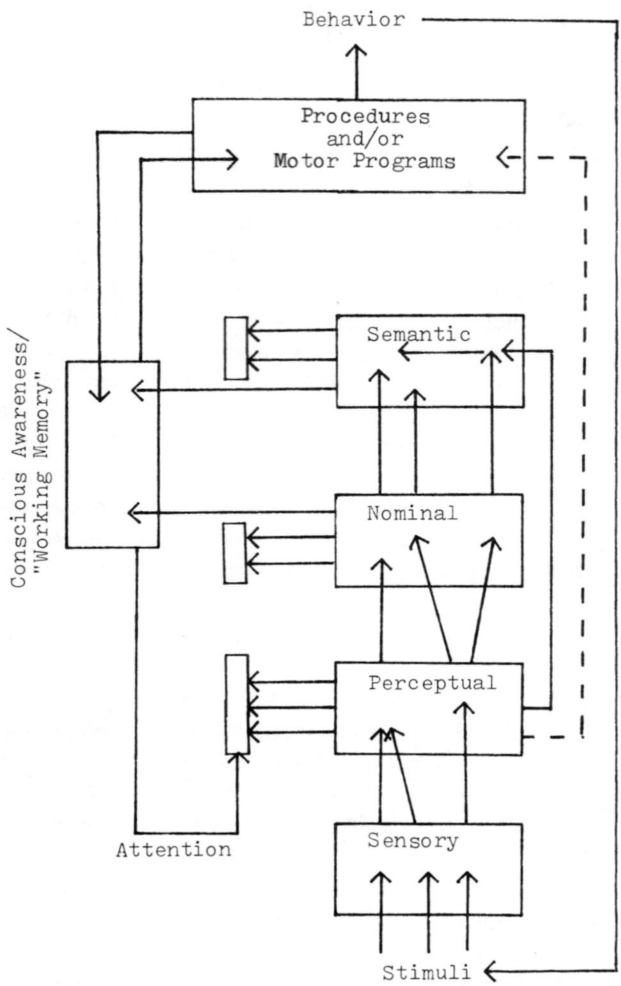

FIGURE 6.4. The Activation-Suppression Model.

but expectations regarding anticipated stimuli as well (as when NURSE activates *doctor*).

Following Marcel (1980, 1983a) and Yates (1985), it is assumed that representation in conscious awareness normally mediates between stimulus recognition and overt behavior although highly automatized behaviors such as walking may be guided perceptually with little representation in conscious awareness (suggested by the dotted line in the figure). It seems likely that the functions of "working memory" (Baddeley & Hitch, 1974) are subsumed by those of conscious awareness. Accordingly, it is assumed that representation in conscious awareness can activate procedures which modify what is represented (for example, when adding 748 + 693 in one's head). Anderson (1976) in particular has argued for a necessary distinction between procedural knowledge (how to do things) and declarative knowledge (what things are). In Anderson's ACT model and other theories based on "production systems" (Newell, 1973), a short-term buffer analogous to working memory provides the interface between the two types of knowledge.

Yates (1985) suggests that what are represented in awareness are abstracted constructs of the world which maximize the sensory information accounted for while minimizing the number of constructs necessary for the account to be complete. Consequently, what interpretation of a stimulus is selected will depend on its context and prior expectations—an interpretation which is consistent with context accounts for more information than one which does not. Thus, in the sentence "The man fished from the river bank," the word *bank* is more easily accounted for if it is interpreted as meaning "shore" than if it is interpreted as a place to deposit money. On the other hand, in the absence of any strongly biasing context, a word may be most easily "accounted for" if it is interpreted according to its most frequent usage. Presumably, what is selected must also depend on consistency with goals and expectations. To return to the example of a chair, I will be aware of its perpendicular edges and surfaces if I wish to draw it, but not if I am looking for a place to sit.

Perhaps the only novel proposal here concerns the role of attention in the selection of what is represented in conscious awareness. Most theories of attention have assumed that selection is achieved by the direct allocation of some processing resource or capacity to the relevant, attended information (e.g., Broadbent, 1958; Deutsch & Deutsch, 1963; Kahneman, 1973; Keele, 1973; Norman, 1968; Norman & Bobrow, 1975; Posner, 1978; Shiffrin & Schneider, 1977). However, the work by Tipper (1985; Tipper & Cranston, 1985; Allport et al., 1985), Neill (1977, 1979; Neill & Westberry, 1987), and others demonstrates that attention entails the active inhibition of specific distracting information. Thus, the facilitation of processing relevant information may be indirect: Interference from competing activations may be suppressed. And by allowing selected information to be represented unimpeded in conscious awareness, the probability may be increased that other relevant associated information will be activated as well.

Finally, as represented by the arrow from "Behavior" to "Stimuli" in Figure 6.4, we are reminded by Gibson (1979) and Neisser (1976), whose theories bear no resemblance to the present one, that behavior does not simply begin with a stimulus. Rather, the organism is always in a cyclical interaction with the environment, such that behavior provides new information about objects and events in the world, requiring constant reinterpretation and updating of the content of awareness.

7

A Context-Sensitive Frequency-Based Theory of Meaning Achievement

DAVID S. GORFEIN AND ANDREA BUBKA

The basic problem for the psychologist interested in any form of human communication is how meaning is achieved by the organism. The present chapter has a twofold purpose: (1) to present evidence for the role of frequency in resolving semantic ambiguity and (2) to elucidate a theory of frequency action that has generality for human information processing. We will argue that the most important role in understanding the processing of words is that the processing will depend on the frequency of the word. Robinson's classic statements (1932) of the *law of frequency* were recently updated by Slamecka (1987) in the following words:

> Since that time, psychologists have considerably extended the list of effective variables, but the impression that I receive from my review is that these other variables tend to play out their roles superimposed against a larger background, which reduces them almost to local eddies that are swept along in the irresistible tide of repetition increments (p. 128)

We believe the data with respect to the processing of homographs support a similar statement; i.e., the law of frequency will apply to the task.

In the first part of this chapter we will review five studies conducted in our laboratory that we believe consistently call for a frequency principle to interpret their results. In the second part of this chapter, we will offer an explanation of those results in the form of a theory of how and why frequency operates in language processing.

Frequency Defined

In the definition of frequency we follow the convention described under characteristics of materials in Chapter 1 (p. 10). We distinguish between polarity (the relative frequency of each of the meanings of a homograph) and frequency in print as derived from normative studies like that of Kucera and Francis (1967). We treat these two measures as independent, and design our studies to test a full range of both polarity (from balanced to unbalanced homographs) and normative frequency (from low to high). Polarity represents an intra-individual difference and is not merely a result of averaging subjects who differ with respect to the dominant association. Thus an individual who responds in word association in the secondary direction with respect to an item that is highly polarized in the group will tend to change to the alternate (primary) meaning when asked to produce subsequent associations to that word. On the other hand, if an association is in the normatively primary direction, subsequent associations tend to stay in that direction. Homographs of more balanced polarity produce changes in meaning in continuous association, as shown in the normative study of Gorfein, Viviani, and Leddo (1982). In a similar fashion, test-retest scores were more stable in the study of Geis and Winograd (1975) for highly polarized homographs.

Frequency and the Ambiguity Decision

We begin with experiments in which the participant's task is to decide whether a given letter string is a homograph (i.e., does it, the letter string, have two or more distinct meanings or fewer than two meanings?). Historically, the earlier studies employing the ambiguity task were among the very few to study a full range of word frequency and polarity in single studies (Forster & Bednall, 1976; Hogaboam & Perfetti, 1975). Recently, we (Cooper, Gorfein, & Bubka, 1988) had the occasion to employ the ambiguity task in an attempt to elucidate some apparent contradictions between the results of Hogaboam and Perfetti and those of Forster and Bednall.

Specifically, Hogaboam and Perfetti (1975) primed their ambiguity decisions with a sentence context and analyzed all the response times obtained, while Forster and Bednall (1976) presented words singly and analyzed only correct response times. The most conflicting result would appear to be the absence of a polarity effect in the Forster and Bednall study and the large effect of polarity in the study by Hogaboam and Perfetti. We believed there would be an interaction of homograph polarity and Kucera-Francis frequency in such manner that for balanced homographs the errors and reaction times would be largely independent of Kucera-Francis frequency. However, as polarity increased, secondary meanings would become more difficult to achieve, especially when the overall (Kucera-Francis) frequency of the homograph was low. We examined these effects on the same materials in two experiments. In Experiment 1, single words were presented for ambiguity decision, whereas for Experiment 2, the words were primed by a related or unrelated item. Both studies presented nonwords as well. The conditions of the two experiments are outlined in Table 7.1. The materials employed were three levels of homographs (polarity: balanced 50–65%, middle 66–85%, and unbalanced 86–100%). Within each of these levels

TABLE 7.1. Design of Experiments 1 and 2.

Experiment 1.

Targets: 80 homographs, 12 nonhomophonic homographs, 66 unambiguous words, and 46 pronounced nonwords

Procedure: Target's presented singly for ambiguity decision

Experiment 2.

Targets: Same as Experiment 1 but primed for 75S with related item or re-paired to form unrelated pairs as shown below

Type of material		Related	Unrelated
		Primary meaning	
80 homographs	Prime:	SAVINGS	RAILROAD
	target:	BANK	BANK
12 nonhomophonic homographs (Hetereophones not included in analysis)		Secondary meaning	
	Prime:	RIVER	TEACH
	target:	BANK	BANK
		Words	
66 unambiguous words	Prime:	Minister	COLESLAW
	target:	Priest	PRIEST
		Pseudowords	
46 pronouncable nonwords	Prime:	MINISTER	COLESLAW
	target:	PREEST	PREEST
204 prime target pairs			

there were some instances of low Kucera-Francis frequency (less than the natural log value of 2), medium frequency (logs from 2 to 4), and high frequency (above a log of 4). There were also a number of unambiguous words of the same frequency range and a set of nonwords constructed from the unambiguous words.

Table 7.2 presents the response times and errors as a function of frequency and materials for the unprimed condition. Following the procedure

TABLE 7.2. Decision time in milliseconds and proportion of errors (in parentheses) as a function of material in the unprimed ambiguity task.

	Materials					
	Homographs			Mean	Unambiguous	
	Balanced (50–65%)	Middle (66–85%)	Unbalanced (86–100%)	Homograph (50–100%)	Words (100%)	Nonwords (0%)
Frequency						
Low	1625(.17)	1845(.32)	2024(.48)	1831(.32)	1930(.17)	—
Middle	1836(.25)	1719(.24)	1935(.32)	1830(.27)	1990(.20)	—
High	1710(.19)	1847(.27)	1973(.37)	1863(.28)	2103(.23)	—
Mean	1744(.20)	1804(.27)	1977(.39)	1842(.29)	2008(.20)	1073(.01)

of Hogaboam and Perfetti, all response times are included in the analysis in order to reflect the length of all decisions.

Our major focus is on the analysis of the error data for the homographs as a function of frequency, i.e., the polarity by frequency interaction. In particular, the homographs which are low frequency in use and which are highly unbalanced produce performance (52% correct) that does not differ reliably from chance. With respect to the main effect of polarity, the data are quite striking, with error rates increasing as homographs become increasingly unbalanced. Decision latencies follow the pattern of errors.

It is interesting, in terms of modeling the data, to look at the error rates and decision times for the unambiguous words. With respect to frequency, both response latency and errors increase as frequency increases. We can see two alternative explanations of these data. One is that the participant uses a familiarity criterion to decide whether a search for a second alternative meaning could be fruitful. A second explanation is that the participants genuinely have more difficulty making the ambiguity decision for higher-frequency entries. For the unambiguous word, the former explanation would only account for the latency data. The latter view is discussed in terms of our theory in the section Accounting for the Data, below.

In the second experiment, half of the items presented for ambiguity processing were primed with a related word. In the case of the homographs, these primes were related to either the primary or secondary meaning equally often and re-paired to form unrelated primes. For the nonwords the prime was related to the word from which it was derived or similarly re-paired. Thus, the procedure was like that of the first experiment with the addition of a prime (related or unrelated).

On the basis of our "race" model (Gorfein & Bubka, 1985), it was hypothesized that the secondary prime would improve ambiguity-decision performance at all levels of polarity, whereas a primary prime would have little influence and might even have a negative influence.

For the unambiguous word items, there was once again a trend for frequency to influence decision latency and error rates in the same manner. The mean response latency and errors (in parentheses) were 1896 (.12), 1829 (.20), and 1988 (.20) from low to high frequency, respectively. Priming had no reliable effect. Once again, nonword decisions were much faster than word decisions and had very low error rates, 1218 ms (.02).

Table 7.3 reports the data for the homographs. Consistent with the data for unprimed homographs, the data for unrelated primes show an effect of both polarity and frequency, with the highest overall error rate (0.58) occurring for the unbalanced low-frequency homographs. With respect to Experiment 1, where words were unprimed, the decision latency for unrelated primes was slightly longer, but error rates were about the same.

Priming with related primes produces some very interesting effects with respect to error rates. While secondary primes (Table 7.3c) produced significant improvement with respect to errors as compared with unrelated

TABLE 7.3. Decision time in milliseconds and proportion of errors (in parentheses) for the homographs presented in the primed ambiguity task.

	Homograph polarity			
	Balanced (50–65%)	Middle (66–85%)	Unbalanced (86–100%)	Mean (50–100%)
		a. Unrelated prime		
Frequency				
Low	1772(.27)	1922(.34)	2135(.59)	1943(.40)
Middle	2006(.34)	1851(.18)	2118(.27)	1992(.26)
High	1990(.21)	2111(.27)	1951(.39)	2017(.22)
Mean	1923(.27)	1961(.26)	2068(.42)	
		b. Primary prime		
Frequency				
Low	1727(.15)	1762(.33)	1928(.53)	1806(.34)
Middle	1919(.32)	1952(.27)	1999(.48)	1907(.36)
High	1617(.38)	1827(.30)	1863(.41)	1769(.36)
Mean	1754(.38)	1847(.30)	1980(.47)	
		c. Secondary Prime		
Frequency				
Low	1670(.15)	1846(.27)	1810(.36)	1775(.26)
Middle	1906(.20)	1822(.17)	1960(.30)	1896(.22)
High	1699(.17)	1789(.24)	1880(.24)	1789(.22)
Mean	1758(.17)	1819(.23)	1883(.30)	

primes, the primary prime had negligible effects and indeed seemed to increase errors. Both primary and secondary primes seem to enhance decision speed.

Thus, the principal findings with respect to the ambiguity decision are those of the interaction of frequency and polarity. The lower the frequency of the secondary meaning, as estimated by the product of the Kucera-Francis frequency of the letter string (homograph) and the normative proportion of secondary word associations, the more difficult the ambiguity decision. A search model of ambiguity decision like that of Forster and Bednall (1976) (see also Forster, Chapter 9, this volume) would predict the findings with respect to decision time. A search model with a deadline to stop searching could predict the error rates. However, the high rate of failed searches (incorrect rejections) is troubling in our view for any model that proposes a search mechanism.

The Meaning(s) Achieved

The crucial problem for the student of language processes is understanding what meaning is achieved by language processes. As mentioned in Chapter 1 of this volume, the problem is by no means a simple one. The tasks in which we study meaning are not themselves transparent, and the performance does not necessarily indicate which meaning is finally arrived at. In the literature, we are told that the meaning present may vary as a function of the posthomograph interval with both meanings of a bipolar homograph present at or shortly (200–400 ms) after the homograph, and ultimately only the primary meaning in the unprimed task and the contextually appropriate meaning in the primed persist after a longer interval (cf., Onifer & Swinney, 1981; Simpson & Burgess, 1985; Simpson, Chapter 2, this volume).

In order to evaluate meaning achieved after a variety of tasks, Bubka (1988) developed the relatedness experiment. In experiments of this type, shortly after the completion of the processing of a homograph, e.g., DUCK (i.e., the required response to that item is made), a word is presented, e.g., SWAN, with the instruction that the participants must decide if that word is related to the homograph that had just been processed. The probe words are related to one or the other meaning of the homograph (primary or secondary) or are unrelated. The simplicity of the idea is that to the degree that the homograph has already achieved a meaning state appropriate to the probe, the decision should be faster and more accurate. Further, the identical probe may follow the homograph in a variety of contexts. Thus, any differences obtained across contexts can be attributed to the task constraint and not to the homograph-target relationship alone or to the nature of the relatedness task. The studies reported in Bubka's dissertation and in a follow-up study we conducted all ask what manipulations favor one meaning state or the other.

In the third experiment we report here, we were interested in the meaning achieved in lexical decision. The priming effects observed in lexical decision are considered an indication of lexical access, although the exact processes by which access occurs, and what meaning is achieved, are debatable. Since the ambiguity-decision task is transparent to the meanings achieved, the two tasks (lexical decision and ambiguity decision) were compared in terms of performance as measured on a relatedness decision that followed the orienting task on a homograph.

When presented with a word in an ambiguity-detection task, the participant decides whether the word has one meaning or more than one meaning. The homographs used in this study have only two meanings; therefore, presumably both meanings will have been achieved when an ambiguous word is presented and a correct response is produced.

In the lexical-decision task, the participant decides if a string of letters is a word or a nonword. Retrieval of one meaning is logically sufficient to make a lexical-decision judgment. If the string of letters has some meaning and a lexical entry has been found, then it must be a word. Lexical access may or may not be exhaustive. Table 7.4 gives an outline of this task.

The orienting task (ambiguity decision, lexical decision), a between-subjects variable, preceded the relatedness-decision task. In the relatedness task, the participant decided if a word was related in meaning to the

TABLE 7.4. Lexical, ambiguity, and relatedness decision in Experiment 3.

	Orienting task			
	Lexical decision		Ambiguity task	
	Homograph	Nonword	Homograph	Nonhomograph
	a. Primary meaning			
	BANK	FANK	BANK	CAT
Relatedness decision	MONEY	XXX	STREAM	XXXX
	b. Secondary meaning			
	BANK	FANK	BANK	CAT
Relatedness decision	STREAM	XXX	STREAM	XXX

homograph presented for lexical or ambiguity decision. Response latencies and error rates of the relatedness decision should depend on the meaning(s) accessed for the homograph as a result of the orienting task. If the results are similar on the relatedness decision across orienting tasks, then it is reasonable to conclude that an exhaustive process occurs during lexical decision since it must occur for ambiguity decision. On the other hand, if differences result, this would support the idea of some form of process that achieves only a single meaning.

The main variable of interest is the effect of target type on the relatedness decision after each orienting task. If an exhaustive-access process is not occurring during lexical decision, then there should be a larger difference between primary and secondary relatedness decisions after the lexical decision than after the ambiguity decision. This difference would be found in response latency and error rate data. If only one meaning is achieved during lexical decision, then more errors and longer latencies should be found for the unaccessed meaning.

It is reasonable that if differences are observed, they will be determined by the polarity of the homograph. The most frequent meaning of the homograph should be the meaning that is achieved post-lexical decision. Response latencies and errors should increase for secondary-meaning targets for relatedness decisions as polarity increases. In the same manner, they should decrease as polarity increases when a primary-meaning target is presented for relatedness decision.

The results were analyzed in terms of the difference between primary and secondary targets in the relatedness experiment. The results indicate that the outcome of the decision process under the two tasks are entirely different. As shown in Table 7.5, there were larger differences between the primary- and secondary-meaning targets for relatedness decision after the lexical decision than after the ambiguity decision, and these differences

TABLE 7.5. Performance across homograph polarity as a function of the orienting task (ambiguity or lexical decision) and dependent variable. Scores represent difference scores (primary target − secondary target).

	Polarity of homograph		
Dependent variable	Balanced	Middle	Unbalanced
a. *Decision time* (milliseconds)			
Ambiguity	−155	−92	−237
Lexical	−117	−210	−344
b. *Proportion of error*			
Ambiguity	.10	.06	.24
Lexical	.08	.17	.35
c. *Sensitivity (d′)*			
Ambiguity	−.31	.04	1.15
Lexical	−.28	.50	2.04

grew with polarity. Latency data showed greater differences in the lexical decision as well, but this effect was not statistically reliable.

Since we only analyzed correct reaction times, the failure to obtain a reliable orienting task by target by polarity interaction may have been due to the significant interaction obtained in the error rates creating an item selection effect. The signal detection analysis indicated that there was more sensitivity toward the secondary-meaning target after the ambiguity decision than after the lexical decision. The difference scores, together with a decreasing response latency and error rate as polarity increased in lexical decision, indicate that in an unprimed lexical decision, only one meaning is achieved, usually the primary meaning.

In Experiment 3, we established that in contrast to the ambiguity-decision task the result in unprimed lexical decision is not exhaustive; rather, often the most frequent meaning is achieved. A second experiment employing the relatedness-decision task (Experiment 4) was designed to examine the effect a prime has on the meaning achieved in lexical decision. It has been hypothesized by most of the lexical-access theorists that context influences the achievement of meaning. Since we found in Experiment 3 that the polarity of the homograph had a large effect, Experiment 4 examined the effect that context had on the process. Does context determine the meaning, or is polarity more important to the process, or do the two variables interact in some way?

As shown in Table 7.6 the participant's task in Experiment 4 was to perform a lexical decision on a homograph (or a nonword) after viewing a prime, which was a word related to one of the meanings of the homograph. After the lexical-decision task, the subject made a relatedness decision between a primary- or secondary-meaning target word and the homograph which was presented for lexical decision. The meaning of the prime and the target word for relatedness decision was always consistent. That is, it was

TABLE 7.6. Lexical- and relatedness-decision Experiment 4.

	Prime conditions	
	Related	Unrelated
	a. Primary meaning	
Prime	SAVINGS	RAILROAD
Lexical decision	BANK	BANK
Relatedness decision	HONEY	HONEY
	b. Secondary meaning	
Prime	RIVER	TEACH
Lexical decision	BANK	BANK
Relatedness decision	STREAM	STREAM
	c. Control—association	
Prime	TOBACCO	MOON
Lexical decision	SMOKE	SMOKE
Relatedness decision	CIGAR	CIGAR
	d. Control—nonword	
Prime	SAVINGS	RAILROAD
Lexical decision	FANK	FANK
Relatedness decision	XXX	XXX

never the case that a primary-meaning prime preceded the lexical decision and a secondary-meaning target was presented for the relatedness decision. The inclusion of this type of trial would have left open the possibility of a strategy in which participants would consciously access both meanings of the homograph. The design, however, does favor any model that depends on the context for meaning selection. That is, to the extent that meaning achievement is context-sensitive, the meaning presented as a prime should be the meaning that is available post-lexical decision and post-access.

To the extent that meaning achievement is not context-sensitive or context-independent, the role of polarity should influence performance as it did in the unprimed lexical-decision portion of Experiment 1. Therefore, under a context-determined process, no differences between primary and secondary targets for relatedness decision or for balanced and unbalanced homograph conditions are predicted. If polarity affects lexical access, such that the primary meaning is accessed even under secondary-meaning context conditions, then differences should result between target types. Greater differences should result under unbalanced homograph conditions than balanced homograph conditions, since, for the latter materials, primary and secondary are somewhat arbitrary.

The results indicate that priming was influential in the task. Relatedness decisions were faster when the prime was related than when it was unrelated. Context is an important variable in lexical access, since it facilitates the process. However, the results shown in Figure 7.1 do not indicate that context solely determines access, since they are for correct decisions only. An analysis of errors is necessary to round out the picture.

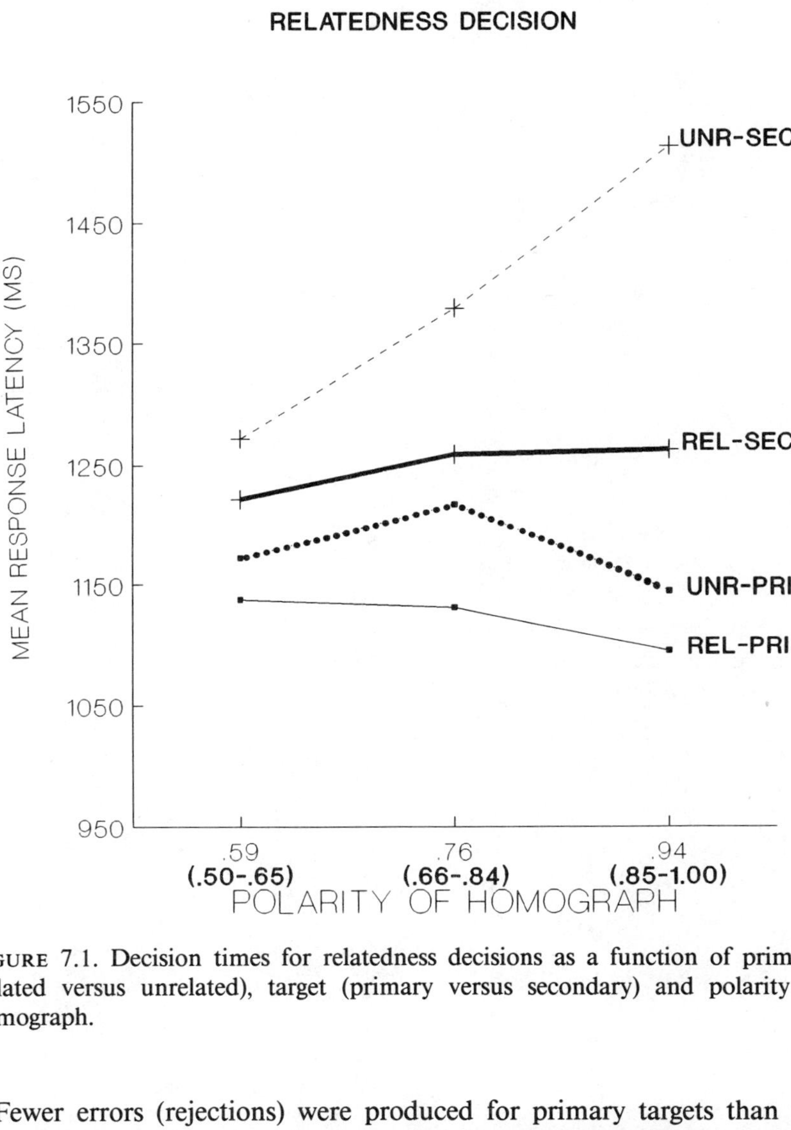

FIGURE 7.1. Decision times for relatedness decisions as a function of priming (related versus unrelated), target (primary versus secondary) and polarity of homograph.

Fewer errors (rejections) were produced for primary targets than for secondary targets on the relatedness-decision task. Also, fewer errors resulted for balanced homographs than for unbalanced homographs. As can be seen in Figure 7.2a, error rates for the secondary targets increased across polarity, while the rates for the primary targets did not differ across polarity.

Two types of errors can occur in a relatedness experiment. An error can result from a false alarm, i.e., saying "yes" when the pair is, in fact, unrelated, and from an incorrect rejection, i.e., saying "no" to a related pair. Therefore, in order to separate errors due to participants adopting a bias toward certain conditions, a signal detection analysis was performed

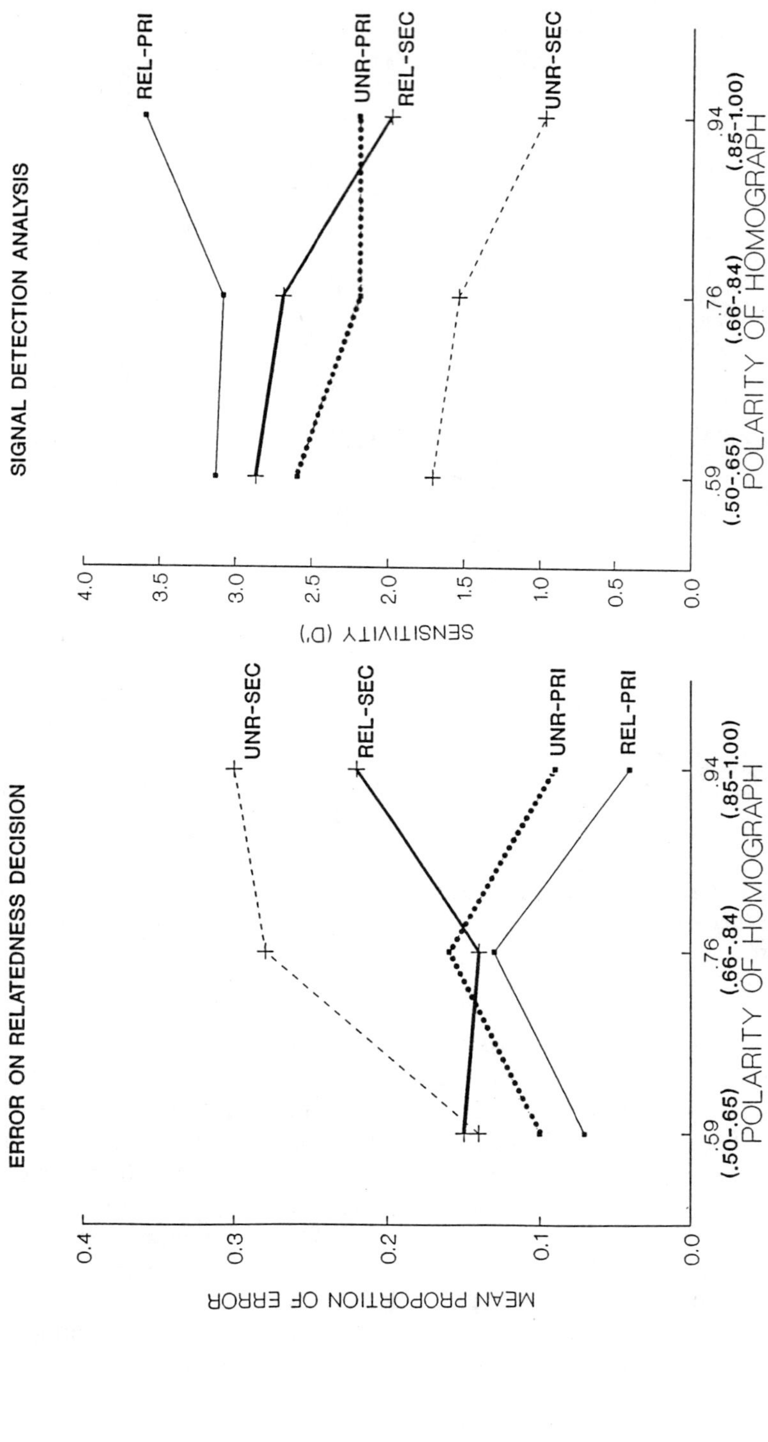

FIGURE 7.2. Performance with respect to errors as defined by incorrect rejections of related targets (Figure 7.2a) and a signal detectability analysis of d′ or sensitivity (Figure 7.2b) as a function of priming (related versus unrelated), target (primary versus secondary) and polarity of homograph.

and is shown in Figure 7.2b. The signal detection analysis suggested that the primary and secondary prime produced equal sensitivity toward the target for the balanced homograph condition. However, for the unbalanced homograph condition, the primary-meaning target sensitivity increased with polarity, while for the secondary meaning, there was a decrease in sensitivity for those targets.

We can conclude that participants were slower and erred most often when the items were unbalanced and where the relatedness decision was directed toward the secondary meaning. This suggests that the primary meaning was more often available at the time of the relatedness decision. Priming was effective in that response latencies were shorter and fewer errors were produced for those items that were primed. Priming in the secondary direction was more facilitative than in the primary direction, although priming was not so effective as to equalize performance on primary- and secondary- relatedness decisions.

In summary, the two relatedness experiments (Experiments 3 and 4) have shown that the lexical access of homographs is determined by the context, polarity level, and particular task involved. Context aids meaning achievement, but context does not overshadow the polarity of the homograph.

Since context facilitated the selection of a particular meaning but did not determine it entirely, Experiment 5, a third relatedness experiment, was conducted in an attempt to increase the influence of the prime in meaning achievement. An experiment almost identical to Experiment 4 was arranged. The only change from the previous study was that following Besner and McCann's procedure (1988), the lexical-decision target was distorted in that the letter string was written in alternating case (e.g., wOrD), always beginning with a lowercase letter. Distorted targets for lexical decision should be responded to slower than undistorted targets in lexical decision. Besner and other investigators postulate that pattern distortion slows the rate of processing in a letter identification process which precedes or is part of the lexical-decision process. Since distorting the lexical-decision target makes it harder to access meaning, we hypothesized that lexical access in this task should utilize the context more than in an undistorted situation.

Figure 7.3 shows the effect on the lexical decision under normal (7.3a) and distorted presentation (7.3b). The distorted lexical decision results in longer latencies with a more pronounced priming effect than the undistorted lexical decisions we obtained in Experiment 4.

Figure 7.4 shows the results in terms of errors and signal detectability on the relatedness decision in this study. More important is the comparison of this study to Experiment 4, and this comparison can be seen by comparing the error rates (Fig. 7.4a) and sensitivity (Fig. 7.4b) with the corresponding panels in Figure 7.2. The distortion manipulation has raised d' slightly, with the greatest advantage occurring for the balanced homograph condition.

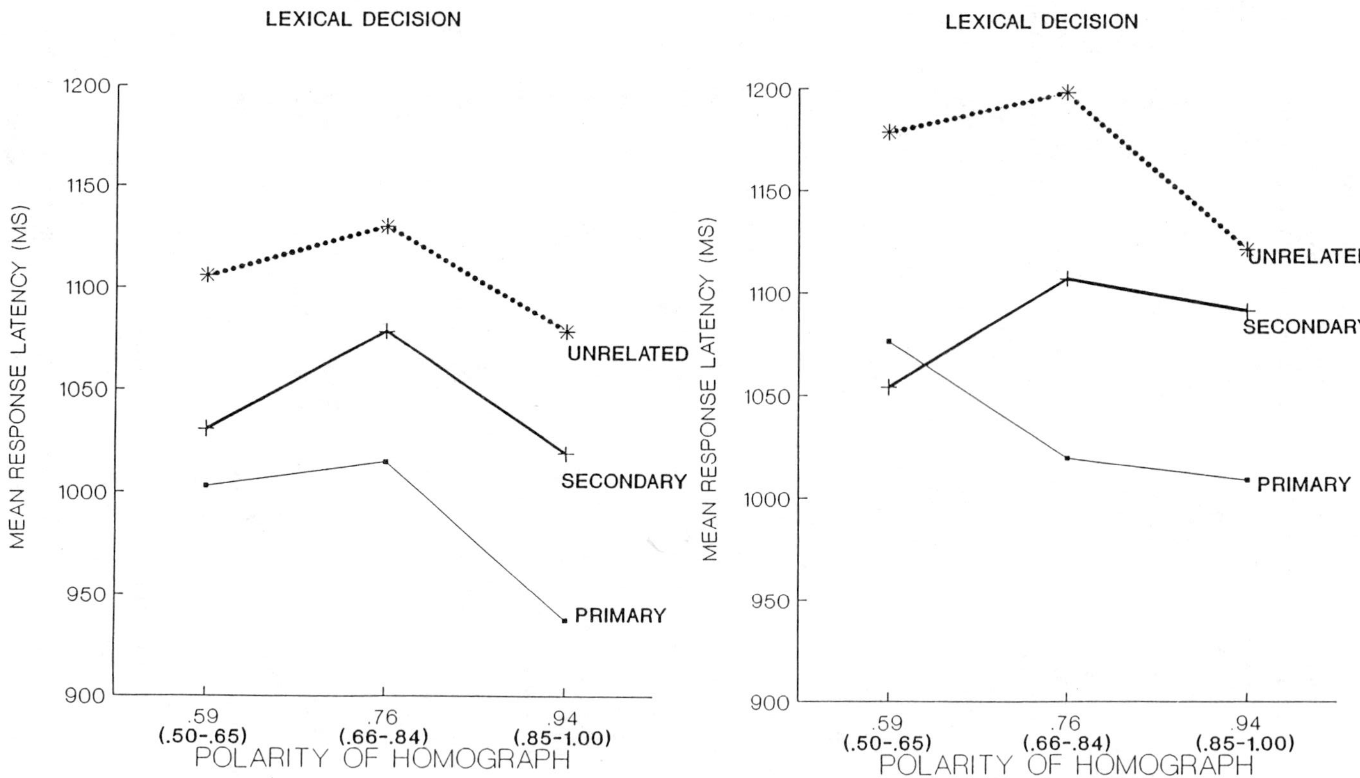

FIGURE 7.3. A comparison of lexical decision latency for undistorted homographs from experiment 3 (Figure 7.3a) to distorted homographs (Figure 7.3b) as a function of priming (primary and secondary related or unrelated) and polarity of homograph.

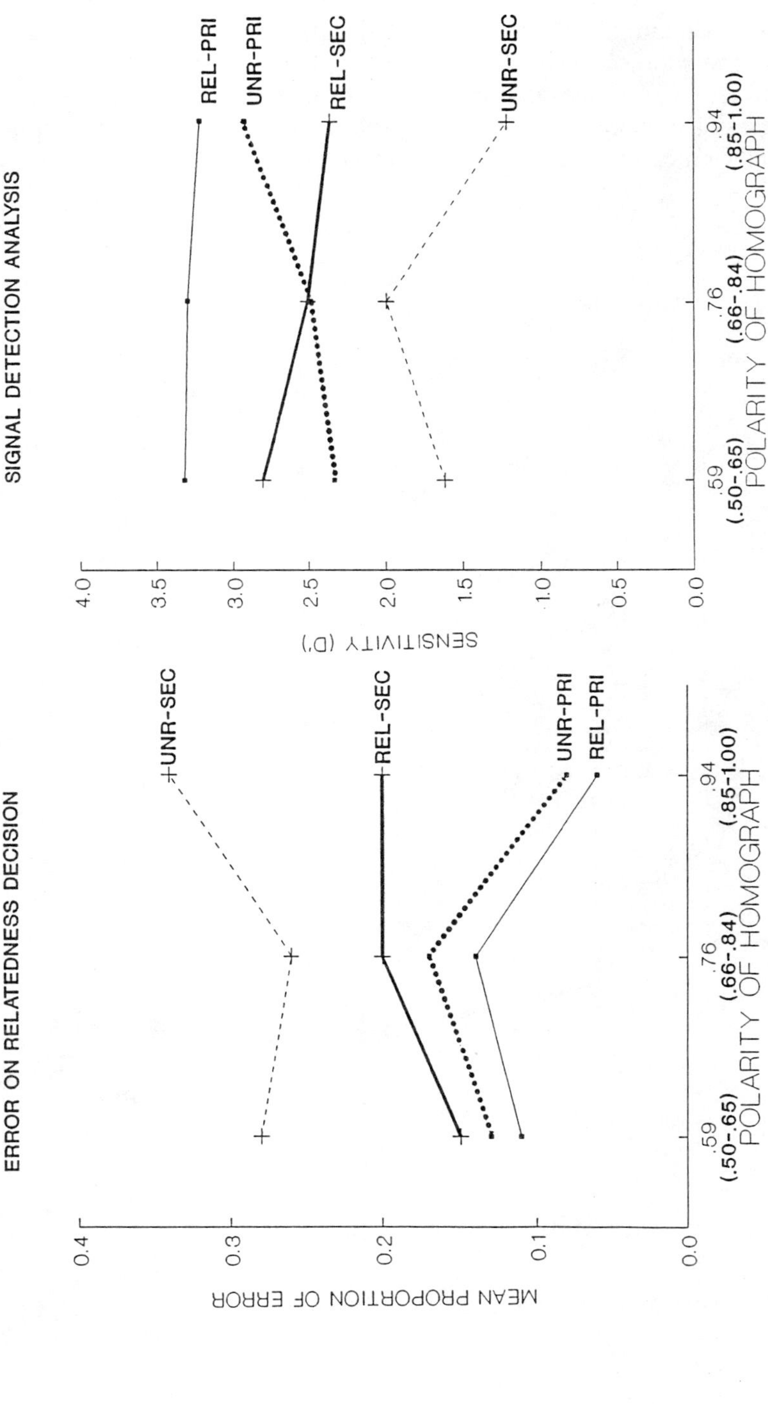

FIGURE 7.4. Performance on the relatedness decision in the distortion experiment with respect to errors as defined by incorrect rejections of related targets (Figure 7.4a) and d′, sensitivity in a signal detection analysis (Figure 7.4b) as a function of priming (related versus unrelated), target (primary versus secondary) and polarity of homograph.

In comparing Figures 7.1 and 7.5, we see that the response latencies present a similar picture with faster responding all around occurring with the distortion manipulation and with the greatest priming advantage accruing for the balanced and middle homograph conditions.

In summary, distorting the homographs for lexical decision produces a slightly greater influence of context, but the frequency variable is still the major determiner of meaning when the polarity of the homograph is unbalanced.

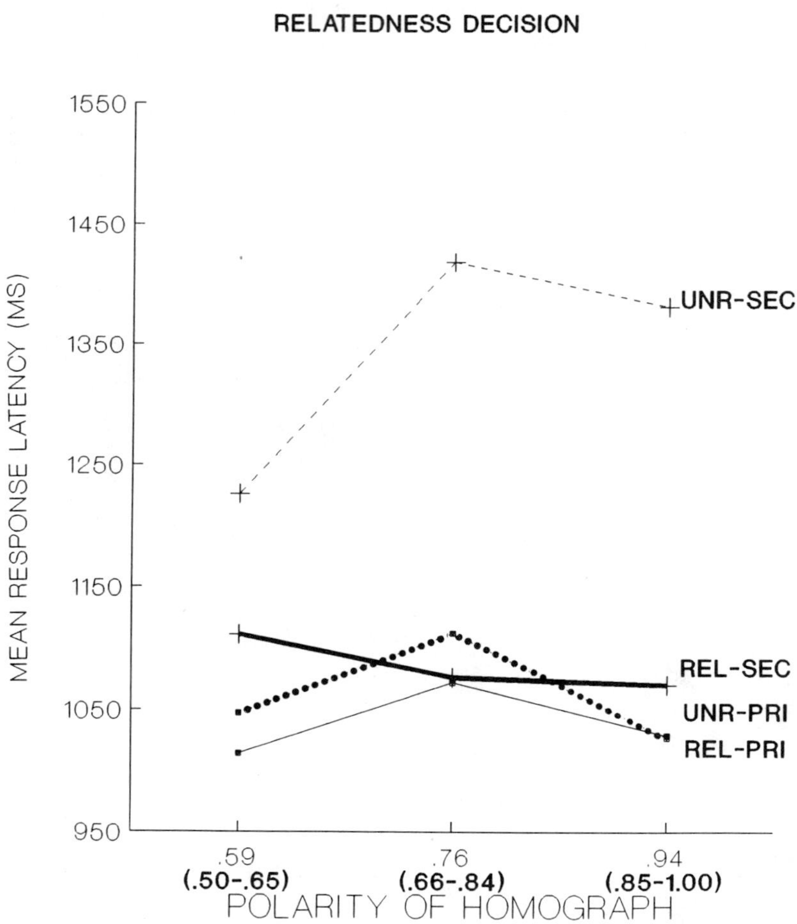

FIGURE 7.5. Decision times for the relatedness decisions in the distortion experiment as a function of priming (related versus unrelated), target (primary versus secondary) and polarity of homograph.

The Effects of Frequency and the Need for an Alternative Theory

Over the five experiments we have reported, we have seen that it often seems to be difficult to achieve the secondary meaning of a homograph. Thus in Experiments 1 and 2 we demonstrated that when Kucera-Francis frequency was low and the homograph was unbalanced (secondary frequency is low), participants have great difficulty in ambiguity decision. In the subsequent experiments the results of a relatedness-decision task were best interpreted as a failure to achieve secondary meanings especially in the lexical-decision task when the meaning measured was secondary and the homograph highly polarized. Thus as we suggested in the introduction to this chapter, there is a need to pay more attention to frequency and polarity in our theorizing.

In reviewing the current state of the field in Chapter 1, we suggested that there were five alternative classes of models extant in the field (see Chapter 1, Table 1.1). A converging theme at the Semantic Ambiguity Conference was that none of the existing models accounted for all of the data. In particular, the presence and absence of semantic context effects seemed to follow no well-understood rule. We reported the failure of subjects to have available the appropriate meaning for the relatedness task even when the context supported that meaning. Tabossi (Chapter 3, this volume) reported powerful context effects that seemed to rule out exhaustive access. Forster concluded (Chapter 9, this volume) that context can influence order of retrieval of meanings, and Simpson and Kellas (Chapter 4, this volume) suggested that once one meaning was achieved, the other was harder to obtain.

At the time of the conference, we favored a search model that placed high-frequency meanings at an advantage, as they would, on the average, occur earlier in a frequency-ordered search (Gorfein & Bubka, 1985). Nevertheless, we believed (unlike the ordered-access theorists) that context might make an entry more accessible in the search, as an appropriate prime might shorten the search for the less frequent entry. However, we could not articulate a mechanism for this shortened search. In the present chapter we abandon many of our previous assumptions and offer a model that solves the problem.

A Theory of Meaning Achievement

In 1981 I proposed a mechanism for spreading activation and the interaction of environmental and semantic context (Gorfein, 1987; Gorfein & Viviani, 1981). That view was applied primarily to episodic memory tasks, with a specific attempt to explain performance in the Brown-Peterson short-term memory task (see Gorfein, 1987). Here we will attempt to extend the theory to the achievement (selection) of meaning in semantic memory contexts.

Listed below are the seven basic principles of the theory (as described in Gorfein, 1987):

1. Words are represented by an ordered set of attributes.
2. The processing of a word activates a number (N) of attributes; the number is limited by (a) task constraints—the number necessary to meet the requirements of the task—and (b) the time available, if it is less than the time needed to meet the task demand.
3. In isolation, the first N attributes of a word are activated.
4. The *set principle:* Processing a word in the context of active attributes will result in the use of those attributes to the extent that the word possesses attributes in common with those that are active.
5. Attributes are activated an amount (S) that is determined by the time available and the task's requirements. Use of a matching attribute results in an increment in activation, while a nonmatch decrements the activity of an active attribute.
6. Activation of an attribute is accompanied by the permanent marking of the attribute with a sampled number of elements of the current environmental context from a universe of potential contextual elements. Context is used in a manner equivalent to the "stimulus sample" in stimulus sampling theory as proposed by Estes (1950).
7. Activation decays over time as a function of initial strength. The probability that an attribute remains active over a period of K seconds is an exponentially decreasing function of the length of the period and an increasing function of initial strength. Therefore, the probability that an attribute active at time T is still active K seconds later can be defined mathematically as equal to $e^{-K/S}$.

In reviewing that model and extending it to semantic memory, we are impressed that the nature of the task could influence the stimulus sampling model. In episodic memory—short-term memory (STM)—it makes sense that the principal retrieval information should be environmental-contextual. After all, that is the nature of episode (cf. Tulving, 1983). To paraphrase the instructions for a Brown-Peterson task, the participant is instructed to judge (recognition form) or recall the *last item* presented for memory. Therefore, a search for environmental context information (information similar to "now") is reasonable. On the other hand, in the semantic memory tasks, the principal search set should be composed of semantic stimuli, as they are most likely to supply answers to the question "Is it a word?" or "Does this letter string have more than one meaning?"

If we examine the information available for retrieval in an unprimed lexical or ambiguity decision, we see that the principal stimulus available is the letter string provided for decision. Under this circumstance, the retrieval could consist of entries in the system associated with this stimulus sample. Modularity (see Chapter 15, this volume) may be preserved under this system by redefining the lexicon as we have described below. Conversely, the retrieval can be from the semantic memory system. In the case of the primed-decision task, the stimulus sample would contain the letter-string stimulus and the active attributes of the prime as well as environmental elements. This suggests the following revision in the theory:

Principle 4 (Revised). The set principle: The stimulus sample employed in retrieval will include the active attributes at the time of retrieval in addition to the environmental contextual elements.

In this revised view, the retrieval cue, a stimulus sample, will contact memory entries most like those in the sample. Therefore, the compound retrieval cue will act like the set principle did in our previous theorizing and select meaning entries for a word presented, which will tend to support the active attributes.

The role of the sample would be to cue relevant entries in the memory system for the task at hand. Following the recent suggestion of Anderson (1987) that such a memory system might be constructed in a rational manner, we would expect that such a system would try to maximize the likelihood of achieving a correct answer while minimizing the number of false entries searched. This adds an eighth and final principle:

Principle 8. The retrieval system in semantic memory will generate a search (candidate) set of entries from the lexicon that meets a criterion of potential utility for the task demands.

In retrieving entries for a candidate set, then, a strength rule will be followed where the probability of an entries retrieval will be a function of the similarity of an entry's contextual markers to that of the current stimulus sample. Entries will come into the candidate set at a rate (speed) commensurate with their contextual strength. In computer jargon, memory is content-addressable.

By setting a criterion for utility we would expect such a system to be sensitive to task demands. Thus, a speeded task might lead to a more narrow retrieval plan, while a high penalty for incorrect answers might lead to a broader and slower search due to a widened definition of the set of relevant cued objects.

The Nature of the Lexicon

From our new viewpoint, we feel we have detected the fallacy in our previous thought (and the thinking of a number of others) with respect to the content of the lexicon. We feel that we have fallen into the same trap that led Collins and Quillian (1969) to localize property information at the highest (most general) node to which it applied in their semantic network.

We, as they, have assumed cognitive (storage) economy. In retrospect we now think that the lexicon contains multiple entries for a word not unlike the dictionary entries for most words. Even the modest college dictionary the authors use contains in excess of 25 entries for the word *hand.* Such a multiple-entry proposal is not as extreme, in terms of the number of entries created, as the random-walk model of Landauer (1975) or the replication memory model of Bernbach (1970). Since entries will be cued by the environmental stimuli (i.e., memory is, in general, content-addressable), the additional entries make life no more difficult than does an unabridged dictionary make word retrieval more difficult than a pocket dictionary. In fact, it may be argued that the precision gained may make the system too perfect and unable to account for failures of retrieval.

It should be noted, for those devoted to the modularity hypothesis, that in order to preserve modularity we can locate the multiple entries in the lexicon. Nothing in principle changes if we were to suggest that a word has multiple nodes in a semantic network.

Thus we are proposing a multiple-entry memory with a retrieval cue which selects more than one entry for examination based on the similarity of that cue to memory entries. We will now show that such a system accounts for the data we report and the other data of interest to students of lexical ambiguity.

Accounting for the Data

In the context of a particular task, the letter string (homograph) provides the principal cue for retrieval in the absence of priming. Background (environmental) stimuli provide secondary retrieval values, which in the absence of previous experience with those contextual elements (i.e., on the first occurrence of that letter string in that context) will not influence the performance. This follows from an analysis of the retrieval problem as being not unlike the retrieval problem in Pavlovian conditioning, extending Rescorla and Wagner's (1972) analysis to this situation. We would expect that the cue's validity will depend on past experience (i.e., how often under those conditions the cue has predicted a particular meaning). In general, the background stimuli in the absence of the letter string will have an asymptotic value near zero (see Rescorla & Wagner, 1972, pp. 86–93).

In the presence of the letter string, the background as part of a compound will be associated with the most frequently useful meanings. Thus, we would anticipate that for each of the *n* entries associated with a letter string, the string and its compound would have a value associated with it predicting the utility of the entry. These values would be consistent with the past experience of the organism, and thus the more frequent entries will have higher values. Both the absolute and relative frequency of the experience of each entry may influence this outcome. Since the letter string is present for all cases, its strength will be more or less asymptotic. However, the background stimuli in a context will fluctuate from environment to environment and indeed from moment to moment under Estes's stimulus sampling rules and thus will have a smaller number of associations with each entry. Thus, the compound of a homograph string in a particular background may not always reflect the same entry as the homographic elements of the array. Therefore, the probability of retrieving any particular entry as the first will vary from the normative frequency of that entry but, in general, reflect that order.

In the lexical-decision task the retrieval system will present, for inspection to consciousness, entries reflecting this order. Since any of these entries is lexical, the first one inspected will meet the task demands. This meaning will be the one "brought to consciousness," and thus conscious experience will tend to reflect the relative frequencies of the meanings.

In ambiguity decision the system will presumably inspect more entries. As mentioned above, entries with a low absolute frequency will have a utility value associated with them which may be quite small. Under speed instructions, the retrieval criterion (number of entries selected for the candidate set) may be limited in such manner as not to include the low-frequency occurrences. We would anticipate this occurring when the frequency of experience with the letter string (homograph) was low and the relative experience with the two distinct meanings was very unbalanced. Such a mechanism accounts for the error distribution in our unprimed ambiguity experiment.

In general, higher-frequency homographs will have a larger search set associated with them, since more senses of the word will have been experienced in sufficient numbers to meet a criterion for inclusion in the inspection set. To the degree that the homograph is polarized with respect to its distinct meaning, we would expect longer searches since the system will inspect more items on the average before finding either an entry that meets the criterion of a second distinct meaning or the bottom of its list. If there is an upper limit on entries in the candidate set, it is possible that a second distinct meaning will not be included in the set, resulting in an error. For unambiguous words, the number of entries generated will, on the average, be greater for more frequent words, and as a consequence, searches of these sets will be longer on the average than for less frequent words.

In context, according to the revised set principle, the entries will be generated by three factors in the stimulus sample: the letter string, the active attributes, and the background stimuli–letter-string compound. This will alter the distribution (order) of the entries in the candidate set and in many cases alter the composition of the set.

The data from the primed lexical-decision-relatedness experiments (undistorted and distorted) suggest that there are limits placed on the efficacy of the prime in lexical decision at least when it is a single word. This conclusion follows from the contrast of the priming-relatedness effect in undistorted and distorted lexical decision. One possible explanation of this is that in lexical-decision experiments the familiarity of the string is directly available and dominates (as suggested by Balota and Chumbley, 1984, but see Forster's Chapter 9 in this volume). Alternatively, it may be that in many cases the letter-string member of the stimulus set is so strongly connected to the entries associated with primary responses that the prime information is insufficient to place a primed entry at the top of the hierarchy of potentially useful responses. Thus, distortion either can make it difficult to assess familiarity or can slow the word integration process down enough to have the prime-partial information compound help form the word, and thus increase the likelihood of a primed entry being first in the order. However, in any event, the gain is small. Further research on the nature of the prime, and perhaps an increased amount of distortion, would help us understand the circumstances in which the secondary meaning is achieved.

In ambiguity processing where meaning is sought by the subject, we would anticipate the prime having a greater influence. Thus, the secondary prime would greatly increase the possibility of including in the candidate set those entries associated with the secondary meaning in the set generated. To the extent that the homograph was a highly polarized one, a secondary prime would not significantly reduce the likelihood of including in the candidate set those entries associated with the primary meaning of the homograph. On the other hand, a primary prime for highly polarized homographs may increase the error rate, as the prime may assure that all entries in the criterion set are related to the primary sense. In fact in the signal detection analysis of the primed ambiguity experiment, we saw a tendency to less sensitivity when the homograph was primed by a word related to its primary sense.

The facilitation of the related decision by an appropriate prime in Experiments 4 and 5 is notable but consistent with the theory proposed. The task is post-access for the homograph and occurs at a time interval when theories of the spreading activation type (cf. Collins & Loftus, 1975) suggest activation should have decayed. However, we have argued elsewhere (Gorfein, 1987; Gorfein & Viviani, 1980) that the duration of activation is task-dependent (see theory principle 5 above). In the relatedness task it is to the participant's advantage to keep the selected entry active long enough to make the relatedness decision easier. To the extent that facilitation was obtained by priming, and it was, this view of activation duration was supported.

In addition to explaining our own findings, we need to explain the principal finding that supports the major alternative model—that of exhaustive access. As indicated in Chapter 1, the cross-modal priming task (Onifer & Swinney, 1981; Swinney & Prather, this volume, Chapter 12) produces what seems to be priming of both meanings of a homograph immediately following presentation of that homograph in sentence context. Two alternative possibilities are suggested by this model to account for those data. One is the possibility that the context is not strong enough to guarantee that the first instance in the candidate set is appropriate to the sentence. This would result in a probablistic distribution of instances, and therefore, would lead to what looks like exhaustive access by the averaging of some solely primary and some solely secondary instances. This view argues that with sufficiently strong priming, only one meaning (the content-appropriate meaning) will be accessed. Tabossi's (1988a) data (see also Chapter 3 in this volume) are generally supportive of this view. Alternatively, there may be sufficient activation produced by having a related entry or entries anywhere in the candidate set to produce priming for brief intervals following the homograph even though only one meaning is selected. Under this view, Tabossi's results would occur whenever the prime was strong enough to ensure that no (few?) entries in the candidate set are related to the unprimed meaning. We tend to favor the former proposal but have not yet achieved unambiguous evidence to support this view.

A number of converging trends (Gorfein & Walters, Chapter 5 this volume; Simpson & Kellas, Chapter 4 this volume; Walters, 1988) have suggested that the first occurrence of an ambiguous word in a situation may result in the inhibition of performance with respect to a subsequent presentation, when that presentation is intended to evoke the alternative meaning.

According to the present theory, a stimulus complex of the ambiguous word and a sample of the environmental background is formed. This ambiguity-background complex will become attached to the entry selected on that trial. When an item recurs in the same background environment it therefore will tend to evoke the same entry. To the degree that the same entry is appropriate to the task demands performance will be facilitated. When as in the case of the Simpson and Kellas manipulation that entry is inappropriate performance will be inhibited. Since the same entry is initially accessed on second occurrences, the stimulus-background association will be strengthened even though another entry is ultimately selected. Thus on the third occurrence of the ambiguity there is a tendency to favor the reselection of the entry selected on first occurrence.

The Ratcliff-McKoon Model

As we were preparing the final draft of this model, Ratcliff and McKoon's (1988) retrieval theory of priming appeared in print. The authors stopped to examine in what way our model differed from theirs. In fact the differences may be small, and we welcome the concurrent support. The differences while small are not negligible. While the Ratcliff-McKoon model does not specify which aspects of a prime are formed into a compound, our model suggests that only those attributes (elements) still active at target presentation will serve to promote retrieval. We have presented evidence for this view in short-term memory studies of homographs (Gorfein, 1983; Gorfein & Viviani, 1981). Further research in our laboratory is being conducted to extend those findings to priming tasks. Our model makes the nature of the lexicon important, while the Ratcliff-McKoon model does allow for existing associations in memory to influence performance. Finally, in our focus of interest, homography, we attribute important effects to frequency of experience when considered in conjunction with background environmental stimuli as well as the semantic stimuli which are the focus of the Ratcliff-McKoon model.

Summary

Elsewhere in this volume (Simpson & Kellas, Chapter 4) a number of relevant arguments for a feature-constraining view of context have been cited. Other individuals, as cited by Simpson, have offered minitheories of word retrieval. Our theory may, on the surface, appear similar to the views of those others and, indeed, that of Simpson and Kellas. However, we believe that the conditioning-retrieval route we adopt provides a mechanism that is quite different from the formal model (the logogen model of Morton, 1964) from which theories like that of Simpson and Kellas derive. Specifically, our theory does not require different resting states of a logogen system but instead makes the strength-of-context-to-response connection the determiner of probability of retrieval as well as speed of retrieval of a lexical entry.

Thus, we have a model consistent with a well-established body of literature in the functionalist tradition, i.e., most, if not all, of the memory literature from Ebbinghaus to the cognitive revolution. The present model is distinguished from the exhaustive-access models in being sensitive to semantic context and strongly influenced by prior experience, in terms of meaning frequency. We believe it can account for the data in the field, and does so by postulating a mechanism that is adaptive as well as consistent with other processes. Finally, by making use of an extended lexicon, it maintains modularity (see the discussion in Chapter 15) without sacrificing context sensitivity.

Part III Representation

Homographs are an interesting problem to those interested in how items are represented in knowledge. The representation of a homograph is, of course, only a special case of the issue of how our words connect to our experiences. This section contains two data-driven papers addressed to resolving this issue. In Chapter 8, Marilyn Smith leaves the lexical ambiguity literature to confront representation from the point of view of the bilingual and offers tools to sharpen our analytical skills. In Chapter 9, K. I. Forster seeks to handle the paradoxes of search models with respect to the role of frequency and its implications for representation.

In addition to these authors who tend to be close to their data, Part III includes a magna theory of representation proposed by Barsalou and Billman, in Chapter 10. Starting from a view of concept stability and instability, they seek to relate experience to the types of storage, from frames to scripts, achieved. Thus they offer a framework for viewing a person's complete knowledge system.

Finally, in Chapter 11 of this section, Robert Hoffman addresses the meta theory of representation and seeks to bring to the consciousness of researchers of ambiguity the assumptions they make.

8

Accessing the Bilingual Lexicon

MARILYN CHAPNIK SMITH

For a long time, cognitive psychologists have been debating the nature of language representation in the bilingual. The question being debated goes something like this: Does comprehension depend upon the activation of a common language-free conceptual representation, or is comprehension in some way language-specific, allowing semantic information for each language to be activated independently? Variations of this question have been applied to a variety of issues related to cognitive representation. It is applicable whenever functionally equivalent stimuli are represented in physically different formats, such as when a concept is represented pictorially or verbally, when a word is written or spoken, when a written word appears in uppercase or lowercase, when synonyms of a given concept are considered, etc. A problem central to all these examples is the extent to which the processes involved in comprehension are specific to the particular form of representation or are common to all related forms of representation.

Arguments have been put forward in support of both views of bilingual functioning. Thus, for example, Kolers (1978, 1979) has argued that the representation of information reflects the way in which it was acquired. Since language is a means of acquisition, it follows that the representation of the information must be language-specific. In contrast to Kolers, who has argued for representation as process, others, such as Morton and his colleagues (Clarke & Morton, 1983; Morton & Patterson, 1980), see representation as abstracted from process. The question of interest then becomes whether a particular representation is unique to a given language or whether it is accessed by both languages.

Models of Bilingual Lexical Representation

In this paper I adopt Morton's view of representation as abstracted from process, and explore the nature of this representation in bilinguals. An illustration of alternative characterizations of bilingual lexical organization

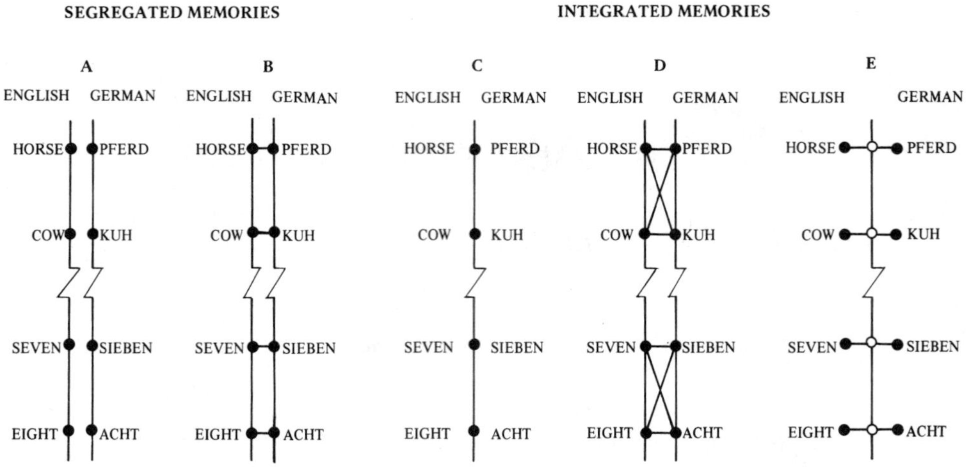

FIGURE 8.1. Models of bilingual lexical representation (from Meyer and Ruddy, 1974 and Potter, So, Von Eckart and Feldman, 1984).

is provided in Figure 8.1 (models a through d are reproduced from Meyer and Ruddy, 1974; model e is based upon Potter, So, Von Eckardt, & Feldman, 1984). Models a and b exemplify two versions of a language-specific model. In a no links exist between the storage locations of words belonging to different languages. Given a bilingual person's ability to readily translate words from one language to another, such a representation appears unlikely. In b the links connect only the direct translations of words.

In contrast, models c, d, and e exemplify integrated language models. In c there is a single common conceptual representation which would be accessed by either lingual format of the word. This model would reflect the type of representation suggested by McCormack (1976, 1977), who has argued in favor of a language-free characterization of bilingual representation. He suggests that information is stored as a complex of features or attributes in a single memory store, with language representing one of these attributes. In d the lexical representations of associated words are connected directly between as well as within languages, whereas in e the only connections between the two languages as well as within a given language are via an underlying language-free conceptual system. Model e differs from the others in postulating that it is possible to separately activate information about meaning (via a conceptual node) and information about more physical aspects of the word (via a surface node).

The Repetition Priming Paradigm

A few years ago several of my colleagues and I (Kirsner, Smith, Lockhart, King, & Jain, 1984) conducted a series of experiments to evaluate these models of bilingual lexical representation. The general approach adopted in these experiments was based upon the repetition effect—the facilitated processing of a repeated stimulus relative to the processing of a novel stimulus (e.g., Forbach, Stanners, & Hochhaus, 1974; Kirsner & Smith, 1974). The usual explanation for repetition priming is that the underlying representation of an item is activated during initial presentation and that this activation persists for some period of time, thereby facilitating the processing of that item when it is re-presented. To the extent that functionally equivalent stimuli presented in two different forms involve common representational units for recognition or classification, this will be reflected in a reaction-time (RT) advantage for repeated items as compared with RT for new items. If the RT advantage is unaffected by attribute change, as in the example of words printed in uppercase and lowercase (Scarborough, Cortese, & Scarborough, 1977), it may be inferred that—initial processing excepted—both formats access common underlying representations. If, however, the RT advantage is either reduced (Kirsner & Smith, 1974) or abolished by the attribute change, it may be inferred that separate representational units are involved in the processing of that item.

The experiments which we conducted employed the repetition priming paradigm to investigate the nature of lexical representation in the bilingual. Typically, the experiments consisted of two parts: an initial study session followed by a later test session. During the study session a given word was presented in one of two languages, in most cases either English or French. During the test phase some of the words were identical to those presented during study (within- or same-language repetition), some were translations of words presented during study (between- or different-language repetition) and some were new words that had not previously been presented at all (control condition).

Our first experiment addressed the question of whether lexical decisions for *translations* of previously studied words were facilitated. In an initial study session, the subjects were presented with a list of letter-strings and were asked to decide whether or not these strings spelled real words. In the later test session, the subjects were again given a list of letter strings and were again asked to perform a lexical-decision task. The average lag between study and test of a given word or its translation was approximately 30 minutes. The data for this experiment are presented in Table 8.1. The average RT for the within-language condition was 603 ms, for the between-language condition 643 ms, and for the control condition 646 ms. Although there was clearly a within-language repetition effect, lexical-decision times were no faster for translations of previously presented words

TABLE 8.1. Repetition priming data (in milliseconds).[a]

Experimental tasks				
Task at study	Task at test	Within language	Between language	Control
Lexical decision	Lexical decision	603	643	646
Translation	Lexical decision	667	668	745
Sentence generation	Categorization	849	900	914

[a]From a series of experiments conducted by Kirsner, Smith, Lockhart, King, and Jain (1984).

than for novel words, indicating an absence of any between-language repetition effect. Thus, these data argue against model c, in which a single lexical representation is shared by both lingual-forms of a word.

In light of this clear absence of cross-language facilitation, we began to wonder if there were any conditions under which between-language transfer *would* occur. Would facilitation be detected under conditions in which we *knew* that translation had occurred? To test this, a follow-up experiment was run in which subjects were *explicitly* instructed to generate translations during the study phase. In order to ascertain that a translation had in fact been generated, subjects were required to provide orally both the initial letter and the total number of letters in the translation. As in the previous experiment, lexical decisions were made during the test phase. The data for this experiment are also shown in Table 8.1. In contrast to our first study, priming effects here were just as great for the between-language conditions as they were for the within-language conditions, with RT values of 667, 668, and 745 ms for the same language, different language, and control conditions, respectively. Hence, if steps are taken to ensure that the translation of a presented word *is* activated, cross-language facilitation of lexical decision occurs. The absence of any facilitation in Experiment 1 indicates that such translation does not occur automatically; rather, it appears to be under strategic control.

Having ruled out model c, the next two experiments attempted to differentiate between models b and d. To do so, semantic priming was investigated: the facilitated processing not of identical concepts (*horse-horse* or *horse-pferd*) but of *related* concepts (such as *horse-cow* or *horse-kuh*). Subjects were shown two letter strings simultaneously and were asked to decide if they both spelled words. The strings were either in the same language or in different languages and, in the case of words, were either semantically related or unrelated. (In this experiment the two languages were English and Hindi.) It is a well-established finding that a lexical decision about two same-language words is made more rapidly if the words are semantically related (Meyer & Schvaneveldt, 1971). The question of interest was whether semantic relatedness would also facilitate lexical decision for *different* language words. In agreement with an earlier study by Meyer and Ruddy (1974) (which used English and German words), the decision that two strings were genuine words was indeed made more rapidly if the two words were related, even if they were in different languages.

These data, reproduced from Kirsner et al. (1984), are shown in Figure 8.2. The occurrence of mixed-language semantic priming indicates that there is considerable integration of the two different language representations. These data therefore serve to rule out model b, thereby leaving models d and e as the best candidates.

In the above study of semantic priming, the two words were presented simultaneously. In contrast, if the prime and target are presented sequentially, several studies suggest that the demonstration of semantic priming may be crucially dependent upon the time interval between the two related words. Thus, for example, in experiments by Tanenhaus, Leiman, and Seidenberg (1979) and by Swinney (1979) which employed ambiguous words as primes, it was found that whereas targets related to both meanings of the word were immediately facilitated, after a short interval only targets related to the contextually appropriate meaning persisted in demonstrating facilitation. In other words, several types of associated stimuli may become activated upon presentation of a prime, but their rate of decay may differ.

Does the decay of semantic connections within a language follow the same time course as those between languages? To investigate this issue, an

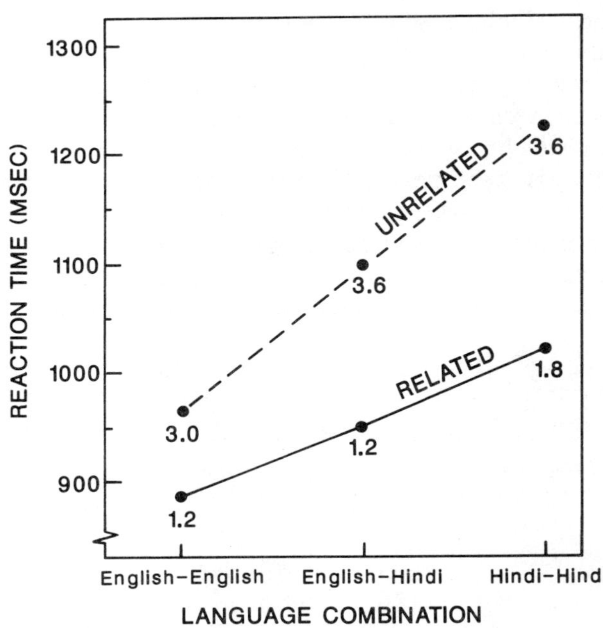

FIGURE 8.2. Lexical decision times for pairs of related and unrelated words in same or different language conditions (from Kirsner, Smith, Lockhart, King & Jain, 1984).

experiment was run in which time delay between prime and target was systematically manipulated. The procedure employed was the continuous lexical-decision task: Subjects were presented successively with French and English words and nonwords, which were followed after various lags by semantically associated words in either the same or the alternative language. The data for this study appear in Table 8.2. At lag 0, the data are comparable to those found with simultaneous presentation: Although same-language priming is of greater magnitude, there *is* nonetheless significant between-language priming as well. Although the priming effect was significant only at lag 0 for both within- and between-language conditions, there is a trend for facilitation to persist longer in the within-language condition. It thus appears that although there are connections between the two languages, as suggested by model d, cross-language activation which relies on these connections is relatively short-lived.

The final experiment in this series focused on evaluating model e. When translation is carried out, a subject must do two things: firstly, think about the *meaning* of the word, thereby activating the conceptual node, and secondly, produce the lingually appropriate format of the word, thereby activating the surface node. What is the relative contribution of these two components to repetition priming? Is emphasis on meaning in the absence of direct translation sufficient to result in cross-language repetition priming? According to model e (Figure 8.1), the only connection between the two lingual representations of a word is via an underlying conceptual system. In this model, semantic analysis of a word clearly necessitates activation of the language-free conceptual node. Hence, if semantic analysis of a word in language 1 is required during study, then this should benefit a second task which requires semantic processing of the same word in language 2. In this experiment we attempted to determine whether extensive activation of the concept node was sufficient to benefit the later semantic processing of the alternative lingual format.

To emphasize meaning, subjects were asked during phase 1 to generate a sentence (in the language of the presented word) so as to demonstrate

TABLE 8.2. Mean reaction time (milliseconds), facilitation (milliseconds), and errors (percentage) as a function of test language, priming language, and lag.

Language		Lag			New
Priming	Test	0	2	32	
English	English	589 (61) 2.1%	624 (26) 2.1%	628 (22) 3.1%	650 3.5%
French	English	606 (44) 1.0%	639 (11) 2.1%	626 (14) 2.1%	
French	French	546 (78) 2.1%	604 (20) 2.1%	605 (19) 3.1%	624 4.2%
English	French	576 (48) 1.0%	629 (−5) 2.1%	617 (7) 2.1%	

understanding of its meaning. In phase 2 they were asked to decide whether those words (or their translations in the between-language condition) represented objects which were animate or inanimate. The data resembled those of Experiment 1: The means for the same language, different language, and control conditions, shown in Table 8.1, were 849, 900, and 914 ms, respectively. In other words, although there was considerable within-language facilitation, there was no evidence of cross-language facilitation. One interpretation of these results is that there is no separate language-free concept node, thereby arguing against model e. There is, however, another possibility. Perhaps the rates of decay for the surface node and the concept node are different, with much faster decay for the concept node. If this were the case, then it might still be possible to demonstrate cross-language repetition priming effects at longer delays if a task could be found which showed greater persistence of facilitation than the lexical-decision task. Several recent studies suggest that the word fragment completion task fulfills this requirement.

Word Fragment Completion to Investigate the Bilingual Lexicon

Whenever one gets a null effect, in this case an absence of bilingual repetition priming with delayed sequential presentation of prime and target, there is always the worry that the procedure simply was not sufficiently sensitive to detect the facilitation. For this reason I was intrigued by the word fragment completion task. In this task subjects are asked to fill in the blanks in a letter string so as to form a word, for example, n_ _bo_ n or _ib_ar_ (for *newborn* or *library*). This is a task which is highly sensitive to repetition priming effects: The likelihood of subjects correctly completing a word is significantly improved if they have been exposed to that word at an earlier stage in the experiment (Tulving, Schachter, & Stark, 1982). It is even the case that amnesiacs who have no conscious recollection of the initial presentation of the words demonstrate facilitation—in fact, as much facilitation as normal subjects demonstrate! Clearly, this is a task that is highly sensitive to prior presentation of a stimulus. Further, these facilitation effects are quite long-lasting and have been noted even after several days.

Although there is considerable evidence that word fragment completion relies heavily on data-driven processes (Roediger & Blaxton, 1987), John Bassili and I (Bassili & Smith, 1986) have recently demonstrated that it can also be used to demonstrate prior *conceptual* activation, even in the absence of physical presentation. In our experiments, subjects were asked to read sentences such as "The plumber slipped an extra $10 into his wife's purse" and were instructed to make a trait attribution about the plumber's personality. We found that word fragment completion of *generous* was facilitated relative to a control group who had not made such inferences. (This experiment did not involve bilingual presentation.) Thus, in addition to being sensitive to data-driven processes, word fragment completion can also serve as an indicator of prior conceptually driven processing. Perhaps, then, it would be sensitive enough to pick up bilingual priming effects (if any existed).

Two previous studies (Durgunoglu & Roediger, 1987; Watkins & Peynircioglu, 1983) have examined cross-language repetition priming effects using word fragment completion as the dependent measure. In both these experiments subjects read long lists of words in either English or Spanish and then attempted to complete English word fragments which corresponded either to previously presented words or to translations. The data from these priming studies were similar to our lexical-decision repetition priming data: There was considerable within-language priming but an absence of any cross-language priming.

However, it may not be only the task that is used during the test—i.e., word fragment completion—that is important. The way in which subjects *process* the stimuli at study may also be relevant. Recently, Levy and Kirsner (1988) demonstrated that the processing of words in the context of meaningful text had different memorial consequences from the processing of isolated words in a list. Perhaps when a word is processed in a sentential context there is relatively greater activation of its conceptual aspect than when the word is processed in isolation. If there is in fact a language-free conceptual node separate from the surface node, then processing the words in sentences might increase the likelihood of activating this component. Following this reasoning, this experiment was designed to maximize the likelihood of detecting cross-language repetition priming effects by providing study conditions which maximized conceptual processing and test conditions known to be very sensitive to repetition priming.

Students in Toronto who were enrolled in a French-immersion high school, where all classes are taught in French, participated as subjects in this study. Subjects were given a set of 18 sentences to read at a rate of 10 seconds each. Half the subjects read them in English, and the other half read them in French. The sentences employed are shown in Table 8.3.

Subjects were told that each sentence implied a particular item. Their task was to make that inference. For example, if they read the sentence "Fish attacked swimmer," they were to make the inference *shark.* I used this particular set of stimuli and instructions for two reasons. Firstly, instructing subjects to make an inference encouraged reading the sentences at a semantic level, thereby increasing the likelihood of activation of a language-free conceptual representation if one existed. Secondly, it allowed me to further explore the use of word fragment completion for assessing prior inferences, namely, the effect of making an inference in one language on word fragment completion in the same or the alternative language.

Subjects read the sentences in either English or French and then per-

TABLE 8.3. Sentences presented for study.

English	French
Fluid contented newborn	Liquide qui satisfait un bebe
Building kept books	Edifice qui sert a garder des livres
Fuel propelled car	Carburant qui fait avancer les voitures
Fish attacked swimmer	Poisson qui attaque les nageurs
Conveyance flew passengers	Appareil qui transporte les passagers dans les airs
Person guarded flock	Personne qui garde le troupeau
Mammal chewed birch	Mammifere qui mache le bouleau u
Box held body	Boite contenant un corps
Headgear safeguarded motorcyclist	Sorte de chapeau qui protege un motocycliste
Woman defended criminal	Femme qui defend un criminel
Boat travelled underwater	Bateau qui va sous l'eau
Animal helped cowboy	Animal qui aide le cowboy
Offender stole jewellery	Criminel qui vole des bijoux
Meat commemorated Thanksgiving	Viande commemorant l'Action de Graces
Organ circulated blood	Organe qui circule le sang
Worker delivered mail	Travailleur qui distribue le courier
Utensil sliced tomato	Ustensile qui coupe les tomates
Clothing repelled downpour	Manteau protegeant contre la pluie

formed a word fragment completion test in either English or French under instructions to complete the fragment with the first word that came to mind. Four groups of subjects were run, two under same-language conditions (study English, test in English; study French, test in French) and two under different-language conditions (study English, test in French; study French, test in English). Subjects were given 30 seconds to complete each fragment. Half the word fragments were based on words which the subject had just *read* in the study sentences (such as *swimmer*) and half were based on words which the subject would have *inferred* (such as *shark*). The lag between initial study and test of a given item was approximately 5 minutes. Four control groups completed the identical word fragments in English or French after having read (in either English or French) a set of similar but totally unrelated sentences under the same "infer" instructions.

Results

The data showing improvement in performance (i.e., priming) as a function of having been exposed to the relevant stimuli during study are presented in Table 8.4. These data represent the percentage difference in performance on word fragment completion for the experimental and control groups under same- and different-language conditions. It may be observed that there was significant priming not only in the same-language condition (an average of 26.5%), but in the different-language condition as

TABLE 8.4. Percentage priming in WFC test.

	Study items		
	Actually presented items	Inferred items	Mean
Within language	28.4	24.5	26.5
Between language	15.2	23.9	19.5
Mean	21.8	24.2	

well (an average of 19.5%)! Although priming was significantly greater in the same-language data condition, separate analysis of the different-language data confirmed that this priming effect was also highly significant. Hence, performance on word fragment completion of a given item benefited from prior exposure to that item either through actual presentation or through inference, even if the prior exposure was in the alternate language. This result is in marked contrast to the earlier findings, and suggests that under appropriate processing instructions and/or measurement conditions, it is possible to find evidence for activation of a common language-independent node. These data point to model e as best describing the organization of the bilingual lexicon.

The data on priming of inferred concepts are also of some interest. Word fragment completion was improved not only when subjects had read the words during study but also when the words had been inferred. In fact, percentage improvement was just as great for concepts which were inferred as it was for those items which had actually been read. These data provide confirmation of the Bassili and Smith (1986) finding that word fragment completion is a sensitive indicator of the occurrence of prior inference, and that word fragment completion is therefore not restricted to the experimental investigation of stimuli which were actually physically presented. It further indicates that at least some of the priming effect in word fragment completion must reside in a conceptual node in addition to any effect resulting from prior activation of a surface node.

For actually presented items, the relatively greater priming for same-language items (28.4%) than for different-language items (15.2%) suggests that some proportion of the priming depends on reactivation of the surface node. However, this finding is difficult to understand in light of the fact that same-language priming of inferred items, for which there is *no* surface node activation, is almost as great (24.5%) as same-language priming of presented terms. This finding suggests that activation of a given node may not be "all or none"; rather, the magnitude of activation may be under strategic control. Perhaps under instructions to make an inference (as was employed in the study) there is relatively greater activation of the conceptual component than of the surface component, thereby giving greater benefit to inferred concepts. By this reasoning it would appear that the boost in activation is sufficient to compensate the inferred items for the lack of surface node activation.

The Effect of Context: A Direct Comparison of Isolated Words and Words Embedded in Sentences

The word fragment completion experiment provided clear support for cross-language repetition priming: Although the priming of actually presented words was greater in the same-language condition, significant priming was also found in the different-language condition. This result contrasts with that of Watkins and Peynircioglu (1983) and of Durgonoglu and Roediger (1987), who also used word fragment completion and found repetition priming only under same-language conditions. The important issue now was to determine what it was about this experiment that differed from the two earlier studies, thereby resulting in the occurrence of cross-language priming. One way in which the present experiment differed from those studies was in the way the stimuli were processed. In the present experiment the test stimuli were embedded in sentences, and subjects were instructed to read them so as to draw an inference, thereby requiring that the words be read for meaning. In contrast, the earlier two studies had subjects read lists of words for a later memory test.

The aim of this experiment was to determine more directly the effect of the initial mode of processing on between-language priming effects. To do this, two groups of subjects were compared. The first group resembled those of the first study—they read 36 short sentences in one language under "inference" instructions. In contrast, the second group read a list of 36 unrelated words under memory instructions. These list words were selected such that half had appeared in the sentences read by group 1 (such as *newborn* or *building*), and the other half would have been inferred by these subjects (such as *milk* or *library*). For subjects reading the list, there was no distinction between actually presented and inferred words; by necessity, *all* had been actually presented. Both groups then completed the same word fragment completion test. This test consisted of word fragments composed from both new and old items. For subjects who had received list presentation, old items corresponded to words that had appeared in the study list. For subjects who had received sentence presentation, half the old items were words which had actually been presented in the sentence (such as *swimmer*) and half were words which subjects had inferred (such as *shark*).

It should be noted that in contrast to the between-subjects design employed to assess priming in the previous word fragment completion experiment, in this experiment a within-subjects design was used, so that for each subject the word fragment completion test contained an equal number of new and old items. Further, presentation time was reduced so that subjects in the sentence condition had 180 seconds (5 seconds per sentence) to study the sentences, whereas subjects in the list condition were given 40 seconds to read the list (approximately 1 second per word).

A second variable of interest was the effect of the amount of time which had elapsed between initial processing and the word fragment completion test. Kirsner et al. had systematically varied lag between study and test, and found that introducing a delay of several seconds eliminated semantic priming effects. However, the effect of delay on repetition priming was not explored. In order to assess the effect of test delay on same- and different-language repetition priming, the subjects in this experiment were given *two* 36-item word fragment completion tests: one test immediately after study and a second test approximately 30 minutes later. Each word fragment completion test consisted of 18 new items and 18 old items. For subjects who had received sentence presentation, half the old items corresponded to words which had been inferred and half to words which had actually been presented. Half the study items were tested on each test (early or late), with counterbalanced assignment of items to test.

Unlike the high school students who served as subjects in the previous experiment, subjects in this experiment were French-English bilinguals living in Montreal who were studying at the University of Montreal to be professional translators. Thus, their ability in the two languages was more closely balanced than that of the subjects in the earlier experiment.

Results

Effect of Time Lag

Although word fragment completion performance was somewhat better with immediate testing than with delayed testing, the effect of time delay did not interact significantly with any other factor. Most notably, between-language priming did not show greater decline with delay than within-language priming. Tulving et al. had previously found little decline of within-language priming for word fragment completion even after 7 days, and this result extends this finding to the between-language condition as well. Consequently, the effect of time delay was not considered further, and all data presented are averaged across the two testing intervals.

Effect of Context

Priming was calculated by subtracting performance on word fragment completion of new items from those which were based on previously studied items. Priming data are shown in Figure 8.3.

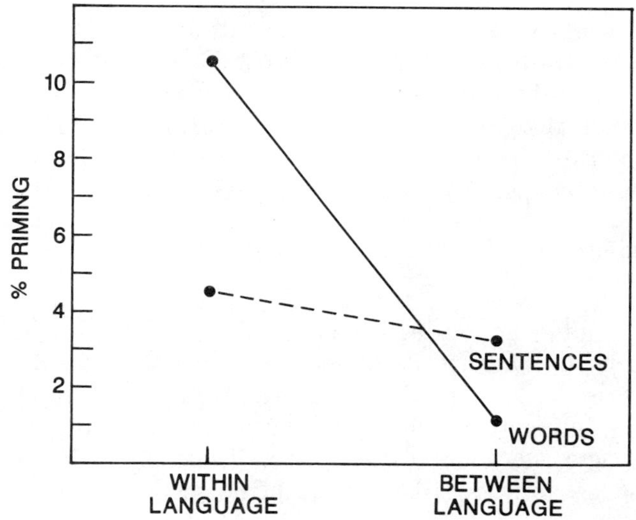

FIGURE 8.3. Same and different language priming of word fragment completion as a function of whether the word had been studied in the context of a sentence or a list.

Sentence Presentation

When the stimuli were studied in the context of sentences, the data resembled those of the previous experiment in demonstrating significant priming for both within- and between-language conditions. In fact, in this study the magnitude of priming was small but comparable for within-language (4.5%) and between-language (3.4%) conditions. As in the previous study, there was no significant priming × stimulus type interaction: Words which had been inferred were primed to the same extent as those which had actually been presented.

Overall, the magnitude of the priming effect was greatly reduced in this study compared with the previous study. There are several possible reasons for this. One factor may be the length of the initial study list. Subjects in this experiment were given twice the number of sentences to study—36 compared with 18 in the earlier study. Perhaps as the number of items presented increases, the relative facilitation of any one item declines. Further, study time was reduced by half in this experiment, a factor which may have resulted in a reduction of the surface node contribution. Another way in which this study differed is that subjects served as their own controls, so that each word fragment completion test contained an equal number of new and old items. In the previous experiment all the test items were old for the experimental group. This difference may have induced different strategies in the two groups of subjects, possibly encouraging subjects in the first experiment to attempt to recall the words from the studied sentences in order to perform the word fragment completion test. Such a strategy would be less likely in the second study, where half the words were new. The important thing, however, is not the overall magnitude of priming between the two experiments, but rather the pattern of priming. In both studies, there was significant between-language priming.

List Presentation

In contrast to the sentence data, which in essence replicate the previous study, the results were strikingly different when the stimuli were presented as isolated words. Under these presentation conditions, the data replicate nicely those of Watkins and Peynircioglu and of Roediger and Blaxton. As may be seen in Figure 8.3, the occurrence of repetition priming is totally dependent upon language combination. There is significantly greater within-language priming (10.6%) than there is between-language priming (1.1%).

In comparing the two context conditions, it is interesting to observe the magnitude of the facilitation effect. When the stimuli were presented in the same language, magnitude of priming was much greater when isolated words were presented than when the words were studied in sentences. In contrast, magnitude of priming was comparable under the two context conditions in the different-language condition. Roediger and Blaxton (1987) have recently argued that word fragment completion is primarily sensitive to the repetition of data-driven processes, i.e., those processes which correspond to the encoding of the stimulus. If we argue that the between-language conditions provide only for the repetition of conceptually driven processes, then these data support Roediger in suggesting that a large part of the repetition effect is based on data-driven processes.

The small between-language component indicates a much smaller role for conceptually-driven processes. The finding of comparable levels of facilitation in same- and different-language conditions with sentence processing suggests that words are encoded differently in the context of sentences than they are in isolation, with greater emphasis on the conceptual component in the sentence condition. It appears then that the strategy adopted during encoding results in differential memorial activation. When individual words are read for memory (in the context of lists), data-driven processes are activated to a greater extent than when they are read for meaning in the context of sentences. Similar results have recently been found by MacLeod (1988). There was more priming of words in a fragment completion task if the words had been studied in a to-be-learned list than if they had been read in meaningful passages.

Jacoby (1983) has reported data which corroborate this suggestion. When subjects perform a perceptual identification task for a set of words after having either read or generated the words in an earlier study phase, their data indicate a "reverse" generation effect. Subjects are able to identify a greater proportion of words which were read during study than of those which were generated during study. This contrasts with the typical generation effect found with recall, where generated words are better recalled than words which were read. It thus appears that asking subjects to generate an inference during the reading of sentences activates processes which are similar to those which are activated in the more usual "generation" experiment in which they are asked to generate a particular word. Interestingly, under our generation instructions the level of facilitation is comparable both for the inferred items (which subjects generated) and for the actually presented items (which subjects read). Thus it is not only the physical presentation of the stimulus but the way in which it is processed which determines later facilitation effects.

Conclusions

At the beginning of this paper, several models of bilingual lexical representation were presented. Through a series of experiments by Kirsner et al. (1984), it was possible to eliminate some of these models. Since lexical decision about a word in one language did not facilitate lexical decision to a translation of that word, we were able to rule out model c, a model which postulated a single underlying lexical representation for both lingual formats of a word. The occurrence of between-language semantic priming allowed us to narrow it down even further, since neither model a nor b would allow for such cross-language facilitation effects. One experimental observation appeared to rule out model e: A between-language task which required semantic analysis of the stimulus during study (sentence generation) failed to facilitate the processing of that stimulus during a later test which also required semantic analysis (categorization). It was argued that the existence of a common conceptual node to which both lingual formats had access would have resulted in priming of the categorization task regardless of language.

Two additional experiments were conducted to provide a more extensive test of model e. Perhaps the processing of a stimulus causes activation in both the surface node and the conceptual node, but the rate of decay is faster in the latter. If this were the case, then only same-language priming would appear, since in this condition subjects could benefit from whatever surface node activation persisted, even if there was little remaining conceptual node activation. A fairer evaluation would involve a test which can detect activation over fairly long delays. Recent experiments suggest that word fragment completion is sensitive to priming even after relatively long lags (Tulving et al., 1982). Hence, a bilingual priming experiment was conducted in which subjects were asked to complete fragments of words to which they had been exposed either directly or via an inference during an initial study phase.

The first question was whether repetition priming effects could be demonstrated using word fragment completion under conditions in which the conceptual node was activated in the absence of activation of the surface node, regardless of the issue of bilingual representation. The answer to this was "yes." When sentences were presented for study under instructions to make an inference, the magnitude of priming for the inferred items was as great as that found if the item had actually been presented for study. Consequently, we could now look at the issue of between-language repetition priming.

When words were studied for meaning in the context of sentences, later word fragment completion for those words was facilitated, not only for fragments in the same language but for translations of those words as well. These data constitute the first experimental evidence for between-language priming using word fragment completion, and suggest that model e, which postulates a common conceptual node to which both lingual formats have access, is the best model of bilingual lexical representation. The final experiment addressed the issue of why earlier studies which had also used word fragment completion had failed to demonstrate cross-language priming.

In this study, items were presented for study in the context of sentences about which they had to make an inference. In contrast, the two earlier word fragment completion studies had presented test items in the context of word lists, with instructions to study the items for a later memory test. To determine whether the nature of the processing task was crucial, in the last study we directly compared the two processing conditions. When words were presented in the context of sentences, once again a small but significant priming effect was found for both between- and within-language conditions. However, when the words were presented in a list context, only the within-language condition facilitated word fragment completion. Hence, the nature of the study task is clearly an important variable.

The data from the last experiment suggest that the mode of initial processing may determine the relative amounts of activation of the surface and conceptual nodes. When isolated words are studied in a list format, most activation occurs in the surface node, with relatively little in the conceptual node. Since word fragment completion is especially sensitive to surface node activation, this condition results in maximum within-language repetition priming. However, the absence or reduction of conceptual node activation leads to a corresponding absence of cross-language facilitation. In contrast, when words are studied for meaning, there is on the one hand reduced activation of the surface node and on the other hand increased activation of the conceptual node. Since word fragment completion is sensitive primarily to surface node activation, repetition priming effects are severely reduced. However, the facilitation which occurs as a result of activation of the conceptual node benefits word fragment completion of both the studied item and its translation.

In summary, the set of experiments as a whole suggests that model e provides the best description of lexical representation in the bilingual person. This model postulates a separation of surface and semantic information, such that there are language-specific surface nodes which in turn feed into a common, language-independent conceptual node. Kirsner and Dunn (1985) have recently attempted to delineate which aspects of language are represented in the surface node, and suggest case, typefont, script, and voice of speaker. The absence of cross-language priming with lexical decision suggests that there is greater persistence of surface node activation, with activation at the conceptual node being relatively short-lived.

In studies of bilingual representation, the question of interest is how two words with different surface forms (i.e., language) but common meaning are represented. In contrast, studies of semantic ambiguity consider the question of how two items with the same surface form but different meaning (depending on context) are represented. Many of the studies in this volume suggest that there is activation of *both* meanings of a semantically ambiguous word but that the rate of decay is much faster for the contextually inappropriate meaning. Differential rates of decay for different kinds of information are also suggested by our bilingual data. However, our suggestion is that the rates of decay for surface and conceptual information differ, with the former showing greater persistence. Given the finding that ambiguous stimuli activate two conceptual nodes, it would be interesting to explore activation of the contextually inappropriate meaning using the sensitive word fragment completion task. Finally, one cannot help but wonder about the pattern of activation of an ambiguous word in one language on the priming in the second language. The permutations and combinations seem endless!

Acknowledgment. I am indebted to Derek D. Besner for his insightful comments on an earlier draft of this paper.

9

On Knowing How Many Entries

KENNETH I. FORSTER

The research reported here concerns a problem that on the face of it has little or no connection with ambiguity. The problem in question is the supposed nonexistence of word frequency effects in semantic categorization tasks, and the implications of this phenomenon for theories of lexical access. However, as we pursue this issue, it will eventually become clear that the theoretical implications of the results may call into question our understanding of how ambiguity is represented in the lexicon, and how those lexical representations are accessed.

Background

The argument starts with Balota and Chumbley's (1984) proposal that the word frequency effect might not be an access effect at all, but might be yet another of the growing list of effects attributed to the post-access-decision stage of the lexical-decision task. What Balota and Chumbley found was that in a semantic categorization task (e.g., "Is DOG an animal?"), there was no reliable frequency effect for "no" decisions. That is, decision times for words with a high frequency of occurrence were not significantly faster than for words with a low frequency of occurrence. Since categorization must involve lexical access as a first stage, it should exhibit strong frequency effects, if frequency really affects the access stage, as widely assumed. Since this result was not obtained, the obvious inference is that frequency must be affecting the lexical-decision task in some other way altogether.

The suggestion made by Balota and Chumbley was that the frequency effect might be playing a role at the decision stage, rather than the access stage. They proposed an alternative decision procedure based purely on the familiarity of the stimulus, not on whether it was associated with a lexical entry. If it is assumed that familiarity can somehow be assessed independently of, and more rapidly than, lexical status,[1] then highly familiar stimuli could be classified immediately as words and highly unfamiliar stimuli could be classified as nonwords, without there being any need to wait to discover whether a lexical entry existed. The effectiveness of this strategy depends on the partial correlation between familiarity and lexical status in the typical lexical-decision experiment: No nonwords are highly familiar, and no words will be highly unfamiliar (since great pains are taken to avoid such items). The consequence of this strategy is that an apparent frequency effect is generated, since low-frequency words fall into the middle range of familiarity and hence cannot be classified until their actual lexical status has been discovered.

However, this spurious frequency effect would not be expected in a semantic categorization task, since there is no correlation at all between familiarity and the correct response in this task. That is, the familiarity of the stimulus DOG is completely irrelevant to the question of deciding whether dogs are musical instruments. Hence a frequency effect (really, a familiarity effect) occurs for the lexical-decision task but not for the semantic categorization task.

As pointed out by Shoben (1982), this attenuation of the frequency effect in the semantic categorization task has been reported many times over the years, beginning with Wilkins (1971), so the findings reported by Balota and Chumbley are certainly not controversial. Indeed, we have obtained similar results ourselves (Forster, 1985). So it seems that the issue is not whether such an effect occurs, but rather, what are the conditions under which it occurs, and what is the correct interpretation.

At this stage, it is most important to get one thing clear: When we speak of a frequency effect in the semantic categorization task, we are referring to the nonmembers only, i.e., items that do not belong to the category in question. For members of the category, it is not hard to think of reasons why the correlation between decision time and frequency might be reduced. For example, the low-frequency item *anchor* might receive a considerable boost if the category was *found on a ship;* i.e., the category might directly prime the target item. On the other hand, the category *weapon* might have the opposite kind of effect on the high-frequency item *foot,* due to the fact that feet are not very good exemplars of weapons. So, as Balota and Chumbley themselves point out, the more crucial cases are the nonmembers.

However, our own experience has been that frequency effects are sometimes readily obtained for nonmembers—too readily in fact, for there are some circumstances where a frequency-ordered search model also predicts no frequency effect. To illustrate this, I will draw on the results from previously unpublished experiments by Elizabeth Bednall and myself.

---

[1]This is not an easy assumption to defend. The very notion of familiarity implies that some preexisting representation of the stimulus has been activated.

The Category-Search Model

Our initial aim was to test whether semantic categories could be searched directly, as proposed by Landauer and Freedman (1968) and others. The essential idea behind this category-search model is that semantic categorization decisions can be made by consulting precompiled lists of exemplars. Thus, to decide whether a peach is a fruit, a list of fruits (or perhaps edible objects) could be searched directly, without ever having to access the lexical entry for *peach*. Since these lists might also be frequency-organized, we might expect a frequency effect (or perhaps a typicality effect) for "yes" responses. But if "no" responses were made by failing to find any category entry for the target word, then no frequency effect would be expected, since the "no" decision would be initiated at the completion of an exhaustive search of the category. Thus the results obtained by Balota and Chumbley are also compatible with the category-search model. On this interpretation, the absence of frequency effects in a semantic categorization task is completely irrelevant to the lexical-decision task, since the search and decision procedures in the two tasks are completely different.

However, the initial experiment designed to test this prediction from the category-search model (reported in Elizabeth Bednall's doctoral dissertation, Bednall, 1978) met with no success at all. The category used was "parts of the body," with 30 members and 30 nonmembers of either high frequency (above 119 per million) or low frequency (below 7 per million). Each test item was presented for 500 ms, and subjects indicated their decision by pressing either a "yes" or a "no" key. Twenty subjects were tested. The results are shown in Table 9.1.

Nonmembers took longer to categorize than members, as the category-search model would predict. However, there was a strong and reliable frequency effect of 59 ms for "no" responses, $\min F'(1,32) = 18.49$, $p < .001$. The frequency effect for "yes" responses was smaller (21 ms), as one might have expected, but even this was still a significant effect, $\min F'(1,28) = 4.55$, $p < .05$.

Since we were reluctant to give up the category-search model entirely, we looked for some way to explain the unwanted frequency effect for nonmembers. We proposed that there were in fact two ways of making a categorization response: one by direct search of the category, the other by

TABLE 9.1. Mean category decision times and percentage error rates as a function of frequency for members and nonmembers of the category *parts of the body*.

	High frequency		Low frequency	
	RT	% error	RT	% error
Members	558	2	579	3
Nonmembers	604	1	663	5

finding the lexical entry for the target, which would then provide the necessary semantic information to enable an inference about category membership to be made. If both procedures are run in parallel, then we expect to find a strong frequency effect whenever the lexical route wins out. For members of the category, this may happen only occasionally (say, for low-typicality items), but for nonmembers it may be a common occurrence.

Since this was a rather ad hoc argument, we attempted to define a boundary condition that would specify when the lexical route should be the fastest. The condition we chose was how tightly clustered the category was. This notion is far from being rigorously defined, but the intuitive idea seemed fairly clear. Tight categories are represented by precompiled lists that are well-defined, are highly integrated, have all their members listed, and can be searched rapidly and accurately. Loose categories, on the other hand, are represented by lists that are ill-defined, are loosely integrated, may not have all members listed, and can only be searched slowly and unreliably. Under the assumptions of the category-search model, these categories would lead to quite different outcomes in a categorization experiment. For a tight category that can be searched very rapidly, category search may well be faster than the lexical route, and decisions can safely be based on the outcome of category search alone. So for this type of category, both "yes" and "no" responses may be controlled by the category search. But for a loose category, the category search is slow and inefficient and is less likely to be faster than the lexical search. Further, it cannot be relied upon, especially for nonmembers, since all members of the category are not necessarily listed, and hence a negative outcome would be ambiguous. Thus, decisions in this case are more likely to be based on the lexical route and are therefore more likely to show frequency effects.

Initially, it seemed that the category *parts of the body* was fairly well defined. But when we started to consider whether the liver, a fingernail, or an eyebrow was a part of the body, we began to realize that it was not quite so clear-cut. So it might be the case that only a fairly standard set of "core" items would be listed as members of this category, with items such as *liver* not being listed at all, in which case it would be unwise to base a "no" decision on the failure of the category search. Instead, the lexical entry would have to be checked before responding "no," thus producing a strong frequency effect.

So what would be an example of a category where this was not the case? The case we picked was *number names* such as *four, thirteen,* etc. This is obviously a fairly tight category and is certainly well-defined in that it seems hard to imagine anyone coming across a previously unrecognized exemplar of this category, whereas one might imagine not having thought of a liver as being a body part. So maybe in this case a "no" decision could be based on a failure of the category search, in which case we would expect no frequency effect at all for "no" responses.

Categorization with Tight and Loose Categories

The next experiment compares the nonmember frequency effect for the tight *number names* category with another category which we felt was reasonably loose, namely, *color names.* The reason for considering *color names* to be a loose category is that almost any object or substance that has a distinctive color can be thought of as a color name but would never be included on a list of standard color names, e.g., ivory, peach, apricot, coffee, chocolate, lemon, etc.

Each of the 20 subjects was tested on both categories, but testing was blocked by category, with order of testing counterbalanced. In the number category task, there were 15 members (single-word number names between 1 and 20) and 15 high-frequency and 15 low-frequency nonmembers; for the color category task, there were also 15 members, and a set of 15 high-frequency and 15 low-frequency nonmembers matched for frequency with the nonmembers in the number category, making a total of 90 items in all. The results were as shown in Table 9.2.

As can be seen, there is virtually no frequency effect at all (4 ms) for nonmembers using the number category. However, the very same frequency contrast (frequencies were closely matched across categories) yielded a significant 41-ms effect for nonmembers when the color category was used, min$F'(1,25) = 5.60$, $p<.05$, with the interaction between frequency and category also being significant, min$F'(1,29) = 4.65$, $p<.05$.

These results provide quite striking support for the predictions derived from the extended category-search model. However, one might want to question whether the relevant difference between the color and number categories is really one of "tightness." For example, it could be pointed out that although the number category is well-defined, the members of that set could not be searched, since there are infinitely many of them, and hence there is no way for decisions to be based on category search. However, this assumes that the list in question contains a separate entry for every number, so that *three hundred and seven* and *seven hundred and three* would have separate entries. But if the list contains only the primitive vocabulary of number names (all those number names consisting of a single unhy-

TABLE 9.2. Mean category decision times and percentage error rates for members and nonmembers of the categories *number names* and *color names* as a function of word frequency.

	Members		Nonmembers			
			High freq.		Low freq.	
Category	RT	% error	RT	% error	RT	% error
Numbers	473	7	488	4	492	3
Colors	538	14	551	2	592	9

phenated word), then number categorization can still be done by search of a relatively small category.[2]

But regardless of how one feels about the extended category-search model, or the notion of tight and loose categories, these results nevertheless show clearly that frequency effects can be demonstrated for nonmembers in a categorization task. Further, they suggest that the size of this effect varies as a function of the type of category used.

Implications for Ambiguity Representation

We now arrive at the point where the argument begins to have relevance for the topic of ambiguity. Let us assume that the presence of the frequency effect for nonmembers indicates that a search for the lexical entry is required before a judgment can be made, and ignore for the moment the question of why the number classification task removes this requirement. The crucial issue that needs to be raised now is as follows. When a lexical search is involved, a frequency effect will only be generated if the search is self-terminating, i.e., if the information in the entry is transferred to the decision-making system immediately, and the decision is then made without waiting for any further evidence to be collected. But given that many words have more than one lexical entry, why is it not necessary for the decision-making system to wait until an exhaustive search of the lexicon has been completed? For example, to decide that the ambiguous word PALM is not a color name, it is necessary to consider both meanings before a decision can be reached. Even that is not enough, because there may be yet another entry for PALM, and hence it is necessary to exhaust all possibilities. So, even for an unambiguous word like YEAR, the search must proceed past the entry for YEAR in case another entry exists, and go on until all lexical entries have been searched. Hence we should never observe frequency effects for nonmembers in a category task, no matter what the category, since a frequency effect can only be produced by a self-terminating lexical search.

So we have, in a sense, tripped ourselves up. In order to show that the absence of frequency effects in categorization tasks did not undermine the assumptions of a frequency-ordered lexical-search model, we showed that:

a. Such an effect would be expected if decisions could be based on the outcome of a category search.
b. Where category search is unreliable (as in the case of a loose concept), frequency effects can be demonstrated.

---

[2]The positive items in this experiment were all one-word names such as *fifteen, twelve, two,* etc., so it was possible to reach the correct decision by category search. However, quite different processes might come into play if the names also had to be evaluated syntactically, as in *three-twenty, sixty-twelve,* etc.

But when we take into account the question of ambiguity, we come full circle. Because the possibility of ambiguity means that a lexical search would always have to be exhaustive, we now say that the result reported by Balota and Chumbley is exactly what a frequency-ordered search model would predict. Thus it is not necessary to postulate category search to explain the Balota and Chumbley result—even if lexical search is always involved in categorization, one would still not expect to observe frequency effects for nonmembers. So now we have the reverse problem: How do we explain the presence of a frequency effect for loose categories?

One might be tempted to solve the problem by denying that an exhaustive search is required in a categorization task. We could propose, for instance, that both meanings of an ambiguous word are listed under the one header. This seems reasonable since the search is supposed to be purely form-based, and so long as there is no variation in form, there should be only one entry. Thus, both meanings of PALM are listed together in the same entry, and we can therefore decide that neither meaning of PALM is a color without having to search any further. The same goes for an unambiguous word such as YEAR. There is only one meaning listed in the lexical entry, and because we know that any other meanings would also be listed at this location, there is no need to carry the search past this point; a "no" decision can be made on the basis of a self-terminating search, producing a frequency effect. Hence everything hinges on how we know how many entries a word might have (hence the title of the paper).

The problem with this line of argument is that we already have clear evidence from data reported by Forster and Bednall (1976) that the search is exhaustive. In these experiments, subjects were asked whether a word had more than one meaning or not. The possible search paths required to decide this question are shown in Figure 9.1, where L1 and L2 are the

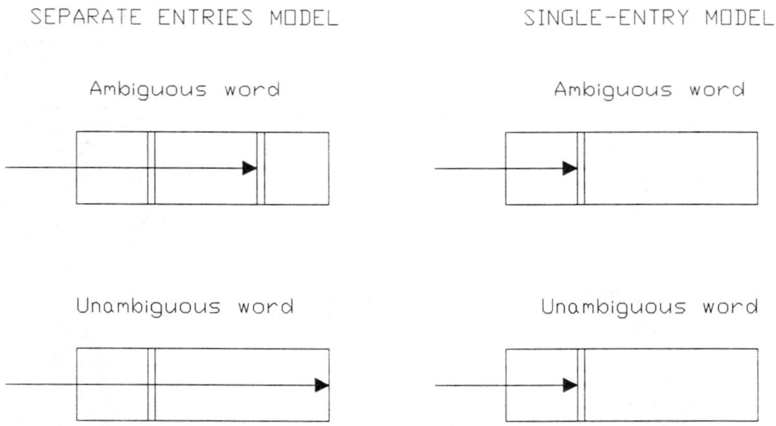

FIGURE 9.1. Search paths for ambiguity decision when entries for ambiguous words are separately listed (left panel), and when both are listed jointly (right panel).

dominant and subordinate lexical entries, respectively. Under the assumption of separate entries, the search path required to make an ambiguity decision terminates at L2 for homographs, but for unambiguous words, the search path must be exhaustive. This means that unambiguous words should take longer to classify than homographs, which was in fact the case (1094 ms versus 961 ms). As well, unambiguous words should show no frequency effect, which also proved to be the case, the obtained frequency effect being very small (5 ms) and nonsignificant, even though the same words in a conventional lexical-decision task showed a significant 46-ms frequency effect. Further, it does not appear that the task itself prevents the observation of a frequency effect since the homographs did exhibit significant frequency effects (43 ms).

These results are very difficult to interpret if we try to argue that both meanings of a homograph are listed under the one entry, as shown in the right panel of Figure 9.1. If this were the case, then access of L1 would be all that was required to establish whether a word was ambiguous or not. If a subentry exists, then a "yes" decision can be initiated immediately, but if there is no subentry, then the correct response is "no." In both cases, a self-terminating search is all that is required, and hence a strong frequency effect should be observed for both ambiguous and unambiguous words.

Exactly the same results are obtained when a more natural task is used, which does not require the subject to report how many meanings a word may have (Forster & Bednall, 1976, Experiment 2). Instead, we simply ask whether minimal phrases such as *the house* or *to year* are legal expressions. Essentially we are asking whether a word can be used as a verb or as a noun, and hence it is called a syntactic function decision. By choosing homographs that can be either verbs or nouns, we can effectively control whether L1 or L2 is accessed. Thus *to care* takes less time to evaluate as legal than *the care,* which reflects the fact that *care* is used far more often as a verb than as a noun. The critical test for our purposes comes with negative instances such as *to wife* or *the avoid.* By the model, it should be necessary to conduct an exhaustive search before we could definitely say that *wife* is not a verb, or that *avoid* is not a noun, and hence the "no" items should not show a frequency effect. This appeared to be the case—the small 20-ms effect in the expected direction was not significant, despite the fact that when the same items were presented as positive instances, i.e., *the wife* and *to avoid,* the frequency effect was very strong (75 ms). Additional support came from a further condition in which ambiguous nouns were included as negative instances, e.g., *to pupil, to volume.* It was expected that these items would take much longer to reject than unambiguous items such as *to avoid,* since there are two independent possibilities to be evaluated rather than just one. This was the case. But more importantly, these items also failed to show any significant frequency effect, the small effect of 5 ms being in the wrong direction.

So the position is this. We assume that there is a certain parallel between the following three situations: (1) deciding that WIFE does not refer to an object that is a member of the category fruit, (2) deciding that WIFE does not have more than one meaning, and (3) deciding that WIFE does not belong to the category of verb. The parallel is that in each case the subject is given the task of locating information that is not contained in any lexical entry for that word. On the assumption that entries are stored quite independently, this situation forces an exhaustive search which should eliminate any frequency effect. This is generally true for all three tasks. However, it is clearly not true for semantic categorization with the "loose" categories reported in Tables 9.1 and 9.2, where a self-terminating search appears to be involved. It is this problem that we now attempt to resolve.

Self-Terminating Search with Loose Categories

To explain why the search is sometimes self-terminating rather than exhaustive, we could adopt a suggestion made earlier by Bednall (1978). She pointed out that in a semantic categorization task the subjects might fail to make any allowances for the possibility of ambiguity. Adopting a strategy of a self-terminating search that examines only the contents of L1 would not, after all, produce very many errors in most experiments. For example, failing to consider that BAT has more than one meaning matters little if the task is to say whether it belongs to the category *fruit*. Bednall went on to show that the latencies for "no" responses in a categorization task were the same for ambiguous and unambiguous words, which suggests that subjects were in fact basing their decisions on the content of L1. However, this result is also compatible with the proposal that an exhaustive search is required for both, and since Bednall did not test for a frequency effect in this experiment, the results are inconclusive.

Following up this issue, Catchpole (1987) pointed out that subjects will only notice the need for an exhaustive search when L2 contains the desired information, as in the example of classifying BRIDGE as a member of the category *game*. Usually, experimenters avoid including items of this type, and hence subjects may never notice that they need to conduct an exhaustive search. To test whether this was the case, Catchpole measured the frequency effect for the same set of nonmembers for two groups of subjects tested under different conditions. For both groups, the category was *living thing*, but for one group, one-third of the positive items had the category information represented in L2 rather than L1, e.g., PERCH, the remaining positive items being unambiguous. For the other group of subjects, these 18 ambiguous items were replaced by frequency- and length-matched unambiguous positive instances. The results are shown in Table 9.3.

The data for the positive instances indicate that the search must have continued past L1. The ambiguous positive instances took longer than the unambiguous positive instances, which would be expected if L2 is being

TABLE 9.3. Mean categorization times (milliseconds) and percentage of error rates for the category *living thing* as a function of the presence or absence of ambiguous examplars[a].

	Ambiguous exemplars			
	Present		Absent	
	RT	% error	RT	% error
Members				
Ambiguous	589	20	—	—
Unambiguous controls	—	—	551	5
Nonmembers				
High frequency	588	5	597	3
Low frequency	654	23	663	9
Frequency effect	66		66	

[a]Data taken from Catchpole (1987).

accessed, rather than L1. Also, if the search never went past L1, the error rates for the 18 ambiguous exemplars would have been 100%, whereas it was in fact only 20%. Despite this, subjects who were given ambiguous exemplars still showed a significant 66-ms frequency effect for the nonmembers, which was exactly the same size as the frequency effect for the group receiving unambiguous exemplars. Further, the former group of subjects were not any slower in rejecting nonmembers than the latter. If anything, they were faster. Thus, finding a frequency effect for nonmembers has nothing to do with whether subjects perceive the need to do an exhaustive search or not.

So this attempt at resolving the problem fails. However, there may be another way of putting the issue. The original suggestion was that subjects were able to get away with a terminating search because of the absence of ambiguous exemplars. But suppose we suggest instead that the information about potential ambiguity is represented so that subjects do not need to carry out an exhaustive search, even if ambiguous exemplars are included. What would this mean?

It might mean that once L1 is located, the decision-making system has the capacity to detect whether another entry in a particular semantic domain exists or not. Thus, for example, if the category is *parts of the body,* then once the lexical entry for the test item YEAR is accessed, the decision-making system would be able to tell that there was no other entry having anything to do with parts of the body, and hence no further search would be required. But if the task was an ambiguity decision, or the syntactic function task, where the semantic field is not known in advance, then there is no way to determine whether there is another entry without doing an exhaustive search.

Before we consider how this state of affairs could arise, let us consider which facts this proposal covers, and which remain outside its scope. First, we can explain the absence of frequency effects for negative instances in the ambiguity decision and the syntactic function tasks, since there is no information about the semantic field to which L2 would belong, and hence an exhaustive search is required. But in semantic categorization tasks, there is advance information about the semantic field, and hence the search can be self-terminating. This will explain the results reported here for loose categories, but we would need further principles to explain why the typical result in past semantic categorization experiments has been a weak or nonexistent frequency effect (Shoben, 1982), and we also need to explain why there is no frequency effect at all when the category is *number names,* as in Table 9.2.

Catchpole (1987) obtained an interesting result that may help us understand why previous studies have obtained weak frequency effects. He found that frequency effects for negative items were very weak when the category changed from one trial to the next, as is typically the case in these types of experiments (e.g., Balota and Chumbley, 1984). However, when only one category was used throughout the experiment (as was the case in the experiments reported here), strong frequency effects for nonmembers were obtained. This suggests that the special technique of using the category information to make inferences about the existence of L2 requires a certain amount of continuous practice with the category. When the category changes from trial to trial, this test for the existence of L2 cannot be applied.

The second point is more difficult to cope with, because one might imagine that "tight" categories such as *number names* would be ideally suited to this technique, or at the very least, no worse than other categories. Perhaps the problem here is that number names do not form a semantic field in the same way that animal names do. Thorp (1986) has in fact already obtained some evidence that the size of the frequency effect for nonmembers depends on the semantic properties of the category. He contrasted categories whose exemplars are natural and nominal kind terms (as defined by Schwartz, 1979). Very roughly, natural kind terms correspond to naturally occurring objects, whereas nominal kind terms involve man-made objects.[3] Thorp found stronger frequency effects when the concept was a natural kind term than when it was a nominal kind term.

This evidence does no more than add a measure of plausibility to the general argument that semantic properties might be important. Applied to our current problem, we would have to argue that the special test for the existence of L2 can only be used when the semantic field is appropriate to a

[3]One test is corrigibility. It is conceivable that we could discover that gold is not what we all thought it was; hence, *gold* is a natural kind term. But it is inconceivable that we could discover that pencils or tables are really quite different objects from what we had thought since they have a functional definition; hence, *pencil* and *table* are nominal kind terms.

natural kind term, e.g., colors, body parts, animals, birds, plants, etc. To explain the results in Table 9.2, we would have to argue that number names are nominal kind terms, which does not seem at all unlikely from the corrigibility test suggested by Schwartz. However, a great deal more evidence would be required before anything at all could be concluded. We would need, for instance, to consider other "tight" categories, such as the days of the week or terms denoting time, to see whether they also have similar properties. These notions are clearly speculative, and they are only mentioned here to give some impression of where this problem could lead.

What Is the Mechanism for the Special Test for L2?

A more critical problem, however, is to make some proposal for the mechanism by which this hypothetical technique might work, since the utility of the search model depends critically on its ability to suggest new interpretations of data. What we need is a mechanism that would enable a subject's decision maker to be in a position to reach the following type of conclusion:

"At this moment, I do not yet know whether YEAR is ambiguous or not, but I do at least know that its other meaning (if it has one) could not be a fruit."

On first consideration, this seems like a very strange thing to know. However, consider the following possibility. If we assume the distinction between access, or index files, and the master lexical file (Forster, 1976), then it is possible to imagine that the L1 entry for a homograph in the master file contains some kind of semantic code which acts as a cross-reference to the subordinate meaning. There are two possibilities to consider. First, this cross-reference might be in the form of a pointer to L2, which would give the system direct access to L2. This has the virtue of explaining why Forster and Bednall (1976) found that access time for L2 was uncorrelated with the frequency of usage of L2, but it would incorrectly predict that access time for L2 should be highly correlated with access time for L1, which does not appear to be the case in the Forster and Bednall data. An alternative possibility is that the cross-reference is not an actual pointer, but acts merely as a flag to indicate (a) that there is another meaning to consider and (b) what broad semantic category this meaning falls into. Essentially, this flag acts as a warning signal—a warning to wait until all the evidence is in before final commitment. This might be especially useful in sentence processing, since the semantic properties of the general topic of the sentence (or key words in the preceding material) could be matched against the cross-reference flag in L1 to see whether it is likely that there is an L2 that will fit the context better than L1.

This will explain why terminating searches are possible for categories such as *color names* or *parts of the body.* But what about the *number-names* category? Merrill Garrett (personal communication) has proposed that the code in which the cross-reference flag is expressed may be very limited, and it is only when the semantic properties of the category being used are expressed in the same vocabulary as the cross-reference flags that it is possible to use the flags. That is, the concept of color or the concept of body parts can be expressed in a notation that can be directly compared with cross-references. However, the concept of number name cannot be so expressed.[4]

This approach would obviate the need to propose a category search altogether. Semantic categorization could always be done by lexical search, but whether a frequency effect is observable or not will depend on the semantic properties of the category being tested. Attractive though this proposal might be, there are still some difficult issues to cope with. For example, a cross-reference flag should make an exhaustive search unnecessary in the ambiguity decision task, since the absence of any flag would make it clear whether any L2 at all existed. Hence there should be a frequency effect for unambiguous words, but this is not the case. One possible reason is that the cross-reference flag may not be a reliable indicator of ambiguity. For example, it may be present only for some words and not others, and hence the absence of a flag is ambiguous. Or it could be that the cross-reference itself is ambiguous. Sometimes it refers to an L2, but other times it refers to associated entries. For example, L1 for PALM might contain something like:

[see also: <plants(tropical)>]
[see also: <body parts(hand)>]

Most entries would now contain cross-references, and hence the unambiguous word would have no special status.[5] Neither of these solutions is particularly appealing, but perhaps the absence of an immediate solution to this problem should not rule the general model out at this stage.

Another problem that needs to be considered is the underlying reason for the apparent clumsiness of the system. What is it about the lexical system that prevents both L1 and L2 from being accessed simultaneously? As we have seen, there are compelling reasons for concluding that this is how it must be, provided one accepts the general principle that frequency controls access time. But until one can give some independent justification

---

[4]The results of Thorp (1986), discussed earlier, would clearly be relevant here.
[5]Note that this problem would not arise for the syntactic function task since the cross-reference flag indicates semantic properties, not syntactic category.

for this property of the system, the theory must remain ad hoc to some degree.

Context-Driven Selective Access

There may be another way altogether to think about the problem. It has been suggested many times that the main function of interlexical associative links is to permit selective access to the contextually relevant meaning. Such a mechanism provides a simple basis for the special test procedure for L2, as shown in Figure 9.2. If selective access occurs, then the first entry to be accessed will always be the contextually relevant entry. So in a categorization experiment, the category acts as a context, and primes the meaning that is relevant to the category (if there is one). This means that if the first entry accessed is *not* relevant to the category, then there can be no other entry that *is* relevant (otherwise it would have been accessed first). Hence the decision-maker need not wait until an exhaustive search has been completed. This would explain how the decision-maker could know that there was no other entry relevant to some specified semantic category, but not know whether there was another entry (regardless of category), thereby explaining the absence of frequency effects in ambiguity decision for unambiguous words. However, it would not explain why the number category does not work in the same way as other categories, since associative connections between the category *number* and all number names must surely be comparable to the connections between the category *colour* and the colour names.

Leaving this problem aside, there is, of course, another worry about this explanation, and that is that it violates the principle of autonomous lexical access (Forster, 1979), and is totally inconsistent with a considerable body of evidence using the cross-modal priming technique suggesting that lexical access is *non-selective* (Onifer and Swinney, 1981; Seidenberg, Tanenhaus, Leiman, & Bienkowski, 1982; Swinney 1979; Tanenhaus, Leiman, & Seidenberg, 1979).

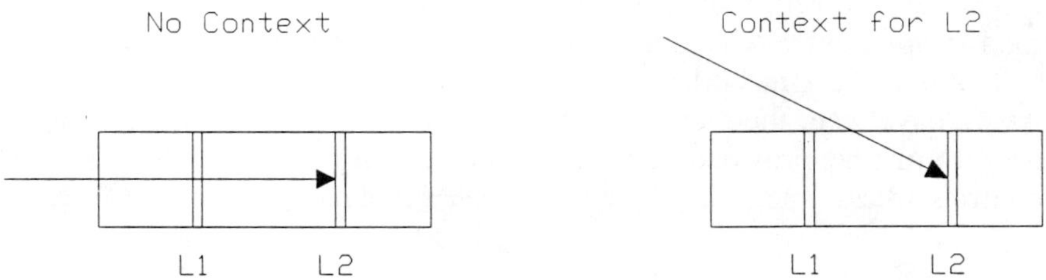

FIGURE 9.2. Selective access for L2. When no context is provided, L1 is accessed before L2, but when context relevant to L2 is present, L2 is accessed independently of L1.

There may be a weaker version of selective access that will do just as well, but will still be consistent with the cross-modal priming evidence. The strong version of selective access insists that the inappropriate meaning is never accessed or activated in any way. The cross-modal priming evidence rules this out since it shows clear activation of the inappropriate meaning. But there is a weaker version of selective access, in which the context merely changes the order in which entries are passed on to higher levels of analysis, as shown in Figure 9.3.

Although L1 is accessed before L2, a context-bias toward L2 may alter the time taken to transfer this information on to higher levels, where decision making is done (Forster, 1979). This would mean that the first meaning relayed to the decision maker was always the most appropriate meaning, which fulfills the conditions for the special test for L2.

How could context have such an effect? To remain within the spirit of an autonomous, modular language processing system, we must avoid proposing interlevel effects. So we really need to propose that the lexical processor itself can determine whether an entry is relevant to the context. Since lexical processors are informationally encapsulated (Fodor, 1983), and know only about lexical entries and their contents, we are restricted to contexts that can be expressed in terms of interlexical associative links. This is true for the case we are considering, since the category is generally denoted by a single word rather than a complex phrase. Thus it is at least plausible that the lexical processor could determine whether a given lexical entry was relevant to a category such as *animal* by checking whether the entry was linked to the entry for the word *animal.* The same goes for other categories such as *furniture, vehicle,* etc. Even those categories that require more than one word, such as *precious stone* or *living thing,* could be treated as being lexicalized. Given this, the lexical processor would then have to assign some kind of priority, so that lexical information that was clearly related to the context was communicated to higher-level systems more rapidly than information that was unrelated to the context. By way of analogy, we could think of the lexical processor as having two communica-

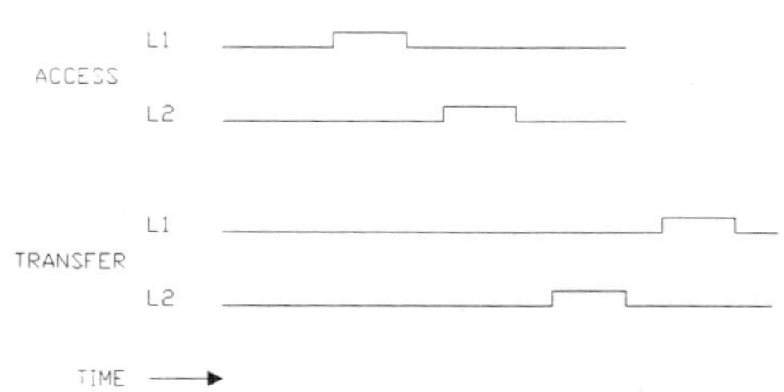

FIGURE 9.3. Selective Transfer: Although L1 is accessed before L2, information about L2 may be transferred to higher decision-making levels before L1, if the context is appropriate to L2.

tion channels—one for high-priority information and the other for the rest.

A corollary of this view is that if the category were expressible only as a complex predicate, then the lexical processor would have no way of knowing which entries were related to this category and which were not. For example, suppose the category were *things that an eagle could plausibly fly down onto.* The best the lexical processor could do would be to give priority to entries linked to *eagle* or *fly,* which would cover very few of the positive cases. Hence the theory predicts that the nonmembers for a category such as this would fail to exhibit a frequency effect, since the decision maker can no longer assume that the first entry will be the one that is relevant to the category, and must wait until an exhaustive search has been completed.

On the negative side, we still cannot explain why the number category shows no nonmember frequency effect. As we have remarked before, the entries for the number names would all be linked with the entry for *number,* and hence the special test for L2 would be operative. Further, this account seems to be inconsistent with the results of Holmes (1979), who found that ambiguity detection times were faster when context favored L2 rather than L1, suggesting that L1 was always the first entry to be checked against the context. In the selective transfer model, the opposite result appears to be the most plausible. However, on close examination, it can be seen that this is not necessarily the case. When context favors L1, ambiguity-detection time will depend on the access time for L2 plus the transfer time for L2 on a low-priority channel. But when context favors L2, the decision maker will usually receive information about L2 before L1, and hence detection time will depend on access time for L1 plus transfer time for L1 on a low-priority channel, which must be shorter than the transfer time for L2 on the same type of channel.

Theoretical Synopsis

We now attempt to link these various ideas into a single model, and present a summary of the results (see Table 9.4). The first point to note is that none of the proposals we have considered apart from the category-search model explains why the number category fails to produce a nonmember frequency effect. For this reason, the idea of a category search is retained in the model.

We propose that a category search is possible only for a very narrow class of categories. These are precompiled categories that have relatively few members but are used very frequently. Normally, category membership is decided by making an inference from the information in the lexical entry for the exemplar, but for some special cases, it is faster to search a precompiled list of all members. For these categories, nonmembers are classified at the completion of an unsuccessful category search, and hence we do not expect a frequency effect for these items. These categories are referred to as Type I in Table 9.4, and the number-names category is the only instance we have considered. Other possible examples might be days of the week or months of the year.

For the remaining categories, where there is no precompilation, positive instances are identified by inference from the contents of the lexical entry for the test item. This class breaks down into two types, according to whether negative instances can be identified only after an exhaustive consideration of all possible entries. In Type II situations, the experimental task conditions are such that the category gives advance information about the likely semantic properties of the target entry, if it exists. This makes it possible to reach a decision after the first entry is accessed, without waiting until an exhaustive lexical search has been completed. This produces a strong frequency effect for nonexemplars. In Type III situations, however, the category is defined in such a way that there is no advance information about the semantic properties of the target entry, which forces the decision-making system to wait until an exhaustive search has been completed. Examples of this type are ambiguity detection (where the members of the class of ambiguous words have no semantic properties in common), syntactic categorization (the class of nouns or verbs are similarly heterogeneous), or semantic categorization with a category defined as a complex predicate (e.g., *things an eagle could plausibly fly down onto*). Since the search is exhaustive, no frequency effect for nonexemplars is expected.

So far, we have not stated why the possibility of avoiding an exhaustive search depends on the way the category is defined. One proposal exploits the presumed existence of semantically coded cross-references to other related words or other senses of the same word. If the first-accessed entry for a word contains no cross-reference with a semantic code that matches the category, then there can be no other task-relevant meaning of this word, and the "no" decision can be made immediately. The other proposal

TABLE 9.4. Summary of experimental results and the presumed methods for categorizing nonmembers.

Categorization task	Frequency effect for nonmembers	Decision criterion for nonmembers
Type I		
Number names	4 ms	Failure of category search
Type II		
Colors	41 ms	Lexical entry contains no link to category—search terminates after first entry
Body parts	59 ms	
Living things	66 ms	
Type III		
Ambiguity	5 ms	Failure to locate relevant entry after exhaustive search
Syntactic category	20 ms	

is that the category can prime the transfer mechanism so that category-relevant information is always the first to be considered, hence making it unnecessary to wait for any further information.

Both of these proposals depend on much the same properties of the task. In order for the category to act as a prime for the transfer process, it must have some semantic or associative connection to all its members. Categories such as the class of ambiguous words or the class of nouns obviously do not have this property. But this also means that there is no way to interpret the cross-references between the accessed entry and other entries related to it.

Experimental Tests of Exhaustive Search

Recent developments in priming techniques (Forster, 1985) suggest an interesting way to test some of the assumptions of the model fairly directly. The technique involves testing for the presence or absence of masked identity priming (Forster, 1985; Forster & Davis, 1984). If a word in uppercase letters is presented for lexical decision and is immediately preceded by the same word presented very briefly in lowercase letters, a strong facilitation effect is observed even though subjects are usually unable to report the prime. However, no such effects are observed for nonword target items. The same effect occurs in an episodic "old-new" classification task, but only if the target word is an "old" item. That is, if subjects study a list containing the word DOG, but not the word HOUSE, and then are asked to make speeded "old-new" classifications of subsequently presented words, then the "old" response to DOG will be faster if it is preceded by a masked presentation of *dog*, but the "new" response to HOUSE will receive no such benefit from the prime *house.*

The general rule for interpreting such effects is as follows. Identity priming occurs if there is a preexisting representation of the test item in the memory system being tapped by the task. Nonwords show no priming when the task is a lexical decision, because they are not represented in lexical memory. Similarly, in an old-new task, there is no episodic representation of HOUSE to be primed, and hence no priming takes place. There is a lexical representation, and that is primed, but since the state of that representation is irrelevant to the task, no effect is observed. Following Forster and Davis (1984), we assume that priming alters the state of an entry so that information can be extracted from it more rapidly on a subsequent occasion.

Applying this rationale to the categorization task yields the following interpretive rule: Priming occurs whenever the decision is directly based on the information extracted from a primed entry. So when the correct decision is "yes," priming should always be obtained, since the decision is based on the information extracted from the lexical entry for the test item.

But for "no" items, the situation is more complex. If the decision is based on the failure to find the relevant entry, then no priming should occur. So the Type I and Type III cases in Table 9.4 should show no priming for "no" decisions. However, Type II cases should show priming, since the decision here is based on the information extracted from the entry. Therefore, whenever there is a frequency effect, there should be a priming effect to match it.

The available evidence is suggestive only. Forster (1985) found approximately equal priming for both "yes" and "no" items in a classification task, where the criterion was whether the designated object was bigger than a brick. Since it is most unlikely that anyone has a precompiled list of objects bigger (or smaller) than a brick, category search cannot be used, and hence we must be dealing with either a Type II or Type III effect. Of these two possibilities, Type III seems more likely, since cross-references would hardly specify size relative to a brick, nor does it seem very likely that the category could prime all the exemplars. Along this line of reasoning, there should be no priming for "no" decisions, so something is wrong. However, the nature of the category used here is rather different. For example, it is not at all clear that an exhaustive search would be required for a "no" decision—discovering that *pin* refers to an object that is smaller than a brick seems sufficient grounds for responding "no" immediately. Indeed it seems absurd to delay the response until it has been established that *pin* does not also refer to another object that is bigger than a brick (whereas a waiting game seems entirely appropriate if one is tempted to deny that *bridge* refers to a game because one has accessed the other meaning). So it may be that this is an indeterminate case. What is more crucial is a repetition of the color-names and number-names categorization experiments. For the color-names task, we should get priming for both members and nonmembers since both show frequency effects. However, for the number names, only the positive items should show priming since the correct response to the negative items is inferred from the failure of category search. Similarly, there should be no priming for negative instances in the ambiguity decision task and the syntactic function task since the response is determined only after an exhaustive search of the lexicon, and is not triggered by the recovery of information from a lexical entry.

In conclusion, it should be pointed out that the model of semantic categorization proposed here has been motivated solely by the attempt to interpret the waxing and waning of the frequency effect in terms of lexical-search theory. As it happens, the model deals more with the procedures for making decisions than with lexical access, and is therefore quite neutral about the access mechanism. Thus, if we were to try to explain the results in terms of a spreading activation model for ambiguity resolution such as that described in Seidenberg et al. (1982), we might end up with much the same model. For example, instead of using a term such as *exhaustive search,* we might say that the deadline for making a decision is extended by a duration greater than the longest firing latency of any word detector. However, the fact that these issues do not speak to the question of which kind of access model is right does not diminish their importance. The account we have offered here could still be wrong, in which case there is something fundamentally misguided about the way we assume ambiguity is represented and accessed, or about the way we interpret frequency effects, or both.

10

Systematicity and Semantic Ambiguity

LAWRENCE W. BARSALOU AND DORRIT BILLMAN

The central issue in the study of semantic ambiguity has concerned whether all senses of a polysemous word are initially accessed as opposed to only the contextually relevant sense. As a simplifying assumption, many theorists assume implicitly that the content of each retrieved sense is static, containing the same information across retrievals. Other theorists make this assumption explicitly (e.g., Fodor & Pylyshyn, 1988, p. 45). But when investigators have assessed the stability of individual word senses, they have generally observed variability in the information retrieved. Reports of semantic variability in retention include Anderson and Ortony (1975), Anderson, Pichert, Goetz, Schallert, Stevens, and Trollip (1976), Barclay, Bransford, Franks, McCarrell, and Nitsch (1974), Geis and Winograd (1975), Greenspan (1986), Thompson and Tulving (1970), and Tulving and Thompson (1973). Reports of semantic variability in lexical access include Barsalou (1982), Conrad (1978), Johnson-Laird (1987), Tabossi (1988), Tabossi and Johnson-Laird (1980), and Whitney, McKay, and Kellas (1985). A review of variability in the representations that underlie decision making can be found in Kahneman and Miller (1986).

We distinguish strong from weak semantic ambiguity. Strong semantic ambiguity (for lexical units) occurs when a single word refers to multiple categories. "Spring" exhibits strong ambiguity because it refers to a season, a type of mechanical device, and a water source. Weak ambiguity occurs when a word refers to a single category but the information retrieved for the category varies. Although "dog" has only one standard sense, it may access *large, brown,* and *mean* on one occasion and *small, white,* and *nervous* on another. We assume weak ambiguity also occurs for each sense of a word that exhibits strong ambiguity. The *insect* sense of "bug" may access *black, poisonous,* and *crawls* on one occasion and *yellow, harmless,* and *glides* on another.

The amount of weak semantic ambiguity that occurs for individual word senses is surprisingly high. Barsalou (1987, 1989) and Barsalou and Medin (1986) review work that has systematically assessed the extent to which the representations of categories vary between and within individuals. Different individuals often appear to represent the same category in substantially different ways. When individuals produce definitions for words, the overlap in propositions between two individuals' definitions for the same word is only 44% on the average. When individuals judge typicality for categories, the judgments of one subject typically only account for about 25% of the variance in the judgments of another subject for the same category. When individuals judge whether entities belong to categories, they frequently disagree on the membership of particular entities. Within the same subject, category representations vary less but still vary substantially over time. When the same individual produces definitions for words, only 67% of the propositions in one session are produced in a second session 2 weeks later. When the same individual judges typicality for categories, judgments in one session only account for around 65% of the variance in judgments 2 weeks later. When the same individual judges whether entities belong to categories, surprising numbers of membership decisions change over a 1-month period.

These assessments of between- and within-subject agreement have typically been performed while holding context as constant as possible. All subjects experience the same experimental context, and a given subject experiences the same experimental context in both sessions. However, when context is manipulated, even more substantial changes in category representation occur. When different subjects judge typicality from different points of view, they represent the same categories in very different manners. Roth and Shoben (1983) demonstrate similar effects through manipulating sentence contexts.

Although weak ambiguity appears robust, care must be taken in interpreting these findings. After reviewing various interpretations, Barsalou (1989) concludes that instability probably does not reflect underlying differences in the content of category knowledge. Different individuals appear to have highly similar category knowledge in long-term memory, and a given individual's knowledge in long-term memory appears to remain fairly stable over time. Instead, differences in the *accessibility* of category knowledge in long-term memory produce instability: The information retrieved to represent a category on a particular occasion is the small subset of category knowledge that is currently most accessible. At any point in time, the most accessible information in a category may vary widely between individuals, even though they share common knowledge. At any two points in time, the most accessible information in a category may vary widely for the same individual, even though the content of underlying knowledge has not changed. Because the most accessible information varies, the information retrieved to represent a category in working memory varies, thereby producing instability. The reader should note that we will use the term "representation" throughout this paper in referring to temporary representations of categories in working memory, as well as to stable category knowledge in long-term memory. The particular sense we intend on a given occasion will be clear from context.

Barsalou (1987, 1989) suggests that frequency, recency, and context are responsible for differences in accessibility. Frequently processed information is more accessible than infrequently processed information. Recently processed information is more accessible than less recently processed information. Contextually relevant information is more accessible than less relevant information. Because these three factors vary dynamically between and within individuals, they produce variation in the knowledge activated for a category.

It is important to note that some degree of stability typically accompanies instability. Complete lack of agreement rarely occurs for definitions, typicality judgments, or membership decisions. Instead, some agreement always remains. Barsalou (1982, 1987, 1989) proposes that some category knowledge is context-independent, being automatically activated across all contexts to produce stability. Information acquires a context-independent status when it has been consistently mapped to a category frequently enough to develop an automatic relation with the category (Schneider & Shiffrin, 1977; Shiffrin & Schneider, 1977).

Overview

Although most theorists agree that a complete cognitive theory requires assumptions about both representation and processing, in practice, work often focuses more on one than the other. It is probably fair to say that work on both strong and weak ambiguity has focused more on processing than representation. Work on strong ambiguity has primarily focused on the selective versus multiple access issue without worrying much about the representation of word senses. Work on weak ambiguity has primarily focused on how the retrieval of category information varies between individuals, within individuals, and across contexts. In this paper, we develop a theory of knowledge that emphasizes representation, although we also include processing assumptions.

The theory we propose is tentative in the sense that we have not collected extensive data to support it directly. Prior work that we each have performed motivates this theory but does not test it. Nevertheless we believe that much work in the literature indirectly supports our proposal, and we will cite this work as we proceed. Most importantly, we view our theory as having value in organizing a diversity of findings in the literature and as providing directions for future research.

We begin by motivating and defining the construct of *systematicity*. After briefly reviewing related work on correlated attributes, we define two structural forms of systematicity that we believe underlie human knowledge: *attribute systematicity* and *value systematicity.* We then discuss the relation between frames and systematicity (Minsky, 1975), the role of higher-order relations in systematicity (Gentner, 1983, 1988), and the relation between decomposition and systematicity (Fodor & Pylyshyn, 1988). In the section on benefits of systematicity for processing, we propose that systematicity is central to important uses of knowledge. We show how systematicity can facilitate the learning of categories, enable the generation of inferences, and produce stability in the retrieval of category information. In the section on systematicity in primitive forms of knowledge, we propose that systematicity underlies three primitive forms of knowledge: *ontological kinds, basic object frames,* and *basic event frames.* We argue that these three forms of knowledge are acquired effortlessly and naturally from experience during early childhood. In the section on systematicity in abstract forms of knowledge, we propose that more abstract forms of knowledge develop later from these primitive forms, requiring more complicated cognitive processing. These abstract forms include *generalized actions, scripts, taxonomic superordinates,* and *goal-derived categories.* Consequently, our theory addresses developmental progressions in knowledge, as well its structure.

Although we touch on a variety of processing issues in presenting this theory, our emphasis will be on the retrieval of information during the construction of category representations. As we discuss various types of knowledge, we will consider how systematicity could produce stability and instability in the representations of each. We will also discuss possible roles that these stabilities and instabilities play in the semantic representation of nouns and verbs. In the section on integrations and extensions, we integrate our main points concerning the evolution of knowledge and the stability of category representations. We then extend our analysis to stability during the comprehension of texts. In the last section, we assess our proposal and note its limitations.

Systematicity

Correlated Attributes

Our construct of systematicity is closely related to Rosch's (1973, 1978) ideas on the structure of the environment and its role in natural categories. Rosch noted that perceived attributes in the physical world do not occur independently of one another. Instead attributes enter into correlations to produce the "correlational structure of the environment" (Rosch, Mervis, Gray, Johnson, & Boyes-Braem, 1976, p. 385). For example, the attribute of *wings* is not equally likely to occur with all other attributes. Instead *wings* is correlated with *beak, feathers,* and *nest building* but not with *scales, roots,* or *requiring batteries.*[1]

Rosch and her colleagues further argued that these correlational patterns underlie natural categories in a number of important ways. In category acquisition, people form categories around sets of things that share correlational structure (Rosch et al., 1976). A category such as *birds* stands out in the environment because its exemplars generally possess the same correlated attributes. In contrast, people do not construct categories that violate these correlations. For example, people do not acquire a category that is the union of *birds* and *cars,* because no common set of correlated attributes generally occurs across members of the union. But because *birds* and *cars* individually embody sets of correlated attributes, people form categories around each of these two sets.

Rosch and her colleagues extended this idea to account for category goodness and category structure. Good categories embody many correlated attributes and share few correlated attributes with competing categories. Basic-level categories, such as *bird, apple,* and *shirt,* are privileged because their respective members share many correlated attributes that do not occur in contrast categories (e.g., *fish, banana,* and *shoe,* respectively). For category structure, correlated attributes determine how central an exemplar is in its category (Rosch & Mervis, 1975, p. 602). Prototypes and typical members are central because they match the category's attributes or its "family resemblance structure." For example, *robin* is typical because it has many of the correlated attributes associated with *birds* (e.g., *small, sings, flies*); whereas *ostrich* is atypical because it does not have many of these correlated attributes.

Actually Rosch and her colleagues never measured correlations between attributes directly. Instead they only assessed the role of independent attributes in category learning, preference, and structure. However, a correlation between each of several individual attributes and a category does not imply that the attributes correlate with each other. Nevertheless, a fair amount of direct evidence has accrued since then to support the importance of correlated attributes, as we review next.

The line between the real and imaginary often follows correlational structure. Mythological animals are typically composed by disrupting actual correlations, and even children show sensitivity to the anomalous nature of such animals (Nash, 1982). Similarly, disrupting well-established correlations in natural kind categories poses a serious dilemma for biologists (Gould, 1985). During the nineteenth century, the first reports that

---

[1]Rosch and her colleagues actually used *feature* in refering to what we call *attribute.* Their use of *feature* and our use of *attribute* so far are ambiguous, because either could refer to an attribute or one of its values (e.g., an attribute could be either *color* or *red*). Later in this section, we distinguish between attributes and values explicitly.

platypuses lay eggs and nurse their young caused great uproar. Biologists were divided into two camps: Either the platypus lays eggs but does not nurse, or it nurses but does not lay eggs. The apparent pairing of these properties violated such strong beliefs about correlations that 30 years of empirical validation were necessary for its acceptance. In a laboratory setting, Malt and Smith (1984) similarly found that undergraduates' typicality judgments of natural categories are sensitive to property correlations. Subjects rate birds that preserve a common correlation as more typical than birds that disrupt it (e.g., the correlation between *neutral color* and *living by the sea*).

Medin and his colleagues have provided extensive arguments for the importance of correlated attributes in categorization. According to the Medin and Schaffer (1978) context model, configural information such as correlated attributes and exemplars enters into category membership decisions. The substantial support for this and other exemplar models is consistent with the importance of correlated attributes (cf. Brooks, 1978, 1987; Estes, 1986a, 1986b; Hintzman, 1986; Jacoby & Brooks, 1984; Nosofsky, 1984, 1986). More directly, Medin, Altom, Edelson, and Freko (1982) have found that correlated attributes facilitate generalization.[2] Medin, Wattenmaker, and Hampson (1987) have further found that causal principles encourage the use of correlated attributes in category formation (cf. Murphy & Medin, 1985).

Billman, Richards, and Heit (1988) note that generalization in accord with correlated attributes does not actually mean that people are inducing and directly using correlations in categorization decisions. Instead people might be good at generalizing categories with correlated attributes simply because these categories optimize the similarity of new exemplars to old exemplars during generalization. New exemplars may be more similar on the average to categories with correlated attributes than to categories without correlated attributes. Thus correlated attributes could facilitate generalization through similarity even when people do not explicitly induce and use correlations.

Billman et al. assessed whether correlated attributes affect category generalization when the similarity between new and old exemplars is controlled. If correlated attributes determine categorization when similarity is not a factor, this would suggest that people are indeed inducing correlations. These experiments focused on what people learn from observational, incidental exposure to exemplars, when they are not intentionally learning

---

[2]We use *generalization* when referring to how people extend knowledge from previous category members to new category members (e.g., from previously experienced dogs to new dogs). Whereas many authors refer to this as *transfer,* we use *transfer* when referring to how people apply knowledge from a previously experienced category to a new and different category (e.g., from calculators to computers).

a category or trying to learn rules. Instead the exposure task was exemplar memorization, a task that focuses on differences between exemplars rather than on their commonalities. Subjects were only told that categories were involved after the final exposure to exemplars. If subjects induce correlations under these conditions, then the tendency to do so would appear quite robust.

The learning exemplars in one set of experiments were pictures of animals that instantiated a correlation between two body parts. In one stimulus set, *striped curved tails* always co-occurred with *round green heads;* whereas *blue puffy tails* always co-occurred with *jagged yellow heads.* Thus values for the attributes of *head* and *tail* were correlated. In another set of experiments, the exemplars described individuals on attributes such as *university, intended profession, sport, hometown,* and *ethnic background,* two of which were correlated. Here, for example, values for *school* and *sport* might covary, with students from *Berkeley* playing *tennis,* and students from *Columbia* playing *volleyball.* Both the attributes and values composing the correlations were completely counterbalanced to control for possible differences in attribute and value salience, as well as for preexperimental biases toward particular correlations. In some experiments, the correlations between attributes were perfect; in others they were not. The complexity of exemplars, both individually and as a group, varied across experiments.

The generalization test following exposure assessed whether or not subjects selectively used the correlated attributes in generalizing a category to novel exemplars. On each trial, subjects decided which of two novel exemplars was more likely to have come from the same category as the original exemplars. One novel exemplar preserved the correlational rule available in learning, and the other disrupted it. Both exemplars, however, were equally similar to the originally learned instances. Exemplar similarity was matched on a stringent measure that controlled the distribution of attribute matches and matches of attribute combinations between a test exemplar and the learning set. Thus, these tests assessed whether subjects show sensitivity to correlated attributes when similarity to the learning exemplars remains constant.

Subjects generalized in accord with correlated attributes. Individual subjects either used the correlation consistently in generalizing or performed at chance, producing a bimodal distribution of scores. Across these experiments, about half the subjects learned and used the correlated attributes when the correlations were perfect, and about a quarter learned and used the correlation when it was not perfect (these proportions are substantially higher than one would expect by chance). Thus, even in a covert and nondirective learning task, some subjects abstracted and used correlated attributes. These experiments provide direct evidence for the importance and availability of correlated attributes even in situations where abstraction is not encouraged. In more explicit learning situations, people would probably induce correlations even more readily (cf. Medin et al., 1987).

Attributes and Values

At this point we need to introduce more precise terminology. Most prior work on categories and correlation refers to the characteristics of exemplars simply as "features," "properties," or "attributes." However, our analysis requires the well-known distinction between attributes and the values they assume (also see Smith & Osherson, 1984; Smith, Osherson, Rips, & Keene, in press). This distinction explicitly captures the idea that some properties (values) specify contrasting levels or special cases of another property (the attribute). For example, the values of *round* and *square* specify special cases of the attribute *shape.* This distinction is clearest when both attributes and values have monomorphemic labels (e.g., "color" and "green"). However, an unlimited variety of more complex attribute-value relationships exists (e.g., values of *automatic station scanning* and *preset station settings* for the attribute of *station tuning mechanism* in *stereo receivers*).

Specifying what can be an attribute is an old and difficult problem (Armstrong, Gleitman, & Gleitman, 1983). Identifying relevant attributes from the set of possible attributes is comparably difficult (Carey, 1985; Lakoff, 1987; McCauley, 1987; Murphy & Medin, 1985). Furthermore, whether a property is an attribute or a value is not simply a matter of logical analysis. For example, *leg* might be a value for the attribute of *limb,* contrasting with *wings* and *fins*; or *leg* might be an attribute with different values for *people, horses,* and *dogs*; or *leg* might be a relatively undifferentiated property (e.g., to an infant who has seen only human legs). As Garner (1974) noted, the specification of a property as an attribute or value intimately depends on the set of entities currently under consideration. We further assume, along with many others since Hubel and Wiesel (1962), that biological as well as contextual factors dictate the specification of attributes and values.

Systems of Correlations

We propose that there is more to optimal category structure than isolated correlations. Instead, we propose that a system of correlations—what we refer to as "systematicity"—produces category coherence and structure (Billman, 1983, 1985; Billman & Heit, in press; Billman, Heit, & Dorfman, 1987). As we suggest next, systematicity produces coherence both at the level of attributes (attribute systematicity) and at the level of values (value systematicity). As we discuss throughout the remainder of this paper, attribute and value systematicity appear to play central roles in both the structure and processing of knowledge.

Attribute Systematicity

Attribute systematicity (AS) is assessed solely in terms of attributes—it has nothing to do with attribute values. AS is the extent to which all members of a category have values on the same attributes, regardless of whether members have the same or different values. As AS increases, the probability of any two attributes co-occurring in a member approaches 1. Consider Figure 10.1a. Exemplars E1, E2, E3, and E4 exhibit high AS because they share attributes A, B, C, and D. In contrast, exemplars E5, E6, E7, and E8 exhibit low AS because they only share attribute Q.

Throughout we refer to predictive relations as "correlations." However, we do not intend to limit our discussion to linear correlations between multivalued attributes whose values fall on ordered scales, such as *height* and *weight*. Instead, we also need to consider relations between other sorts

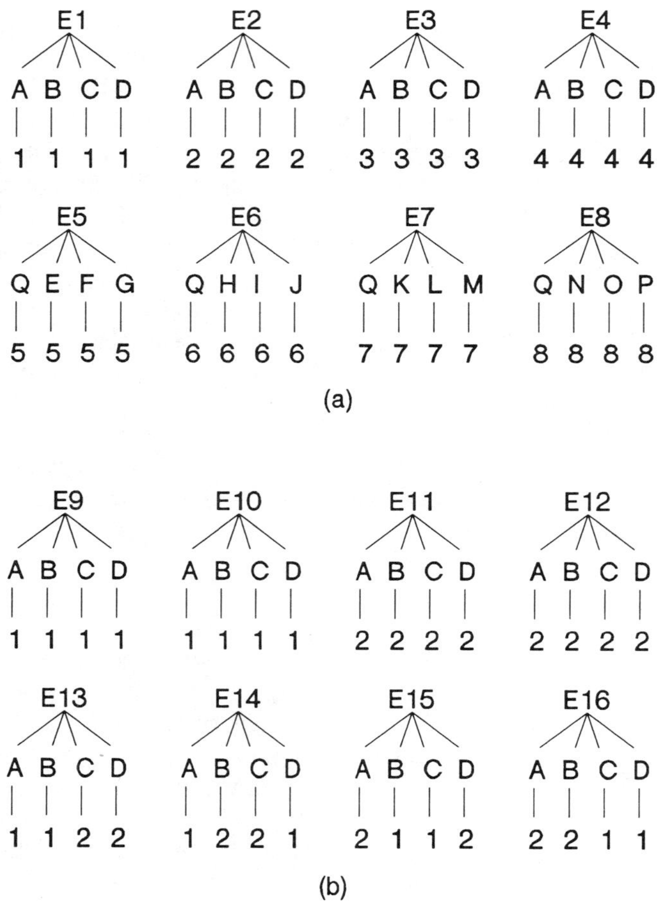

FIGURE 10.1. (a) Exemplars E1, E2, E3, and E4 represent a category with high AS; exemplars E5, E6, E7, and E8 represent a category with low AS. (b) Exemplars E9, E10, E11, and E12 represent a category with high VS; exemplars E13, E14, E15, and E16 represent a category with low VS.

of information, such as whether *wings* co-occur more often with *feathers* than with *gills.* Hence conditional probabilities across a table of predictive and predicted information are a more exact expression of what we have in mind.

There are many possible measures of systematicity. For example, AS could increase with the number of attribute correlations that fall above some minimal value; or AS could increase with the percentage of attribute correlations above some minimal value; or AS could increase with the number of attribute correlations that involve the most predictive attributes. These examples are certainly not exhaustive. For example, more informative measures would include information about the levels of attribute correlations, as well as their number.

Natural categories vary widely in AS. For example, *dog* has high AS because most members have values on the same attributes (e.g., *legs, fur, color, weight, temperament*). *Artifact* has low AS because most members do not have values on the same attributes (e.g., *wheels, pockets, handles, roof*). Categories that intuitively display a high level of coherence typically seem to have high AS. We suspect that AS is closely related to what Rosch and her colleagues had in mind when stressing the importance of correlated structure.

Obviously a critical problem in assessing AS is specifying the relevant attributes. One can obtain high or low AS for the same category, depending on the attributes chosen. Later, when we discuss specific forms of knowledge, we suggest principled ways of selecting relevant attributes.[3]

Value Systematicity

Value systematicity (VS) depends on and is enabled by AS, being computable only across exemplars that share attributes. VS is the extent to which values of one attribute predict values of another, averaged over pairs of shared attributes. As VS increases, the average probability that the values for one attribute predict the values for another attribute approaches 1.

Consider Figure 10.1b. Exemplars E9, E10, E11, and E12 exhibit high

---

[3]It is important to distinguish between attributes that could apply to a category member versus ones that could not. Although cars do not have wings, they possibly could. On the other hand, although cars do not reproduce, it is impossible that they could. Consequently, it makes sense to say that a car has the value of *no value* for *wings,* but it does not make sense to say that a car has the value of *no value* for *means of reproduction.* If *no value* is allowed as a value for *either* kind of attribute, then measuring attribute systematicity becomes difficult if not impossible, because categories like *vehicle* have high attribute systematicity (i.e., all *vehicles* would have values, not only for *wheels, propellers, engines,* and *pedals,* but also for *beaks, fur,* and *means of reproduction*). But following Barsalou and Bower (1984), we assume that people normally do not include attributes having *no value* in category representations. Consequently we expect that AS is best defined only over those attributes that have a value other than *no value.*

VS because the values for attributes A, B, C, and D are mutually predictive. If the value of A is known to be 1, then one can infer that the values of B, C, and D are also 1; whereas if the value of A is known to be 2, then one can infer that the values of B, C, and D are also 2. In contrast, exemplars E13, E14, E15, and E16 exhibit no VS because the values for A, B, C, and D are not mutually predictive. Knowing the value of A does not provide any information about the values for B, C, and D. Measuring the predictive relations and systematicity that underlie VS can take many forms, as was just discussed for AS.[4]

Natural categories vary widely in VS. *Animal* has high VS because values for shared attributes often appear correlated (e.g., values for *locomotion, limb, reproduction, temperature regulation*). *Artifact* has low VS because values for shared attributes often appear uncorrelated (e.g., values for *material, shape,* and *color*).

Frames and Subcategories

We assume that AS and VS are central to "carving nature at its joints." Not only do people acquire information about patterns of AS and VS across entities, they also use this information to create categories. For example, certain categories may be salient because they have high AS: A set of entities stands out as a group because the entities share values on the same attributes. *Bird* may stand out because its exemplars share a large number of attributes, providing them with high AS.

A stable pattern of attributes can be represented as a frame (Minsky, 1975; Rumelhart & Ortony, 1978). A frame consists of a stable set of variables that are integrated by an invariant set of relations and that take on different values across exemplars. The frame for *chair* might contain spatially organized variables for *seat, back, legs,* and *arms* that take on different values across individual chairs. These variables, or slots, are essentially what we refer to as "attributes," and their relatively stable presence across exemplars constitutes high AS. Some theorists assume that a frame simply contains an unordered list of attributes. Following other theorists, we assume that relations connect a frame's attributes, integrating them into a pattern of systematicity. In later sections, we discuss spatial, temporal, causal, and intentional relations that organize frame attributes.

Within a category having high AS, various subcategories may stand out

---

[4]One could assess VS only for attributes common to *all* category members. For *vehicle,* VS could be assessed for *weight* and *color* because they are common to all exemplars; however, VS would not be assessed for *wings* and *wheels* because not all exemplars have them. Alternatively, VS could be assessed over any attribute that applies to *some* category members (e.g., *wings* and *wheels* would be included for *vehicle*). We opt for the latter so that we can discuss VS in categories having low AS, such as *vehicle.*

because exemplars exhibit VS across the frame's shared attributes. In *bird,* for example, *duck* contains a fairly stable pattern of values across the attributes of *mouth, neck, feet, locomotion,* etc. Other subcategories such as *eagle* and *hummingbird* contain different stable patterns of values. Whereas some categories exist because their members share a common frame (e.g., *birds*), others exist because they share a set of correlated values that instantiate a frame (e.g., *duck*). Shipley (1988) proposes that people are predisposed to believe that a particular attribute for a category (e.g., *diet* for *animal*) has a homogeneous value for each of its subcategories (e.g., *bananas* for all monkeys, *honey* for all bears). These "overhypotheses," as Shipley refers to them, reflect a bias to increase VS in category knowledge.

Consequently AS and VS are intimately related. AS represents a frame that remains relatively invariant across a category's exemplars. VS reflects the extent to which the variability of values across frame attributes is systematic and predictable. High AS in a category enables and often accompanies high VS in its subcategories. Both contribute to the overall coherence of a category. Regardless of how one ends up distinguishing attributes and values, we believe that AS and VS will combine in this manner to produce category coherence.

Higher-Order Relations

So far, we have only addressed first-order relations between attributes. But as Gentner (1983, 1988) notes, higher-order relations often integrate first-order relations. Imagine that Wanda prevents children from stealing apples by buying a dog. This situation can be represented as: PREVENT [BUY [*Wanda, dog*], STEAL [*children, apples*]]. As can be seen, the higher-order relation, PREVENT, integrates the two first-order relations, BUY and STEAL.

We assume that higher-order relations are central to conceptual organization, often being organized around hidden causal attributes that interrelate first-order relations. For example, if we observe Wanda buying a dog, we might infer that she has the goal of preventing her apples from being stolen, where this goal is a hidden causal attribute. After reviewing various literatures, Murphy and Medin (1985) and Wellman and Gelman (1988) conclude that hidden causal attributes are used ubiquitously in acquiring and organizing knowledge (also see Medin et al., 1987; Wattenmaker, Dewey, Murphy, & Medin, 1986). Numerous empirical results in the social cognition literature, especially regarding trait inferences, further attest to the importance of hidden causal attributes (see Fiske & Taylor, 1984, for a review). As we discuss throughout this paper, hidden causal attributes contribute to systematicity in many domains.

Gentner (1983, 1988) uses "systematicity" in referring to the role of higher-order relations in analogical reasoning. In her structure-mapping theory of analogy, systematicity is the extent to which higher-order relations are common to the base and target domains of an analogy. Good analogies have many higher-order relations in common, whereas poor analogies have few. Gentner's construct of systematicity is similar to ours in that higher amounts of integration are increasingly optimal. One difference is that we focus less on the height of higher-order relations and more on the breadth of first-order relations (i.e., how densely attributes and attribute values are interrelated). However, full development of our approach requires assessments of higher-order relations as well. Another difference is that we are interested in the statistical degree of correlation between attributes. For example, systematicity in Figure 10.1 can vary continuously as the average correlation across all possible attribute pairs varies. In contrast, the relations in structure-mapping theory typically represent the presence or absence of conceptual relations. In many cases, these all-or-none relations represent logical or physical necessities in the structure of a domain.

Decomposition

One might suppose that an implementation of systematicity would essentially be equivalent to a connectionist network (McClelland & Rumelhart, 1986; Rumelhart & McClelland, 1986). In both, relations might simply reflect correlational strength and nothing else between all possible pairs of representational units. If so, then implementations of systematicity would not allow decomposition, as noted by Fodor and Pylyshyn (1988). But as we discuss later, the relations in AS and VS simultaneously represent correlational strength *and* conceptual relations (e.g., spatial, temporal, causal, and intentional relations). Consequently, our view of systematicity supports decomposition in the sense that Fodor and Pylyshyn raise. The various elements in a pattern of systematicity can be extracted and recombined in rule-governed manners to form new representations. Although we do not propose productive mechanisms for doing this, our representations support them.

Because we only propose connections between attributes that are positively correlated, our construct of systematicity differs further from standard connectionism. To make our account connectionist in this regard, we would have to include connections between attributes that are negatively correlated (i.e., inhibition). If these relations were unlabeled, they would complicate decomposition (Fodor & Pylyshyn, 1988). One possibility would be to include negative relations only when they are explicitly noticed. Because these relations are not passively established, as they would be in a connectionist system, they might typically be labeled by relations that express contrast, mutual exclusivity, or impossibility. In general, by only representing correlations that are conceptually labeled, we capture some statistical learning capability, while retaining decompositionality.

We disagree with Fodor and Pylyshyn (1988, p. 68) that the statistical information represented by correlations between attributes is rarely relevant to human cognition. Even cursory readings of the literature in cognitive and social psychology reveal how ubiquitous statistical information is in human knowledge and performance. Although people often do not process frequencies and probabilities in a statistically normative manner, they nevertheless are extremely sensitive to this information, from the most perceptual to the most conceptual sorts of processes. The papers in Kahneman, Slovic, and Tversky (1982) and in Sternberg and Smith (1988) clearly document the extensive role that statistical information plays in human decision making and reasoning.

The statistical nature of our labeled relations differs in another important regard from what Fodor and Pylyshyn (1988) have in mind. Fodor and Pylyshyn appear committed to the view that semantic relations are utilized according to the rules of logic. For example, once something has been placed in a particular category, attributes related to the category are logically entailed; they must be part of its representation (e.g., pp. 41–48). In contrast, our statistical relations are not processed strictly according to the rules of logic. Instead we assume that much of the quasi-logical character that people impose on relations has its basis in probabilistic reasoning and intuitive theories.

Probabilistically, a system with access to correlational information might infer that relations whose correlations fall above some threshold (e.g., .90) are entailed. What this threshold might be is an empirical question. But once statistical relations become interpreted in this manner, logical labels may be attached to them. People's intuitive theories of the world may also impose a quasi-logical character on relations. As numerous theorists have proposed, such theories often cause people to believe that certain relations are necessary or have other logical interpretations during various forms of reasoning and decision making (Carey, 1985; Cheng & Holyoak, 1985; Lakoff, 1987; McCauley, 1987; Murphy & Medin, 1985; Rips, 1988). People may impose such interpretations on relations even when the correlations underlying them are low or nonexistent (Chapman & Chapman, 1969; Murphy & Medin, 1985). Strength of belief reflects both theory and observation.

Consequently, we adopt virtues of both the connectionist and symbol processing frameworks. The correlational nature of our relations provides us with some of the statistical information that makes connectionist systems powerful learners. But because these relations are also conceptually labeled, they support compositional symbol processing.[5]

---

[5]Fodor and Pylyshyn (1988, pp. 37–41) also use the term *systematicity*. For them, *systematicity* refers to the principle that the ability to understand one idea entails the ability to understand certain other ideas. Understanding "Doug loves Luke" entails understanding "Luke loves Doug." Fodor and Pylyshyn's concept of systematicity, although related, is thus distinct from ours.

Benefits of Systematicity for Processing

Why might systematicity be an optimal organization for human knowledge? We next discuss how systematicity benefits three important uses of knowledge: learning, inference, and retrieval. In our discussion of retrieval, we consider various ways in which systematicity can produce stability and instability in category representations.

Learning

If systematicity structures the environment (Rosch et al., 1976), and if organisms have evolved to seek this systematicity, then AS and VS in a conceptual domain should facilitate category learning. In contrast, the absence of systematicity should make learning difficult. We consider the roles of AS and VS in turn.

Attribute Systematicity

Imagine that a learner, with a bias toward seeking systematicity, tries to identify which pairs of attributes co-occur in a new category. Consider the three categories in Figures 10.2a, 10.2b, and 10.2c. As indicated by the dashed lines, exemplars in any of these three categories can have either of two values (1 or 2) on any of 12 attributes (A through L). However, not all attributes need be present in a particular exemplar. The solid lines represent those pairs of attributes that tend to co-occur frequently with one another across exemplars. In Figure 10.2a, for example, attributes A, B, K, and L are connected by the six possible correlations between them to form a pattern of AS. Pairs of attributes that are not connected may never co-occur or may co-occur unreliably. We make no assumptions in these examples about correlations between attribute values.

Imagine that a learner receives exemplars from the category represented in Figure 10.2a and tries to identify attributes that frequently co-occur (i.e., attributes that co-occur in the same exemplars, regardless of their specific values). As soon as the learner detects any of the six correlations in Figure 10.2a, a bias toward systematicity would facilitate detecting the remaining five correlations. How might this bias work? Billman and Heit (in press) suggest that it takes the form of *focused sampling*. Although Billman and Heit only address focused sampling in learning VS, it can be readily extended to learning AS: As evidence about co-occurring attributes accumulates, assume that attributes in any undiscovered co-occurrence relation are likely to co-occur with the initially discovered co-occurring attributes. When one regularity is discovered, assume it is related to whatever other regularities may exist.

Imagine a learner first detects the correlation between A and B in Figure 10.2a. A bias toward systematicity predicts that other attributes in the

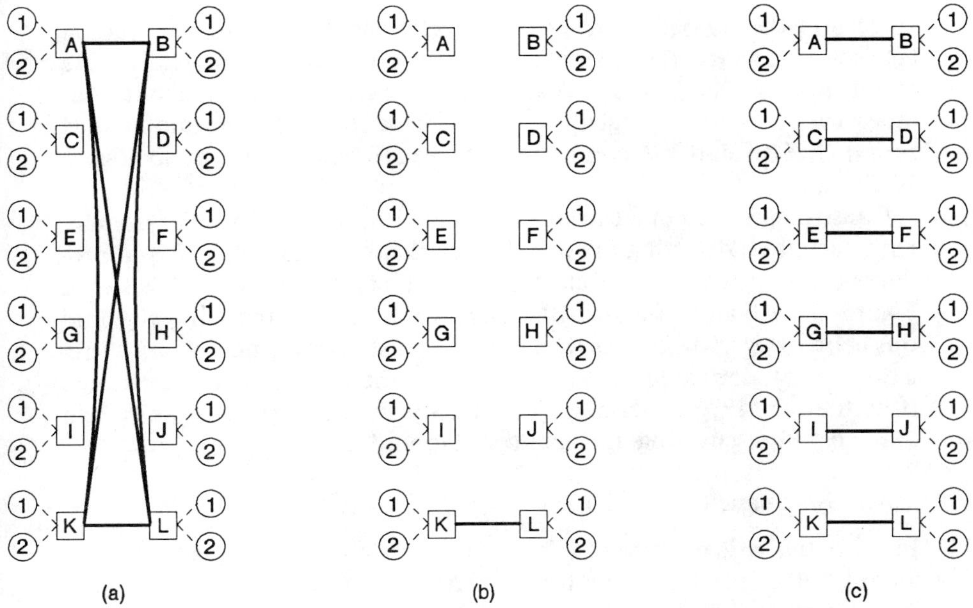

FIGURE 10.2. (a) Attributes A, B, K, and L generally co-occur across category members to form a pattern of AS. (b) Only attributes K and L co-occur across category members. (c) Six pairs of attributes are correlated across category members but do not form a pattern of AS.

category entering into a co-occurrence relation also co-occur with A and B. By focusing attention on A, B, and the attributes with which they co-occur, it becomes easier to identify the five remaining correlations (A-K, A-L, B-K, B-L, K-L). For example, even the most distant correlation—between K and L—is easily acquired after discovering the A-K, A-L, B-K, or B-L correlation. By biasing search to A, B, and the attributes with which they correlate, a learner expends less effort searching for nonexistent correlations. Because neither G nor H would be found to co-occur with either A or B, little effort would be made to look for a correlation between G and H. If G and H *did* co-occur, learners with a bias toward systematicity might in fact miss it.

In contrast, consider Figure 10.2b, where the only attributes that frequently co-occur are K and L. The only way to find this correlation is to search the entire space of possible correlations, because no other structure draws attention to the relevant attributes. In the process, many more negative cases would be tested than for Figure 10.2a (e.g., G-H). Figure 10.2c demonstrates that the organization of correlations—not just their number—is critical for systematicity and its benefits in learning. Even though the category in Figure 10.2c has the same number of correlations as the category in Figure 10.2a, the organization of the correlations in Figure

10.2c provides no help in detecting correlations. Finding the correlation between A and B, for example, provides no assistance in finding the correlation between K and L. A and B provide no information about what other attributes are correlated. Thus the entire space of correlations must be searched to find the correlation between K and L, just as in Figure 10.2b.

Consequently, AS in a category, combined with a bias to seek systematicity, facilitates detecting the correlations that constitute the AS and produces category coherence. Detecting the K-L correlation is much easier in Figure 10.2a than in Figures 10.2b and 10.2c. The primary drawback to this heuristic is that it biases the learner against discovering isolated correlations. But to the extent that the structure of the environment is correlated (Rosch et al., 1976a), seeking systematicity should provide more benefit than cost in discovering attribute correlations.[6]

Value Systematicity

Imagine that a learner, with a bias toward seeking systematicity, tries to identify which pairs of attributes have correlated values in a new category. As we discussed earlier, discovering co-occurring sets of attribute values within a category is important for establishing its subcategories. Consider the two categories in Figures 10.3a and 10.3b. Solid lines between lettered squares represent those pairs of attributes that tend to co-occur frequently with one another across exemplars. Because attributes A, B, C, D, E, and F are all interconnected in Figures 10.3a and 10.3b, the two categories have the same pattern of AS. Solid lines between numbered circles represent values that are correlated with one another across exemplars. In Figure 10.3a, the solid line between A-1 and B-1 means that whenever A has value 1, B is likely to have value 1. Dotted lines between values represent values that co-occur to some extent but that are not correlated. In Figure 10.3a, the dotted lines from C-1 to D-1, D-2, and D-3 mean that whenever C has value 1, D can take any of its three values. Because C-2 and C-3 are

[6]We only claim here that focused sampling predicts facilitation when subjects receive no external feedback about the correctness of their responses during learning. Instead of relying on external feedback, a learner, who is using focused sampling, generates predictions about additional attribute correlations whenever a correlation is detected. Internal feedback about these predictions is provided by testing whether they are confirmed in observed exemplars. The result is that any individual correlation is learned faster when other cues covary with it. Facilitation from correlated cues contrasts with predictions and findings from learning *with* external feedback. In several studies with external feedback, learning a given correlation appears to be independent of (Trabasso & Bower, 1968) or inhibited by (MacKintosh, 1975; Zeaman & House, 1963) the presence of other correlated cues. Consequently the presence or absence of explicit feedback may moderate the effects that systematicity has on learning.

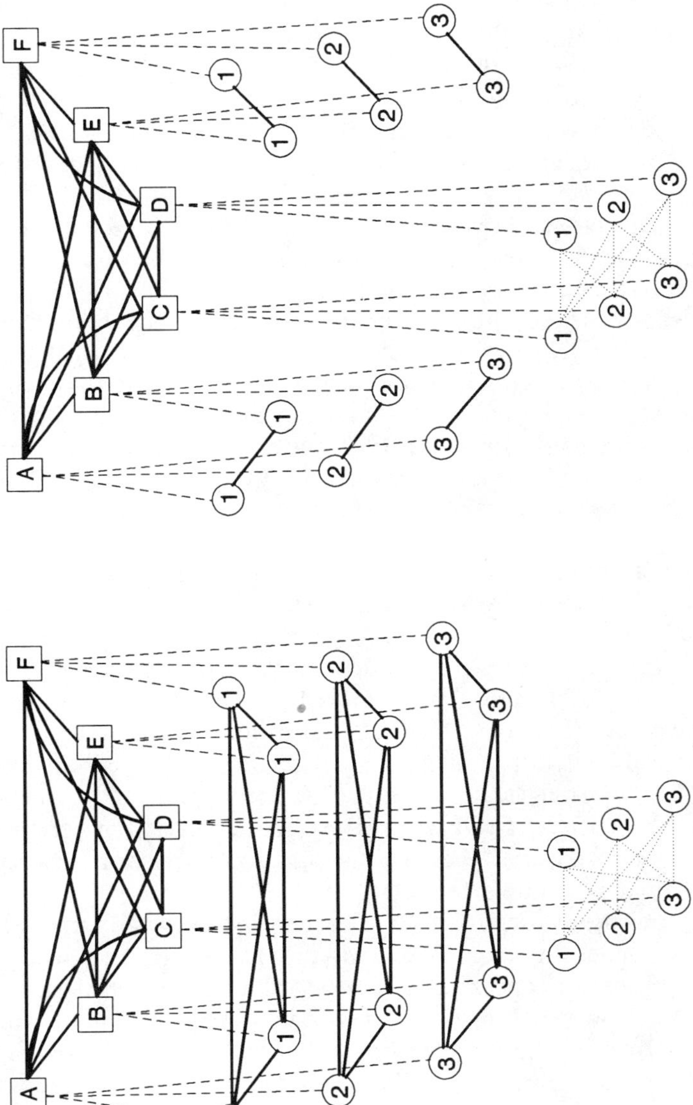

FIGURE 10.3. (a) Values for attributes, A, B, E, and F are inter-correlated to form a pattern of VS. (b) Two pairs of attributes have correlated values but do not form a pattern of VS.

similarly related to D-1, D-2, and D-3, the values for C and D are not correlated. The reader should assume that attribute pairs for which no connections between values are shown are actually connected in the same way as the values for C and D (i.e., values for all these pairs of attributes are uncorrelated). We have not shown these dotted lines in order to keep Figures 10.3a and 10.3b simple. For example, each value of A in Figure 10.3a sometimes co-occurs with each value of C such that the values of A and C are uncorrelated.

As can be seen, VS is higher in Figure 10.3a than in Figure 10.3b. In Figure 10.3a, the values of A, B, E, and F are correlated. If the value for A is 1, then we can predict that the values for B, E, and F are also 1. If the value for E is 2, then we can predict that the values for A, B, and F are also 2. Once the value for any of these four attributes is known, the values of the remaining three can be predicted.

In contrast, consider Figure 10.3b. Here only two pairs of attributes have correlated values: The values of A are correlated with the values of B, and the values of E are correlated with the values of F. Because these two correlations do not enter into a pattern of systematicity, much less prediction is possible. If the value for A is 1, then one can only predict that the value for B is 1—no predictions can be made for the values of C, D, E, or F. Consequently, VS is substantially lower in Figure 10.3b than in Figure 10.3a.

If learners are biased to seek systematicity, then it should be much easier to detect correlations between attribute values in Figure 10.3a than in Figure 10.3b. If a learner first detects the correlation between the values for A and B in Figure 10.3a, then this will facilitate detecting the correlation between the values for E and F. If the learner primarily searches for correlations involving attributes already found to have correlated values, all correlations will be detected, and unnecessary tests will be minimized. For example, because the values of neither A nor B correlate with the values of C or D, little effort will be made to find a correlation between the values of C and D. Again, if there were an isolated correlation between the values of C and D, it could be missed.

In contrast, consider Figure 10.3b. If a learner first detects the correlation between the values for A and B, this will provide no help in detecting the correlation between E and F. Because the values of neither A nor B correlate with the values of E or F, search will not focus on E and F and allow their correlation to be detected easily. Instead this correlation can only be detected by searching the entire correlation space. In the process, many more negative cases would be tested than for Figure 10.3a (e.g., testing the values for C and D).

If learners have a bias toward seeking systematicity, then VS in a category has the parallel strength and weakness of AS: VS facilitates the discovery of correlations that constitute systematicity but inhibits the discovery of isolated correlations.

Empirical Support

Billman and Heit (in press) show, computationally, that focused sampling facilitates converging on systematicity. But do people actually benefit from systematicity in the manner suggested by focused sampling? To explore this issue, Billman and her colleagues investigated adults' ability to learn the rules of a miniature, artificial language (Billman, 1983, 1985; Billman, Heit, & Dorfman, 1987). Because systematicity underlies many linguistic categories, language learning is a good place to look for focused sampling. Rich patterns of VS between semantic, morphological, phonological, agreement, and distributional attributes typically specify categories such as *noun, masculine noun,* and *noun phrase.* Consider English verbs. Their attributes include inflection with *ing,* inflection with *ed,* multiple arguments, negation with *not,* and reference to actions. Because values for no single attribute perfectly predict any linguistic category, systematicity among many attributes might be the basis for inducing these categories from the available input (Maratsos & Chalkley, 1980).

Subjects in these experiments were exposed to miniature artificial languages by observing sentences and scenes. In some conditions, the linguistic categories were specified by patterns of VS, as in Figure 10.3a. Different categories shared attributes but contrasted on their values, with values being correlated across attributes. For example, noun categories in one set of experiments were specified by correlated values for *referent type, stem vowel,* and *ending type.* In the comparison condition, the same categories were based on only one set of correlated values instead of three.

Following learning, subjects' sensitivity to each correlation was assessed when it had occurred in isolation versus when it had occurred as part of a systematic set of relations. Thus learning the identical correlation was compared with or without systematicity. If people use focused sampling, then systematicity should facilitate acquiring the target correlation, because identifying any correlation should lead to the target. But if people do not capitalize on the informativeness of an identified correlation, then systematicity should not help.

The experiments mimicked natural language acquisition in several crucial respects. All structures in the artificial language occur in some natural language but are unlike English or other common Indo-European languages. During learning, subjects watched animated displays accompanied by descriptive sentences in "Neptunese." Subjects received no tutoring or feedback about the target correlations or linguistic categories but simply observed the input sentences and scenes. Five experiments were run using several different grammars. In some, the contrasting categories were analogous to noun subcategories. In others, they were relational categories with contrasting phrase structure rules, somewhat analogous to verbs and prepositions.

Across experiments, subjects were more likely to learn a target correlation when it occurred in a pattern of systematicity than when it occurred in isolation. This suggests that learners have procedures, not only for discovering correlations, but also for selectively converging on systems of correlations. If the environment, either physical or linguistic, does provide rich "correlational structure," as Rosch and her colleagues suggested, then it is not surprising that evolution has produced this sort of learning mechanism.

INFERENCE

There are at least two different forms of category-based inference: inferring that known category information applies to a new exemplar, and inferring that new information found in an exemplar applies to a category. Systematicity facilitates the ability to draw both inferences.

Category-to-Exemplar Inferences

Imagine that Figure 10.2a represents the attribute structure of a category. If we discover that some new entity has attribute K, the systematicity underlying this category enables us to infer that the entity is likely to have attributes A, B, and L. In contrast, imagine that Figure 10.2b or 10.2c represents the attribute structure of a category. Now if we discover that some entity has attribute K, we can only infer that it also has attribute L. The same amount of given information for a new entity produces more inferred information in Figure 10.2a than in Figures 10.2b and 10.2c. As AS increases for a category, the power to produce attribute inferences increases.

VS similarly supports category-to-exemplar inferences. Imagine that the shared attributes in Figure 10.3a represent the frame for a category and that the three correlated sets of values represent three of its subcategories (e.g., A-1, B-1, E-1, and F-1 represent one subcategory). If we discover that some entity has value 1 for attribute A, we can infer that it has value 1 for attribute B, E, and F as well. In contrast, consider Figure 10.3b. If we discover that some entity has value 1 for attribute A, we can only infer that it has value 1 for attribute B. The same amount of given information produces more inferred information in Figure 10.3a than in Figure 10.3b. As VS increases for a category, the power to produce value inferences increases.

Gelman and Markman (1986, 1987) demonstrate the importance of categories in inference. When people discover that an entity belongs to a category, they assume that this licenses a variety of inferences about the entity: Attributes observed for previous category members are likely to be true of the newly assigned member. We suggest later that natural kinds and highly specific categories may typically have higher systematicity than artifacts and less specific categories. Interestingly, Gelman (1988) reports that these high-systematicity categories encourage greater inferencing than these low-systematicity categories. Consequently, systematicity appears related to drawing category-based inferences: Once we know that an entity belongs to a particular category, we are increasingly likely to infer that it exhibits category attributes to the extent those attributes are systematically related.

Exemplar-to-Category Inferences

Upon discovering that some new attribute is true of a known exemplar, people may use systematicity to draw inferences about the attribute's scope of application. One possible heuristic is to identify the exemplar's dominant category, retrieve the frame (AS) associated with that category, and integrate the new attribute into the predictive relations that the frame represents. If people are biased to seek systematicity, they may initially assume that the new attribute correlates highly with other attributes in the category's frame. Upon discovering that a particular person has a spleen, for example, children may retrieve the frame for *human* and integrate *spleen* into it.

Of course, the degree to which such inferences are drawn also depends on the particular attribute. Upon discovering that a particular car has a gas filter, people may infer that all cars have gas filters. But discovering that a particular car has a television would probably not lead to an analogous inference. People's intuitive theories of the world must be central in determining which attributes become generalized (Carey, 1985; Keil, 1987; Lakoff, 1987; McCauley, 1987; Murphy & Medin, 1985; Rips, 1988; Schank, Collins, & Hunter, 1986). The degree to which such inferences are maintained also probably reflects experience. Someone might find it plausible to infer initially that all cars have gas filters, only to modify that inference later upon discovering that some cars do not.

The integration of novel attribute values appears similar but different. If a new value is encountered for an attribute that has typically had some other value across category members, the new value may not be generalized. Discovering that a 1966 Volkswagen Bug has an oval steering wheel will probably not lead to the inference that all 1966 Bugs have oval steering wheels. Instead, previous experience with round steering wheels will dominate. But if the new value is for an attribute never before encountered, the value may be integrated with preexisting correlated values that specify the category, assuming it seems plausible to do so. Discovering that a 1982 Toyota Celica has rear disc brakes will probably lead to the inference that all 1982 Celicas have rear disc brakes, along with four-cylinder engines, rear-wheel drive, and other correlated values.

The point is that systematicity may guide the integration of new attributes and values into knowledge. A new attribute may typically be integrated into the frame (AS) for the exemplar embodying the attribute, when the attribute could plausibly apply to other category members. A new value may similarly be integrated into the appropriate set of correlated values.

Retrieval

Stability

Our central thesis is that systematicity underlies the stability of category representations. Consider how the AS in Figure 10.2a might produce stability. As we discussed earlier, the connections between attributes simultaneously represent correlational strength and conceptual relations. In the following examples, we further assume that these connections transmit spreading activation, where the amount of activation is some function of correlational strength (cf. Collins & Loftus, 1975). Imagine that attribute A in Figure 10.2a becomes active. Because A is associated with B, K, and L, activation spreads from A to these other attributes. They in turn send activation back to A and to each other, with activation passing back and forth among attributes over time. In this synergistic or quasi-connectionist manner, the pattern of attributes settles into a stable, mutually reinforcing pattern of activation.

Why would this synergistic activation of attributes produce stability? Imagine on one occasion that only K were initially active. Imagine on another occasion that only L were initially active. In both cases, the same pattern of attributes—A, B, K, and L—would eventually emerge. Regardless of which attribute is initially active, activation settles into the same pattern of attributes. Because the information activated initially for a category may vary widely, systematicity in category knowledge ensures that some stability occurs across its representations in different contexts. Along these lines, Whitlow, Smith, and Medin (1982) report that sentence sets with correlated predicates lead to better retrieval, reducing interference (fan effect) among associated items.

VS similarly produces stability. Imagine that each set of correlated values in Figure 10.3a represents a subcategory (e.g., A-1, B-1, E-1, and F-1). If A-1 becomes active on a particular occasion, activation spreads from A-1 to B-1, E-1, and F-1 to produce a stable, mutually reinforcing pattern of activation. Regardless of which value is initially active, the same pattern will always be activated for the subcategory, thereby providing its representations with stability.

Context-Independence

If a pattern of attributes or values occurs frequently enough across category members (i.e., systematicity is sufficiently high), it may develop an automatized status. When the same attributes or values occur for most members of a category, a structural change takes place in memory such that these properties are always included in category representations. This relation between consistent mapping and obligatory (automatic) activation has been widely documented in the attention literature (e.g., Schneider & Shiffrin, 1977; Shiffrin & Schneider, 1977). Barsalou (1982, 1987, 1989) refers to information that acquires this status as being "context-independent" and proposes that it provides one kind of core information for categories.

Explanatory Attributes

Attributes may often become context-independent after being frequently perceived in exemplars (e.g., *wings* for *birds*). However, other attributes that are often hidden from view may also become prominent because they explain surface attributes (Wellman & Gelman, 1988; also see Carey, 1985; Fiske & Taylor, 1984; Keil, 1987; Lakoff, 1987; McCauley, 1987; Miller & Johnson-Laird, 1976; Murphy & Medin, 1985; Nelson, 1974, 1978; Rips, 1988; Schank et al., 1986). Examples of such attributes include spiritual essences, personality traits, cognitive abilities, internal organs, genes, atomic structure, and so forth. Explanatory attributes may generally provide higher-order organization of lower-level relations, as discussed earlier.

To the extent these hidden attributes frequently play a role in the comprehension and representation of exemplars, they may acquire an obligatory, context-independent status. But to the extent they are rarely utilized in processing, they may typically remain inactive. Because the chemical composition of H_2O is rarely relevant to our interactions with water, for example, it does not acquire a context-independent status. Consequently, information that is logically or epistemologically fundamental in some sense does not necessarily have to be present in category representations (cf. Putnam, 1977). Instead, information may only be context-independent to the extent that it is frequently perceived and/or relevant to interacting with category members. This does not imply that people cannot retrieve and use more fundamental information in relevant situations. Nor does it imply that people's normal representations are explanatorily incoherent.[7]

Instability

Instability in retrieval can also be understood in terms of AS and VS. Consider Figure 10.2a. Because attributes A, B, K, and L occur across most category members, they are strongly interconnected. As defined earlier, other pairs of attributes idiosyncratically co-occur but not systematically

---

[7]Obviously our view implies that people typically do not represent categories in a classical manner, namely, with necessary and sufficient attributes. This implication is consistent with the last 20 years of categorization research (Medin & Smith, 1984; Mervis & Rosch, 1981; Oden, 1987; Smith & Medin, 1981).

(e.g., B-C, G-H, J-K). Assume that these idiosyncratically co-occurring attributes are connected by weak pathways that transmit small amounts of activation. Consequently, when A, B, K, and L are activated via their strong pathways, they send small amounts of activation to attributes C through J. Because these latter relations are weak and do not form systematicities, they compete for the limited activation remaining. The attributes that eventually become activated may vary, depending on which receive the most activation on a particular occasion. Although A, B, K, and L are always activated, thereby producing stability across contexts, these attributes may additionally activate D and G on one occasion but F and J on another, thereby producing instability.

Low VS produces instability in a similar manner. Consider the subcategory defined by the correlations between values A-1, B-1, E-1, and F-1 in Figure 10.3a. If A-1 becomes active, it produces stability in representations of the subcategory by also activating B-1, E-1, and F-1. But because these values are not strongly associated to values for attributes C and D, the values activated for C and D may vary, thereby producing instability across contexts.

VS can also produce instability in another way. Consider the category represented by the frame in Figure 10.3a, that is, the set of exemplars that share attributes A, B, C, D, E, and F. As discussed earlier, this frame provides stability for category representations at the attribute level. However, representations of this category may also contain value information, even if it is irrelevant to defining the category. On one occasion, A-1, B-1, E-1, and F-1 may be active; but on another A-2, B-2, E-2, and F-2 may be active, thereby producing instability. Correlated patterns of values activated in this manner produce instability because they compete with one another for activation during retrieval. When representing *bird,* for example, people may not simply activate *bird* attributes but may also instantiate them with values for a particular subcategory (e.g., *sea gull* on one occasion and *bluejay* on another).[8]

However, if one set of correlated values occurs much more frequently than all others, it may provide a set of *default values* for the frame. Under these circumstances, the default values may generally dominate the competition between correlated sets of values. As a result, the default values may reduce instability and increase stability in representations of the category specified by the frame.

Finally, correlated sets of values may provide *norms* by which current events are judged (cf. Kahneman & Miller, 1986). Certain values of an event—those that are immutable, according to Kahneman and Miller—

[8]Value instability again implies that people do not represent categories in a classical manner. Instead, people often instantiate attributes with values that overly specify the category (Anderson, Pichert, Goetz, Schallert, Stevens, & Trollip, 1976).

may be used to access a pattern of values in a frame containing the immutable values. Other values in this pattern then provide predictions about their counterparts in the current event. If the predicted and observed values match, the event is normal; if they mismatch, the event is surprising. Because many patterns of correlated values exist within a single frame, many possible norms can be constructed, one for each pattern of values. Moreover, each pattern of values can serve as a norm for any value in the pattern that might be viewed as immutable on a particular occasion.

Determinants of Instability

What factors underlie the competition that produces instability? We assume that three determinants of activation play central roles: frequency, recency, and context (Barsalou, 1987, 1989). We further assume that these determinants affect retrieval through standard associative mechanisms found in spreading activation models.

Attributes and values vary in how frequently they occur for a category. We assume that frequent attributes and values are most likely to be activated, all other factors being equal. To the extent that attributes and values vary across exemplars, they compete, and more frequent information dominates. If people differ in the attributes and values they frequently experience, instability occurs between individuals.

Attributes and values vary in how recently they have occurred for a category. We assume that recent attributes and values are most likely to be activated, all other factors being equal. Because recent attributes and values vary across people for the same category, instability occurs between individuals. Similarly, because recent attributes and values vary at different points in time for the same person, instability occurs within individuals.

Attributes and values vary in how relevant they are to the current context. We assume that attributes and values currently relevant are most likely to be activated, all other factors being equal. We assume that context effects emerge from patterns of systematicity: When part of a systematicity occurs as context, it activates other parts of the systematicity that are currently inactive. For example, knowing that an animal *lives in trees* and *flies* serves as context to activate related attribute values such as *feathers* and *beak* in the frame for *animal.*

Systematicity in Primitive Forms of Knowledge

We next explore how AS and VS manifest themselves in human knowledge. In this section, we consider the systematicity that underlies three primitive forms: *ontological kinds, basic object frames,* and *basic event frames.* By "primitive," we mean that these three forms of knowledge arise naturally and effortlessly from experience during early childhood. In a later section, we propose that more abstract forms of knowledge evolve from these primitive forms. In our discussions of basic object frames and basic event frames, we explore their propensity for producing stability and instability in category representations.

Ontological Kinds

Ontology concerns the fundamentally different kinds of things in existence. We assume that fundamental kinds exist and that some of these are ever-present and unavoidable in human experience and activity. As a result, we believe that evolution has biologically prepared human cognitive systems for perceiving and understanding these ontological kinds. In particular, we suggest that *location, time, agent, action* and *object* are five ontological kinds that fundamentally structure human experience. These five kinds have been widely noted by philosophers, linguists, and psychologists as being central to language, knowledge, and thought (see Miller & Johnson-Laird, 1976, for a review). After we summarize our rationale for including these kinds in a fundamental ontology, we contrast our approach with the one taken by Keil (1979, 1981).

Location. Every event that an individual experiences occurs in a location. Moreover, there is one invariant domain of locations that every human habitates, namely, earth. Although we do not all experience the same locations, those we individually know all have the same local Euclidean properties and are interconnected spatially in an invariant configuration. It is now widely believed that evolution has endowed humans with neurological specialization for navigating this environment (e.g., O'Keefe & Nadel's, 1978, 1979, work on spatial mapping of the hippocampus). This biological preparedness for perceiving and navigating space can be construed as knowledge of an ontological kind. It seems reasonable to assume that infants come into the world ready to understand that locations are points in space and that these points differ fundamentally from other kinds of things in experience.

Time. Every event occurs at some time. Adults may often fix the time of an event with respect to abstract temporal systems for minutes, hours, days, weeks, months, and years. In the absence of such knowledge, infants may often fix the time of events with respect to meaningful cycles and patterns in their lives (e.g., eating, sleeping, day/night, schedules of parents). Moreover, the temporal position of an event may often be encoded relative to other events occurring within the same temporal window (e.g., an infant might code being picked up as occurring after seeing a parent enter the room). Much work on animal conditioning can be viewed as having investigated the parameters of relative temporal coding.

Agent and Action. Infants learn quickly that they are agents who can produce actions on the world to achieve goals. Consequently, it seems reasonable to suppose that infants understand agency and action at an early age. Moreover, such understanding may readily extend to recognizing external agents and their actions. We suspect that children's readiness to perceive causality (Baillargeon, Spelke, & Wasserman, 1985) is closely related to their ability to perceive agency.

Object. Actions are typically performed on objects. Infants pick up rattles, throw food, cuddle stuffed animals, and so forth. In general, the understanding of *agent* and *action* seems closely bound with an understanding of what agents act on, namely, objects. By "object" we do not mean the category of "physical objects" in Keil's (1979, 1981) ontology, namely, physical entities that are inanimate, well-bounded, and movable. Instead, for the remainder of this paper, we will use "object" when referring to entities on which agents act. We will use "physical object" when referring to the physical sense of "object." These two senses are correlated in that many of the things on which people act are physical objects. Spelke's (1982) finding that infants understand the physical sense of *object* at a very early age therefore appears consistent with our view.

Intuitive Theory of Intentional Events

Because humans have evolved in an environment where *location, time, agent, action,* and *object* are ever-present, they may have developed biological predispositions for using these kinds. Moreover, these kinds may constitute the fundamental ontology of human experience, at least in infancy. Additional ontological kinds probably develop later. Of these, we imagine that *mental events* and *instrument* are universal and necessary, given most humans probably understand them after sufficient development.

We believe that *location, time, agent, action,* and *object* are central concepts in an intuitive theory that people have of intentional events. According to this theory, an intentional event occurs whenever an agent performs an action on some object in a particular location at a particular time. We assume that this intuitive theory is available early in infancy and structures infants' understanding of their interactions with the world. As we propose shortly, this intuitive theory also constrains the development of other primitive forms of knowledge.

Roles versus Essences

Our ontological kinds differ somewhat from those in Keil (1979, 1981; also see Sommers, 1959, 1963). Keil's ontology appears heavily driven by logical and scientific concerns. His ontological kinds conform to formal criteria (e.g., the *M* constraint) and often appear based on scientific distinctions (e.g., between *plant* and *animal*). In contrast, our ontological framework is not an attempt to provide an objective or formal account of the kinds of things in existence. Instead our ontological kinds are more related to how people perceive their interactions with the world. Although some of Keil's kinds overlap with ours, some of his others rely on cultural and scientific theories acquired after infancy (e.g., *plants* versus *animals*). Instead, we assume that our five kinds have a biological basis in the human cognitive system and emerge early in infancy to support initial interactions with the environment.

Perhaps the fundamental difference between our ontological kinds and Keil's is that ours concern how people perceive the *roles* of entities in intentional events, whereas Keil's concern how people perceive the *essences* of the entities in existence. In our scheme, *apple* would be classified as an *object,* because apples often serve as objects on which agents act. In Keil's system, an apple would be classified as a *plant,* which defines its essence.

We believe that people develop both sets of distinctions. However, we believe that people's knowledge of many essences often develops later than *location, time, agent, action,* and *object.* Moreover, much of people's knowledge of essences may be better construed as belonging to their knowledge of taxonomic superordinates. As we discuss in a later section, taxonomic superordinates are abstract categories that organize the kinds of things in the world according to their essences. Although taxonomic superordinates are usually assumed to be categories like *tool, vehicle,* and *fruit,* we believe that many of the ontological kinds in Keil (1979, 1981) are also taxonomic superordinates (e.g., *plant, human, animal, living thing, artifact*).

Systematicity

What attributes define the categories of *location, time, agent, action,* and *object?* This is a very difficult problem. Similar to Johnson-Laird (1983, 1987), we believe that these categories are specified in cognitive systems well below the level of consciousness. Although humans have the cognitive machinery to recognize these kinds, it is not available for inspection. We suspect that theoretical analyses, similar to those on syntactic mechanisms, could be performed on ontological kinds. We do not attempt such analyses here (cf. Keil, 1979, 1981).

However, we assume that a set of co-occurring attributes defines each ontological kind to provide it with AS. For example, *physical, movable,* and *causal* appear to co-occur as attributes of *agents.* Because these attributes co-occur across many agents, they provide some AS for the category. Whatever the attributes happen to be, we suspect that the human cognitive system is biologically prepared to perceive them as a correlated set that defines the ontological kind. Because we do not have much to say about the attributes that underlie ontological kinds, we also do not have much to say about their VS. Nor do we have much to say about their stability and instability. Our main point is that ontological kinds provide a primitive form of knowledge that probably depends to a large extent on biologically based AS. As we discuss in later sections, this knowledge appears central to other forms of knowledge.

Basic Object Frames

Basic object frames are another primitive form of human knowledge. We assume that they represent a more specific level of categorization than ontological kinds and rely much more on experience. Basic object frames represent basic-level categories of physical objects, agents, and locations. In general, a basic object frame captures the topological structure that generally occurs for a particular kind of physical entity. We first address the partonomies that represent exemplars, where "partonomy" refers to an exemplar's topological structure. We then address how these partonomies are generalized to form the basic object frames that represent basic-level categories. Finally, we address how subordinate-level categories and mental models for physical systems develop from basic object frames.

Exemplars

We assume that an innate perceptual system "parses" the topological structure of a physical entity into visual primitives.[9] We adopt Biederman's (1987) proposal that the biologically based primitives in visual perception are geons. However, our argument would probably remain unchanged if visual primitives turn out to take some other form. Geons are generalized-cone components such as blocks, cylinders, and wedges derived from five robustly detectable properties of two-dimensional images (curvature, collinearity, symmetry, parallelism, and cotermination). As shown in Figure 10.4a, six geons represent the typical airplane: one cylindrical geon for the body, two large triangular geons for the wings, and three smaller triangular geons for the tail. Biederman (1987) presents numerous arguments for why geons might be the elemental attributes of visual perception.

The geons extracted from a visual stimulus are integrated by spatial, part-whole relations to form a hierarchical partonomy (cf. Palmer, 1977, 1983). In the partonomy for a human body, geons for fingers and the palm are integrated by spatial relations into a hand, which is then integrated by another spatial relation with the arm, which is then integrated by another spatial relation with the body. These partonomies integrate the parts of a physical entity according to their spatial relations and nestings. We assume that Gestalt mechanisms of perceptual organization play a central role in

[9]We realize that we are glossing over important epistemological issues concerning the veridicality, or "realism," of perception. For convenience, we assume that perception is reasonably veridical and that the structure of perceptions typically bears a strong correlation with the structure of physical entities.

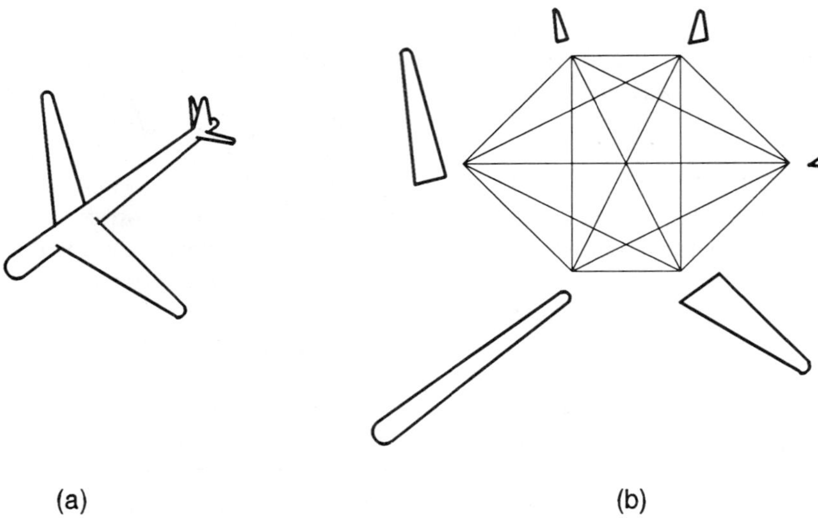

FIGURE 10.4. (a) The configuration of geons for *airplane.* (b) The AS between the attributes (geons) for *airplane.*

this process. Miller and Johnson-Laird (1976), Markman and Seibert (1976), Nelson (1978), and Tversky and Hemenway (1984) discuss partonomies in perception and categorization. Chafin and Herrmann (1987) and Winston, Chafin, and Herrmann (1987) present a taxonomy of part-whole relations.

The partonomy for an individual exemplar usually exhibits perfect systematicity. Because the same geons are always present for the exemplar across situations—unless its physical structure changes—each co-occurs with all the others, as shown in Figure 10.4b. As we discussed earlier for decomposition, the relations in Figure 10.4b do not simply represent correlations but also represent conceptual relations, in this case, spatial relations. We assume that spatial relations do not originate in conscious, effortful computation. Instead, they originate implicitly and automatically during the operation of biologically based perceptual mechanisms (cf. O'Keefe & Nadel, 1978, 1979). Consequently, we assume that two relational forms of information are computed for geons that co-occur in a partonomy: correlational information and spatial information.

Basic-Level Categories

Imagine that a person experiences different exemplars that have the same partonomy. We assume that this shared partonomy is induced to form a *basic object frame.* The geons in the partonomy become attributes in the frame and take on different values across exemplars. A child encountering several different airplanes that have the same partonomy might induce a basic object frame for *airplane.* Encountering several different humans should similarly produce a basic object frame for the human body.

As noted by numerous investigators, basic-level categories are privileged: They are learned earlier in development than other categories; they are processed more quickly; and they are used more often for labeling (Jolicoeur, Gluck, & Kosslyn, 1984; Mervis, 1987; Murphy & Brownell, 1985; Murphy & Smith, 1982; Rosch et al., 1976; Tversky & Hemenway, 1984). Rosch et al. (1976) concluded that the basic level's optimality reflects its informativeness and parsimony: Categories at the basic level capture much information with a relatively small number of categories. However, Tversky and Hemenway (1984) reassessed Rosch et al.'s arguments and concluded instead that basic-level categories are optimal because they share the same components in the same configuration (i.e., basic object frames). More recently, Biederman (1987) has argued that geons are the primitive attributes underlying partonomies at the basic level. Consequently, there is some controversy over what constitutes the basic level.

We believe that the basic level may be relative to particular categorization processes: Different taxonomic levels may be optimal for different processes. We therefore distinguish between a *perceptual basic level* and an *informational basic level.*

The perceptual basic level contains those categories processed the fastest and therefore made first during the perception of a stimulus. If a configuration of geons is the first information available for an exemplar, then the category defined by this basic object frame should be perceptually basic. According to this view, the perceptual basic level does not change with expertise, contrary to Rosch et al. (1976). Because more specific categories share the same basic object frame, they compete with each other during categorization and thereby slow processing (for relevant evidence, see Jolicoeur et al., 1984; Murphy & Brownell, 1985; Murphy & Smith, 1982). In contrast, different categories at the basic level compete less because they do not share a basic object frame.

An implication of this view is that basic object frames determine the basic level in perception, independent of the conceptual and linguistic organization of categories. As a number of investigators have noted, atypical members of basic-level categories are categorized faster at the subordinate level than at the basic level (Biederman, 1987; Jolicoeur et al., 1984; Murphy & Brownell, 1985; Tversky & Hemenway, 1984). Consider *rocking chair,* which does not share the basic object frame associated with the majority of chairs. Rather than being initially categorized with the basic object frame for *chair,* rocking chairs are categorized with their own basic object frame. As a result, categorizing them into *rocking chairs* proceeds more rapidly in perception than categorizing them into *chairs.* Initial access into the conceptual system appears to occur through categories defined by basic object frames.

Categorization need not stop at the perceptual basic level. Whereas novices may stop at this level because it is the easiest to process, experts may continue categorizing a stimulus to an informational basic level, namely, to more specific categories that carry more information. Thus the informational basic level may vary with expertise, even though the perceptual basic level remains constant. The informational basic level may also be more important to language than the perceptual basic level. As noted by Cruse (1977), speakers select categories that optimize reference according to pragmatics of the current situation. In some situations, categories below the basic level may best communicate the speaker's intended meaning. In others, categories above the basic level may be preferable.

Privileged Status of Basic Object Frames

Categories at the perceptual basic level exhibit high AS because their members contain the same attributes (geons) in the same configuration. Even though the values for these attributes vary across exemplars in *length, color, texture,* etc., the same partonomic attributes always co-occur. If cognitive systems are biased toward discovering patterns of systematicity, as we proposed earlier, then acquiring categories at the perceptual basic level should be facilitated.

Moreover, because the detection of geons and spatial relations is biologically built into perceptual mechanisms, the information necessary for acquiring basic object frames is available very early in development. Learning and conscious attention are not central to utilizing geons and spatial relations successfully. Instead basic object frames are induced effortlessly and reliably from experience with the physical world. Because geons and spatial relations are privileged in the cognitive system, we believe that basic object frames are fundamental to human knowledge and play a central role in many other forms of knowledge.

We noted earlier that a fundamental problem in accounting for AS and VS is specifying the critical attributes in induction (Armstrong et al., 1983; Carey, 1985; Goodman, 1955; Lakoff, 1987; McCauley, 1987; Murphy & Medin, 1985; Schank et al., 1986). For basic object frames, this problem appears manageable: The relevant attributes are simply the primitive shape attributes of visual perception. If one believes that Biederman's (1987) account is correct, then the problem is essentially solved, because Biederman specifies a relatively complete set of possible primitives. The related problem of how to identify the relevant relations between attributes also appears manageable. Here we can simply assume that spatial, part-whole relations are sufficient (O'Keefe & Nadel, 1978, 1979). For both the attributes and relations in basic object frames, evolution appears to have solved the relevance problem for us.

Subordinate Categories

Within basic-level categories, more specific, subordinate categories may develop for salient patterns of VS. In *bird,* for example, salient patterns of

VS may produce *robin, pigeon,* and *bluejay.* Subordinate categories may provide natural contrasts with each other because they share a basic object frame but differ on the values of its attributes.

The values that define subordinate categories, rather than being the basic shapes that constitute geons, may often provide additional information about geons (e.g., *size, texture*). Biederman (1987) argues that the visual system needs more time to extract this information than geons. If so, then subordinate categories should generally take longer to identify than basic-level categories. Moreover, because subordinates of a basic-level category share a common basic object frame, discriminating and learning them may generally be more difficult than learning the basic-level category. The literature on basic-level categories has produced similar conclusions (Jolicoeur et al., 1984; Mervis, 1987; Murphy & Brownell, 1985; Murphy & Smith, 1982; Rosch et al., 1976; Tversky & Hemenway, 1984).

Returning to our earlier discussion of exemplars, they too can be viewed as sets of correlated values, where the values are more specific than those that specify subordinate categories. Viewing exemplars as sets of correlated attribute values is similar to Medin and Schaffer's (1978) and Hintzman's (1986) relational view of exemplar representation. Although we believe that people store extensive information about exemplars, we do not believe, as these theorists apparently do, that exemplars are stored independently of one another in memory. Instead, because exemplars of the same basic- or subordinate-level category share a basic object frame, they are integrated into memory as correlated sets of attribute values that instantiate the same frame. Because many exemplars instantiate a frame, much potential for interference between them exists (see Barsalou, 1988, for an example of how events can be represented in this manner).

Hidden Parts and Mental Models

People often know more parts for a physical entity than those that compose its exterior. Internal parts may be directly perceived on some occasions (e.g., cutting a piece of fruit, disassembling a car engine). Or knowledge about them may be acquired indirectly through hearsay and instruction (e.g., studying the internal organs of the human body in school). To varying extents, people may integrate the spatial locations of internal and external parts (e.g., noting that the brain is in the head and that the heart is in the chest). In this sense, the representation of internal parts is a natural extension of the basic object frames that underlie categories at the perceptual basic level.

However, the representation of internal parts may often produce causal and temporal relations between attributes in basic object frames (e.g., the brain causes the limbs and sense organs to move; food passes from the stomach to the intestine). Causal and temporal relations, coupled with basic object frames, form "mental models" that can simulate the behavior of category members. Given an input to such a model, one can manipulate attributes and relations of the basic object frame to predict intermediate states and final outcomes (Gentner & Stevens, 1983; Johnson-Laird, 1983; Rasmussen, 1986). We assume that these internal parts often impose higher-order structure on lower-level relations, as we discussed earlier (cf. Gentner, 1983, 1988). Internal parts also appear central to the intuitive theories that people have about categories (e.g., Keil, 1987; McCauley, 1987; Murphy & Medin, 1985; Rips, 1988; Wellman & Gelman, 1988).

Stability and Instability

A number of hypotheses concerning stability and instability follow from our analysis. In most cases, not much evidence exists to assess these hypotheses. Therefore they should be viewed as issues for future research. Similar subsections on stability and instability in later sections provide hypotheses of a similar ilk. For reviews of the current evidence, see Barsalou (1987, 1989).

Basic object frames should provide a major source of stability for basic- and subordinate-level categories. Because the same geons occur for most members of the category, this pattern of AS should become well entrenched in memory. Generally when an exemplar of *airplane* occurs, the same geons apply. Moreover because these geons apply in most contexts, they become consistently mapped to "airplane" such that reading or hearing it activates these attributes in a context-independent manner. When Barsalou, Spindler, Sewell, Ballato, and Gendel (1987) performed a content analysis of subjects' word definitions, they found that parts were frequently mentioned (cf. Rosch et al., 1976; Tversky & Hemenway, 1984).

For subordinate categories and exemplars, VS should provide further stability. Because correlated sets of values specify subordinates and exemplars across contexts, these sets should become well entrenched in memory. Every time one's pet *golden retriever* is encountered, a similar set of attribute values is present. Later, in constructing representations for this exemplar, its correlated set of values should provide additional stability beyond the basic object frame associated with *dog*. Consequently, representations of subordinates and exemplars should exhibit more stability than representations of basic-level categories.

Variability in value information should produce instability. If basic-level categories are primarily specified by basic object frames, then much potential exists for instability at the level of values. Consider representations of *chair*. The representation on one occasion might specify that the legs are *short, brown,* and *rough;* whereas on another it might specify them as being *long, white,* and *smooth*. As we discussed earlier, the activation of different values may depend on frequency, recency, and context.

Representations of subordinate categories and exemplars may also exhibit variability in values. But because these representations exhibit some stability in value information, there should be less potential for variability.

Instead, variability in value information should become increasingly subtle.

Basic Event Frames

We assume that basic event frames are another primitive form of knowledge. As we discuss later, both children and adults appear to extract basic event frames naturally and effortlessly from experience. We first address the partonomies that represent individual events. An "event partonomy" represents the various parts of an event (e.g., the agent, action, object, location, and time) and their relations to one another, (e.g., spatial, temporal, causal, and intentional relations). We then address how these partonomies are generalized to form the basic event frames that represent what we will refer to as "summarized events."

Individual Events

Following our previous discussion and Barsalou (1988), we assume that a physical event includes entities from multiple ontological domains. A typical event includes an agent, action, object, location, and time. Consider the example in Figure 10.5a: A child (agent) plays catch (actions) with a

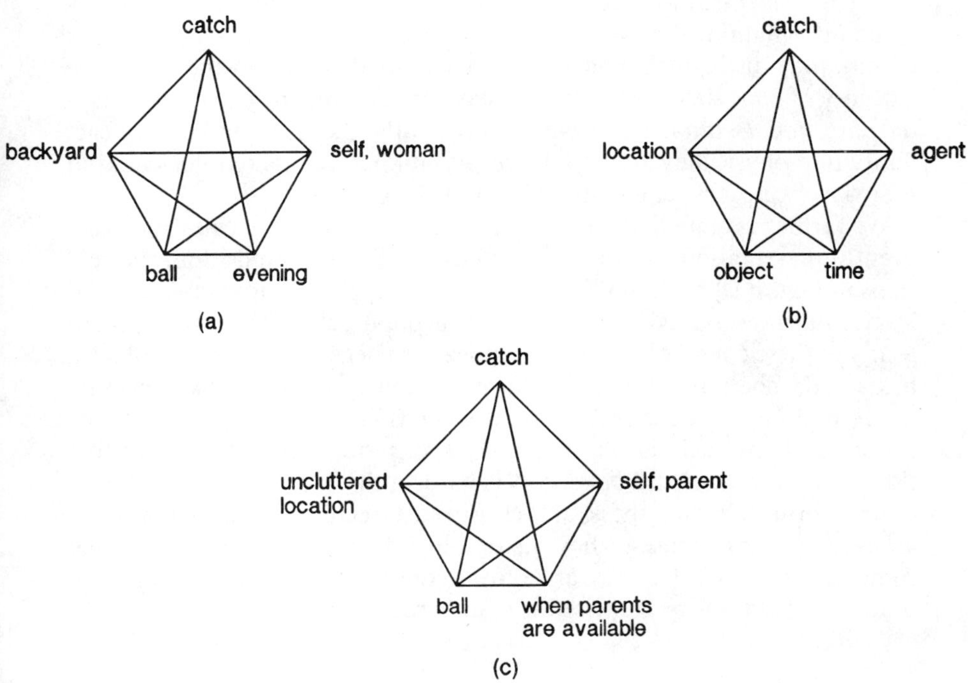

FIGURE 10.5. (a) A basic event frame. (b) A generalized action. (c) A generalized action with two goal-derived categories.

woman (agent) using a ball (object) in a backyard (location) in the evening (time). In other words, the parts of a physical event are the relevant ontological entities. We assume that events may often have additional parts, such as *instruments, patients,* and *experiencers.* To simplify our presentation of event partonomies and basic event frames, we do not consider them here.

We assume that people categorize the entities in a physical event at two levels. First, each entity is classified according to people's intuitive theory of intentional events.[10] Consequently, the relevant entities are classified as *agent, action, object, location,* and *time.* Second, each entity is classified more specifically at the basic level. For example, the physical ball in the event for Figure 10.5a is classified both as *object* and as *ball;* the actions are classified both as *actions* and as *catch.* Consequently, the ontological kinds can be seen as attributes that take the basic-level categories as values.

We assume that basic-level categories exist in every ontological domain. People have been shown to have basic-level categories, not only for physical objects, but also for people (Cantor & Mischel, 1979), locations (Tversky & Hemenway, 1983), and activities (Rifkin, 1985). Although we are not entirely clear at this point what the basic-level categories are in each ontological domain, nor on what structural principles underlie them, we assume that there is a preferred or "basic" level of categorization in each.

We further assume that the representations of event entities include value information. If a ball is part of an event, values for *color, size,* and *texture* may distinguish it as a particular individual within the basic-level category of *ball.* Value information may similarly distinguish exemplars of *agent, action, location,* and *time.* Consequently, the representation of each entity in a physical event includes information about its ontological kind, basic-level category, and distinguishing values.

We further assume that relations integrate the basic-level categories in an event representation. As we discussed earlier for decomposition, the relations in Figure 10.5a do not simply represent co-occurrence between basic-level categories but also represent conceptual relations between them. Many of these conceptual relations appear privileged by virtue of biological bases in the cognitive system. We have in mind spatial relations such as *on, in, at,* and *beside;* temporal relations such as *before, after,* and *co-occurs;* causal relations such as *cause, enable,* and *prevent;* and intentional relations such as *intend* and *believe.* It is hard to think of relations any more basic or primitive than these, and clearly such relations must be applied to an event to make sense of how its ontological entities interact. Although some of these relations may arise from conscious and effortful computation, we would not be surprised if many are assigned implicitly and auto-

[10]Although we only address intentional events in this paper, we assume that children may learn to understand nonintentional, or "natural," events by assimilating them to their knowledge of intentional events.

matically during the experience of an event (cf. Hasher & Zacks, 1979; Johnson-Laird, 1983, 1987; Michotte, 1963; Miller & Johnson-Laird, 1976; O'Keefe & Nadel, 1978, 1979).

Consequently, conceptual relations integrate the representations of the ontological entities in an event to form an event partonomy (Abbot, Black, & Smith, 1985; Barsalou & Sewell, 1985; Bower, Black, & Turner, 1979; Nelson, Fivush, Hudson, & Lucariello, 1983; Nelson & Gruendel, 1981). Higher-order relations may further integrate lower-level relations to create hierarchical relational structures (cf. Gentner, 1983, 1988).

Summarized Events

Imagine that a child experiences several events, each having the same partonomy as Figure 10.5a. For example, the ball might differ across events, the woman might differ across events, the backyard might differ across events, and so forth. But in all cases, each event involves playing catch with a woman using a ball in a backyard during the evening. We assume that the shared partonomy is induced to form a *basic event frame* that represents the category of events sharing this structure. The basic-level categories in the partonomy become attributes in the frame, taking on different values across individual events. Note that the basic-level categories serve as *attributes* in this manner while simultaneously serving as *values* for the ontological kinds of *agent, action, object, location,* and *time.* Basic event frames appear similar to the event knowledge that Rosch (1978) explored.

Event categories like these are close to what many theorists have referred to as "scripts" (Schank & Abelson 1977). However, we reserve "script" for a more complicated form of event knowledge to be discussed later. Instead basic event frames, such as the one in Figure 10.5a, underlie "summarized events." Barsalou (1988) reports that summarized events are ubiquitous in adult knowledge. In describing events from a past time period, adults recall things like "I drank wine in Paris cafes with friends in the afternoon after classes." These summarized events generalize over a very specific type of event that occurred repetitively in a person's experience and that was idiosyncratic to the person (or to a small group of people). Consequently, summarized events constitute an idiosyncratic form of generalized knowledge.

Analogous to the partonomy for an individual event, we assume that spatial, temporal, causal, and intentional relations integrate the attributes (basic-level categories) of a basic event frame. We also assume that goals often provide higher-order relations that integrate first-order relations. In all cases, relations carry both conceptual and correlational information. Furthermore, a basic event frame constitutes a mental model that supports "simulations" of that kind of event: Given initial-state values for certain attributes, it may be possible to "run the model" and generate intermediate- and terminal-state values for the event. It may also be possible to run such models in reverse, given terminal-state values as input.

Privileged Status of Basic Event Frames

Basic event frames exhibit high AS because the events that instantiate them have the same attributes integrated by the same relations. Even though the values for these attributes vary across specific events, the same basic-level categories always occur as attributes, and the same conceptual relations always integrate these attributes. If cognitive systems are biased toward discovering patterns of systematicity, as we proposed earlier, then acquiring basic event frames should be facilitated.

Moreover, the attributes and relations that compose basic event frames may be available early in development. Because the acquisition of basic-level categories is privileged (as proposed earlier), the attributes that specify basic event frames are readily available. Similarly, if spatial, temporal, causal, and intentional relations have biological bases in cognitive systems, then the relations that structure basic event frames should also be readily available. As a result, people may induce these frames with little computation or supporting knowledge. As we suggest in the next section, several forms of abstract knowledge appear to evolve from basic event frames.

Developmental psychologists report that acquiring generalized event knowledge occurs early and effortlessly during early childhood (Nelson et al., 1983; Nelson & Gruendel, 1981). Children as young as 2 and 3 acquire generalized event representations for frequently experienced events. Moreover, children often acquire these representations from as few as two similar events. Because these investigators have utilized methodologies that rely on language, it is possible that evidence for generalized event representations might be found at earlier ages. As any parent can testify, infants quickly develop expectations about familiar events. The developmental evidence is therefore consistent with the claim that basic event frames are a relatively primitive form of knowledge.

We noted earlier that strong constraints on attributes and relations in vision may make the induction problem tractable for basic object frames. Similar, although lesser, constraints exist for basic event frames. If the relevant attributes are basic-level categories in ontological domains, then this provides some constraint on attributes: The set of relevant attributes is whatever basic-level categorizations have been made in the current context. If the relevant relations are spatial, temporal, causal, and intentional relations, then this provides some constraint on relations.

However, these constraints are insufficient. In Figure 10.5a, for example, a doghouse in the backyard may be irrelevant to playing catch and should not be included. One way to rule out irrelevant basic-level categories like this is to include only categories that are related to the intentional actions of the event. Actions may typically provide a major source of constraint on attributes and their relations to one another. In Figure 10.5a, for example, if neither participant gets on the doghouse during catch, never throws the ball in there as part of the game, and so forth, then the doghouse is unrelated to the actions of the event. On the other hand, if doghouses typically enter into the actions, then *doghouse* should become an attribute.

Subordinate Events

The values of the attributes in a basic event frame are representations of particular ontological entities (e.g., particular balls, women, backyards, times of evening). Regardless of variability in values, all events sharing the basic event frame have high AS, because they share the same relational configuration of basic-level categories as attributes. VS may be high or low depending on whether the values of these attributes are correlated across events. If values for *ball* are highly predictive of values for *woman, backyard,* and *time of evening,* then the category has high VS. Playing catch with a tennis ball could typically co-occur with Aunt Mary in her backyard in the early evening; whereas playing catch with a softball could typically co-occur with Mom in the family backyard in the late evening. To the extent such patterns of values exist, subordinates of a summarized event may develop.

Although the values of summarized events often vary, they may also remain constant. For example, playing catch may always involve Mom and a particular softball (constant values) but occur in different backyards and at different times of evening (varying values). When values remain constant, they reduce variability, thereby decreasing the potential for VS across subordinate events. To the extent that values vary for *all* attributes, and to the extent that these values are correlated, a basic event frame exhibits maximum VS.

Stability and Instability

Basic event frames should provide a major source of stability in the representations of summarized events. Because the same basic-level attributes occur for most instances of a summarized event, the pattern of systematicity they represent should become well established in memory. For subordinate events, VS should provide further stability. Subordinate events should exhibit more stability than summarized events because instances of a subordinate event share both attributes and values, whereas instances of a summarized event share only attributes.

Variability in value information should produce instability. Even though the basic event frame for a summarized event provides its representations with stability, its attributes may take on different values across contexts. When thinking about the summarized event for playing catch in Figure 10.5a, a child may retrieve values for *Aunt Mary* and *tennis ball* on one occasion but retrieve values for *Mom* and *softball* on another. Different values may become activated simply as a function of frequency, recency, and context.

Representations of subordinate events may also exhibit variability in value information. But because these representations exhibit some stability in the values common to their instances, there should be less potential for instability. Instead the variability of value information should become increasingly subtle.

Systematicity in Abstract Forms of Knowledge

We turn next to more abstract forms of knowledge that evolve from the primitive forms: *generalized actions, scripts, taxonomic superordinates,* and *goal-derived categories.* In general, as the abstractness of a category increases relative to primitive forms of knowledge, the following phenomena occur: (1) The total number of attributes that could be true of *some* category member increases; (2) the total number of attributes true of *most* members decreases (i.e., AS decreases); (3) the attributes common to a category become increasingly abstract; (4) the conceptual relations integrating common attributes become conceptually weaker; (5) VS decreases across attributes common to all members. For these reasons, abstract forms of knowledge are not as salient and easy to learn. Individuals may therefore vary widely in the attributes induced for these categories and in the relations integrating them. We will argue that people's intuitive theories about the world play their most important role in structuring these abstract forms of knowledge (Carey, 1985; Keil, 1987; Lakoff, 1987; McCauley, 1987; Murphy & Medin, 1985; Rips, 1988; Schank et al., 1986).

Generalized Actions

We begin with generalized actions because other forms of abstract knowledge appear to be derived from them. As we just discussed, basic event frames are readily acquired event partonomies, whose attributes are basic-level categories in the ontological domains that compose physical events. These basic-level categories specify which entities from their respective ontological domains occur in the events that the frame represents. In Figure 10.5a, for example, the basic-level category *backyard* specifies that instances of this summarized event only occur in backyards and not in other locations.

Generalized actions develop when the entities from an ontological domain do not fall within a single basic-level category. Playing catch might occur in a street, in a playground, and in a living room—not just in backyards. Consequently, *backyard* (Figure 10.5a) might become maximally generalized to specify that playing catch simply occurs in some *location* (Figure 10.5b). Similarly, if *time* varied across all times of day, then *evening* (Figure 10.5a) might generalize to *time* (Figure 10.5b). When values in ontological domains vary widely, a generalized action category develops for *catch,* whose attributes remain specific only in the action domain (as shown in Figure 10.5b). The other nonaction attributes generalize to ontological kinds (and also to taxonomic superordinates and goal-derived categories, as discussed shortly).

Generalized actions should be more difficult to acquire than basic event frames, because they require exposure to a wider range of events. However, generalized actions maintain a high degree of AS, because the same attributes apply to all events: All events that are instances of a generalized action category have a common action and the same generalized attributes. The particular basic event frames that instantiate a generalized action may further provide it with high VS, because the value for one attribute may often predict values for others. If the object for *catch* is a football, then this somewhat predicts that the location is a football field, that the agents are male, and that the time is afternoon.

We assume that generalized actions underlie the representations of many action verbs. The argument structures of action verbs often map onto the attributes of generalized actions. For "throw," verb arguments for *agent, object, location,* and *time* map onto the analogous attributes in the corresponding generalized action.[11]

Not all attributes of a generalized action need be explicitly realized when the corresponding verb occurs in a sentence. Although the inclusion of some generalized action attributes as verb arguments is obligatory, the inclusion of others is optional (cf. Tanenhaus & Carlson, 1989). For example, sentences with the verb *buy* must include an agent and an object but do not require a locative, as the following examples demonstrate respectively:

John bought sandals in Taos.
*bought sandals.
*John bought.
John bought sandals.

Arguments that are not obligatory may nevertheless be strongly implied,

---

[11]As we discussed earlier, our analysis of event attributes excludes important attributes such as *instrument, patient,* and *experiencer* for simplicity. We similarly exclude the analogous verb arguments from our discussions of verbs here and later. We simply note several possibilities concerning their origin. First, these remaining attributes may exist in an infant's intuitive theory of intentional events from the start, just like *agent, object,* etc. Second, they may only develop as a more differentiated understanding of events develops. Third, they may emerge directly from the process of language acquisition.

and comprehenders may typically infer their presence even though they are not explicitly stated (Schank, 1975). In the above example, it is implied that John bought the sandals from someone, that the purchase took place at a particular time, that John had a goal in buying the sandals, and so forth.

Stability and Instability

The stability of generalized actions affects the stability of both verbs and nouns. For verbs, stability primarily reflects two sources. For action verbs such as *eat* and *push,* a common action occurs for all instances, thereby providing a source of stability. A second source of stability is verb arguments that typically map onto generalized attributes, which can include ontological kinds, taxonomic superordinates, and goal-derived categories. For *eat,* the *agent, location,* and *time* arguments map onto the ontological kinds for *agent, location,* and *time,* respectively. An *instrument* argument maps onto the taxonomic superordinate of *eating utensils.* An *object* argument maps onto the goal-derived category of *food.*[12] Because these verb arguments and their associated categories are almost always relevant whenever the generalized action occurs, they become consistently mapped to it and thereby provide stability.

We note again that not all attributes in a generalized action are obligatory in sentential realizations of a verb's argument structure. But because nonobligatory attributes are generally implied, they may be present in a verb's semantic representation and provide a source of stability. Consequently, verb stability reflects systematicity between a common action, obligatory arguments, and implied arguments, all of which correspond to the attributes of a generalized action. Verbs generally exhibit high AS because a common action and a set of arguments co-occur across most instances of that event.

Variability for the values of verb arguments appears responsible for much of the instability in verbs. The values for arguments can vary widely across uses of a verb, thereby producing instability. For *eat, object* could be *won ton soup, location* could be *Chinese restaurant, instrument* could be *spoon, time* could be *evening,* and so forth. Or *object* could be *sandwich, location* could be *park, instrument* could be *fingers,* and *time* could be *midday.* Each of these scenarios might be associated with a basic event frame that represents a repeated kind of event in an individual's experience. Because these frames share the value of *eat* for *action,* the generalized

---

[12] *Food* is not a taxonomic superordinate because it is defined more by function than by essence. Instead, *food* cuts across several taxonomic superordinates, picking out subsets from *animals, plants,* and *natural, inanimate substances* (e.g., *salt*). The selection of these subsets is based on optimizations such as *nutritious* and *nontoxic,* as described later for goal-derived categories.

action for *eat* integrates all of them. Given that many basic event frames may be associated with the generalized action for a verb, instability can be substantial. When *eat* is represented on one occasion, values from the basic event frame for *eating Chinese food* might instantiate its abstract arguments. On another occasion, values from *eating deli food* might instantiate them. Consistent with our proposal, Gentner (1981) and Gentner and France (in press) report that verbs exhibit considerable instability, perhaps much more than nouns.

Not only do generalized actions produce stability in verb representations, they can also produce stability in noun representations. Because organisms and artifacts often perform a common action, or have a common action performed on them, the generalized action should become well entrenched in memory for the corresponding noun. Instances of *bird* often fly, and instances of *hammer* often are used to pound things. To the extent that a generalized action applies frequently to a noun category across contexts, it should provide a further source of stability. In Barsalou et al.'s (1987) content analysis of noun definitions, attributes of generalized actions were frequently mentioned.

On the other hand, generalized actions can also produce instability in noun representations. A given noun category may often enter into many different kinds of generalized actions. *Car* is associated with generalized actions for driving, getting gas, washing, repairing, packing, crashing, towing, and so forth. Because *car* is associated with all of these generalized actions, each is potentially retrievable on any given occasion. Depending on their relative frequency, recency, and contextual relevance, different generalized actions may be incorporated into the representation of *car*. On one occasion, getting gas may be retrieved because it was done recently. On another, repairing may be retrieved because the current topic of conversation is the high cost of having things repaired. Instability from generalized actions should increase to the extent a category enters into a variety of activities, none of which dominate. Generalized actions should provide stability only if one generalized action applies to a noun category or if one generalized action occurs at a substantially higher rate than others that also apply.

Scripts

Generalized actions are highly similar to what Schank and Abelson (1977) and Schank (1982) refer to as "scenes," namely, the components of scripts. In fact, Schank (1982) often refers to scenes as "generalized actions." Scripts are typically a sequence of generalized actions that combine to achieve a goal (Abbot et al., 1985; Barsalou & Sewell, 1985; Bower, Black, & Turner, 1979; Galambos & Rips, 1982; Nelson et al., 1983; Mandler & Murphy, 1983; Nelson & Gruendel, 1981; Schank, 1982; Schank & Abelson, 1977). For example, the script of eating at a restaurant involves the generalized actions of entering the restaurant, being seated, reading a menu, ordering, eating, paying, and so forth. Because scripts are more complex than generalized actions, it seems reasonable to assume that their development follows the acquisition of the generalized actions that compose them.

AS in scripts reflects the common configuration of generalized actions that occurs in a particular script. However, this AS may sometimes be relatively weak, given the wide variety of tracks that can occur through a scripted activity (Schank, 1982; Schank & Abelson, 1977). For example, one does not always order hors d'oeuvres in restaurants, one sometimes pays before eating rather than after, and so forth. Consequently, AS may not be as strong as in more primitive forms of knowledge. However, there may still be high degrees of VS, because the values for one generalized action often seem to predict the values of others. If the value for *hors d'oeuvres* is *escargot,* this predicts that the *main course* is more likely to be *frog legs* than *burritos* and that the *tip* is more likely to be *large* than *small.*

Stability and Instability

Stability in scripts reflects three factors: the extent to which the same set of generalized actions occurs in all instances of a script; the extent to which relations among these generalized actions remain invariant; and the extent to which each generalized action is stable itself. Highly routinized activities, such as manufacturing procedures, should show more stability than less routine activities, such as eating at restaurants.

Taxonomic Superordinates

Whereas generalized actions and scripts may evolve naturally from experience, taxonomic superordinates such as *fruit* and *furniture* may be the outcome of more effortful and analytical thought. Taxonomic superordinates may often only result from formal education and other types of cultural transmission. Moreover, they may develop for a variety of reasons and may depend heavily on intuitive theories that are culturally specific (Carey, 1985; Keil, 1987; Lakoff, 1987; McCauley, 1987; Murphy & Medin, 1985; Rips, 1988; Schank et al., 1986). We believe that the purpose of taxonomic superordinates is to organize basic-level categories in ways that reflect cultural and scientific beliefs about the structure of the world.

As discussed earlier, we believe that many of the categories previously classified as ontological (e.g., Keil, 1979, 1981) are taxonomic superordinates. Categories such as *artifact, plant,* and *animal* seem more oriented to capturing the essences of certain kinds of things than to being primitive constructs that organize human experience. Consequently, taxonomic superordinates, according to our scheme, compose multilevel structures that organize the kinds of things in existence according to their essences. These categories include very abstract superordinates (e.g., *artifacts, living things*), as well as more specific superordinates (e.g., *clothing, fruit*).

For natural kinds, taxonomic superordinates often appear based on an abstract partonomy that is common to a related set of basic-level categories. People's lay knowledge of *plant* may include an abstract partonomy that contains *foliage* and *roots;* similarly their lay knowledge of *mammal* may include *vertebrae* and *mammary glands.* These partonomies are abstract because they are not defined in terms of the geons that specify basic-level categories. Moreover, the attributes in these partonomies may often be hidden and play explanatory roles with respect to external attributes. To some extent they may underlie a mental model for the category, as discussed earlier for basic object frames.

These abstract partonomies may be difficult to learn for a number of reasons. First, the attributes themselves are often abstract and nonobvious perceptually. Second, AS is not as high as it could be because there typically are some attributes not common to all members (e.g., some *fish* have *scales,* but not all). Third, relations between attributes often seem to represent co-occurrence rather than stronger conceptual relations (e.g., most people may believe that *vertebrae* and *mammary glands* simply co-occur for *mammals*). Fourth, attributes and relations that integrate them may be heavily dependent on cultural and the scientific theories. For example, a theory in our culture places *whales* and *dolphins* in the taxonomic superordinate *mammals;* whereas theories in other cultures place *whales* and *dolphins* in *fish.* Not knowing the relevant theory may make it difficult or impossible to learn the category.

Taxonomic superordinates seem to develop differently for artifacts, where function seems more important than parts. For *clothing,* it is difficult to find any common part. Instead, what all clothing has in common is more closely related to function; namely, *clothing* is something one puts on, wears, and removes from one's body. For *tools,* common parts are again difficult to find, and again common functions seem important (i.e., *tools* are artifacts used to make and repair things). Consequently, taxonomic superordinates for artifacts appear related to generalized actions that represent functions. Generalized actions also appear important to taxonomic superordinates for biological kinds, given that generalized actions are often central to their description (e.g., birds *fly;* fish *swim*).

The attribute selection problem may be most severe for taxonomic superordinates. As discussed earlier, biologically based cognitive mechanisms appear to facilitate induction of the attributes and relations that underlie ontological kinds, basic object frames, and basic event frames. In contrast, biological constraints appear to play a much weaker role in acquiring the AS that underlies taxonomic superordinates. Instead, intuitive and scientific theories appear to play the central role in identifying the relevant attributes and relations for these categories. As a result, taxonomic superordinates may vary more with culture and expertise than do categories whose attributes and relations are constrained by biological bases. Moreover, instruction may typically be necessary before these attributes and relations can be utilized to structure one's knowledge of the world.

The attributes and relations central to a culture's theories should also be central to maintaining the coherence of its world view. Following Goodman (1955), attributes and relations that have become entrenched for a culture should be preferred in further attempts to induce new structure about the world. This may be especially true when making new inductions in poorly constrained domains.

Stability and Instability

Taxonomic superordinates often occur within a particular ontological domain. For example, *fruit* is a superordinate within *object, tool* is a superordinate within *instrument,* and *outdoor location* is a superordinate within *location* (Tversky & Hemenway, 1983). In these cases, factors that produce stability in an ontological kind should also produce stability in its taxonomic superordinates. The attributes that specify taxonomic superordinates should provide an additional source of stability. The abstract partonomies and generalized actions that specify taxonomic superordinates for natural kinds may produce stability in these superordinates. The generalized actions that specify taxonomic superordinates for artifacts may produce stability in these superordinates.

However, some taxonomic superordinates occur in multiple ontological domains. For example, *human* belongs to both *agent* and *object; car* belongs to both *object* and *instrument.* In these cases, ontological information should provide instability. Representations of *car,* for example, may include *instrument* information on one occasion and *object* information on another.

For all taxonomic superordinates, basic-level categories provide a major source of instability: Across different occasions, different basic-level information may be included in a superordinate's representation, even though this information is irrelevant to specifying the superordinate. Consider *clothing.* On one occasion, the basic object frame for *shirt* might be activated; whereas on another occasion, the basic object frame for *pants* might be activated instead. Although the attributes for *object* and the generalized action(s) that define *clothing* provide stability, the variable presence of lower-level information that is irrelevant may provide instability.

Goal-Derived Categories

Goal-derived categories result from optimizing the attributes of event representations and ensuring that the values of these attributes are compatible (Barsalou, 1983, 1985, 1987). Some goal-derived categories may be well established in memory from much experience; whereas others may be "ad hoc," having been constructed to achieve a novel goal (Barsalou, 1983). Because many different kinds of attributes occur in event representations, many kinds of goal-derived categories can be formed. Goal-derived categories can be derived from the ontological kinds and taxonomic superordinates that serve as attributes in generalized actions (e.g., from *location* or *eating utensils*); goal-derived categories can be derived from the basic-level categories that serve as attributes in summarized events (e.g., from *backyard* or *ball*); goal-derived categories can be derived from the subordinate categories that serve as attributes in subordinate events (e.g., from *tennis ball*). Figure 10.5c demonstrates two goal-derived categories—*uncluttered locations* and *times when parents are available*—that have been derived from attributes in the generalized action for *catch.*

Many goal-derived categories are produced by optimizing an event attribute. Optimization involves finding ideal values that category members should approach to maximize goal success (Barsalou, 1985). In *uncluttered locations,* ideally the location should have zero clutter, so that the participants will not have to work around things in the air and on the ground. The goal-derived category is produced by combining the ideal, *uncluttered,* with the ontological kind, *location.* Goal-derived categories can similarly be constructed by combining optimizations with other kinds of event attributes. In Figure 10.5a, the basic-level category *backyard* could be optimized to form *uncluttered backyards.*

Many other goal-derived categories are produced by propagating constraints between the attributes of an event representation. A constraint is a value of one event attribute that restricts the values of another attribute (cf. Fox, 1987; Stefik, 1981). In *times when parents are available,* the value of *agent* restricts the possible values of *time* (see Figure 10.5c). The goal-derived category is produced by combining the ontological kind *time* with the constraint *agent = parent.* Goal-derived categories can similarly be constructed by propagating constraints to other types of event attributes. In Figure 10.5a, the basic-level category *evening* could be constrained by *agent = parent* to form *evenings when parents are available.*

Stability and Instability

The construction of a goal-derived category essentially begins with an event attribute, which is then combined with relevant optimizations and/or constraints. Consequently, the factors that produce stability in event attributes should also produce stability in goal-derived categories. If the event attribute is an ontological kind, then it should provide less stability than if it is a basic-level category. The optimizations and constraints that define goal-derived categories provide additional stability. Because this information is stated explicitly in the category description, it should be present in representations of the category across situations.

Goal-derived categories exhibit much potential for instability, because many basic-level categories instantiate each. Consider *locations that are uncluttered.* On one occasion, the basic-level category for *backyard* may be activated; whereas on another, the basic-level category for *park* may be activated instead. Although ontological information for *location* and the optimization, *uncluttered,* provide stability, the variable presence of lower-level information that is irrelevant produces instability.

Integrations and Extensions

In the previous two sections, we covered a lot of ground exploring systematicity in various kinds of knowledge. In this section we first attempt to summarize and integrate the main points. We then explore one final set of implications concerning the role of systematicity in text comprehension.

Evolution of Systematicity in Knowledge

We made a number of proposals regarding the evolution of knowledge. They are summarized in Figure 10.6. We proposed that ontological kinds are the first to develop because they underlie infants' intuitive theory of intentional events. This theory enables infants to parse their experience into ontological kinds that support functional interactions with the environment. Basic-level categories evolve rapidly in development because the attributes and relations that underlie them are readily available (e.g., geons and spatial relations for basic object frames). Summarized events develop next, utilizing basic-level categories as the attributes of basic event frames. We assume that these three forms of knowledge are primitive because the attributes and relations that compose them have biological bases.

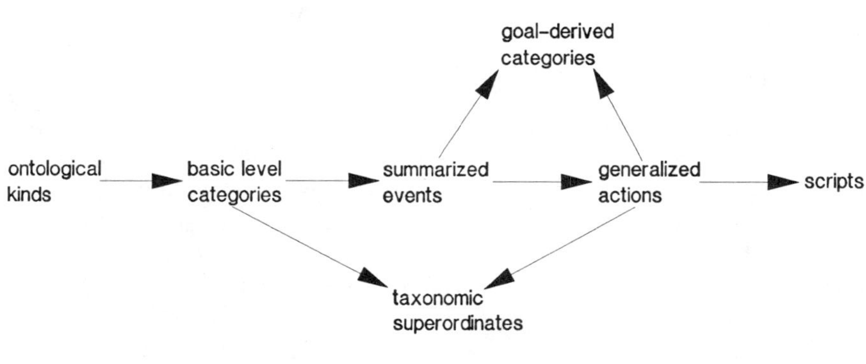

FIGURE 10.6. Proposed evolution of knowledge from primitive to abstract forms.

Four forms of abstract knowledge evolve from the three primitive forms. Generalized actions evolve from basic event frames as the values experienced for *agent, object, location,* and *time* become increasingly broad. Scripts develop after experiencing stereotypic configurations of generalized actions. Taxonomic superordinates develop from abstract partonomies that evolve out of basic object frames and from generalized actions that specify functions. Goal-derived categories develop from optimizing the attributes of event representations and ensuring that the values of these attributes are compatible.

Sources of Stability in Category Representations

We made a number of proposals concerning the role of systematicity in stability. We summarize these proposals in Table 10.1. The row headings refer to various forms of knowledge. The column headings refer to various sources of systematicity that can provide stability. Each source of systematicity is defined by the type of attributes, values, and/or relations that compose it. An X in a cell of the table indicates that the form of systematicity in the column generally provides stability for the form of knowledge in the row. An (X) indicates that the source of systematicity may sometimes provide stability but not always.

Ontological AS

As shown in Table 10.1, we assume that ontological AS provides stability for all forms of knowledge. We assume that the attributes underlying ontological kinds, whatever they may be, provide them with stability. Every time an ontological kind is represented, a common core of attributes specifies it. Ontological AS also provides stability for those taxonomic superordinates, basic-level categories, and subordinate categories that generally fall within a single ontological kind (e.g., *fruit, apple,* and *golden delicious* all generally fall into *object*). Because the exemplars in each of these categories are all of the same ontological kind, they exhibit high AS for the attributes defining that kind. However, ontological AS does not provide stability for those taxonomic superordinates, basic-level categories, and subordinate categories that fall into multiple ontological kinds (e.g., *human* as an *agent* and an *object*). In these cases, ontological AS provides a source of instability. Similarly, ontological AS only provides a source of stability for those goal-derived categories that were derived from a single ontological kind (e.g., *uncluttered locations*).

Ontological AS also indirectly provides stability for generalized actions, summarized events, subordinate events, and scripts. Because all events include *agent, action, object, location,* and *time* as attributes, the ontological AS that provides these attributes with stability also provides stability in event representations.

TABLE 10.1. Sources of stability in category representations.

Form of knowledge	Source of stability								
		Physical object attributes and relations			Event attributes and relations				
	Ontological AS	Abstract partonomy	Geon AS	Geon VS	Intentional-event AS	Common action	Basic-category AS	Basic-category VS	Scene AS
Ontological kinds	X								
Taxonomic superordinates	(X)	(X)			(X)	(X)			
Basic-level categories	(X)	(X)	X		(X)	(X)			
Subordinate categories	(X)	(X)	X	X	(X)	(X)			
Goal-derived categories	(X)	(X)	(X)	(X)	(X)	(X)	(X)	(X)	
Generalized actions	X				X	X			
Summarized events	X	(X)	X		X	X	X		
Subordinate events	X	(X)	X	X	X	X	X	X	
Scripts	X				X	X			X

Note: An X in a cell specifies that the source of systematicity in the column generally provides stability for the form of knowledge in the row. An (X) specifies that the source of systematicity may sometimes provide stability but not always.

Physical Object Attributes and Relations

Abstract partonomies provide stability for some taxonomic superordinates, basic-level categories, and subordinate categories. For example, the abstract partonomy that specifies *mammal* also provides stability for basic-level categories (e.g., *dog*) and subordinate categories (e.g., *golden retriever*). Because the same abstract partonomy applies to categories at all levels, it potentially provides each with a source of stability. Abstract partonomies do not appear to provide a source of stability for many other superordinates, basic-level categories, and subordinate categories (e.g., *tool*). Some goal-derived categories that have been derived from a taxonomic superordinate (e.g., *fast-growing plants*) also benefit from the stability provided by an abstract partonomy.

Abstract partonomies indirectly provide some summarized events and subordinate events with stability. Factors that produce stability in basic-level categories also produce stability in event representations that have basic-level categories as attributes. Because abstract partonomies provide stability for some basic-level categories, they may thereby provide stability in some summarized events and their subordinates.

Geon AS provides basic-level and subordinate categories with stability, because all members of these categories share the same configuration of geons (i.e., basic object frame). To the extent that geon AS extends internally to include hidden, explanatory parts, the resultant mental model may also provide stability. Geon AS also provides stability for those goal-derived categories that have been derived from basic-level categories. Geon AS indirectly provides stability in summarized events and subordinate events. As just described for abstract partonomies, factors that produce stability in basic-level categories also produce stability in these event representations.[13]

Finally, geon VS provides subordinate categories with further stability, because all members share common value information. Geon VS also provides stability for those goal-derived categories that have been derived from subordinate categories. Geon VS indirectly provides subordinate events with stability. Because subordinate events are specified by values for basic-level attributes, factors that produce stability for subordinate categories also produce stability for subordinate events.

---

[13]We only address basic-level categories in Table 10.1 for *physical objects, agents,* and *locations.* As discussed earlier, we assume that basic-level categories also exist for *time, action,* and other nonphysical ontological kinds, even though we do not know the attributes that specify these basic levels. If we did, then "geon AS" in Table 10.1 would be changed to include the other types of AS that specify the basic level in these nonphysical domains. A similar caveat holds for "geon VS" in the next column of Table 10.1

Event Attributes and Relations

The ontological kinds that constitute people's intuitive theory of intentional events—*agent, action, object, location,* and *time*—form what we refer to in Table 10.1 as "intentional-event AS." Because these five ontological kinds generally co-occur, taking on different values in specific events, they form a pattern of AS for all intentional events. Intentional-event AS provides a source of stability for all forms of event knowledge in Table 10.1. The attributes composing intentional-event AS can be expected to occur in any generalized action, summarized event, or subordinate event. Because scripts are composed of generalized actions, intentional-event AS also provides them with stability through the stability of their generalized actions.

"Common action" in Table 10.1 refers to a common action that occurs across all instances of an event type. The representation of this action provides stability in generalized actions, summarized events, and subordinate events. Because scripts are composed of generalized actions, common actions indirectly provide scripts with stability through the stability of generalized actions.

Intentional-event AS and common actions also provide stability for some taxonomic superordinates, basic-level categories, and their subordinates. If one of these categories is highly associated with a particular function, then the generalized action that represents this function may become context-independent (e.g., *pound* for *hammer*). Because intentional-event AS and a common action specify the generalized action and provide it with stability, they also provide stability for the category. However, intentional-event AS and common actions provide a source of *instability* for categories associated with multiple functions, none of which dominate. Goal-derived categories also benefit from the stability provided by a generalized action, if the category they are derived from is associated with a dominant function.

"Basic-category AS" in Table 10.1 refers to the correlated configuration of basic-level categories that specifies a basic event frame. These frames provide stability for summarized events and their subordinates. They may also provide stability for goal-derived categories to some limited extent, when the constraints that define goal-derived categories are basic-level instantiations of the constraining attributes (e.g., when *location* = *beach* and *time* = *evening* produces *evening beach clothing*). "Basic-category VS" in Table 10.1 refers to the correlated patterns of values that specify subordinates of a summarized event and give them stability. These patterns may also provide stability for goal-derived categories, when the constraints that define them are subordinate-level instantiations of the constraining attributes (e.g., when *location* = *rocky beach* and *time* = *summer evening* produces *rocky beach clothing for a summer evening*).

"Scene AS" in Table 10.1 is the extent to which the generalized actions that constitute the scenes of a script co-occur. If the same scenes co-occur frequently in the same configuration, they provide a script with stability.

Problems in Predicting Stability

In this section we have listed various sources of stability for particular forms of knowledge. But if a form of knowledge is associated with more than one source of stability, do all of them together combine *cumulatively* to produce stability? Consider basic-level categories. According to Table 10.1, ontological AS, abstract partonomies, geon AS, X intentional-event AS, and common actions all provide basic-level categories with stability. If so, then basic-level categories should exhibit more stability than taxonomic superordinates, which have one less source of stability. Similarly, basic-level categories should exhibit less stability than subordinate categories, which have one more source of stability. These predictions rely on the assumption that various sources of stability accumulate monotonically. If the cumulative assumption is correct, then Table 10.1 provides explicit predictions concerning the relative stability of various forms of knowledge.

Alternatively, people may not take advantage of all available sources of stability. Certain sources of stability may often be irrelevant to normal uses of a particular category and therefore not evolve into a context-independent core of information. For example, abstract partonomies may generally not be relevant to basic-level categories that have them. When interacting with one's dog on a daily basis, one rarely has to consider the abstract partonomy that defines *mammal.* If people are selective in the sources of stability they utilize, then this complicates drawing predictions about stability from Table 10.1. To assess the relative stability of various kinds of knowledge, one would need to have a theory of how various sources of stability are selected.

There are two other complications for predicting stability that we do not pursue here. First, the number of sources that provide stability for a form of knowledge in Table 10.1 is not necessarily a good index of its stability. Instead, one needs to consider the *complexity* of the knowledge as well. Consider summarized events in Table 10.1, which have three more sources of stability than basic-level categories. Because basic-level categories constitute the attributes of summarized events, summarized events are more complex than basic-level categories. A comparison between basic-level categories and summarized events is meaningful only if they can be normalized for complexity.

Second, it does not necessarily follow that any cell in Table 10.1 *without* and X or (X) represents a source of *instability.* Although some of these empty cells may constitute a source of instability for a form of knowledge, some may simply be irrelevant. Although we have not attempted to identify sources of instability here, meaningful predictions concerning stability cannot be made without taking these sources into account.

Stability in Text Comprehension

So far, we have primarily addressed the relative stability of various forms of knowledge. In doing so, we have implicitly assumed that the sources providing stability remain relatively constant across a task or processing episode. In this final section, we briefly consider how sources of stability change over time.

Words and Attributes

We propose that a primary purpose of many words is to activate relevant attributes. When a noun is read or heard for the first time in a text, it may activate ontological attributes, part attributes, and event attributes. When a verb is read or heard for the first time, it may activate attributes for arguments, along with information about the action. These initially activated attributes provide global information about the referent of the word, providing a rough idea of what the speaker or author has in mind as the intended meaning. Consequently, the primary stability for words read out of context should be for attributes. In contrast, stability should be low for the values of these attributes, unless the word has specific meaning at the value level (e.g., subordinate-level categories and proper names).

Texts and Values

A primary purpose of texts may be to provide values for the ambiguous attributes activated by lexical units. Once a noun is first mentioned, values may be added later through predication, as in the following example for *dog:*

Michele went to the Humane Society to get a dog. The one she selected was large and had floppy ears.

In this example, the text provides values for the attributes of *size* and *ears.*

Values are also frequently assigned through modifiers of a noun head, as in the following example:

Michele went to the Humane Society and selected a large dog with floppy ears.

In this case, the values are provided by an adjective and a prepositional phrase in the noun phrase. Smith et al. (in press) also suggest that values are assigned to attributes of a head noun in this manner (but see Medin & Shoben, 1988; Murphy, in press).

When a verb occurs, values for obligatory arguments may be provided in its sentence, and implied arguments may be provided in accompanying sentences, as in the following example for *sleep:*

Michele's dog, Chelsea, had to live outside but had a nice doghouse. At night, Chelsea usually was able to sleep quite well. Michele had bought her a nice dog pillow filled with cedar chips for a bed.

In this example, the argument for *location* is filled by a value from the previous sentence (*doghouse*). Other arguments for *agent* and *manner* are filled by the sentence containing "sleep" (i.e., the *agent* is *Chelsea,* and the *manner* is *well*). A third argument, *sleeping surface,* is filled in the final sentence (on a *dog pillow filled with cedar chips*). In general, the stability of nouns and verbs may increase over the course of a text through various linguistic devices that provide values for unconstrained attributes.

Patterns of VS may further facilitate the process of instantiating attributes with values. Because values are often correlated with one another, receiving a value for one attribute may generate plausible inferences about correlated values for other noninstantiated attributes. Consider *pounded* in the following sentence:

Michele pounded nails all day to build Chelsea a doghouse.

In this sentence, values for the attributes of *material* and *instrument* are not specified for "pounded." However, the value for the *object* (*nails*) is correlated with values for the *material* (*wood*) and the *instrument* (*hammer*). In this manner, explicitly provided values may imply unmentioned values that participate in patterns of VS. To the extent that these patterns of VS are shared and stable, they should increase the stability of texts.

It is important to note that texts, besides providing values, may also provide attributes for words in certain situations. Words that have low AS may often have their values specified by surrounding text. Consider *gift* in the following sentence:

Sarah received an unusual gift for her birthday. It was a small, round, thin piece of metal that one puts in a light socket to extend the life of light bulbs.

In the process of providing values, the second sentence also introduces attributes for *size, shape, thickness, material,* and *function* that were not specified by *gift* (e.g., *gift* can also refer to events and living organisms).

Texts may also add unusual attributes to nouns that normally have high AS. Consider *raft* in the following example:

Henry put axles and wheels on his raft so that he could tow it to the lake without having to put it on a trailer.

Here attributes for *axles* and *wheels* are added to those normally associated with *raft.* Even though texts may primarily provide values for attributes activated by lexical units, they may also introduce attributes.

Text Position and Stability

To the extent that texts produce stability, the stability of certain words should increase over the course of a text. Repeated words may often gain in stability as increasing amounts of value information accumulate. This may be especially true for proper nouns (e.g., "Chelsea") and definite descriptions (e.g., "the doghouse Michele built") that occur repeatedly. Consequently, different readers should increasingly represent these nouns similarly, and the same reader should increasingly represent something similarly across contexts. Johnson-Laird (1987) provides a similar view of semantic refinement during text comprehension. Other words that refer to less important referents may only be mentioned occasionally and briefly. Because they have fewer values specified, they may typically exhibit lower stability between and within individuals.

Stability across text positions may also be associated with the use of indefinite and definite reference. When referents are introduced, they are often introduced through indefinite reference, as for *dog* in:

Michele bought a dog.

However, later references to the same dog must be made with definite reference, as in:

The dog was thrilled to have a real home.

Indefinite references may typically serve the purpose of introducing probable attributes of the referent. Definite references, on the other hand, may typically refer to referents whose attributes have at least begun to be instantiated with values from the text.

Conclusion

We have tried to show how the simple construct of systematicity permeates human knowledge. We have argued that AS and VS interact to provide coherence in categories. AS reflects people's attempts to identify aspects of categories that are relatively invariant and to integrate them into frames. VS reflects people's attempts to organize the variability within the context of a frame into meaningful configurations of values that specify subcategories. In the extreme, exemplars represent individual configurations of values that instantiate a frame and its subcategories. We are not the first to stress the importance of relational information in human knowledge (see Gentner, 1983; 1988; Johnson-Laird, 1983; Medin et al, 1982, 1987; Medin & Schaffer, 1978; Medin & Shoben, 1988; Miller & Johnson-Laird, 1976; Murphy & Medin, 1985).

We have also attempted to specify constraints on attributes and relations. These constraints suggest that certain types of systematicity should be fundamental (e.g., basic event frames), that others should be derived from them (e.g., generalized actions), and that still others may be relatively unconstrained (e.g., taxonomic superordinates). In general, we have tried to show how the development of knowledge may result from interactions between a mechanism that seeks systematicity and constraints on relevant attributes and relations.

As we noted at the start, we have not tested this theory directly. However, we cited a great deal of evidence throughout that motivates and often supports it indirectly. We believe that this theory integrates a wide variety of findings on human knowledge and that it provides numerous testable predictions (e.g., various claims about the evolution of knowledge, the content of category representations, the production of inferences, the stability of category representations).

Clearly many unanswered questions remain. First, for this theory to be complete, it will first be necessary to assess systematicity in various kinds of knowledge. Do attributes and relations exhibit the kinds of systematicity we suggest here? Second, we have a long way to go before we have adequately described the various kinds of knowledge and their relations to one another. What exactly are the fundamental ontological kinds, and what attributes specify them? What exactly are the relational structures that integrate the attributes of basic object frames, basic event frames, and generalized actions? What categories provide the basic level in domains such as *action* and *time?* Third, direct evidence is needed for our claims about the biological bases of privileged attributes and relations. Are configurations of geons as readily induced and utilized as we suggest? Do basic-level categories constitute the attributes of primitive-event categories? Are the spatial, temporal, causal, and intentional relations that integrate events applied effortlessly and implicitly during the experience of events? Fourth, it will be necessary to develop statistical measures of systematicity. What particular measures most closely reflect human sensitivity to systematicity? Fifth, it will be necessary to assess directly how systematicity affects acquisition, inference, and retrieval. Is systematicity as central to these processes as we suggest? How do various sources of stability and instability combine to produce category representations in working memory? Sixth, just how does one develop a computational model that exhibits all these benefits of systematicity? Furthermore, how does one build a connectionistlike model that is sensitive to statistical information yet exhibits decomposition along the lines we suggest? This theory in its current form may raise more questions than it answers.

Acknowledgments. Work on this chapter has been supported by National Science Foundation Grant IRI-8609187 and Army Research Institute Contract MD A903-86-C-0172 to Lawrence W. Barsalou and by National Institutes of Mental Health Grant R23HD2052201A1 to Dorrit Billman. We are grateful to Adele Abrahamson, Christopher Hale, Joel Martin, Robert McCauley, Douglas Medin, Brian Ross, Liz Shipley, and Edward Smith for their helpful comments. Address correspondence either to Lawrence W. Barsalou or to Dorrit Billman (now at Georgia Institute of Technology), School of Psychology, Georgia Institute of Technology, Atlanta, GA 30332.

11

Some Ambiguities in the Study of Ambiguity

ROBERT R. HOFFMAN

Researchers agree that there are different kinds of ambiguity and that ambiguity occurs at a number of levels of language. Everyone agrees that the different kinds and levels can be defined and researched. However, a number of terms are relied upon heavily in explanations of ambiguity—*lexicon, retrieval, search, activation, access, inhibition, interference,* and *representation*—and researchers have major disagreements about the meanings of these explanatory terms. It may seem curious that the various technical terms that are used in the scientific analysis of lexical ambiguity are themselves ambiguous in meaning. For instance, what is the "conceptual meaning" of a word? One would be hard-pressed to find any two cognitive psychologists who would fully agree in their answers to this question. Not only are the meanings of the scientific terms left open, but the terms themselves are usually (and rather obviously) reliant on underlying metaphorical concepts. Examples would be the "suppression" of meanings or the "interference" of mental processes.

Goals of this Chapter

My immediate goal in this chapter is to say something about the meanings of the key theoretical terms—lexicon, retrieval, search, activation, access, inhibition, interference, and representation. However, to fully understand the meanings of these terms, I have to take the reader on a somewhat dizzying tour of a number of philosophical issues. Although these issues go well beyond the specific topics of this volume, the issues put the key terms into perspective. My purpose is to remind experimental psychologists of the ontological, epistemological, and methodological issues involved in their theorizing and research on the topic of lexical ambiguity.

My Point of View

Philosophers and scientists usually lament and protest when they notice that a particular bit of scientific theorizing is imprecise in meaning. Anyone with even the slightest inclination toward logical empiricism and operationalism would assert that "good" scientific theorizing should be just as precise and just as clear-cut as the experimentally derived data on which the theorizing is based. Indeed, an ideal theory would be logical at least, mathematical at best. So scientists are chastised when their theories seem flabby.

My own point of view is that ambiguity of scientific terms is a necessary aspect of all human problem solving. Conceptualization itself is inherently dynamic and involves reasoning heuristics that go well beyond the bounds of classical or deductive logic. In fact, ambiguity of scientific terms is quite healthy for science. At any point in the development of a methodological paradigm or a school of thought, open-endedness of scientific meaning leads to further research and refinements of theoretical ideas (Hoffman, 1985; Hoffman & Nead, 1983). Indeed, it has come to be recognized in the philosophy of science that metaphoric ambiguity plays a critical role in attempts to "fix the meanings of scientific terms" (Kuhn, 1979, p. 414).

The Organization of This Chapter

I begin with the two key terms, *ambiguity* and *lexeme,* and describe some of the meanings that seem to be utilized by various theorists and researchers. I then launch into a discussion of some basic questions that are raised by the modern cognitive science approach to word meaning. This leads to a discussion of some issues involving the concept of "mental representation." I conclude with some recommendations about how theorists might analyze their own theorizing. The ideas I present here are food for thought. I will leave the topic as we find it, ambiguous.

What is *Ambiguity?*

The English word *ambiguous* derives most immediately from the French *ambiguité,* which comes from the Latin word *ambiguus.* This word combined the stems *ambi-* ("on both sides") and *agere* ("travel" or "drive"), which taken together mean to "wander about" or to "drive on both sides" (Mish, 1984; Partridge, 1966). The metaphor in operation here is that of someone who is traveling and reaches a choice point—there are two or more different ways to go, and the traveler has some reason to go each of the various ways.

Human beings often conceive of choice in terms of the traveler's selection of alternative pathways along a journey (Kovecses, 1988; Lakoff, 1987; Lakoff & Johnson, 1980; Parker, 1982). To cite just one of the numerous instances which Lakoff and his colleagues have documented, lovers sometimes say (on the positive side), "He follows her everywhere," or "He can't go on without her," or "Look how far we've come." On the negative side, lovers may say, "Our relationship has reached a crossroads," or "We're just spinning our wheels," or "We've gotten off the track," or "It's been a long, bumpy road." In all of these cases, the complex relationship of love or marriage is conceived in terms of journeys and pathways. It is no coincidence that cognitive scientists, all too human, conceive of the complex and somewhat abstract concept of memory in terms of "associative path" and "network search" theories of meaning and memory (Hoffman, Cochran, & Nead, 1989).

Since the incorporation into English of the word *ambiguity,* the word has lost its reference to journeys and paths. As some might say, the word has become "literal." Literally, then, *ambiguous* means "doubtful or uncertain especially from obscurity or indistinctness . . . capable of being understood in two or more possible senses or ways," (Merriam-Webster, Inc., 1984). The word *ambiguity* refers in particular to the ambiguity of linguistic meanings.

The Varieties of Semantic Experience

What does it mean to say that meaning is ambiguous? To answer this, I rely on the journey metaphor. A path or journey might involve wandering or "driving on both sides" for a variety of reasons:

1. Although the alternative paths may be clear, one may lack directions and therefore be uncertain about which path to choose.
2. The directions refer to the general heading, but one needs information about specific landmarks.
3. The directions refer to specific landmarks, but fail to convey a sense of the general direction.
4. The director is deliberately misleading the traveler "down a garden path." The directions make no sense, and the traveler has to backtrack.
5. The path itself becomes obscure or indistinct, and one does not know where to go.
6. The major routes are clear, but one needs information about the minor pathways or side streets.
7. The path itself is actually a trap or maze. There's no way out. The traveler has been set up, and winds up going in circles.
8. The director goofed. The directions explicitly convey something other than what they were intended to.
9. The directions are not sufficient or coherent. The traveler is forced to make deductions or other inferences to avoid getting lost.
10. The directions are phrased cryptically like some treasure map or Sherlockian puzzle. The traveler has to figure out where to go.

Comprehending a word, or a phrase, or a sentence, or a bit of prose, or a conversation, is rather like following a path. In both activities, one can get lost. One can be misled. On the other hand, one can deliberately choose to wander, choose to get lost. Carrying this particular possibility over as an analogy to meanings and ambiguity: One can choose to deliberately utter ambiguities, perhaps for the sake of irony or humor. One of our favorite examples is the letter of recommendation which said "This person performed adequately. He is leaving. We are satisfied."

Following through on the analogy, there is a variety of distinctly different ways in which linguistic meanings might involve ambiguity. These are shown below. Obviously I've set things up here—each of the various distinctions about meaning that have been proposed by linguists, psychologists, and others can be identified as one of the types of wandering listed previously.

1. *Polysemous meaning:* A word has multiple and distinct meanings. Each of the meanings is clear, but one does not know which one to use or apply in a given situation. For example, when taken out of context, "He went toward the bank" could be referring to a river bank or to a savings bank.
2. *Sense versus reference:* The essence (what the word means) may differ from the ostension (what the word "points to" or "stands for"). For example, the concept of love has a meaning that goes beyond specific instances of loving behavior.
3. *Core versus context:* The meaning of a statement as such differs from the meaning when taken in its full context. Thus, a statement like "He was voracious" means one thing in the context of human appetite, but quite another in the context of shark behavior. If defined in a vacuum, the word *book* might mean one thing, but when a tome is used as a doorstop, *book* would mean something slightly different.
4. *Grammatical versus ungrammatical meaning:* A string of words can be syntactically well-formed and comprehensible, or it may be ill-formed and more or less comprehensible ("anomalous"). Examples would be strings such as "The odorless child inspired a chocolate audience" and "Sensible ideas distrust politicians."
5. *Conceptual versus associative meaning:* Conceptual meaning is inherently unclear or indistinct. It relies on mental nebulosities such as prototypes, schemata, abstract concepts, and perceptual sets. It exists in minds. On the other hand, associative meaning is an operationally defined concept. It is dependent on the empirical demonstration of particular semantic relations and associations to particular words. It exists primarily on paper as in word frequency and associative norms.
6. *Primary versus secondary meaning:* The dominant or most frequent meaning differs from alternative less dominant or less frequent meanings. Some heterophones make good examples. When shown the word *wind* out of context, most people might be inclined to assume that one means wind as in "windy day" rather than the less frequent meaning of wind as in "wind the clock."

7. *Closed versus open meaning:* The meaning of a message is closed if comprehension reaches an immediate and satisfactory conclusion. Open meaning is meaning without an obvious resolution or completion. Examples of this are: "The horse raced past the barn fell" and "The sailor ate the submarine." Early in such sentences, one is set up to comprehend one thing, but later in the sentence something appears that gives one pause. The sentence as a whole suddenly seems anomalous. Only after one backtracks and thinks it over does a coherent meaning begin to appear.
8. *Intended versus understood meaning:* The meaning intended by a speaker or writer is not the meaning that is understood by the listener or reader. An instance of this occurs every time a program crashes and the programmer swears at the computer: "Don't do what I say, do what I mean!"
9. *Explicit versus implicit meaning:* The meaning as explicitly stated differs from the meaning as can be elaborated, on the basis of knowledge other than that contained in the explicit statement. A good example is a favorite of psycholinguists: Common indirect requests such as "Can you tell me the time?" and "Can you pass the salt?" can be answered by a simple "yes," but the answerer would no doubt be considered rude.
10. *Literal versus figurative meaning:* The actual meaning is literal, like the entry in a dictionary. The literal meaning of words is what they point to or stand for. Figurative meaning involves illogical comparisons of unlike things. The sentence "He drove through a red light" does not mean what it says literally. The sentence "He is a wolf" is literal in reference to a tour of a zoo, but is a metaphor when in reference to an adventuresome human male.

As this list of semantic distinctions suggests, philosophers, linguists, and psychologists have distinguished many different types of meanings. Here, I have expressed these distinctions through an analogy based on the etymology of the word *ambiguity.* So far, so good. But complications do arise. To return to the journey metaphor, one can wander for more than one reason. One could be lost *and* could lack information about specific landmarks. One could have directions that specify only the general heading *and* could encounter indistinct paths. In the same way, any of the various types of ambiguity could be in effect at a given time. For instance, a researcher might hold that polysemy can characterize sense but not reference, another researcher might hold that primary meaning *is* associative meaning, another might hold that literal meaning *is* referential meaning, another might hold that associative meaning *is* conceptual meaning, and so on. In such combinations, one distinction is defined in terms of others, and there are many possible combinations. It is therefore obviously important for researchers and theorists to be clear on what they mean by their concepts.

My examination of the word *ambiguity* has led directly to a discussion of semantics, and has revealed the variety and richness of some of the terms and distinctions that are made. Now, what about the word *lexicon?*

What is a *Lexeme?*

The English word *lexeme* is a technical term in linguistics and psycholinguistics. According to etymologists, it derives ultimately from the Greek word *legein,* meaning "to say" (hence *legend*), and *lexis,* meaning "word" or "speech" (Mish, 1984; Partridge, 1966). Its usage in English derives more directly from the Greek phrase *lexicon biblion,* denoting a word or phrase book or a bibliography. Anything that is "lexical" is something that relates to the words or the vocabulary of a given language. Thus, a *lexeme* is a meaningful linguistic unit, usually a vocabulary item in a language but sometimes a morpheme. As used by modern linguists, the term *lexicon* denotes any collection of words or morphemes—whether it be a collection of Sanskrit cognates for proto-Indo-European words or a collection of the terms used by cognitive psychologists. Usually, a lexicon lists words, presenting them in alphabetical order, and usually the primary entry for each word consists of the word's definition or "essential" meaning.

Obviously, any collection of words is collected for particular purposes. For example, the student of Sanskrit is interested in the evolution of languages, and so is likely to focus on changes in the pronunciation of words with similar meanings across various languages over a broad span of time. In general, the purposes of each lexicographer will determine: (1) the nature of the entities that are denoted by the entries in the lexicon, (2) the form of the entries, (3) the organization of the entries, and (4) the form and nature of any characteristics of the entries.

Lexicons—in the sense of tablets, scrolls, dictionaries, atlases, encyclopedias, word lists, foreign language phrase books, bibliographies, and the like—have been a part of human experience for centuries and have been widely familiar in Western civilization since the Renaissance. Given the concrete, familiar nature of lexicons, it is natural that the concept of a "lexicon" would be used as a way of describing the ineffabilities of language and mind. A good example of the use of the mental dictionary metaphor in theorizing about language can be found in Vico's *New Science* (1725/1970, Sec. 43; see Pompa, 1982, pp. 151–153). Throughout the history of cognitive psychology there has appeared a general metaphor theme: *The mental representation of meanings (of words, pictures, symbols) has the character of a lexicon.*

Since there are different types of lexicons, one can generate different instances of the metaphor theme, such as the specific comparison of stored word meanings to encyclopedias, or to filing systems. Furthermore, the various specific metaphors each suggest additional possibilities, such as the idea of different types of "search" through the mental lexicon. For instance, Clark and Clark (1977, Chapter 11) explicitly compare the relative merits of the mental dictionary and mental encyclopedia notions.

The term *lexeme* is taken to mean widely different things by different theorists. Titchener (1915, Chapter 5) proposed that meanings consist of a "core" of elemental sensations plus their associated "contexts." Many theorists propose that the internal structure of lexemes consists of semantic attributes or features, and their values (e.g., Katz & Fodor, 1963). Some theorists propose that lexemes represent meaning in terms of relationships, that is, "nodes" with "pointers" to other lexemes (e.g., Lindsay & Norman, 1977, Chapter 10). Some theorists propose that lexemes include phonemic, phonological, or articulatory information as well as semantic information (e.g., Fromkin & Rodman, 1988, Chapters 4, 6). Some theorists propose that lexemes contain information about the syntactic roles of words (e.g., Foss & Hakes, 1978, Chapter 4). According to some researchers, the entries in the mental lexicon contain all three types of information: phonological, syntactic, and semantic (e.g., Clark & Clark, 1977, Chapter 11). On the other hand, some researchers argue that the lexicon of words-as-concepts is stored separately from the lexicon of words-as-utterable-things (e.g., Penfield & Roberts, 1959). The *logogens* of Morton (1964) and the *geons* of Biederman (1987) consist solely of primitive perceptual features, and are somehow linked up to a separate semantic system.

Although hypothetical lexeme entities go by various names and are assumed to contain various sorts of information, a majority of theorists assume that their lexeme entities are the stored meanings of words. That is, it is the semantic content of the lexemes that is critical, especially with regard to lexical ambiguity.

As the relational "nodes and pointers" definition of the structure of lexemes suggests, different researchers are free to propose different ways in which lexemes are interrelated. Researchers who retain an associationistic point of view have proposed a number of different types of associative connections—causal, temporal, correlational, "higher-order," and logical (e.g., entailment). To some researchers, lexemes are interrelated in that they all have a "frame" structure, each lexeme with its specifying "slot" values. Like the windows in a house, the frames are all alike, yet each offers its own particular information about the world. To other researchers, lexemes are clusters of features whose semantic similarity is reflected by their proximity in some sort of knowledge space. Like the almonds in a chocolate bar, they float in a morass of meaning relations. To other researchers, lexemes are believed to be entries in a network. Like the crossings in the strands of a spider's web, lexemes are the intersections of the various associative pathways.

To most theorists, the logic of lexeme interrelation is categorial. The categories could be "natural," as in a family-genus-species taxonomy of ordinates and superordinates, or a divisioning into "ontological kinds." In any event, the categorization is somehow rational, if not logical, and is certainly an idealization. Like the steps and arches in some huge Platonic hierarchy of forms, "the general" rises above "the particular," while "the particular" supports or underlies "the general." Over the many centuries since their invocation, the notions of "hierarchy" and "logic" have become commonplace (especially in academia). It comes as little surprise that the familiar notions of logic and hierarchy are relied upon heavily in philosophy, linguistics, and psychology to help in understanding the ineffabilities of language and semantics. (For a review of the uses of logic metaphors for language and semantics, see Hoffman, MacCormac, Lawler, & Carroll, 1989.)

Most cognitive scientists share a core set of assumptions, a general philosophy that can be dubbed "lexemism." Lexemism hinges on the belief that words and the semantic elements of which they are composed are the basic units of language and remembering. The assumptions of this view have been characterized as the "atomization of meaning" (Bolinger, 1965; Hall, 1972) and as the "literalist" approach to meaning (Honeck, Voegtle, Dorfmuller, & Hoffman, 1980). The ontological and epistemological assumptions of lexemism are presented in Table 11.1.

The ostensive purpose of this set of assumptions is to give researchers a handle on the problem, "What are the units of the analysis of memory and meaning?" But this mental lexicon is no simple bibliography. The assumptions assert the existence of unit entities and subentities. These are ontological assumptions. The assumptions also relate the units to awareness, and they assert particular ways in which the units "capture" meaning, knowledge, and learning. These are epistemological assumptions.

TABLE 11.1. Some ontological and epistemological assumptions of "lexemism."

1. Lexemes are actually existing things, either in the brain or in the mind, or both.
2. Lexemes are phenomena of consciousness and the unconscious.
3. Lexemes are the units out of which phrases, sentences, and other chunks of language are composed.
4. Lexemes are meaningful.
5. Lexemes' internal structure and interrelations have both static ("stored") and dynamic qualities. That is, the structures are changeable but persisting.
6. Lexemes are interrelated ("connected" or "associated") in a way that preserves the meaning of individual lexemes and relates the meanings of different lexemes.
7. Lexemes are decomposable into subelements which preserve the essential feature, meaning.
8. The semantic subelements also exist, in some accessible place.
9. The semantic subelements are complete, context-independent, and universal.
10. Learning is a process of generating new lexemes or new interrelations, or of changing the internal or external structure of lexemes.
11. Comprehending is a process of determining the meaning relationships within and between lexemes (i.e., by means of "calculations" or "logic").
12. Remembering (recall, recognition) is a process of comparing or "matching" sets of lexemes or subelements according to their compatibility of meaning content.

Issues Raised by Lexemism

A number of important philosophical issues reside in the lexemism assumptions. Like alligators eager for a meal, some of the issues are hidden, some are apparent. The remainder of this chapter is an exploration of these issues, in an attempt to clarify the meanings of the key words—*search, access, retrieval, activation, inhibition, interference,* and *representation.*

One issue that is fairly apparent in the lexemism assumptions is the mind-body problem (assumption 1 in Table 11.1). This issue is usually sidestepped by cognitive psychologists, unless their work is particularly tied to physiology or to models that are based on physiological facts or hypotheses. (As is the case for modern "connectionism" and for "modularity" theories. See Chapter 15, this volume.)

Another basic philosophical problem, one that is less apparent, but is nonetheless present in the assumptions, happens to be one of the key paradoxes of meaning. Our restatement of this paradox is based on Searle's (1972) description of the "Chomskyian revolution" in linguistics, but the paradox applies to any structuralist-reductionist approach to semantics, whether logical semantics, linguistic semantics, or psychological semantics:

Either: The theory involves reduction to elements which lack the essential feature (meaning). In this case, the theory fails due to inadequacy—it cannot explain what it is intended to.

Or: The theory involves reduction to units which preserve the essential features. In this case, the theory fails due to circularity. It relies on meanings to explain meanings.

Not only is this a basic philosophical problem, but it is an especially nasty one—except to those who can conjure up meaning as some sort of "emergent."

There is another important philosophical issue that is implicit in the assumptions of lexemism, one that is related to methodology.

From the Lexemism Assumptions to Research Methodology

The assumed entities and processes have their particular hypothetical properties. The properties, in turn, suggest possible things to measure, such as association frequency or comprehension latency. The assumptions also suggest variables that could be manipulated, such as conceptual relatedness or semantic complexity. Once a particular theory or processing model has "fleshed out the bones" that are provided by the assumptions, all sorts of particular methods can be derived and particular predictions made.

For example, if one takes British associationism seriously, one might be tempted to create a task in which people see pairs of items (such as words) and are instructed to learn them as pairs—as in Mary Calkins's (1896) invention of the method of "right associates," which came to be called "paired-associate learning." If one takes seriously the notion of a huge mental "associative network," one might be tempted to look for "backward" associations or "remote" associations in learned lists, as Ebbinghaus did (1885/1964). If one takes seriously the cardinal principles of associationism and frequency, one might attempt to generate tests of "one-trial" learning, as Guthrie did (1935).

The assumptions of lexemism, accompanied by some fleshing out to generate particular processing models, have given rise to a paradigm, in a Kuhnian sense—a paradigm that has typified experimental psychology, and typifies cognitive science today. The issue involved here is a general philosophical issue. That is, it is akin to the mind-body problem and to the paradox of the structural analysis of meaning. However, this issue is unlike the others in that it is as closely related to scientific practice as it is to ontology. Specifically, the issue is methodological: What constitutes evidence that *any* hypothetical mental entity actually exists, and that it actually plays some causal role? The issue of the "psychological reality" of hypothetical constructs pervades this chapter, just as it pervades this volume and the entire field of cognitive psychology.

Why Constructing a Psychological Model Is Like Building a Dagwood Sandwich

My decision to describe various types of semantic ambiguity in terms of types of journeys and paths was quite deliberate. A theme that cuts across this chapter is "Knowing the ineffable in terms of the familiar." It cannot be doubted that metaphor can play an important, if not necessary, role in the etymology of words and idioms, in natural discourse, and in human conceptualization in general—including scientific problem solving. In fact, metaphoric ambiguity is *undoubtedly* the most pervasive type of ambiguity in technical discussions of research on lexical ambiguity.

So far, I have looked at various conceptualizations of lexical meaning and lexical ambiguity. In most cases, the ideas go hand in hand with notions about the nature of the processes that operate on lexemes. For example, the relational definition of the structure of lexicons goes hand in hand with the notion that comprehension and remembering involve following associative paths. What I am getting at here is that the "bones" of lexemism describe the units of analysis, but leave open most of the details of the processes and operations that are needed to produce the kinds of effects and behaviors that are seen in the laboratory. Note the open-ended nature of lexemism assumptions 10, 11, and 12 in Table 11.1. Numerous metaphors have been used to describe the processes alluded to in these three assumptions, and explication of these metaphors reveals the basic meanings of a number of the key terms—search, access, activation, inhibition, and interference.

Spaces

The British empiricists/associationists, such as Hume (1739/1896) and Locke (1670/1959), had a definite penchant for explaining the laws of association in terms of hypothetical mental processes akin to the processes and energies described by physics and chemistry. Thus, the association of ideas was said to occur because of mental "gravity," mental "magnetism," or other "vibratory energies" which "attract" similar ideas and "repel" contrasting ideas in the mental space. Just as planets orbit their suns, just as magnets attract iron filings, just as atoms combine to form molecules, simple ideas combine to form complex and hypercomplex ideas.

Most theories of memory, from the earliest days of psychology onward, are variations of a metaphor of a compartmentalized mental space, with remembering regarded as a "search" through the contents of the space (Roediger, 1980). Once "accessed" (located), the contents can be carried into consciousness ("retrieved"). Specific theories differ in their details (or lack of details) with regard to the particular hypothetical entities and mechanisms. For instance, one could postulate that learning and comprehension consist of "slot-filling operations." One could postulate that there is more than one type of associative connection. One could postulate different kinds of search—serial search, exhaustive search, self-terminating search, massively parallel search, "race" models, etc.

An example of a general theory of cognition that relies on the mental space metaphor is the "levels-of-processing" theory (Craik & Lockhart, 1972). It divides the mental space into higher and lower levels, with "higher" indicating closer to consciousness and comprehension, and "lower" indicating closer to raw sensations and unconscious motor commands. It is common for theories of the mental space to associate consciousness with "up" and the unconscious with "down."

Traces

One might be inclined to link the mental space to its physiological substrate, as Hartley did (1749/1801). In this case, one would be likely to postulate some sort of memory "trace." The metaphor of memory traces was suggested by Descartes as a description of neural processes in sensation and perception. Although Descartes' theorizing was based on Harvey's description of the circulation of the blood, the analogy is to riverbeds and to fluid flow in general. The flow of experience leaves traces in the form of changes in the fluid pathway, which in turn determine the course of future experiences.

A very nice metaphor, this, and it has stood the test of time. Another example of an early trace theory would be J. S. Mill's (1878) theory of "associative strength." A more modern example of a trace theory would be Guthrie's "stamping in" and "strengthening" of associative connections between specific behaviors. More modern still would be all the connectionist models, from Hebb (1949) onward, in which strengths are somehow gauged (these days, in terms of probabilities in the connectionist models).

Electricity

The history of psychology is largely a history of machines (Pribram, 1981). Descartes saw the body as a clockwork mechanism. Wundt and Pavlov saw the nervous system as a set of connections like a telegraph or telephone switchboard. Immediately following World War II the radio was used as a metaphor in the earliest "information theory" psychology, which quickly expanded its conceptual base to include computers (and later still holograms). Given that the nervous system is believed to be somehow like an electrical circuit or communication system, one can suppose that mental or neural processes operate like electrical ones. Thus, for example, neural and mental processes could be turned on and off—memories could be "activated" and the energization of associations could be based on "spreading activation." Also, neural and mental processes could suffer from "interference" just like the interference in radio reception. The concepts of interference and activation are widely used in modern cognitive psychology and in research on lexical ambiguity.

Icebergs

Theorizing by Leibniz (1704/1898) and Herbart (1816/1891) about the unconscious, including the notion of the "threshold of consciousness," helped bring two important metaphors into psychology. One metaphor is the comparison of the mind to a set of rooms. This is a clear manifestation of the mental space theme, and was especially important in Freud's theorizing. The other metaphor that is commonly used to explicate the relation of the conscious to the unconscious is that of an iceberg. According to this metaphor, the mass of memories is constantly below awareness, an "apperceptive mass." The capacity of consciousness (or attention or "working memory") is limited, so that at any one moment only a small subset of ideas can be above the threshold. This metaphor suggests notions such as the "suppression" and "inhibition" of ideas, concepts that have always been current in experimental psychology (cf. Kimble, 1961; Woodworth, 1938).

Making a Sandwich

Psychologists have a wealth of metaphors available to them, but the problem here is *not* the presence of metaphor, nor its overabundance. Rather, it is a problem of undisciplined consumption. Put simply, theorizing in cognitive science is risky if it is underconstrained. Theorists seem to operate under the assumption that they are completely free to pick and choose from among the various candidate hypothetical entities and processes. Thus, building a psychological processing model becomes rather like making a Dagwood sandwich. "What do you want—schemata? Sure, we got schemata. Sorry, no labeled relations today, but we got parallel processing. A side order of prototypes? Sure."

While somewhat whimsical, the cafeteria metaphor is serious in import. Any given theory in cognitive psychology is likely to be a more or less ad hoc mixture of metaphors. One can find theories that combine propositional reckoning with schemata, theories that combine feature hierarchies with templates, theories that define comprehension as the calculation of distances in a semantic hyperspace, etc.

Sometimes, mixed metaphors work, and work well. Perhaps the best example is the merger of the ancient themes "Language is logic" and "Minds are machines" in modern computer models. Computers are machines that do logic, thus giving the mixed metaphor an experiential base (the familiar) with which to describe the ineffable (the mind).

However, mixed metaphors often fall flat, as in the famous Reaganism "The Ship of State is sailing the wrong way down a one-way street." In the case of mixed metaphors in cognitive science, a theorist might combine certain notions without considering whether their basic metaphors are different or even incompatible. Like putting ketchup on a hot dog instead of brown mustard. Some people might like it, but anyone who has studied hot dogs in detail regards ketchupped hot dogs as revolting.

For instance, a theorist might define the inhibition of ideas or meanings by reference to a hypothetical process of interference. But what does that buy you? A radio made of ice? Such a metaphor would probably add little to the conceptual armamentarium of cognitive psychology, and may lead to confusion and communication breakdowns. As a second example, some theories in cognitive science attempt to incorporate Bartlettian or Piagetian schemata into the notions of information processing, but the two basic metaphors are inherently at odds. Schemata are dynamic, motivational things—based on a "plastic" or "organic" metaphor. A thing is a "schematic" if it is an overview, and only partially represents details: Schemata capture meaning in big gulps. Thus, schemata do not fit terribly well within the structured, categorial, logical, detailed framework of information processing models. Any attempt by logicians to specify the internal structure for schemata is likely to appear somewhat ad hoc from the perspective of psychology. In any event, once the logical structures take over, the reasons for invoking schemata in the first place can get lost in the shuffle, and one may end up sacrificing the theoretical power that the schemata concept offers.

The cafeteria strategy of conflating meanings and mixing metaphors might work in cognitive simulation, where one is seeking clever ways of finding computational solutions to tough memory search or inference-making problems. But for the psychology branch of cognitive science, some means needs to be found to constrain the theorizing, to provide it with a clear referential base (Bahrick, 1987). Presumably, any given bit of theorizing in experimental psychology is closely linked to some type of evidence, whether it be the results of a psychological experiment or the output of a computer program that is intended to mimic human learning. But for some reason, cognitive scientists as a group usually don't operate this way. Examples even exist of lengthy discourses on theories of cognition in which it is nowhere explicitly stated whether the theory is supposed to be a theory of how heads work or of how computers work (or both). Hypothetical entities are postulated and combined without any clear evidential motivation for the postulation of either their existence or their combination.

Certainly, decent cognitive theories will be complex and will require a number of hypothetical concepts. A major point of modern psycholinguistics and cognitive psychology is that theories in psychology cannot ignore "the mental." They cannot be so rigid or strictly behavioral as to end up losing parsimony for the sake of simplicity. A "parsimonious" theory, after all, is not just simple; it must include *all* the concepts that are necessary to give a full understanding of the phenomena at hand. However, in recent years the pendulum may have swung too far toward mentalism. It's as if Lloyd Morgan had never shot off his canon. It's as if Ockham had never shaved. And if cognitive theorizing is underconstrained, it might just as well be a branch of philosophy. Pretty much anything goes, and theorizing becomes a game of "out-clevering" the other fellow.

So far, I've explored *ambiguity* and *lexeme* in order to highlight important issues, such as the mixing of metaphors, and in order to point out the basic metaphors that underlie some of the key words (search, access, retrieval, inhibition, and interference). Now I can pull together some other issues that pervade this chapter, and do so by looking at another of the key words.

What is *Representation?*

Another of the key words often used as hard cash is the word *representation.* This concept has also shown up in this chapter, in the general metaphor theme of lexemism ("The mental representation of meanings has the character of a lexicon") and in the philosophical issue, "What constitutes evidence that a theoretical representation has psychological reality?"

The word *representation* derives from the Sanskrit roots *es* and *sat,* meaning "to be real, present, or existing." In Latin, *representare* meant "to be before the mind or in view." There are many kinds of things that can be regarded as representations: photographs, drawings, symbols, logic, mathematics, language, percepts, images. One might regard a black cat as a symbolic representation of evil. An abstract work of art may be appreciated as a hodgepodge of pretty colors, but might also be taken to represent things other than itself, such as Freud's angst. A caricature may preserve none of the actual features of the lampoonee but may nonetheless represent some of his essential characteristics, such as his outrageous eyebrows and ears.

The Stage Metaphor

The concept of representation is a somewhat abstract concept, and it comes as little surprise that numerous metaphors have been used throughout the ages to talk about various kinds of representations: A thing represents something else if both the items can be "mapped" onto one another; a representation is a "translation" of reality; a representation "mirrors" the world.

The word *representation* as a technical term in psychology comes most directly from the German mentalistic psychologies of the 1800s, and specifically the "stage" metaphor for consciousness (Hoffman, Cochran, & Nead, 1989). According to this metaphor, the mind is structured like a theater. One can be on stage, actively participating in the stream of ongoing events, or one can be in the audience, observing thoughts as they go by and making judgments about them. Furthermore, important events can be going on backstage, outside of awareness.

Any phenomenon in which ideas, percepts, images, or meanings appear in awareness is thus called a *presentation* (in German, *Vorstellung*). This is essentially the German psychology analog of American psychology's concept of a percept or image. Something is "set before" the mind for inspection or introspection. A representation is when a phenomenon is re-presented; that is, it is recognized or is dredged up from memory. The *Vorstellung* stage metaphor is a rich one, and was used extensively by European psychologists, including Brentano, Ebbinghaus, and many others.

The Assumptions of Representationalism in Modern Cognitive Science

The general approach taken in modern cognitive science involves a number of assumptions about mental representations: (1) Mental representations can be described in rational terms (i.e., systematic, logical, or even calculational terms). (2) Mental representations are of two types, contents and operations. (3) Contents capture bits of information and knowledge about the world. (4) Contents can represent either the form of stimuli (e.g., the perceptual features of letters, the acoustic features of syllables) or the meaning of stimuli (e.g., word meaning). (4) Mental representations have both static and dynamic qualities. That is, they are "stored," but can be operated upon and thereby altered. (5) Mental operations produce informative changes in both form and meaning contents. (6) All of cognition and perception consists of causal sequences of contents and operations.

The Risks of Representationalism

A number of risks are involved in any theorizing about hypothetical mental representations. I have already pointed out that cognitive scientists are somewhat fast and loose with their metaphorical representation schemes; they mix them in a somewhat unconstrained way. In contrast with the risky mixture of metaphors, its also risky to be an imperialist and push a single representational scheme too far. Sometimes, theorists latch onto a pet formalism or representational concept, and argue that the formalism applies to all of cognition. An instance is the claim that all mental representations must be in the form of schemata since schemata are so computationally elegant or have some other beautiful characteristics.

Risk is certainly involved whenever one reifies a theoretical representation. In general, cognitive scientists regard mental representations as theoretical descriptions of actual mental contents and operations. From the cognizer's perspective, their representations represent the world. But from the theorist's perspective, the theoretical representations represent the cognizer's representation of the world. Two different perspectives are engaged, and it is sometimes difficult to keep them separate. The distinction here is between theories as *descriptions* and theories as *reified representations.* That is, one can assume that a description of mental phenomena is also a representation of what is actually going on in the mind or brain; one can assume that the theoretical representation *is* what the head does.

It takes something of a leap of faith to go from description to reified representation (Bahrick, 1987). To lessen the risk involved, one needs to generate two different sets of evidence: (1) evidence that the hypothetical description is a valid description and (2) converging evidence, *evidence other than (1),* that mental phenomena actually obey the description. Much reification in cognitive science is risky because these two different types of evidence are not provided. Let's look at a few examples of risky reification.

Comprehension Is Calculation. Just because we can use mathematics and probabilities to describe degrees of semantic similarity, that does not mean that comprehension itself is a process involving the computation of distance vectors. Some theorists talk as if they believe exactly that (cf. Sternberg, Tourangeau, & Nigro, 1979). Has anyone ever shown that computations go on in the mind during comprehension?

Schemas as Intentional Agents. Many theories in cognitive psychology rely on the schema concept. Schemata are pretty since they capture knowledge in gulps. In Schmidt's (1975) schema theory of motor skills, schemata are regarded as "abstract" structures, but ones that also operate as intentional agents. They not only guide actions, but initiate them as well. How can one show that an abstract structure is also an intentional agent?

Inhibition and Interference as Mental Processes. How does one actually show that inhibition or interference is occurring? Has anyone ever actually seen them? *Inhibition*—according to the iceberg metaphor—suggests that a process is kept from running, or that a content is kept out of awareness. *Interference*—according to the radio metaphor—suggests that a process is running, but doesn't run properly or doesn't reach its natural conclusion, because some other process is going on at the same time. These are two entirely different possibilities, and no single research method is likely to peg down everything that could be going on. A simple increase in reaction time, or even a pattern of increases and decreases across experimental conditions, may not be enough to actually show that *either* an inhibitory or interfering process is going on. Yet cognitive psychologists often take it for granted that reaction time is a measure of "ease" of comprehension or "degree" of inhibition, or interference, or facilitation.

In all these cases, there is some initial evidence that the description or metaphor can be invoked, but there is little or no additional or converging evidence that the descriptions are "psychologically real."

At a Loss for Words

Certainly, when theorists use one of the key concepts, they are not necessarily experiencing mental images of icebergs or electric circuits or other metaphors. Indeed, some researchers use key terms (interference, inhibition, access, etc.) while explicitly denying *any* metaphors or ancillary meanings. They go to extremes to avoid all the connotations of metaphorical terms, thereby avoiding the reification problem. For instance, a researcher might swear up and down that her use of the word *inhibition* involves absolutely no connotations of any sort of inhibitory processes. A researcher might swear up and down that his use of the word *access* involves absolutely no connotations of contact with consciousness—or absolutely no connotations of access of anything by anything. They insist that by *access* they merely mean *activation.*

Such claims are a testament to the extent to which researchers differ in their views of how various theoretical terms should be used. But if the researchers who deny the ancillary meanings of their terms really mean what they say, they would be acting as true operationalists. They would not talk of inhibition or access or activation at all, but would instead talk of *hypothetical process type 1* or *hypothetical entity type Beta.* Operational definitions are certainly critical in linking theoretical concepts to research methods and results, but theoretical terms can never be successfully defined *only* in operational terms. To do so is to eliminate the meaning of the terms altogether, a sort of linguistic hygienics of psychological theories. It is doomed to fail, because it is the metaphors and the images they suggest that support the generation of hypothetical models, which lead in turn to ideas about research. The metaphors, images, and models that a term suggests cannot be discarded like soiled linen. They cannot be denied, no matter how hard one might try.

Some Recommendations

This exploration suggests two ways in which researchers can try to get clear about the meanings of their terms. One is to try and pull out any hidden assumptions in their theorizing. The list of lexemism assumptions in Table 11.1 can be used as a checklist. Researchers can ask whether they believe each of the assumptions, and if not, how they might choose to reword them. Some cognitive researchers routinely list their postulates, which is a commendable practice. A good example would be Gorfein's listing of the postulates of his "race" model. But listing one's postulates may not be enough if lots of ontological and epistemological assumptions lie hidden in the postulates.

Another way to achieve greater clarity is to perform a propositional analysis of one's theory. Propositional analysis would include a listing of each hypothetical entity and its definition, and each hypothetical process and its definition. The definitions might rely on the metaphors that are implied by the key terms, but if they do not, then one must ask oneself whether alternative terms might be better suited to express the intended meaning. Next, one can ask, "Is each hypothetical entity necessary?" and "Is each hypothetical process necessary?"—if one seeks to avoid a Dagwood-sandwich type of theory. For each proposition, one can also list any evidence that supports or verifies it, if one wishes to minimize the risks of reification.

Though a fairly straightforward process, propositional analysis can be very revealing. I recall reading a major treatise on language in which schemata were invoked and defined as types of prototypes, but at another point in the manuscript, prototypes were defined as types of templates. It wasn't clear until after I had listed all of the propositions that the theory included the conjoint claim: "Schemata are prototypes are templates." When taken out of context and listed separately, the propositions of the theory lost most of their explanatory power—in this case because the theory never really had much to begin with.

Final Thoughts

I began with the goal of pegging down the meanings of the key terms that were relied upon heavily in this volume—*ambiguity, retrieval, search, activation, access, interference, inhibition,* and *representation.* To put these terms and their meanings in perspective, I have taken the reader on a tour of a number of larger philosophical issues, which culminated in a statement of the general assumptions of cognitivism (the lexemism and representationalism assumptions), and some of the risks that these assumptions involve.

The "bones" of the lexemism assumptions may represent the old ghosts of past mentalistic theorizing. However, the lexemism assumptions are, and have always been, incredibly pervasive in mentalistic psychologies and in studies of language. The basic lexemism assumptions may actually represent constraints on the ways in which humans are capable of thinking about the ineffabilities of meaning and language. That's a rather scary possibility. If it is true, the ghost in the machine can look forward to a lease in perpetuity, and we may have to pay the price forever. Only time will tell whether the bones will end up representing the ghosts of our present, and future, theories.

Acknowledgement. Thanks to David Gorfein for prodding me to write these ideas out, and to Tram Neill and Richard Klein for stimulating their refinement.

Part IV Ambiguity in Text

The first paper in this section (Chapter 12) addresses two important issues: development of language skills and the status of modularity, whether it is developed or inborn. David Swinney, a strong supporter of the modularity hypothesis throughout the conference, collaborates with Penny Prather to argue for an early onset of a modular system in children's language processing. They offer a methodological refinement of the cross-model priming task for use as a developmental tool.

In Chapter 13, Whitney and Clark leave the realm of single-word and syntactic ambiguity to carry the approach of ambiguity researchers to the problems afforded by story ambiguity. Thus they examine how individual difference variables influence the construction of an interpretation in passages where the text lends itself to a variety of interpretations.

12

On the Comprehension of Lexical Ambiguity by Young Children: Investigations into the Development of Mental Modularity

DAVID SWINNEY AND PENNY PRATHER

The fundamental questions concerning the human language faculty have traditionally been cast as involving at least: (1) the determination of the general nature of that faculty, (2) an understanding of how that faculty develops, and (3) the determination of innate and learned characteristics of that faculty (see, e.g., Chomsky, 1986). These questions, in fact, represent fundamental issues in the study of all domains of cognitive performance, language or otherwise.

Fodor's (1983) recent delineation of cognitive processes into domain-specific modular routines and domain-general systems offers an important framework within which to consider these general questions about cognitive processes. Briefly, in Fodor's proposed architecture of cognitive processes, basic perceptual systems (e.g., language) are argued to be modular, while more integrative, problem-solving types of processes act across modules. Criterially, "modularity" involves information encapsulation and cognitive impenetrability for processes activated within a perceptual module. Thus, for example, language perception is argued to be a form-driven process, one relying for its initiation only on information of acoustic/phonetic/graphemic form received by the listener/reader, and not on world knowledge or other contextual influences. Descriptively, perceptual processes in modular systems are held to be automatic, very rapid, and autonomous. Much support for the existence of perceptual modules has been developed over the past few years, with a large amount of the work focusing on modularity of smaller and smaller processing units within perceptual systems—submodules, if you will (e.g., Forster, 1979).

One such putative submodule within the language domain, lexical access, has been the focus of work by a large number of researchers (see others chapters in this volume), many of whom have used resolution of lexical ambiguity during language comprehension as a testing ground for claims of modularity. Briefly, such research has focused on examination of whether or not prior contextual information constrains access to the various meanings of the ambiguity when it is heard or read. The overwhelming bulk (but certainly not all) of the evidence from sentence processing studies has supported the modularity position; even in the face of strongly biasing contextual information, multiple interpretations of a clearly polysemous word are accessed automatically by normal adult listeners when they first hear it in a sentence.[1]

Assuming for the moment, then, that lexical access during sentence comprehension for normal adult listeners is best characterized as a modular process, the second and third questions raised above come into play: Is this modularity an innate property of the lexical recognition system, one which is in place in the neonate as part of the functional wiring of the neurological substrate underlying language processing? (The issue of whether it is expressed immediately or developmentally as a part of prescribed maturation of the system represents a separate question.) Or, rather, is modularity an acquired characteristic of the lexicon, the result of practice and developing automaticity? (After all, the descriptive characteristics of a modular system could be obtained through development of a system which becomes so practiced and automatic that its most efficient functioning is maintained purely through extremely rapid bottom-up, contextual-free processing—in short, modular, autonomous, rapid processing.)

Clearly, the answers to these questions will have considerable impact on the answer to the basic question first raised above: namely—the general nature of the process. A formal characterization of language processing may differ considerably depending on whether or not a modular system in the adult is innate, or alternatively, has a developmental history tied to purely practice and/or learning considerations. Similarly, the characterizations of *child* language will differ greatly depending on the answers to these questions. For example, even if there is an innate propensity for a modular system that is not realized in the immature individual (the maturational hypothesis), the lack of a modular system in a child will require descriptions of the child-to-adult transition in language to encompass the discontinuity of these systems with regard to modular perceptual systems.

---

[1]Some recent work by Tabbossi (1988; see also Chapter 3 this volume) has presented a particularly interesting challenge to what has come to be orthodoxy here. However, it does appear that the effects achieved by Tabossi may be reflecting issues dealing with *how much* information related to each meaning is accessed when all meanings are accessed for a word. Schema theory (e.g., Kintsch, 1988) suggests that even if many independent meanings are accessed for each word, the depth of features related to these meanings may be very shallow. Although it may not turn out to be the case upon further investigation, it appears that Tabossi's interesting and exciting effects may be caused because only a few, strongly related features are ever activated upon access for a word, whereas features such as she examined, being a function of schema, are a result of nonmodular post-access processing. See also footnote 3.

Finally, it is important to note that while this paper is focused on language and ambiguity processing, the issues are arguably generalizable to other cognitive systems. Thus, the issues concerning development of modularity for a processing subsystem apply equally to processes as far removed from language (or as closely aligned, depending on your point of view) as object recognition, number perception, attentional processes, and memory. While developmental research has not directly examined the question of whether or not modularity in any domain is acquired, there is some indirect evidence that modularity may be innate in certain instances. Hasher and Zacks (1975), for example, argue that there are two types of automatic (modular) process, those that are innate or prewired and those that are acquired through (over)learning. In their scheme, as in Fodor's, language is considered a privileged domain, that is, one in which automaticity is determined structurally. Similarly, certain automatic properties of attention are deemed innate in this system, while nonmodular, intentional properties of attention are claimed to develop between the ages of 6 and 10 (see Treisman & Gelade, 1980; Treisman & Schmidt, 1982, for examples of a variety of attentional properties). Further, there is a population of children in whom controlled attention (as opposed to automatic properties of attention) develops more slowly than for their peers, children with the formal diagnostic label of *attention deficit hyperactivity disorder* (ADHD). These children show no delays in acquisition of motor, language, and other developmental milestones and no apparent deviance or delay in acquisition of basic skills until entering school. At that time, however, these children show problems in "getting organized" and in "processing language" (e.g., difficulty with complex constructions). Since their inattentiveness (deficits in controlled attention) affects complex linguistic processing but not acquisition of basic lexical and syntactic skills, then it seems reasonable to assume that these latter skills do not require conscious, attentive learning and therefore that their modularity or automaticity may be innate rather than acquired.

Overall, however, there is little empirical data to draw on in discussing merits of the acquired versus innate positions concerning mental modules. The work which we present below focuses on language (and, in particular, on lexical ambiguity) processing in young children, and is aimed at shedding light on the issue of whether or not the modularity of processing displayed by adults in lexical access has a developmental history.

General Methodological Issues

The process under discussion here—lexical access of the meanings of ambiguous words—is first and foremost an unconscious perceptual process. Thus, tasks which are intended to be used to measure such processes should be known to be sensitive to this level of processing. If a task requires conscious introspection/analysis about the lexical-access process, or about the role of the lexical target in the sentence, it will, at best, be a distant and impoverished reflection of this targeted process. Similarly, if the task used to reflect the targeted process "taps" processing at a point temporally removed from the occurrence of the process, it too will only vaguely and indirectly, and perhaps incorrectly, reflect the nature of that process (see Neely, 1977; Prather & Swinney, 1988, for further discussion). Thus, it is critical that tasks be as temporally close to the target as possible (such tasks are typically referred to as *on-line* tasks), and they must require as little conscious introspection as possible about the target and its role in the sentence. In short, we want accurate tasks that add as little to the process under study as possible and tasks that are in a position to reveal temporally evanescent effects. There is no ideal task; all bring their own complications. However, there are clearly distinctions among usefulness of various tasks that do exist. Our review of the literature below and our own choice of tasks reflect these points.

Comprehension and Detection of Ambiguity by Young Children

There exist some studies of children's comprehension of ambiguity in the literature, but they tend to be studies involving the metalinguistic—and hence conscious—ability of children to detect linguistic ambiguity. Kessel (1970), in what may be the first modern research on children's comprehension of ambiguity, used a picture selection task to examine children's ability to detect ambiguities. In this, children were asked to pick the correct one that represented the meaning(s) of the word from a set of four pictures. Kessel argued that his data demonstrated that most children in kindergarten and first grade (the youngest age was approximate 6.3 years) could perceive lexically ambiguous sentences. Using a similar task, Shultz and Pilon (1973) found that their first-grade students only detected about 10% of the lexical ambiguities they were presented with. However, as has been pointed out (see, e.g., Evans, 1976; Wankoff & Cairns, 1987), there were a large number of methodological difficulties that prevent definitive establishment of precisely when lexical ambiguities are available to conscious introspection, at least from these experiments. In studies which closely link the ability to detect ambiguity to the development of Piagetian conservation skills in children, Wankoff and Cairns (1987), using a picture-choice task, discovered that their youngest children (kindergarteners, mean age 5.6) only detect a low percentage of lexical ambiguities in language, while third graders perform quite well on this task. Thus, by age 5 or so, children do not demonstrate behavior that would support a strong belief that they access multiple word meanings upon encountering a lexical ambiguity.

As noted above, however, the question of whether or not children can become consciously aware of polysemy is not at issue here. Rather, the essential question focuses on the nature of their (unconscious) perceptual processing of lexical ambiguities. There are two studies examining this issue with slightly more "on-line" tasks of ambiguity processing in young children that deserve comment. Evans (1976), using a word-monitoring task, asked children to monitor for a target word in a sentence and measured reaction time to detect the target word. These target words immediately followed an ambiguous word in the sentence. (Foss, 1970, and Foss, Starkey, & Bias, 1975, have demonstrated that reaction time to detect such a target word is a function of the complexity of the immediately preceding sentential material, in both children and adults.) In her study, Evans examined kindergarten and first-grade children (divided on the basis of having attained Piagetian-type conservation skills or not) and discovered that, overall, there was a main effect for the ambiguity variable (reaction times to monitor for words following an ambiguity were longer than for those following a nonambiguous control word). The increased reaction times following ambiguities were taken to indicate that the child's processing device was being forced to deal with more than one meaning, and hence performing the monitoring task was slower following ambiguities than controls. At first blush, this evidence appears to lend support to the innate (or, at least, "very early") modularity hypothesis. Since the time that this research was performed, however, it has been demonstrated that monitoring tasks are subject to a number of potential confounds that were not controlled for in this study (see, e.g., Mehler, Segui, & Carey, 1978; Newman & Dell, 1978), and, consequently, the interpretation of these results is not secure.

In another study of lexical access of ambiguity in children, Bowman (1979) used a picture verification task. In this work, a picture was presented during comprehension of the sentence and subjects (children age 6–7) had to make a decision about whether or not the picture was related to the sentence). Unfortunately, although Bowman's results were interpreted as supporting multiple access of meanings for the ambiguity, the data were merely suggestive rather than significant, and this, combined with the fact that her task required an attempt at conscious reflection/integration on the target of inquiry, suggests that these data, also, cannot help us in any absolute determinations of an answer to our basic question concerning innateness of modularity.

The Current Study

Background

Thus, we are still left with the question of whether all (or only one) meanings of an ambiguity are accessed by very young children. The set of studies detailed below is aimed at providing more revealing, fine-grained evidence concerning what information is actually accessed by very young children when they encounter lexical ambiguities during sentence comprehension. Such work required development of a task that children could perform that was sensitive to both the automaticity and short time course of lexical access.

In research with adults, a cross-modal priming task that required either lexical decision or naming of a visual word in order to examine lexical-access processes on-line has proved to be quite useful in this regard (e.g., Swinney, 1979; Tanenhaus, Leiman, & Seidenberg, 1979). Since young children cannot read, it was decided to modify that task to include a picture priming rather than a word priming task. A number of experimenters (e.g., Carr, McCauley, & Sperber, 1982; Kroll & Potter, 1984; Vanderwart, 1984) have demonstrated that words reliably prime pictures, and thus the task is a promising one for subjects who cannot read. The essential characteristics of the task used with children were the same as that used with adults. The task, an on-line, cross-modal, sentence comprehension–picture priming (CMPP) task, was designed to allow evaluation of which meanings of an ambiguous word are available to children as they hear the word in a sentence context. Children were asked to make sentence-unrelated (this is important!) decisions about pictures which were visually presented at a point simultaneous with the offset of an ambiguity in a sentence they were listening to. Their task was twofold: (1) they were to listen to and understand the sentence. They were told that they would be tested often for sentence comprehension. And (2) they were told that a picture would be presented at some point while they were listening to the sentence, and that they were to decide as quickly as they could whether or not the pictured object was something they could eat. An important advantage of this task is that it does not require the child to try to link the picture to the sentence in any conscious way (and, indeed, due to the ratio of related to unrelated pictures throughout the experiment, such a strategy would hurt task performance). The relevant data using this task were the differences between reaction times on pictures that were and that were not preceded by a related word (in our case, an ambiguity) in the auditorily presented sentence. If the child accesses a particular meaning of the ambiguity, then reaction time on the "eat/no eat" task should be faster for a picture related to that meaning of the ambiguity than to the same picture when it is preceded by an unrelated word (e.g., replacing the ambiguous word with a different word in the same sentence). If the child accesses both meanings, then reaction times for pictures related to each meaning should, by the same argument, be faster than their respective controls. Thus, this picture priming task constitutes an on-line measure that can directly reflect activation of meanings for a word in a sentence, much like lexical-decision or naming tasks in the adult literature (see Swinney, 1984, for a review of assumptions in this type of work).[2] It might best be noted here that a great

---

[2]There is a small literature on a putative phenomenon known as "backward priming" (Kiger & Glass, 1983) which has been claimed by Glucksberg, Kreuz, and Rho (1986) to put in jeopardy the interpretation given for the cross-modal results

deal of pretesting concerning the type of decision to be used with children took place. "Something you can eat or not" was chosen as the task because children demonstrated quite definite ideas on the topic in pilot work, and because they could be trained to make this classification; in short, it worked.

---

with adults. This deserves some brief comment here, although several more recent pieces of work demonstrate that the claims for backward priming are not supportable as presented (see, e.g., Burgess, Tanenhaus, & Seidenberg, 1988; Prather & Swinney, 1988). In short, the claim is that the effect obtained by (for example) Onifer and Swinney (1981) is caused by the following: The appearance of the lexical-decision target item related to the contextually irrelevant interpretation of the ambiguity causes reanalysis of the ambiguity which has just been heard in the sentence (and for which only the contextually relevant interpretation was originally accessed, in this view) such that the "other" meaning of the ambiguity then gets activated, which then, in turn, helps the ongoing lexical decision (which started this effect) for that target. This claim hinges on results reported by Kiger and Glass (1983), who obtained an effect in the visual domain (only) of a lexical decision to a word presented initially for 50 ms by a semantically related word that followed such presentation 30 ms later. It is critically important to note that this effect was obtained only with these timing constraints (others were tried, but the effect was not maintained), only for visual-visual presentation (where modality interference effects are notorious), *and* that the effects obtained are far better described as a lessening-of-inhibition effect rather than any sort of priming effect. (To be convinced of that fact, look at the absolute RTs obtained by Kiger and Glass compared with normal lexical-decision RT. Additionally, look at the fact that in their Experiment 1, which contained a "neutral" control, no effect was obtained.) Importantly, many attempts to replicate this effect cross-modally have failed to find *any* evidence of such an effect, and the effect itself in the visual domain has also been remarkably resistant to replication (see, e.g., Prather & Swinney, 1988; Forster, personal communication). Now, Glucksberg et al. performed their experiment *assuming* that there was such a thing as backward priming. They did not, in any sense, provide a test of backward priming. Their results with nonwords are most easily interpretable as effects driven by prior material in the sentence which have nothing to do with the presence of any ambiguity. Further, a careful analysis of the post hoc control conditions run by Glucksberg et al. reveals that their effect seems to obtain clearly in only one of their experimental conditions. Finally, Burgess et al. (1988) have recently demonstrated that the Glucksberg results were a function of the particular conditions they chose. There is simply not sufficient space to give adequate argument about all of these, and other related, issues here. However, it is the case that the general interpretation of the overall results in the literature provided above (in the text of this paper) are secure, and are not susceptible to interpretation by a "backward priming" argument, at least given everything that is currently known about the issue.

Finally, note that the backward priming argument, even if it could have been mounted, would be much more difficult to argue for pictures and words (since we don't know how pictures are coded, and they would have to be coded the same manner as words to "interact in memory," as held by the backward priming argument). In short, this is not an argument that has any current empirical or logical support in terms of the work presented here.

Pretesting Ambiguities and Pictures

Preparation of the materials for the present research involved a good deal of pilot work to assure that both meanings of ambiguous words were familiar to our young subjects and to be certain that the pictures and sentences were easily understood by preschoolers. It was important to establish the children's level of conscious awareness of ambiguities in order to examine the question of whether or not they automatically access those multiple meanings during on-line processing. The procedures used to select materials are described briefly here.

In the first stage of materials preparation, 56 ambiguous words were pretested in three successive stages with 33 children between the ages of 4,0 and 5,6 (all enrolled at the Eliot-Pearson Children's School at Tufts University). Stage 1 involved asking children to give definitions for orally presented ambiguous words. This was done under the guise of a game. Once one definition was given, the child was asked if the word could mean anything else. The second stage of testing, done on a separate day, involved presenting each child with a description of an item for those meanings of ambiguous words that they had not produced spontaneously during stage 1 testing. So, for example, if a child did not spontaneously produce a definition of baseball bat for the word *bat* in stage 1, then in stage 2, the child would be asked, "What do you hit a baseball with?" Finally, in stage 3, for any meanings of ambiguous words that were not demonstrated to be familiar to the child in stages 1 and 2, a third session was scheduled in which the child was shown a picture of the item and asked to name it. From this initial work, 20 lexical ambiguities identified by all children at stage 1, plus 4 additional ambiguities know to all but one child at stage 1 and demonstrated to be familiar to that child under stage 2 testing, were chosen for use in the on-line studies described below.

In the next step of materials preparation, line-drawn pictures representing each meaning of each of the 24 ambiguous words, plus those of a number of other items (to be used for filler sentences), were created. The items and drawings were chosen so that approximately 50% represented edible objects. Each picture was tested for easy and quick recognition on a group of 10 children in the same age range as those participating in the major study described below. This step was done to validate that the pictures were easily identifiable representations of the word meanings. Subsequently, two sentential contexts were created for each of the 24 lexical ambiguities (as well as appropriate filler sentences), and this same group of 10 subjects was used to verify that these sentences were easily understood. Each child was asked to explain what each sentence meant, and sentences were rewritten according to a criterion of ease of understanding based on these children's responses.

Finally, the 56 sentences and accompanying pictures (see detailed materials description in the next section) were presented to 23 college-aged students as an initial pilot test of the cross-modal picture priming (CMPP) sentence comprehension methodology, and in an attempt to replicate effects found for adults with other on-line techniques. In this initial experiment, no effects of any type were discovered; mean reaction time was 489 ms to classify the pictures as edible or not, with no RT difference for either edible versus nonedible classifications or for ambiguity versus control materials. It was apparent from our analyses that floor effects were obtained with adults, and so the pictures were "degraded" by the simple procedure of presenting them with the experimental room lights on. Using this degraded condition, priming was obtained for classifying pictures related to each meaning of the ambiguity for both of the contextual bias conditions, thus replicating results obtained for normal adults with cross-modal lexical-decision and naming studies. At this point it was decided that this methodology could be used to investigate children's access of meanings for ambiguous words in sentential context.

Study of Lexical Access for Ambiguous Words in Young Children

The basic experiment with young children involved use of the CMPP technique briefly described above. We elaborate on the experimental design here in slightly more detail. In this study, subjects (the same group of thirty-three 4- and 5-year-olds used in the pilot work, but tested 2 to 11 months later) heard 56 sentences presented over headphones. Twenty-four of the sentences contained a lexical ambiguity placed in a semantically biasing context. Two different sentence contexts were written for each ambiguity: one biased toward the most frequent interpretation (version 1, experimental) and the other biased toward the least frequent interpretation (version 2, experimental). (Frequency of meanings was determined on the basis of the first definition given during stage 1 testing, described in the preceding section.) A second set of "control" sentences was written in which an unambiguous control word was substituted for the ambiguity in the same sentence frame (version 1 and version 2, control). This word was of the same frequency and length as the ambiguity (age 5 children's frequency norms were used; Carroll, Davies, & Richman, 1971), and was chosen so as to roughly maintain the meaning of the sentences. However, the word itself was not semantically identical to the meaning of the ambiguity. (See the Appendix for an example of the two sets of materials.) Thus, there was a total of four sentence conditions. To prevent repetition of the same ambiguity in different context conditions, four different scripts were prepared, each recorded on one channel of a reel-to-reel tape. The four sentence conditions were counterbalanced across scripts, so that each script included equal numbers of sentences for version 1, experimental; version 2, experimental; version 1, control; and version 2, control. Each ambiguous word was presented in just one sentence context in each script. Finally, a tone marker was placed on the unused (and unheard) channel of the tape for each of the 56 sentences; for experimental sentences, tone placement was always coincident with the end of the ambiguous or corresponding control word.

Each subject heard one of the four scripts at one session, and a second script at a second session 1 week later. The task presented to the subjects was to listen to and understand the sentences they were hearing because they would be asked questions about the sentences; in fact, after every third sentence, they were asked "yes-no" questions about the sentence they had just heard. The purpose of this testing was to keep the subject's attention on the sentences. In addition, the children were told that they had a second task: At some point in the sentence, a picture would be displayed in front of them (via a tachistoscopic shutter attached to a slide projector, triggered by the tone on the audio tape) and the children were asked to decide as quickly as they could whether or not the presented picture was something they commonly ate. They indicated their decision by a choice button press. The same picture was always presented for each ambiguity-containing sentence and its control, and that picture was always something nonedible, i.e., always a negative decision for experimental sentences. (Recall that two sets of pictures were created, one for each of the two interpretations of the ambiguity.) For the nonexperimental filler sentences, pictures were presented that were not related to the sentence, and the pictures were selected for those sentences in a way that maintained roughly a 50/50 balance of edible-nonedible items.

Each of the four scripts was presented in conjunction with each of the two sets of pictures, thus creating eight experimental conditions. Each subject participated in two of these conditions: once with a sentence version containing the ambiguous word and with a picture related to one meaning of that ambiguity and once with a sentential version containing the control word along with the picture related to the "other" meaning of the (nonpresent) ambiguity. (Thus, in the latter case, the picture was not related to anything in the sentence.) These two test conditions were presented at least 1 week apart.

As mentioned earlier, reaction time to decide that a depicted object was edible was assumed to be a function of time to process the picture as well as a function of any possible priming that might occur from the ambiguity in the sentence. Priming could only occur if the relevant meaning of the ambiguous word in the sentence was activated so as to then provide some "prime" for processing of the picture. As mentioned earlier, both pictures and words have been demonstrated to provide similarity and semantic priming, both within-mode (picture-picture) and cross-modally (word-picture) (Vanderwart, 1984; Walls & Siple, 1987). Thus, any priming for decisions to pictures in the presence of the ambiguity compared with decision time for the same picture in the neutral control sentence is

TABLE 12.1. Priming scores (control − experimental) for all 33 children, in ms.

	Picture of:	
	Most freq.	Least freq.
Sentential bias:		
Most frequent	56**	27*
Least frequent	49**	23*

*$p < .06$.
**$p < .02$.

considered evidence of activation of that meaning of the ambiguity in the sentence.

Results

The results are presented in Table 12.1 in terms of priming scores (RT for control minus RT for experimental conditions). As can be seen, there is significant priming for the most frequent interpretation of the ambiguity regardless of the biasing contextual material. There is also marginally significant priming for the least frequent interpretation of the ambiguity under all conditions of contextual bias.[3]

In examining evidence from studies with children, support or rejection of any hypothesis that encompasses a developmental argument typically requires careful scrutiny of data for important trends. Thus, rather than just concluding that these data somewhat weakly support an innate (or very early) modularity claim (i.e., exhaustive, context-independent access appears to be weakly defensible in these data), we decided to examine the data more closely from a developmental perspective.

The children were divided into two roughly equal-sized classes—a

---

[3]It is important to note that the issues addressed in this paper all concern existence proofs—that is, proof of whether there is or is not any priming for "edibility" decisions for pictures related to each of the meanings of the ambiguity. For a large number of reasons, the magnitude of the priming effect is not interpretable. While the mean differences in reaction times which constitute priming do differ in magnitude, it is inappropriate to attempt to interpret these differences with respect to the issues at hand. One of the many reasons for this stems from the fact that the degree of relationship holding between each of the "related" pictures used to probe for activation of meanings of the ambiguity and the ambiguity itself were not equated (a difficult, if not impossible, task given the other constraints on materials in the design of this experiment). So, there may exist a priori differences between the degree of this relationship for these two conditions (primary and secondary). This and other sources of confound preclude any possible interpretation of the magnitude effects of the priming found here. Thus, the only appropriate interpretation of these data centers on the existence-proof aspect of these data—whether there is or is not priming—indicating activation of the various meanings of the ambiguity. For this reason, only priming scores are provided in this chapter.

TABLE 12.2. Priming scores (control − experimental) by age groups:

	Picture of: Most freq.	Least freq.
	a. Younger 16 Ss (age 4.0–4.7), RT in ms	
Sentential bias:		
Most frequent	59**	8
Least frequent	54**	0
	b. Older 17 Ss (ages 4.8–5.6), RT	
Most frequent	54**	47*
Least frequent	44**	46*

*$p < .05$.
**$p < .03$.

"younger" group of 16 children (ages 4.0–4.7 years) and an "older" group of 17 children (ages 4.8–5.6 years). Data for each of these groups were then analyzed separately, and the results can be seen in Table 12.2. As is evident, these two groups perform quite differently.

The older group provides data that look remarkably similar to data for adults; picture decisions for pictures related to both interpretations of the ambiguity are primed, regardless of the contextual bias of the sentence. Certainly, a simple, straightforward interpretation of these data might be that these older subjects are experiencing context-free, exhaustive access of all meanings of an ambiguous word immediately upon hearing it in a sentence. Thus, it looks as though modularity for lexical access is in place at least by age 4.8 years.

The younger children's performance, however, is a different matter. It looks as though there is activation of *only* the most frequent meaning of an ambiguous word for these children at the point tested (immediately after hearing the ambiguity). Notice that this effect is independent of the contextual bias of the sentence; that is, context does not cause the less frequent interpretation of the ambiguity to be activated. Thus it might be claimed that modularity is evident in these youngest children insofar as modularity is defined as contextual impenetrability. However, it also appears that exhaustivity of access might not be a characteristic of young children's lexical-access routines!

There is, however, a plausible alternative interpretation. Research with both older children (10 year olds; Prather, Schmidt, & Marakovitz, 1988) and elderly subjects (e.g., Swinney, Zurif, & Nicol, 1989) has demonstrated that while both of those populations exhibit exhaustive lexical access, access to both primary and (when examined with the elderly) secondary meanings of words is more protracted than access times found for the more typically examined college student population. Similarly, work by Simpson & Lorbach and Simpson & Foster (1983) (1986) argues strongly for a change from automatic to attended processing as children get older, and for the existence of changes in the apparent speed of initial activation with increases in age. It is not clear why access is slowed in these groups. Slowing may be secondary to familiarity (10-year-olds have less familiarity with words and particularly with reading than college students) or to processing speed (older individuals have slower reaction times and slower basic word-finding skills than young normals). In any case, however, lexical access is slowed for young and old individuals relative to college age individuals.

Given this perspective, it seems plausible that the lack of priming for the secondary (less frequent) meaning of ambiguous words for 4-year-olds represents a slow "rise time" of availability to the secondary meaning relative to their older counterparts. By the use of "rise time" we are suggesting that all information stored with a lexical item may be made available for further processing by a sentence comprehension device, but all such information may not become available simultaneously. Thus, while the information related to the more frequent meaning of the ambiguity may be made immediately available upon access for further processing, it may be that, for younger children, it takes time for information related to secondary or tertiary meanings simply to become available. Note that this is not a state of affairs that would argue against modularity: The issue of modularity revolves around demonstrations of information encapsulation and contextual impenetrability. All of our subjects, younger and older, demonstrated information encapsulation. Thus this is simply an issue about the nature of information availability from the lexicon for other processes.

Interestingly, connectionist accounts of access have rise time built naturally into their models, as the frequency of the meanings should control the order of information availability. It may be, in fact, that even for college students there are different rise times for different information sources in the lexicon, but that their processing is simply so rapid and automatic that our on-line techniques have not been sufficiently sensitive to pick up the slightly different rise times that do exist (see Simpson, 1984, for experimental work which did find evidence for this position).

The pattern of activation found here for young children has also been found both in dyslexic readers and in Broca's aphasics. It is well known that "disordered" populations often mimic developmental effects, and these may both be examples of that fact. In the case of dyslexics, Swinney (1982) found slow rise times for phonetic priming (see Seidenberg & Tanenhaus, 1979, for more about phonetic priming) as compared with semantic priming. In the case of Broca's aphasics, the exact same pattern of results (from a very similar study) as found for these younger children has been found for agrammatic subjects (Swinney, Zurif, & Nicol, 1989). Clearly, whether or not appeal to the concept of "slow rise time" is the proper explanation for these data is an empirical matter to be determined by further investigation. Obviously, proof of this issue of rise time (but not that of modularity) will hinge on finding priming for these secondary meanings slightly "downstream" from those for the primary meanings. This work is under way at the present time.

Overall, the results of the present research with preschoolers are most consistent with a modular view of the lexical-access system, where exhaustive, context-free access is the rule rather than the exception, even for relatively young children. Certainly, these data can support the notion that for children at least as young as age 4.0 one finds evidence for the modularity of lexical access, and these data strongly suggest that there is a frequency effect governing the time course of activation of information from the lexicon.

Summary

In these studies with young children, we have found no evidence suggesting that, at any point at least as young as age 4.0 years, lexical access is anything but a modular, informationally encapsulated, contextually impenetrable process. However, we have evidence suggesting that under about 5 years of age, access is not mature in children, leading to more frequent entries being made available before less frequent ones. It is argued, therefore, that different sources of information may be available at different times from the lexicon, but that there is not any evidence supporting a developmental growth of "modularity," even as young as age 4.0 years. Thus, it is reasonable at this point to assume that modularity in lexical processing may be an innate characteristic of human language performance.

Acknowledgments. The authors wish to thank Donnagene Hofmann, Mary-Tara Ward, Debby Brotman, and Esther Robles for their tireless competence in collecting much of the data for the studies presented in this paper. This work was supported in part by NIH Grant NS21806.

Appendix

Sentence versions (bias) for two of the twenty-four ambiguities used in the study. The ambiguity and its control are given in each sentence (/).

A. Bias toward most frequent interpretation:
   1. "The nearsighted girl put her glasses/bundles on the table."
   2. "The baseball player picked up the bat/cap lying in the park."

B. Bias toward least frequent interpretation:
   1. "The thirsty girl put her glasses/bundles on the table."
   2. "The birdwatcher picked up the bat/cap lying in the park."

13

Disambiguation and Cognitive Control

PAUL WHITNEY AND MATTHEW B. CLARK

The main questions driving research on ambiguity have been concerned with the processes that allow for selection of a particular meaning of an ambiguous word in context. As noted in several chapters of this volume, a number of processing models have been proposed to account for the data obtained in such investigations of "lexical ambiguity." Of late, however, interest has begun to turn toward assessing the generality of results on lexical ambiguity for other levels of language processing. The connections among research findings on lexical ambiguity and findings at other levels of language comprehension range from fairly well developed for word recognition (e.g., Simpson, 1984) to only inchoate development at sentence and passage levels. Yet these higher levels also have problems of indeterminacy of meaning that deserve attention (cf. Seidenberg, 1985; Simpson, Burgess, & Peterson, 1988). The problem is not so much the failure of psycholinguists to consider other types of ambiguity as it is the failure to integrate research on different levels of language comprehension. To be more precise, several aspects of the general problem of indeterminacy of meaning have been addressed in psychological research, but often such work is not labeled *ambiguity research*, and it is frequently done without any attempt to consider how the processes uncovered may overlap with those elucidated by work on lexical ambiguity.

Our purpose in this chapter is to make connections between the recent research on lexical ambiguity and some other areas of research broadly concerned with indeterminacy of meaning. We will argue that important connections become especially salient when we take a cognitive control perspective, i.e., when we focus on how the information processing system adjusts to various contextual factors. Thus, we will focus on how people manage information during task performance. This includes not only conscious strategies that people adopt but also more automatic adaptations to contextual constraints. Where possible, we will consider individual differences as well as general information processing principles.

To develop these ideas, we will first present a "modal model" of disambiguation at the lexical level. We will then consider how processes of disambiguation at the lexical level relate to research on how readers employ elaborative inferences to comprehend sentences. Next, some new data will be presented relevant to the process of disambiguation across sentences, i.e., at a thematic level. Finally, we will conclude with speculations on future research directions, including how the current research might relate to problems with ambiguity that arise in text production.

Lexical Ambiguity Research

A number of studies have investigated the time course of activation of dominant and subordinate meanings of ambiguous words in context (e.g., Seidenberg, Tanenhaus, Leiman, & Bienkowski, 1982; Simpson, 1981; Swinney, 1979). Various methods have been employed, but a particularly instructive technique has been to use some form of cross-modal priming. Subjects listen to a sentence containing an ambiguous word and respond, after varying intervals, to a target word related to either a primed or an unprimed meaning of the ambiguous word.

In reviewing research in this area, Simpson (1984) noted that three models of ambiguity resolution had been proposed to account for the results. Some authors argued for a context-dependent model in which the contextually appropriate meaning is selectively activated (e.g., Schvaneveldt, Meyer, & Becker, 1976). An ordered-access model was proposed which assumed that meanings are activated in their order of dominance (Hogaboam & Perfetti, 1975). However, most attention centered on a multiple-access model (e.g., Onifer & Swinney, 1981). According to this view, ambiguous terms are processed in two stages. In the first stage, multiple meanings are activated in parallel regardless of context. In the second stage, the contextually appropriate meaning is selected and activation of other meanings is inhibited.

In Simpson's (1984) review, he pointed out that there is considerable evidence that multiple meanings are activated initially, but it is also consistently found that dominant senses have an advantage in rate or amount of activation. Simpson concluded that none of the three models, in their purest form, provide an adequate account of the data.

More recently, hybrid models that can better account for the data have been offered by several researchers (cf. Gorfein & Bubka, 1985; Neill, Hilliard, & Cooper, 1988; Simpson & Burgess, 1985). For our purposes, the core elements of these models are:

1. The activation of a particular word meaning depends on the strength of the prior association between the meaning and the ambiguous word and the strength of association between the word meaning and the context.
2. Selection of a particular meaning depends on its activation level and current task demands. The idea here is that an important factor in what

meaning is selected and what meanings are inhibited is the task within which the lexical-access processes are embedded. This refers not only to the task being used to measure activation (lexical decision, naming, Stroop) but also to the subject's overall task (understanding connected discourse, responding to word triplets, resolving repeatedly presented ambiguities, etc.).

3. The above processes take place within a limited-capacity information processing system. Thus a major problem for the comprehender is to appropriately deploy attentional resources and to coordinate the activation and inhibition of information in semantic memory with information needed to facilitate ongoing task performance (as managed by working memory).

Clearly, a major theme running through the research in this area is that our attentional resources must be used efficiently to coordinate the multiple sources of information needed to disambiguate words. In the skilled reader, this complex process has become so automated that one only becomes aware of its occasional failures. However, some less skilled readers seem to have difficulties with information coordination at the lexical level (Merrill, Sperber, & McCauley, 1981; Simpson & Foster, 1986). For properties of unambiguous nouns, as well as for multiple meanings of ambiguous nouns, less skilled readers have difficulties with selecting contextually appropriate properties or meanings after initial multiple activation. As we will discuss next, an analogous information coordination problem exists at the sentence level, and it may also present particular difficulties for less skilled readers.

Inferences and Text Comprehension

Over the past 15 years, much of the research on text comprehension has been based on the idea that the reader attempts to construct a mental model of the situation described in the text (Bransford & Johnson, 1973; Johnson-Laird, 1983; Morrow, Greenspan, & Bower, 1987). The mental representation formed during comprehension is thus thought to be a joint product of information from the text and information already in memory. A great deal of research in this area has centered on what elaborative references are made on-line to link text-based information with the reader's preexisting schemata (see Whitney, 1987, for a review).

There is a growing body of evidence indicating that readers are selective in their use of elaborative inferences. Readers make those inferences that help them maintain a clear, coherent model of the text (Garnham, 1982; Goetz, 1979; Whitney, 1987). This can be demonstrated easily in the case of instantiations—inferences about the referents of general terms in context. For example, given the sentence "The fish attacked the swimmer," do readers infer that the attack was by a shark? Anderson, Pichert, Goetz, Schallert, Stevens, and Trollip (1976) found that particular instances (like *shark*) that fit the context were better retrieval cues for sentences with general terms than were the terms that actually appeared in the sentences (like *fish*). They interpreted this result as indicating that readers routinely encode general terms in as concrete a manner as possible.

Their results were inconclusive, however, because the cued recall paradigm can reflect processing taking place at retrieval. Priming studies that tested for instantiations on-line during comprehension provided a much more complex picture. This can be seen in Figure 13.1, which shows the results from an experiment reported in Whitney (1986). In this study, a modified Stroop task was used to determine if typical or atypical category members are activated in biasing contexts. An example stimulus set is shown in Table 13.1. In short, subjects received either a biasing or control sentence followed by the relevant typical or atypical category instance. The subjects' task was to name the color that the target word was printed in. Reaction time on such a color-naming task is a useful index of semantic activation based on the priming context (cf. Dosher & Corbett, 1982; Warren, 1972).

Two aspects of the results deserve particular attention. The expected Stroop interference was obtained when atypical examplars followed atypi-

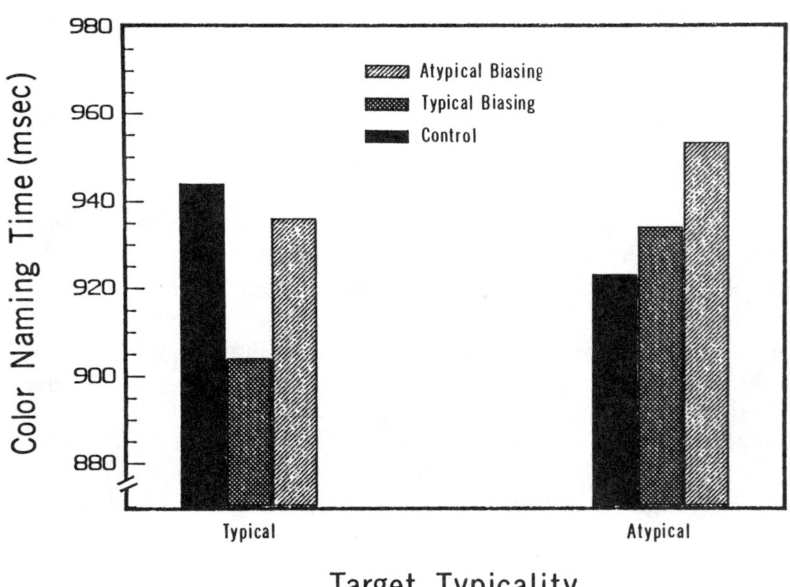

FIGURE 13.1. Mean color naming times (in msec) to typical and atypical exemplar targets after control, typical biasing, and atypical biasing sentences. These data are from Whitney (1986).

TABLE 13.1. Example stimulus set from instantiation research.

Target	Sentence (biasing/control)
	Typical
Trout	The small fish/nugget from the mountain stream ended up in the man's pan.
	Atypical
Shark	The dangeorus fish/explosive moved slowly in the water.

cal biasing priming sentences, but there was significant Stroop *facilitation* when typical exemplars followed typical biasing sentences. This latter effect was the same type of Stroop effect found when Dosher and Corbett (1982) instructed subjects to consciously generate inferences when encoding. Also of interest was the finding that typical examplars showed no activation after atypical biasing primes. This is in contrast to an earlier study by Whitney and Kellas (1984) in which typical examplars were activated regardless of biasing context. However, in the Whitney and Kellas study, the general terms appeared in the sentence predicates and were not the focus of attention.

A plausible interpretation of these results follows closely in line with the hybrid models in lexical ambiguity research. We can think of typical and atypical instances as nodes in a network with connections to a general category. The differences in typicality are represented as different baseline levels of activation. We know that when category terms are processed in isolation, typical and atypical instances are activated in parallel, but typical instances reach higher levels of activation (e.g., Lorch, 1982). When encountered in a biasing context, both the category term and the context serve as sources of activation. If a certain threshold of activation must be reached to give rise to the Stroop facilitation effect, then we would expect that a more strongly biasing context would be needed to show this effect for atypical exemplars because of their lower baseline activation level. Some evidence for this notion is provided in Whitney (1986). Strength of the biasing context was equivalent for atypical and typical biasing sentences, based on a normative task. Yet Stroop facilitation was found with priming of atypical targets only when the atypical targets actually appeared in the priming sentences.

That these results on instantiation are comparable to the work on lexical ambiguity may not seem surprising. After all, the basic problem in both areas involves the resolution of what is meant by a particular term that appears in context. However, the same sort of model of "ambiguity resolution" suggested for the lexical ambiguity and the instantiation results can be extended to more inclusive kinds of memory structures. To use a schema-theoretical example, different subscenes of the overall scene of a restaurant could be connected but with varying resting levels of activation that affect which inferences are made during comprehension (cf. Schank, 1982; Waltz & Pollack, 1985). This idea finds support in research on various kinds of elaborative inferences such as inferences about likely instruments and agents for actions (Garnham, 1982; McKoon & Ratcliff, 1981). Two factors have been shown to be critical in determining whether a particular inference has been made: (1) prior association between the concept in memory and the information in the sentence (see especially McKoon & Ratcliff, 1981) and (2) the task environment within which the reader is placed (e.g., Graesser & Clark, 1985; Reiser & Black, 1982). Both of these factors were, of course, highlighted in our discussion of processing models of lexical ambiguity.

In summary, readers use elaborative inferences to form as explicit a model of a text as possible. However, because of working memory limitations, readers must be selective in their use of inferential processes (cf. Reiger, 1975). Consequently, we make those inferences that reduce the arbitrary nature of connections between text elements and that aid in the construction of a coherent model.

Of course, representations could be constructed with varying degrees of specificity. It seems probable that skilled readers will be constructive to whatever degree is appropriate to fit current task demands (Johnson-Laird, 1983; Whitney, Williams-Whitney, & Hewitt, in press). However, less skilled readers may fail to make appropriate use of elaborative inferences to facilitate sentence encoding (Oakhill, 1982). This is reminiscent of the individual-differences research on lexical ambiguity (cf. Simpson & Foster, 1986).

To summarize: The kinds of inferential processes that facilitate understanding at the sentence level could be considered another case of dealing with indeterminacy of meaning, and in fact, the processes involved show great similarity to those involved in disambiguation at the lexical level. We are currently investigating related processes at the passage level. In our initial work we have been concerned specifically with how the pattern of use of inferences may be influenced by information processing limitations.

A Study of Comprehension of Ambiguous Passages

Virtually every model of text comprehension includes a dual role for working memory. It buffers the most recent propositions to maintain coherence, and it serves as a work space for the coordination of information from various sources (Glanzer & Nolan, 1986; Just & Carpenter, 1980; Kieras, 1981; Kintsch & van Dijk, 1978). Thus, working memory serves to facilitate local coherence as propositions are taken in, and it aids in the manipulation of information needed for global coherence—the formation of a well-connected overall representation (e.g., Britton, Glynn, & Smith, 1985). Not surprisingly, the ability to hold and manipulate information in working memory is related to reading skill (Daneman & Carpenter, 1980; Daneman & Green, 1986; Masson & Miller, 1983).

In the present study, we attempted to determine if individual differences in working memory span (WMS) are related to differences in the ways that readers use inferences to disambiguate text. Our rationale was based on the idea that readers with more limited spans would face a trade-off between using their working memory for achieving a coherent overall representation of the main ideas (global coherence) and using it for connecting together successive propositions from the text (local coherence). If subjects with limited WMS concentrated on the former, they would read in a highly "top-down" pattern. That is, they would generate thematic inferences very early and force the remaining text to fit into the established pattern. Readers who use their limited working memory space to buffer the last few propositions and maintain local coherence will have a reading style that is more "bottom-up." They should make very few predictive inferences but risk forming only a loosely connected overall representation. Readers with larger memory spans should not be faced with the same trade-off between information needed for local and global coherence, and thus they should exhibit a more balanced inference strategy. They should show less early commitment than the top-down reader, and they should be able to repair incorrect early interpretations that are formed. Thus, if they read an unclear or ambiguous passage, we would expect the reader with a good WMS to hold a few likely interpretations in memory and check them against later portions of text (cf. Collins, Brown, & Larkin, 1980).

All subjects in this study were given a standard word span test and the reading span test used by Daneman and Carpenter (1980) to assess working memory capacity. Because the word span test is based mainly on storage capacity, we did not expect it to be related to inference patterns. The reading span test assesses both storage and information manipulation components of working memory and was the measure that we expected to be related to inference patterns.

In the reading span test, subjects read aloud a set of sentences, and at the end of the set they tried to recall the last word of each of the sentences from that set. Subjects had three trials at each of five set sizes: two, three, four, five, and six. The sets were always presented in order of increasing size. A subject's reading span score was the highest set size at which the subject was correct on at least two trials. Half credit was given for passing one trial of a set. So, if a subject got two trials correct on the four-sentence set and one trial correct on the five-sentence set, their score would be 4.5. The test was constructed from 60 unrelated sentences that ranged from 13 to 17 words in length.

In their first session, subjects were administered the word span test and the reading span test. They returned a few days later for a reading task that allowed us to collect verbal protocols from them in a procedure similar to that used by Olson, Duffy, and Mack (1984). Subjects were given ambiguous passages, including some of the ones used by Bransford and Johnson (1973) and Collins et al. (1980). For example, one of the stimulus passages was the "washing clothes" passage used in Bransford's research. Subjects got a passage, untitled, divided into a series of events, with each event on a separate page. Three of the passages remained ambiguous throughout, and three passages had disambiguating information in the last few sentences. The subjects' task in each case was to read a page (event) from the passage and give their interpretation of what was happening in the story. The subjects' responses were recorded on tape so their content could be scored later.

Twenty-one subjects, drawn from introductory classes, participated in the study. The mean word span for the group was 5.33 (SD = .885) out of a possible 7. The mean reading span was 3.69 (SD = 1.40) out of a possible 6. Congruent with Daneman and Carpenter's (1980) work, these two measures were not highly correlated with each other, $r = .21$.

Subjects' responses to the ambiguous paragraphs were rated by two independent judges on each of three five-point scales. The first scale measured the subjects hypothesis generation strategy (HG scale). A low score indicated that specific, concrete predictions were made, and a high score represented general and open-ended predictions. The second scale was a measure of hypothesis monitoring—whether subjects failed to evaluate previous expectations (low score). Scale 3 was complementary to scale 2. It measured the text assimilation strategy—whether the text was distorted to fit previous ideas (low score) or hypotheses were evaluated against new parts of the text (high score). Note that scales 2 and 3 were really the same at the high end but differed at the low end, to pick up both possible aspects of the hypothesized inference patterns for low-WMS readers. Thus, the data of primary interest are the mean rating across passages for the HG scale and a combined scale (C scale), which was the average of a subject's rating on scales 2 and 3. The interrater reliabilities were reasonably good, $r = .82$ for the HG scale and $r = .73$ for the C scale.

Two parallel sets of analyses were performed. One set of analyses was based on the differences among groups formed with a tertile split of the word span scores, and the other analyses were based on a tertile split of the reading span scores. As expected, the only significant effects were found using the reading span scores, and so the word span data will not be treated further here (cf. Daneman & Carpenter, 1980)

Figure 13.2 shows the mean ratings on both scales for the three reading span groups. Differences among the HG ratings were marginally significant, $F(2,18)$, $p = .07$. These are clearly preliminary results with a small number of subjects, so they should be interpreted cautiously at this point. It does seem clear that the lowest-span readers made the most concrete and specific predictions, which is consistent with a more top-down reading style. If, in later studies, the trend toward somewhat more concrete predictions by the highest-span readers holds, it may indicate that high-span readers can make more specific predictions because their better WMSs allow for efficient repair even if a "garden path" is taken. Of course, it may

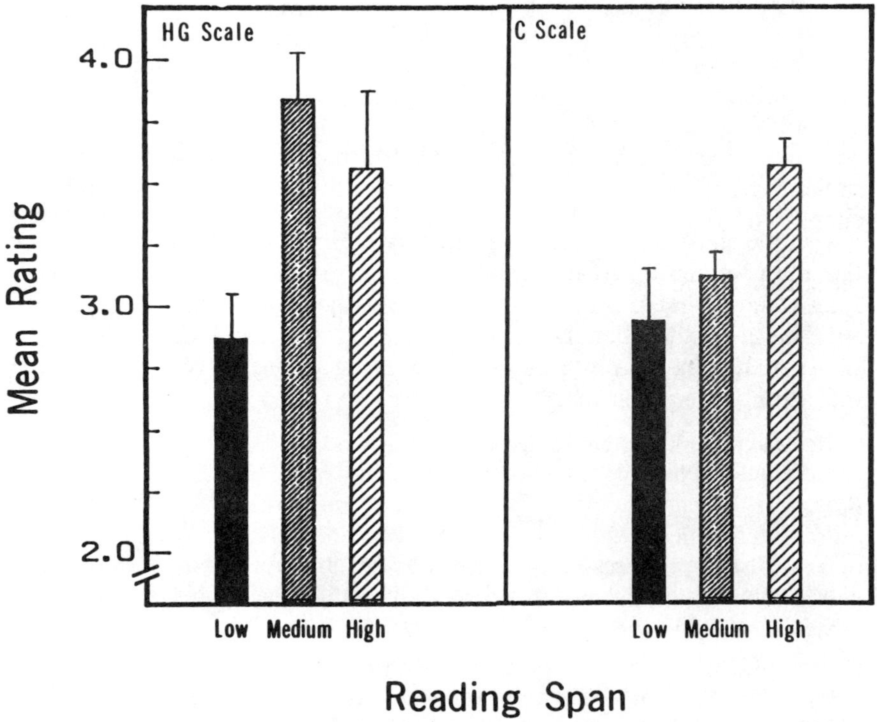

FIGURE 13.2. Mean ratings on the hypothesis generation (HG) and combined (C) scales for story interpretations by readers with low, moderate, and high reading spans. Standard errors of the means are indicated by vertical bars.

turn out that there is no difference between moderate and high-span readers on this scale.

The data from the C scale were more clear-cut. The group effect for this variable was significant, $F(2,18) = 4.55$, $p < .05$, with the high-span group scoring significantly higher than the other two groups (with LSD, $p < .05$). As predicted, readers with high WMS were better able to evaluate incoming segments of text.

These data suggest that individual differences in working memory span are associated with different text disambiguation strategies. Perhaps the best way to illustrate how different the strategies were is to provide an example from the protocols.

One of the stories used (from Bransford & Johnson, 1973) began with a man getting up very early and very quietly to go out walking in a dense forest. One of the low-span subjects interpreted these initial events as:

> He's probably going fishing and he didn't want to wake anybody up. He was excited because he hadn't done it in a long time.

A high-span subject responded:

> Apparently this guy's been looking forward to something all week long and now he's happy because it got here. Wherever he was sleeping it was around other people because he didn't want to wake anybody up.

Obviously, these protocols differ in specificity of the interpretation drawn early in the story. As the story developed, most subjects considered the possibility that the person was hunting or fishing, but certain events served as a subtle signal that something might be wrong with this interpretation: The man walked upstream for a while as if to hide his trail; he was very quiet when he heard other voices; and when he saw a rabbit, he started to raise his gun and then he "thought better of it" and didn't fire. The low-span subject simply used the latter event to decide between hunting and fishing interpretations.

> He saw a rabbit and he wanted to shoot it.
> He should be hunting if he had a gun.

The high-span subject responded with:

> He's got a gun and sees a rabbit. Maybe he's planning on staying a while and he's going to shoot it to eat. If he's a guy getting chased, like an escaped convict, shooting a gun shouldn't be a real good idea.

The high-span subject is apparently keeping two very different possible interpretations open and evaluating the text against these. The low-span subject is doing this to a much lesser degree. The low-span subject's more top-down style becomes very apparent at the conclusion of the story, which reads: "When his brother arrived they would go more deeply into the wilderness. They would go where few had ever gone. It was unlikely the police would find them there." The high-span subject used this part of the passage to confirm the suspicion that the man was running away to hide out. The low-span subject, however, struggled to find a way to interpret this within the "hunting schema" she had selected for the passage:

> It *almost* [emphasis added] sounds like this man was running away from something. Maybe he was helping his brother because it sounds like he's in trouble. But he had been waiting for this so maybe they were just going away and it's the thought of being so far away where no one will see you. Maybe they're poaching. They could be poaching.

This subject has missed many of the details that would make this ending unsurprising as she assimilated everything into a hunting and fishing trip, ignoring several details that did not fit. Finally, she must integrate the rather salient statement about police into this hunting trip story and does so (rather creatively to be sure) by coming up with the idea that they are hunting illegally.

Of course, the data presented here only show that there is an association between WMS and the way the subject goes about disambiguating a text.

We have not demonstrated a causal connection, although, as discussed above, there are a number of theoretical reasons for believing a causal relationship might be involved. We are currently pursuing this question by examining the effect of different working memory loads on inference strategies.

Another question arises, however, if we tentatively accept the likely connection between WMS and text disambiguation style. Simply put, are we placing too much of a theoretical burden on working memory? Our analysis of how indeterminacy of meaning is resolved has included a processing management role for working memory at lexical, sentence, and thematic levels. It may seem that short-term memory limitations are too great for this. This problem is more apparent than real, however, because we are not talking about a working memory buffer that is synonymous with the relatively fixed capacity short-term store in the tradition of Miller (1956). If the cognitive control processes that we have considered here were related to the workings of a short-term store in the traditional sense, then we would expect individual differences in word span to be related to inference strategies. Instead, we are concerned with the ability to maintain information in an active enough state so that it can be used easily to influence ongoing processes. This is a different matter than whether some piece of information is or is not in the buffer. Accordingly, as theorists have tried to understand how the necessary information is made accessible during task performance, the concept of working memory has grown quite complex.

A review of the various architectures proposed for working memory is beyond the scope of this chapter, but two points can be emphasized: (1) The data on working memory's involvement across a wide range of tasks seem to call for the interaction of several elements or buffers guided by some sort of management program (cf. Baddeley, 1986; Britton et al., 1985; Schneider & Detweiler, 1987), and (2) even in reading, not all the information ultimately needed has to be actively buffered. A single concept actively maintained could be used to reinstate a series of propositions stored in long-term memory (see Glanzer & Nolan, 1986).

Conclusions and Speculations

For the present purposes, the key point of our research on ambiguous passages is that the reader is faced with problems of indeterminacy of meaning that overlap with the problems at the sentence and lexical levels. In particular, readers can, and do, deal with multiple possible interpretations. The interpretation of a segment of text is based on current context (recently processed information) and the connections with preexisting knowledge structures (for example, schemata). This information coordination problem must somehow be managed within a limited-capacity information processing system. Individual differences seem to stem from some problems with the information coordination process. These observations dovetail nicely with the core elements of the recent models proposed for ambiguity resolution. We are not arguing that the mechanisms for dealing with indeterminacy of meaning are necessarily the same at all the levels discussed here, but the problems and processes certainly bear more than a superficial resemblance to each other. This becomes especially clear when we view the central problem of ambiguity resolution as one of information coordination and management. Certainly, the central role for such cognitive control processes is made salient by the research on individual differences discussed here. Furthermore, we believe a cognitive control perspective can shed light on a relatively neglected problem in ambiguity research—the production of ambiguous language.

There are, of course, occasions when writers and speakers are intentionally ambiguous, but we are concerned here with unintentional ambiguity in written language. In conversation there is more opportunity for context and feedback from the listener to allow for disambiguation. However, ambiguity in written language often leads to problems in comprehension. In fact, the pervasiveness of ambiguity (at various levels) in written language is no doubt a major factor underlying much of the research reported in this volume. Unintentional ambiguity of meaning, especially in technical materials, is not only pervasive (Nickerson, 1986) but also costly (Faigley & Miller, 1982). Accordingly, this is an area of research that deserves more attention from ambiguity researchers.

With even a cursory review of the literature, it is not too difficult to show how research discussed in this chapter (and elsewhere in this volume) relates to recent findings about the writing process. Once again, we see that the central problem that makes writing difficult is the problem of information management—writers must coordinate information from a number of different sources while composing.

On the basis of protocol studies of writing in various domains, most theorists conceive of the composing process as consisting of three recursively applied phases: planning, translating, and reviewing (e.g., Hayes & Flower, 1980; Kellog, 1987). Planning refers to goal setting and the organization of ideas. Translating is the process of constructing sentence representations from conceptual representation. Reviewing refers to evaluating and editing the written product. Each of these phases is quite taxing on mental resources because of the amount of information that must be kept active in working memory (cf. Kellog, 1987; Whitney & Williams-Whitney, in press).

Writing failures that lead to unclear and ambiguous text can result from problems within each of the phases of composition. For example, in planning the writer must organize the information to be conveyed while keeping track of genre patterns and text conventions for specific writing contexts. Collins and Williamson (1984) found that unclear writing often results from difficulties in adapting to constraints imposed by particular writing tasks. It may be that poor writers have difficulty selecting what information is relevant to the current writing context, just as poor readers seem to have trouble selecting which features of meaning are most applicable to a sentence or passage context (cf. Merrill et al., 1981).

With regard to the translation phase, Dauite (1984) found that syntactic errors often occur in the construction of multiclause sentences in which grammatical information from the early part of the sentence fades from working memory. This results in a mismatch with later grammatical constructions. It is easy to imagine that the same sort of process may lead to "semantic mismatches" that result in indeterminacy of meaning.

Likewise, reviewing is a very demanding process because several levels of analysis must be performed simultaneously while keeping track of the intended audience and the overall goal of the piece. One factor that could lead to failures within the review phase has already been highlighted in the ambiguity literature. When the same ambiguous words are repeatedly presented, it becomes very difficult to retrieve meanings other than the meaning selected previously (see Simpson, this volume, Chapter 2). This is exactly the situation faced by a writer when reviewing a segment of text. It will be quite difficult to see that a reader could interpret the text to mean something other that what the writer had in mind.

Obviously, many more empirical studies of the writing process are needed. Our intent was merely to show that the cognitive control perspective taken here represents a logical way to proceed in looking at the commonalities among research issues and phenomena in the production as well as comprehension of ambiguous language.

In summary, our main point is that there are important connections among the different areas investigating the general problem of ambiguity. These connections become especially clear when resolving indeterminacy of meaning is viewed as a problem of cognitive control, i.e., as a problem of information management and coordination.

Part V Cognitive Science and Ambiguity: An Overview and Expansion

Much of this book represents the product of individuals who are affiliated with Departments of Psychology. It is particularly fitting that Graeme Hirst presents an analysis of the issues raised from the point of view of a leading "consumer" of these ideas, working from the framework of computational linguistics. Not unlike a cognitive science Ralph Nader, Hirst evaluates the product and suggests how the next models might be improved.

Chapter 15 closes the book by addressing the two dominant positions of theorizing that seem to exist at this time. Thus Neill and Klein briefly describe connectionism and modularity and offer a basis for evaluation of their claims to uniqueness and utility. In so doing they open the question again of what data we need to obtain.

14

Computational Models of Ambiguity Resolution

GRAEME HIRST

Research on computer programs for understanding natural language can be both a consumer of psycholinguistic research on ambiguity and a contributor to such work. The fields have different ways of thinking, different concerns, and different criteria as to what counts as a result. I will show that, nevertheless, both fields may profit from cooperation, by giving examples from my own work and that of some of my students showing how issues raised or results obtained in one field can be of use in the other. The examples will include computer systems for lexical, structural, and thematic disambiguation that were inspired by recent psycholinguistic work. I will also show computational work on ambiguities of description attribution and other "large ambiguities" that raise, I will argue, interesting problems for psycholinguists.

Artificial Intelligence and Psycholinguistics

One of the nice things about working in artificial intelligence (AI) is that you have available to you a nice, not-entirely-consistent set of religious doctrines, and can choose among them according to your feelings on any particular day.

When I'm being a hard-nosed computational linguist, I choose the *doctrine of engineering.* What I want to do is create computer programs that "understand" unrestricted natural language input, and I don't particularly care how. If a program embodies any degree of psychological reality, that may be an interesting point, but not one that really matters compared with whether the program, by hook or by crook, does what it is supposed to.

On other days, when the weather is warmer, I turn into a cognitive scientist. Then I work under the *doctrine of science.* I'm not just a software hacker; I'm out for nothing less than an understanding of the very nature of language and language comprehension. My programs must not merely work; they must do it the way people do. And better still, by virtue of their being fully specified operational systems, they must formalize so well the psychological models on which they are based that they shine new light back into psycholinguistics.

But most of the time, my approach is more pragmatic than doctrinaire; I just do whatever I can get away with, knowing that I will be forgiven if it works. For the fact is, even under the doctrine of engineering, trying to model human language and understanding is an awfully good strategy for writing a program; but, more sadly, even when one follows the doctrine of science, the final 10% usually turns out to be a big hack anyway. As often as not, it's the psycholinguists who are to blame for that. I expect them to have all the answers, and they don't. Sometimes they don't even have the questions.

What it comes down to is this: I and others like me are *consumers of psycholinguistics.* We are all out to buy theories and models to use in our programs. But sometimes we can't find what we are looking for, and so we have to build our own. And often, when we can buy, we find that the product is raw and we have to refine it for ourselves. It is our conceit that we therefore do two things for psycholinguistics. First, we provide a market; that is, we ask questions that psycholinguists haven't. Second, we provide a new and different way of both formalizing and testing models. (Both computational linguists and psycholinguists are consumers of theoretical linguistics—but that's a separate story.)

What I will do in this paper is show how cross-disciplinary thinking can work by presenting some work on models of ambiguity resolution that, although computationally oriented, has a strong psycholinguistic inspiration. I will concentrate on my own work and that of my students—not because we are the only people in the business, but rather because I need to be anecdotal in order to demonstrate some of my points about the sociology of science.

Ambiguity and Semantic Interpretation

In my dissertation (Hirst, 1983b, published as Hirst, 1987), my overall goal was to develop an improved approach to semantics for use in natural language understanding (NLU) programs. Fairly early on, it became clear that just inventing wonderful new ways of thinking about semantics would not by itself achieve this goal, because in any NLU system, semantics is just the foundation (*part* of the foundation) on which the rest is built. Unless I could show that the new design for a foundation could support a house on top, it wouldn't be very convincing. Now, I couldn't build a whole house in one thesis, so I concentrated on the parts of it that I thought were the most important (or at least the most interesting), and those were ambiguity resolution—lexical, structural, and thematic. I especially wanted to show that my approach to semantics was generally able to provide the information needed to resolve an ambiguity at the time the ambiguity arose—the immediacy hypothesis.

Put this way, it all seems pretty obvious. That the importance of ambiguity resolution didn't go without saying, however, was shown by much of the earlier work.[1] For example, Woods's procedural semantics (1967, 1968; Woods, Kaplan, Nash-Webber, 1972) took little notice of lexical ambiguity, and structural ambiguity was handled as follows. The parser made an uninformed choice, and if, after the parse was complete, no sensible reading could be found, the parser was asked for another choice. Semantic analysis began only after syntactic analysis was complete, so semantic information could not influence the parse.

Likewise, in theoretical linguistics, Montague semantics (Montague, 1973), from which I drew a lot of inspiration, was concerned with many important semantic puzzles, but said nothing about lexical, thematic, or structural ambiguity. Montague was concerned with other types of ambiguity, such as quantifier scope, and a somewhat perverse feature of his system is that he was able to reduce these to (unintuitive) ambiguities in the derivation—and hence the parse—of the sentence. He did not, however, treat the "traditional" ambiguities of structure.

Lexical Ambiguity

In this section, I want to talk just about the lexical ambiguity parts of the work. I will mention the thematic ambiguity aspects in a later section. Details of the accompanying approach to structural ambiguity are described in Hirst (1984a, 1987); the semantic basis itself appears in Hirst (1983a, 1987).

At the time I was starting this work, lexical ambiguity had been seen in AI mostly as a problem of selectional restrictions or context. Wilks's "preference semantics" (Wilks, 1973), for example, tried to match selectional restrictions of potential word senses, but relaxed the restrictions when nothing fitted, thereby allowing some simple metaphors. In a different approach, Schank (Schank & Abelson, 1977) suggested that contexts ("scripts") had lexicons associated with them, and each incoming word was matched with its unambiguous entry in the predefined lexicon attached to the current context. It seemed to me that there were too many counterexamples to these approaches. It was clear that local cues, and even syntactic constraints, can select a meaning for a homonym that is counter to the prevailing context or selectional preferences. On the other hand, one sense of a homonym can be selected by semantically close words in the context without this being reflected in any selectional restrictions or the invocation

[1]A notable exception is the work of Schank (Schank & Abelson, 1977).

of a Schank-style script. [This is just a particular instance of what I have described as the Boots-And-All Theory of Language Comprehension (Hirst, 1981): Anything that can be used in human language comprehension is. A theory of word sense selection must therefore account for all kinds of resolution cues and their interrelationship.]

Polaroid Words

There were two important influences on the system that I eventually developed.[2] The first of these was work by Philip Hayes (1976, 1977a, 1977b), in which he tried to account for disambiguation through semantic association by following the links in a knowledge representation. This was not a new idea. It had first been proposed in AI by Quillian in 1961 (see Quillian, 1962, 1967, 1968, 1969). What had developed since then were the representations in which association chains could be found—in particular, structures such as frames (Bobrow & Winograd, 1977; Minsky, 1975) and their variants (Schank, 1975; Schank & Abelson, 1977) had been considerably developed. Hayes's CSAW system used associations in a network of frames to disambiguate nouns. (It also used knowledge about case slots and selectional restrictions.) However, Hayes's system did not work in conjunction with other semantic or syntactic processes—the sentence was parsed before CSAW started work. If a choice occurred at any point in disambiguation, the possibilities were considered in parallel; multiple forking was permitted. The system worked only on nouns; verbs were considered to be too complex.

From this, it was only a short step to borrowing from cognitive psychology the more general model of spreading activation to find associations in semantic memory (e.g., Anderson, 1976, 1983; Collins & Loftus, 1975)—a model that had been strongly influenced by Quillian's work in artificial intelligence. Also, I was particularly struck by the problem of negatively primed sentences ("The astronomer married the star"), and wanted my system to be misled by such sentences the same way people are.[3]

---

[2]This is a lie; there were actually three such influences, but I'm only going to discuss two of them here. The third one was Steven Small's (1980) "Word Experts" for parsing and semantic interpretation. I thought that he was correct about control structure with his idea of communicating one-per-word processes. I thought that he was wrong about everything else: what those processes should do, how they should do it, and why they should do it.

[3]At the time, my knowledge of exactly how people reacted to such sentences was purely introspective and anecdotal, and there is a fair amount of individual variation in reactions. Reder (1983) later published a useful study of these sentences. I note in passing that Waltz and Pollack (1985) also claim "correct" handling of such sentences in their connectionist natural language interpretation system. In their case, "correct" means that the system temporarily prefers the primed interpretation, but settles, before processing is complete, on the interpretation consistent with

The second influence was the now-well-known results of Swinney and Tanenhaus, Seidenberg, and their respective colleagues (Onifer & Swinney, 1981; Seidenberg, Tanenhaus, Leiman, & Bienkowski, 1982; Swinney, 1984; Tanenhaus, Leiman, & Seidenberg, 1979), which showed, with some qualifications, that all senses of an ambiguous word are activated, regardless of context—exactly contrary to the Schankian scripts approach that I thought inadequate. Naturally, this encouraged me to create a system in which the same was true.

The system I developed was called *Polaroid Words*.[4] The metaphor of a self-developing photograph was important for the interaction with semantics; just as a partly developed Polaroid photo contains usable information —you can tell a photo of a mountain from that of a person, but you mightn't be able to tell which mountain or which person it is—so a Polaroid Word in process can send usable information on to the parser, the semantic process, or the structure disambiguation procedures. The system has been described in detail elsewhere (Hirst, 1987, 1988; Hirst & Charniak, 1982); I will mention here only the aspects relevant to the points at hand.

Word senses are nodes in a knowledge base built in the Frail frame language (Charniak, 1981a; Charniak, Gavin, & Hendler, 1983; Wong, 1981). Whenever it sees a content word, the system starts activation spreading from the sense or senses of that word through the network of frames and their slots and slot fillers. Whenever one burst of activation collides with another, this is taken as evidence that the senses from which these bursts started are the appropriate ones. For example, in the sentence "Nadia's plane taxied to the terminal," activation starts from the two senses of *plane*: namely, *airplane* and *wood-smoother*; from those of *taxi: ride in taxicab* and *aircraft ground travel*; from those of *terminal: airport building* and *computer terminal*; and from *Nadia*. The aircraft-related meanings will be close enough in the frame network that activation *paths* will meet to form a *chain* between each pair of senses; activation from the other senses will just spread out into the wilderness and die away.

The sentence is read from left to right. If a word is found where one sense has already received activation from a previous word, that fact is considered strong enough evidence to select that sense immediately without

selectional restrictions on the verb—i.e., the system is not really misled at all. Not all negatively primed sentences mislead all people all the time (whenever I mention them in a talk, there always seems to be one person in the audience who can't see the problem), but most of them require conscious error recovery, so I can't see how psychological reality or "correctness" can be claimed for a system that always finds the literal meaning as part of its normal comprehension process.

[4] *Polaroid* is a trademark of the Polaroid Corporation for its range of photographic and other products. It is used here to emphasize the metaphor of a self-developing object, and the system described herein carries no association with, or endorsement by, the Polaroid Corporation.

further consideration; this is what happens in negatively primed sentences, for example. Otherwise, any chain found is taken as evidence, but factors like selectional restrictions are also considered. In all cases, all senses of an ambiguous word are initially "activated." Those that are found to be untenable will be suppressed—perhaps immediately, as in the case of strong activation evidence, or perhaps one by one as they are found not to fit with the requirements of previous or subsequent words.

One point in the previous paragraph needs clarifying: the use of selectional restrictions. In many computational systems, selectional restrictions are the main mechanism for deciding on the ambiguity resolution; systems differ in exactly how much knowledge is used and how much inference from world knowledge is permitted. In Polaroid Words, I tried to minimize the use of selectional restrictions per se, but instead achieve the same effect by having Polaroid Words look at word meanings and simple world knowledge to decide if an assignment is appropriate. That is, the fact that *boy* denotes something animate is not in the lexical entry for the word, but is a fact about its meaning, stored in the system's knowledge base. I do not attempt to characterize exactly what "simple" world knowledge is (this is not formalized in the system), but the intuition is that it includes knowledge that is stored explicitly and close enough to the meaning of a word to be activated when the meaning is. It also includes knowledge that may require a couple of simple inference steps to derive. These contraints are intended to reflect intuitions concerning modularity (cf. Fodor, 1983), although the encapsulation is not perfect.

The reason that I took this approach was that selectional restrictions can get impossibly complex. That is, I am basically in sympathy with Kelly and Stone (1975), who concluded, after trying to construct a system for word sense selection in large text corpora, that selectional restrictions do not work in realistically large systems: "The Procrustean notion of selection restrictions, supposedly stating necessary and sufficient conditions for semantically acceptable combinations of words, is fundamentally misguided" (p. 69).

The problem with selectional restrictions is the rather complicated and arbitrary properties of objects that can be linguistically significant. Two well-known examples: Whether one *boards* a vehicle seems to depend on whether or not one can stand up in it (one can *board* a plane, train, or boat, but not a car or a canoe). Whether the seed of a fruit can be called a *pit* depends on the exact nature of the fruit and the seed. When faced with a new kind of vehicle or fruit (a hovercraft and a chericot, say), people have no trouble using the right words, even though they may not have conscious knowledge of the rules. It is hard to believe there are markings in the mental lexicon for properties like [±*vehicle-one-can-stand-up-in*] or [± *fruit-having-a-large-seed-surrounded-by-a-thick-fleshy-part-and-thin-skin*]; rather, people use world knowledge. The problem with this argument is that while the lexical representation of *hovercraft* may not be marked [+*vehicle-one-can-stand-up-in*], we still have to posit such a marking for the *object* theme of *board.* That seems unavoidable, but I don't think it follows from it that the lexical entries for objects that are boardable need be similarly marked. Why should we expect a priori the property of animacy to be any different?

The pros and cons of Polaroid Words as a psychological model are discussed in detail in the references cited earlier. I should note briefly, however, that one obvious shortcoming of the system is its vulnerability to slight differences in the organization of the frame network—not to mention the unanswered question of what the "right" organization is. (According to the doctrine of engineering, it is the one that works.) The model of spreading activation that I used was also not a very good one, and this issue was taken up by Jim Hendler (1987) in his dissertation.

One point in which Polaroid Words are probably not a very good model is how they behave when they have to hold off making a decision about a word because there is insufficient evidence at the time of its occurrence to choose a unique sense for it. Almost all the psycholinguistic work I found considered only cases when resolution was immediately possible—often, the target word would be the last word of a sentence. I therefore had no data on which to base the behavior of Polaroid Words in cases where a decision had to be deferred. My intuition is that Polaroid Words are somewhat more hesitant to jump to a conclusion on the basis of limited evidence than humans seem to be (see Hirst, 1984b, for more discussion of these issues).

The main point here, however, is not so much the virtue of Polaroid Words as a psychological model, but the interdisciplinary manner in which it was developed. Although my main goal was a computer system that did a certain job, I was strongly influenced by work in psycholinguistics. And I think the work resulted in questions that should interest psycholinguists. Here are some (for more problems and discussion, see the "Exercises for the Reader" in Hirst, 1987):

- Except in the case of strong priming, when one sense is selected by positive data, Polaroid Words generally work by suppressing senses that are ruled out, until only one is left. This seems to be a good way to make sure all possibilities are adequately considered, but is it the way it happens in people?
- Do selectional restrictions live in the mental lexicon, or is real-world knowledge used?
- If they have insufficient information but time is running out, Polaroid Words will try to make the best possible guess about the meaning of a word. How soon and under what circumstances will people do the same (Hirst, 1984b)?
- Polaroid Words look for semantic associations, but they do not use word associations in the traditional sense. Such associations do not include all semantic associations, but do include other kinds of association such as phrase completion (Postman & Keppel, 1970). Fischler (1977) has shown

evidence that activation spreads between both kinds of associates. Are both kinds used in ambiguity resolution? Or perhaps only activation between associates?
- Polaroid Words predict no qualitative processing differences between homonyms and polysemes. But are the two kinds of lexical ambiguity cognitively distinguished, as some psycholinguistic work (Panman, 1982) has suggested?

In addition, Polaroid Words raised questions concerning thematic ambiguity, for, though I haven't mentioned it above, the system addressed this as well as lexical ambiguity; I'll discuss these matters in the section on Thematic Ambiguity.

Lexical Access

In closing the section on lexical ambiguity, I should mention one matter on which computational models may not shed any light, and that is how the lexical entry of a word is accessed. When a computer reads a typed word, it gets a nice string of ASCII characters, and can go straight to the lexical entry, usually by means of some system of indexes and pointers into a data structure; often this system will be built right into the programming language, and the programmer need not even think about how it works. It is implausible that such data structures have any psychological validity (although after talking to Ken Forster I am not so sure of that!), and it is equally implausible that any psychological data could suggest more efficient computational methods, at least for conventional present-day computers. Where the concerns of AI and psycholinguistics do overlap is in the question of exactly what information is accessed and whether lexical access has side effects, such as priming, that will affect later processes.

Parsing as a Race

One area in which there has been great cross-fertilization between computational linguistics and psycholinguistics is in models of parsing, and, hence, in the resolution of structural and categorial ambiguities. Marcus's deterministic parser (Marcus, 1977, 1980) is especially well known in psycholinguistics; it has been cited more than 30 times in the psychological literature.[5,6]

---

[5]The *Science Citation Index* and *Social Sciences Citation Index* list a total of about 46 distinct citations from 1980 to 1987, the sources of 33 of which I judged to be part of the "psychological literature."

[6]In my dissertation work, I was also concerned with structural disambiguation, and how semantic decisions could be added to a Marcus parser. The system that resulted, called the Semantic Enquiry Desk (Hirst 1984a, 1987), had only a modest amount of psycholinguistic inspiration because little of the work at the time could

To give an example of how research in the two fields can interact, I will describe the evolution of the ideas behind a parser developed by a member of my research group, Susan McRoy (McRoy, 1987; McRoy & Hirst, 1988).

The work began in my graduate seminar on computational linguistics, when we read the well-known paper by Frazier and Fodor (1978) on their "Sausage Machine" model of parsing, and the subsequent controversy it generated (Fodor & Frazier, 1980; Wanner, 1980). Frazier and Fodor, you'll recall, tried to account for structural preferences in parsing by means of a two-stage parser. Words were put together in little bundles by a myopic "preliminary phrase packager"; the bundles were then used to build larger structures by the "sentence structure supervisor." Wanner objected that the data could be much better explained in terms of processing in an augmented transition network (ATN) (Wanner, 1980), and the original authors responded at great length (Fodor & Frazier, 1980).

What McRoy observed was that, from a computational perspective, nothing much had been settled at all, for the Sausage Machine was not even specified well enough to be refuted. One of the advantages of a computational approach is that when it comes time to actually write a program, you find out very quickly where the subtle flaws and small holes are in your theory. And while not all theories proposed in the field ever reach the stage of becoming part of a working system, one is expected, if talking about a process and its alleged properties, to describe the process in enough detail that someone could take the description, program it up, and see what happens.[7] Frazier and Fodor, despite the length of their papers (88 journal pages in total), never gave an explicit enough description of the Sausage Machine that one could do this. For example, they said nothing about how the two stages of the parser might communicate with each other. Similarly, although the Sausage Machine was to employ a strategy of "revision as last resort" if it were found to have built a semantically or pragmatically unacceptable structure, they presented no details of how this might work—neither how semantic or pragmatic processes would inform the Sausage Machine of its error, nor how it would carry out the revision. Moreover, Frazier and Fodor's account of minimal attachment was based solely on ad hoc aspects of the grammar.[8]

account for the lexical preference issues raised by Ford, Bresnan, and Kaplan (1982), which I wanted to include in my system. I did, however, use some aspects of the work of Crain and Steedman (1985), but found most of their results unconvincing.

[7]That's just the computational equivalent of telling people how they could replicate your experiment. The principle is often violated in the computational literature, if only because such descriptions must frequently be much too long for the average paper.

[8]Minimal attachment is the alleged preference for attaching a new constituent into the parse tree in the way that uses the fewest possible intermediate nodes. But just how many nodes will be required by any particular kind of attachment depends on the exact rules of the grammar.

Although Frazier and Fodor essentially abandoned the Sausage Machine after the publication of their 1980 paper (Lyn Frazier, personal communication to Susan McRoy), McRoy believed that the general idea of two-stage parsing still held promise from both a psychological viewpoint and a computational viewpoint. Ford et al. (1982) had subsequently presented data showing that structural preferences are lexically conditioned, so any attempt to account for them purely through the structure of the parser must be inadequate. However, this did not affect the more general question of whether two-stage parsing held interesting properties. McRoy therefore decided to develop such a parser. The model would be specified computationally, i.e., as a working program, but would retain psychological reality in that it would be as faithful as possible to the data on human parsing.

Two kinds of constraint that particularly interested McRoy were those of memory and time. The respect for constraints in the amount of memory required, while not usual in computational linguistics,[9] was simply carried over from the original motivation for Frazier and Fodor's "preliminary phrase packager," which could only handle small bundles. The respect for time constraints is more unusual, and was encouraged by Jean-Pierre Corriveau, another of my group, in whose work the role of time is also emphasized (Corriveau, 1987).[10]

While working in the framework of two-stage parsing, McRoy also wanted to account for other data. For example, the lexical preferences of Ford et al. (1982) mentioned above had to be able to influence the parser. And the parser had to be able to talk to processes for semantics, pragmatics, and lexical disambiguation. Thus it seemed that the parser would have many different sources of knowledge that could be offering it advice on how a particular attachment should be made. The various pieces of advice would often be redundant, two or more sources picking up the same cue. Sometimes, however, they might conflict. How was the parser to choose which to believe? Approaches used in previous models included fixed-order ranking mechanisms (most of the traditional systems, not to mention my own (Hirst, 1984a)), mechanisms in which interpretations race to reach a threshold level (most connectionist systems, perceptrons, READER (Thibadeau, Just, & Carpenter, 1982)), and summation or vot-

---

[9]In the doctrine of engineering, if your workstation has 4 megabytes, you don't have to care about memory constraints on the parser's work space. Traditional computational models, such as the ATN, have observed no constraints. Even Marcus's parser, though limited in its look-ahead, assumed unbounded memory, in that its stack was unbounded and its window of visibility could slide arbitrarily far back and forth across the input sentence.

[10]Corriveau's research concerns computational models of text comprehension with an emphasis on psychological validity, and so serves as another example of the interdisciplinary work I wish to promote. However, since it does not emphasize ambiguity, it will not be described here.

ing mechanisms, possibly also with thresholding. Fixed-order rankings for parsing options had been shown to have problems by Schubert (1984), who proposed a summation system that considered the "potential" of various knowledge sources. But this is problematic too. The fact that two sources notice the same cue should not by itself allow their opinion to prevail over a conflicting cue noticed by only one source. So instead, McRoy turned to the role of time, as used in some of the threshold models: The preferred attachment should be the one that is found most quickly.[11]

Thus came the idea of *hypothesizers*. Hypothesizers are small bodies of knowledge about particular aspects of parsing. Whenever an attachment is to be made, they race against one another to determine whether they apply to the particular situation, and if so, how strongly. The time a hypothesizer takes to come to a decision may vary with the dynamic state of the system. For example, the time required may increase with how much of the existing parse tree a hypothesizer has to examine, but priming may reduce the time it would otherwise take to access an item. Unlike the races in some connectionist systems, the hypothesizers do not actively suppress their competition.

The hypothesizers are a combination of the general and the specific across parts of speech. In this way McRoy both handles certain special cases (such as subjects that consist only of a categorially ambiguous plural noun) and exploits generalities (such as attaching words according to selectional information). Since hypothesizers run in parallel and compute their time value internally, it is simply an implementation detail as to how general or specific each one is. The following hypothesizers are among those in the current implementation:

To detect explicit expectations: For example, an item may expect the item following it as an argument, or the item preceding it as a specifier. Information about such expectations is contained in the lexicon. These are minimal attachments and so are very rapid.

To detect plural noun subjects: When a package begins with a word such as *sinks* that could be either a plural noun or a singular verb, the subsequent input of a verb disambiguates the first word and creates a chain of expectations that will link the two words; the plural noun morphology licenses a null determiner, the verbal morphology licenses INFL, and INFL selects a determiner phrase specifier (DP) and a verb phrase complement (VP). This is less rapid than the previous hypothesizer.

To detect possible post-modification: An item X allows an item Y as a post-modifier if, firstly, there is a phrase structure rule linking Y to a projection of X as a post-modifier (e.g., $X \leftarrow XY$), and, secondly, X modified by Y describes an entity that either exists or might exist (Hirst,

[11] Race models of linguistic processes seem to be catching on; cf. the papers by Neill and by Gorfein and Bubka (Chapters 6 and 7 in this volume).

1984a, 1987). These attachments are presumed not to be expected arguments and hence are "nonminimal." It is also preferred to make the attachment as low and as far right in the tree as possible ("right association"), which requires increasing time with increasing distance from such a point. Thus, unless there is priming (which reduces the time needed to check existence), these attachments will also require more time than syntactically expected attachments.

To detect a thematically expected argument or modifier: Thematic expectations are determined by a separate "argument processor" that reports the degree to which the argument is expected. These attachments are the result of verb-frame preferences and thus are more strongly favored than other attachments when there is no priming. The time required by the hypothesizer reflects the fact that more highly expected items are somehow easier to access, or more readily assumed to exist, than less expected items.

To detect the start of a reduced relative clause: This is a nonminimal attachment involving some revision of the current structure, and hence will take quite some time unless there is some sort of priming.

To computer scientists, hypothesizers are appealing because they strongly support modularity in the system, and computer scientists always like modularity. Hypothesizers support modularity by allowing disparate sources of knowledge to be packaged up and treated the same way by the parser. I'm not sure how appealing hypothesizers are to the psychological eye. *Modularity* seems to be a dirty word in some camps and a sacred invocation in others, as Garfield's (1987) collection demonstrates.

At the suggestion of Janet Fodor, McRoy addressed the objection that the Sausage Machine had no principled theory of grammar by using government-binding (GB) theory—in particular, a processing-oriented interpretation of GB developed by Barbara Brunson (1988), another member of the Toronto group. Thus the parser builds structures according to $\overline{\text{X}}$-theory and its knowledge of the direction of headedness in English.[12] To give the parser access to semantic knowledge, McRoy used a simple semantic procedure based on my own (see the section on Ambiguity and Semantic Interpretation), and for lexical disambiguation, she used Polaroid Words (see the appropriate section). (She did not address the question of how revision as a last resort should work.)

If you think that there is any psychological merit to race-based parsing, then many interesting questions immediately arise concerning relative timing. Psycholinguists have never been shy to infer facts about the nature

[12]Note that the use of GB is not intended to imply any special psychological status for that theory. The intent is only that the parser may not be crucially dependent on an ad hoc grammar with odd hacks. GB could be replaced by some other theory without changing the fundamental principles of the parser (we hope!).

and organization of comprehension from measurements of relative processing loads in different situations. Race-based parsing, however, asks for something more subtle. It asks for the relative processing loads of a wide variety of rather small processes within comprehension—not an easy task, but one that would surely be as worthwhile in psycholinguistics as it would be useful in developing this kind of parsing model in computational linguistics. It was a surprise to us that little of these kinds of data were available, and in their absence, McRoy was obliged to use intuition and guesses in her model. (It may be objected that the required data cannot be found at all—that the differences in timing are too small and timings themselves too subject to intra- and inter-individual variation to be interesting or useful. But if that were so, then the way individuals parse a given sentence would be completely random. That is, the race-based model crucially assumes that these relative timings are reliable and consistent across individuals.)

Ambiguities That Psycholinguists Don't Think About

Let me now turn to a slightly different perspective on what computational linguistics can offer psycholinguistics. So far, I have talked about different ways of thinking, and about models and the questions they raise. But it is my observation that problems in ambiguity are sometimes raised and studied in theoretical and computational linguistics long before they attract the attention of the psycholinguistic community.

These problems tend to be what we might call "big" ambiguities—that is, ambiguities that can't be localized at any particular word or any particular decision point in the parser. Rather, they concern the way in which the various parts of a sentence relate to one another, beyond the relations dictated by the syntactic structure of the sentence.

Thematic Ambiguity

Until recently, I could point to thematic ambiguity as an example of one that everyone but psycholinguists cared about. And in fact, I will do so anyway, for even though thematic ambiguity has started to get a small amount of press in psycholinguistics (Stowe, 1988; Tanenhaus & Carlson, 1989), I'd like to claim that artificial intelligence and computational linguistics were there a decade earlier.

The original inspiration, of course, came from linguistics. But Fillmore's (1968) original "case-for-case" paper had an immediate strong influence in artificial intelligence—probably more so than it did in theoretical linguistics. The role of semantic cases in parsing and understanding was developed considerably in the 1970s. See Taylor and Rosenberg (1975) for just one example; for a survey of the research, see Somers (1987). The approaches developed were very compatible with the slot-and-filler knowledge representations that were developed around the same time, such as frames and their variants. Indeed, Charniak (1981b) hypothesized that semantic cases and frames were actually the same thing.

When I was first thinking about the Polaroid Word system in the early 1980s, I was concerned with thematic ambiguity as much as with lexical ambiguity. But despite all the psycholinguistic literature on lexical ambiguity, I saw nothing on thematic ambiguity. In retrospect, this strikes me as a large gap. At the time, I was unconcerned, for in fact, one of my early observations was that no distinction needed to be made between the two types of ambiguity. If one accepted a framelike representation for semantics, then the meanings of content words would always be frames, and the meanings of *case flags*, be they surface prepositions or syntactic position, would always be slots in frames. This led me to adopt the following procedure. Case flags (which are almost always ambiguous) would be disambiguated by exactly the same kind of Polaroid Word processes as content words, except that spreading activation would not be relevant. Furthermore, even syntactic position (the fact of a noun phrase being the subject, the object, or the indirect object of the clause) could be regarded as an ambiguity amenable to this process; one simply created a *pseudo-preposition* that flagged the case of the noun phrase the same way the preposition in a prepositional phrase does. This could then be disambiguated by a Polaroid Word process.

In 1982, I thought that this was pretty neat; I'd got two ambiguities for the price of one, it all fitted very nicely with my approach to semantics, and it reflected the fact that lexical and thematic ambiguities often strongly constrain one another. What's more, I was so pleased with my adherence to the doctrine of science for lexical ambiguity that I didn't give much attention to the fact that my approach to thematic ambiguity made some pretty odd predictions—such as, for example, the basic premise: that lexical and thematic ambiguity are resolved by exactly the same mechanism. The psychological reality of pseudo-prepositions is also probably without foundation!

Since 1982, of course, linguistics has come to put a much greater emphasis on semantic cases, or "thematic relations."[13] A little of the interest has spilled over into psycholinguistics, and we now have evidence from Tanenhaus, Carlson, and their colleagues (Carlson & Tanenhaus, 1988; Tanenhaus, Burgess, D'Zmura, & Carlson, 1987; Tanenhaus & Carlson, 1989) that lexical and thematic ambiguity resolution might be separate processes. But as Tanenhaus and Carlson say, the question of how thematic roles are assigned remains almost untouched by psycholinguistics.

---

[13]The word *case*—never a good choice anyway—had in the meantime been recycled and given a new technical meaning in government-binding theory.

I would, of course, like to suggest that some of the models developed in computational linguistics could be good starting points for answering this question. For example, Polaroid Words, despite my remarks above, still make some useful predictions. As in the case of word senses, all thematic assignments that are possible for a particular NP are activated, and the inappropriate ones disappear as soon as they are found untenable. Most of the information about thematic roles is carried on the verb, but there are also a priori predispositions—for example, even before the main verb occurs, thematic roles that can be assigned to the subject of a sentence will have been activated for the subject. Moreover, the premise that thematic and lexical ambiguity involve the same resolution mechanisms is not dead. The Tanenhaus and Carlson results merely show that recovery from erroneous assignment is easier in one case than the other, but that may have nothing to do with the mechanisms used for the original assignment. Ken Forster has suggested (personal communication) that recovery from thematic role errors could be by table-lookup, since there aren't very many different kinds of error situation; but this shortcut wouldn't work for lexical sense errors. (The question of error recovery was not addressed in Polaroid Words.)

Semantic association, used by Polaroid Words for lexical ambiguities, has no meaning in the case of thematic ambiguities, so selectional restrictions (based on world knowledge, as discussed in the Polaroid Words section) take on a greater importance in thematic role assignment. But this is not to say that the assignment is based purely on semantic coherence. There seem to be rules in English that constrain assignment in other ways. For example, the *instrument* theme can be assigned only to inanimate entities, even though animate entities can be perfectly good as instruments; to say that Ross broke the window by throwing Nadia through it, we have to use just such a circumlocution; we can't say *"Ross broke the window with Nadia." In addition, Barbara Brunson (1986) has shown that preference for a verb phrase or noun phrase attachment of a locative prepositional phrase varies according to whether the subject of the sentence is assigned an *agent* or *experiencer* thematic relation (or both), and this effect can override semantic coherence in the case of strongly agentive verbs. Thus subjects usually assigned an anomalous interpretation to sentences such as "Ross baked the cake in the freezer." (Brunson's results are not included in Polaroid Words.)

Because case and related notions have been used so much in natural language understanding programs, and because they correspond so closely to structures used in knowledge representations in artificial intelligence, psycholinguists may find useful ideas and models in the literature. (Somers's survey, 1987, would be a good entry point.) In particular, the field has considered the issue of how thematic processing relates to syntactic processing. For example, in Marcus's model (1980), the two proceed in parallel (but one is deterministic, the other not); in some other models, such as Wilks's (1973), thematic processing almost completely supplants syntactic processing.

Ambiguities of Intension and Description

De re–de dicto ambiguities are well known in theoretical linguistics, but apparently less so in psycholinguistics. In sentences displaying these ambiguities, a noun phrase could be referring to either an *intension*—an underlying concept—giving a *de dicto* (or *opaque*) reading, or an *extension*—an instance of the concept—giving a *de re* (or *transparent*) reading. Standard examples are sentences like "Ross wants to marry a Swedish woman," where the noun phrase *a Swedish woman* could refer to a particular person Ross fancies, or just to the general concept: whomever Ross marries, he wants it to be a Swedish woman. It should be clear that (unless you believe in the psychological reality of Montague semantics) this ambiguity is not structural. Nor is it lexical, except insofar as one might wish to identify the locus of ambiguity as being in the determiner of the NP, and even so it is clearly qualitatively different from the homonyms usually studied.

This kind of ambiguity is similar to those of *generic* and *specific* readings and of *referential* and *attributive* readings. In the generic–specific ambiguity, sentences such as "The lion is a fierce animal" and "A lion has sharp teeth" could be intended to be true of all lions (the generic reading) or one lion in particular (the specific reading). This is not identical with the previous ambiguity, however; our earlier example cannot be read as meaning that Ross wants to marry all Swedish women. In the referential–attributive case, the speaker may intend to refer to a particular entity, or to whichever (unknown) entity has certain attributes; thus "Smith's murderer is insane" may be intended to refer to a certain known person, or merely to the murderer, whoever it might be (Donnellan, 1966).

The preference for one reading over another seems to be conditioned by both syntactic structure and semantic content. Sidner (1979) gives some suggestions for when a generic reading is preferred over a specific one; I know of no comparable work for intension–extension preferences. In fact, another member of my research group, Brenda Fawcett, had originally intended to study, among other things, this question. Instead, she found the more she looked, the more the ambiguities multiplied, and the result was a study of *ambiguities of description* (Fawcett, 1985; Fawcett & Hirst, 1986).

These ambiguities revolve around the knowledge and beliefs of the speaker and the agents referred to in the sentence, raising the question of to whom a description used in a sentence may be attributed—the speaker or one of the other agents mentioned in the discourse. For example, consider the sentence

1. Nadia wants a dog like Ross's.

This sentence has (at least) seven readings. There are two obvious readings, corresponding to those of the *Swedish woman* example above. These ambiguities, however, cross with an ambiguity about the agent to which the description *a dog like Ross's* is to be attributed: the speaker or Nadia (the *agent* of the verb of the sentence). This gives four readings. To see the four cases, consider the following situations, any of which could be summarized by sentence 1:

Transparent reading, agent's description: Nadia sees a dog in the pet store window. "I'd like that dog," she says. "It's just like Ross's." The speaker of sentence 1, who need not be familiar with Ross's dog, reports this.

Transparent reading, speaker's description: Nadia sees an animal in the pet store window. "I'd like that," she says. Nadia is not aware of it, but the animal is a dog just like the one Ross owns. The speaker of sentence 1, however, knows Ross's dog (and believes that the listener also does).

Opaque reading, agent's description: Nadia feels that her life will be incomplete until she obtains a dog. "And the dog that would be perfect for me," she says, "Is one just like the one that Ross has." The speaker of sentence 1, not necessarily familiar with Ross's dog, reports this.

Opaque reading, speaker's description: Nadia feels that her life will be incomplete until she obtains a dog. "And the pet that would be perfect for me," she says, "Is a big white shaggy dog, with hair over its eyes." Nadia is not aware of it, but Ross owns a dog just like the one she desires. The speaker of sentence 1, however, knows Ross's dog (and believes that the listener also does).

Another complicating factor is the time at which a description is to be applied. The above readings assumed that this was the time of the utterance. The intensional readings, however, could be referring to the dog that Ross will get or (not included in the examples below) once had:

Opaque reading, agent's description, future application: Nadia has heard that Ross will buy a dog. Wanting one herself, and trusting Ross's taste in canines, she resolves to buy whatever kind he buys.

Opaque reading, speaker's description, future application: Nadia finds English sheepdogs attractive, but none are available. She therefore intends to purchase some other suitably sized dog and spend her weekend gluing long shaggy hair onto it. Nadia is not aware of it, but Ross owns a dog just like the one she wants to end up with. The speaker, knowing Ross's dog, can describe Nadia's desire as that of having an object that will at some future time be describable as a dog like Ross's.

The description in an intensional reading may also be used to refer to different entities at different times.

Opaque reading, agent's description, repeated application: Ross buys a new type of dog every year or so. Desperately wanting to keep up with canine fashion, Nadia declares her intent to copy him. Whatever dog Ross has at any given time, Nadia wants to have the same kind.

We were not able to find an example in which repeated application of the speaker's description gives a natural reading. Thus, there are at least seven readings for "Nadia wants a dog like Ross's."[14] The different readings permit different inferences to be drawn. For example, the agent's description readings allow the inference that Nadia *believes* that she (either intensionally or extensionally) wants a dog like Ross's; the other readings do not. Making the distinction is thus crucial for any system that reasons about the beliefs of other agents (such systems being an area of much current concern in artificial intelligence).

One question that must be considered is whether this is in fact a linguistic ambiguity that can be considered in isolation from other thought processes; that is, one might wish to argue that deciding among the interpretations available for sentence 1 is more like nonlinguistic problem solving than language comprehension per se. This line of argument is suggested by the strong role of pragmatic context in the resolution, and the fact that, as mentioned, there is no clear locus or decision point for the ambiguity, nor (notwithstanding my list above) any small, neat set of alternatives sitting in a mental data structure (like a lexicon or grammar) waiting to be chosen from. Thus, for example, attributive–referential ambiguities may be resolved only by seeing whether or not the expression in question has a referent in the listener's model of the speaker's model of the world.

That there is, nonetheless, a linguistic component to (at least some of) these ambiguities is suggested by the influence of words and syntactic constructions on which of the readings is preferred. For example, *de dicto* readings may only appear in *opaque* contexts, such as the complement of an attitude verb ("Ross believes a unicorn is in the garden"), or in the scope of certain modals ("Ross might marry a Swedish woman"). While such contexts are syntactically rather diverse, they are still a relatively small, well-defined set (Fawcett, 1985). In fact, in some languages there are

[14]In Fawcett and Hirst (1986), we discuss a couple of other proposed readings that we do not believe are distinct from those above. Hofstadter, Clossman, and Meredith (1982) analyze a similar sentence for the case where the speaker and the agent are the same, "I want the fastest car in the world," and derive five readings where we predict four. However, their two extensional readings are identical in our analysis, as they differ only in how many separate descriptions the agent has for the entity.

grammatical markers to distinguish opaque contexts (Jackendoff, 1983, p. 214). And Sidner's heuristics for generic readings have already been mentioned.

Our work has not progressed to the stage where we have a model of the resolution of these kinds of ambiguities. (Rather, we have concentrated on suitable semantic representations of the various meanings, and the inferences they do and don't license in various situations.) I mention the work here because it is representative of the kind of "larger" linguistic ambiguity that is being studied now in computational linguistics and that I hope psycholinguistics will soon find itself able to consider.

Scope of Quantifiers and Negation

One other class of "large" ambiguity that deserves at least brief mention is that of the scope of quantifiers and of negation. For example, "Every student brought a lunch" may take a wide-scope or narrow-scope reading of the quantifier *every.* In the former, for every student there is some lunch such that that student brought it; in the latter, there is one single lunch that all the students brought. Clearly the former is the preferred reading here, but there are other sentences of the same structure in which the narrow scope is preferred: "Every student was introduced to a strange little man who stood on a platform in the center of the room." In sentences like this, the preference seems to derive from both the degree of specificity of the existentially quantified noun phrase and, of course, general plausibility. There can also be a syntactic effect—in particular, passive sentences tend to suggest narrow scoping: Compare "Everyone in this room knows two languages" (wide scope preferred) and "Two languages are known by everyone in this room" (narrow scope preferred).

Quantifier-scope ambiguities have received a lot of attention in computational linguistics, as they are particularly common in the kinds of sentences that people tend to ask of databases with natural language interfaces ("List all the students that are in some class every day"). For heuristics for determining scoping preference, see Allen (1987, pp. 283–286).

Another kind of scope ambiguity concerns negation; it is often ambiguous as to what the focus of negation syntactically attached to the main verb is. For example, there are four readings of "I didn't slam the door" (Diane Horton, personal communication):

- Focusing on *I:* "*I* didn't slam the door; *Nadia* did."
- Focusing on *slam:* "I didn't *slam* the door; I closed it quietly."
- Focusing on *the door*: "I didn't slam *the door*; I slammed *the window.*"
- Focusing on the whole proposition: "I didn't slam the door; it's still open."

Research Questions

What would be involved in the study of these kinds of ambiguities? One should, of course, start by gathering some data. At what stage do the various readings become available? Do some take longer than others? Is there always at any stage in the processing one reading marked as the current favorite? How can comprehension be misled, and how well can it recover?

Then we can ask how the system might choose one reading. Computational work has mostly taken the following sort of approach: After complete lexical, syntactic, and thematic analysis of the sentence, derive all the possible readings, and then decide among them on the basis of structural preferences and plausibility. (In the case of a database interface, the plausible readings may be exactly those that can in fact be answered from the database.) This seems untenable psychologically. Often, the number of possible readings is large, and each is expensive to derive. In fact, Hobbs (1983) has suggested that it is not a good idea, even computationally, to derive all readings of sentences that contain several quantifiers (giving a combinatorially large number of readings), as people surely don't—surely can't. Rather, Hobbs proposes, the sentence should be represented in a deliberately vague, "scope-neutral" manner in which an assertion is made of a "typical" member of a set (e.g., the typical student brought a lunch), and appropriate inferences are made from this representation for ambiguities of description. This has a clear appeal as a starting point for a psycholinguistic model.

Conclusion

I have presented several examples of computational work on the resolution of various kinds of ambiguity. What I hope to have shown in so doing is that psycholinguistics and computational linguistics have distinct but overlapping concerns in the study of ambiguity, and that research in each can have application in the other. Although I have limited my discussion to ambiguity, I hope it will be clear that the same argument could be made for many other aspects of language comprehension and generation.

I don't want to give the impression that interactions between the two fields have been limited to the few examples I have given. On the contrary, I believe there are quite a number of researchers who follow the literature of both fields; the conference and journal of the Cognitive Science Society have no doubt helped this along, as has the journal *Language and Cognitive Processes.* Nevertheless, I think that still more interdisciplinary contact could be beneficial for both groups; we do have quite a lot to say to one another.

Acknowledgements. I am grateful to Barbara Brunson, Diane Horton, Susan McRoy, and Murray Watt for their comments on earlier drafts and suggestions for improvements, and to the other conference speakers for stimulating discussions. My dissertation research was supervised and strongly influenced by Eugene Charniak, and supported in part by grants to him from the U.S. Office of Naval Research. Parts of the work described herein were supported by grants from the Natural Sciences and Engineering Research Council of Canada, and from IBM Canada Ltd. Preparation of this paper was supported by a grant from NSERC.

15

Reflexions on Modularity and Connectionism

W. TRAMMELL NEILL AND RICHARD M. KLEIN

As must be clear from the foregoing chapters, the ambiguities of ambiguity resolution remain unresolved. The problem of how context affects the processing of information is still complex and controversial. Recently, the controversy has been heightened by the emergence of two global (and in some respects opposing) approaches to the "architecture" of the mind: "modularity," especially as propounded by Fodor (1983); and "connectionism," as manifested, for example, in the work of McClelland and Rumelhart and their colleagues (McClelland, Rumelhart, and the PDP Research Group, 1986; Rumelhart, McClelland, and the PDP Research Group, 1986). The purpose of this chapter is to review some of the concerns aroused by these two contrasting approaches.

In the introduction to a recent edited volume on modularity, Garfield (1987, p. 17) explicitly accords to modularity the status of a scientific "paradigm" in Kuhn's (1970) sense. On the other hand, Schneider (1987) characterizes connectionism as an important "paradigm shift" for psychology. Both of these claims are probably a bit exaggerated. Despite their differences, the two approaches share many assumptions and metaphors with each other and with cognitive theories which are neither modular nor connectionist. Kuhn, in fact, notes that major paradigm shifts are typically accompanied by changes in what questions are considered suitable for investigation. The questions addressed by modularity and connectionism are, however, remarkably consistent with historical and modern "mainstream" cognitive psychology: How is knowledge represented in memory? What levels of representation are required to account for behavior? How do perceptual processes interact with cognitive processes? What processes are data-driven (bottom up) and what processes are conceptually driven (top down)? How do words activate their corresponding meanings? How do syntax and word meaning interact in language comprehension? How do linguistic and nonlinguistic processes and/or representations differ? What is the time course of information processing? What are the variables which affect information processing, and why? Indeed, much of the published work on both modularity and connectionism has been concerned with modeling the phenomena described in any cognitive psychology textbook!

On the other hand, modularity and connectionism may be legitimately viewed as "meta theories"—theories of how theories should be constructed. As such, they may not be directly falsifiable. Rather, the success of either approach will depend on its usefulness in generating more specific, testable hypotheses. There are, in fact, many strikingly different connectionist theories, and numerous variations on the theme of modularity as well. No claims are intended here as the absolute truth or falsity of either meta theory. Our comments are intended instead to apply at a more speculative level, to considerations which may (or may not) affect the utility of the approaches.

The organization of the chapter is as follows: The first two sections briefly describe some basic features of the modular and connectionist approaches. The third section examines some of the extensive historical roots of the two approaches. This is followed by a direct comparison of the two approaches, highlighting some important similarities and differences. Next, some problems that must confront modular theorists are discussed; a similar section for connectionists follows. Finally, some speculations on the ultimate success of the approaches are offered, along with suggestions of future directions for research.

The Modularity Hypothesis

In his book, *The Modularity of Mind*, Fodor (1983) advances the hypothesis that certain perceptual, cognitive, and linguistic operations function autonomously from each other and from higher, "central" processes. In this scheme, processing is strictly "bottom up": Input from a lower level is automatically processed by the module, and the final result of its computation is then passed to a higher module or to unspecified central mechanisms. A module's computations are unaffected by higher-level context or expectation—the module is "informationally encapsulated." Higher levels also do not have access to intermediate computations between the module's input and output; the module's output is said to be "shallow." The module is characterized as "cognitively impenetrable," reflecting the singularly constrained communication between higher and lower levels.

Fodor argues that processing modules evolved to provide fast, efficient processing of domain-specific information. Such specialization is necessitated by the unique computational requirements for certain brain functions which are not characteristic of the brain as a whole. As a prime example, it is argued (following Chomsky, 1965, 1980) that innate mechanisms have evolved for the syntactic analysis of language. According to the modularity hypothesis, the parsing of a string of words depends entirely on the possible grammatical roles of each word; it is not affected by the meanings of the words or of previous sentences. Using its peculiar computational rules, the syntactic module generates a description of the logical structure of the sentence, which is then passed on to other language comprehension processes. There is no "top-down" guidance of the syntactic parsing by higher-level semantic and pragmatic information.

The modularity hypothesis makes a strong claim to "biological plausibility," appealing to the evidence for localization of functions in the human brain. For example, it is believed that Broca's area, in the left prefrontal cerebral cortex, is important for structuring linguistic input and output. Damage to this area produces "expressive aphasia," but appears to leave comprehension intact as long as meaning can be inferred from the words independently of grammar (Caramazza & Zurif, 1976; Geschwind, 1972). In contrast, damage to Wernicke's area in the left temporal lobe produces "receptive aphasia" in which the patient produces syntactically correct but meaningless utterances, and displays impaired comprehension. Hence, it is natural to think of Broca's area as a "syntactic module" and Wernicke's area as a "semantic module." Similarly, the specificity of other aphasias and agnosias is suggestive of highly independent processing modules.

The modularity hypothesis is consistent with the exhaustive-access and ordered-access theories of word recognition, which assert that the retrieval of meanings is independent of the context in which a word occurs. According to these theories, presentation of an ambiguous word, such as BANK or PALM, results in either the generation of all possible meanings or an ordering of meanings by past frequency of occurrence. The context is then used to select the appropriate meaning for processing at a higher level. Thus, the mental lexicon containing the meaning of words constitutes a Fodorian module, functioning independently of higher-level operations.

As noted in preceding chapters, evidence that context does affect availability of meanings is often difficult to interpret: Both meanings of an ambiguous word may be initially activated, but the context-inappropriate meaning may decay or be inhibited very rapidly. Furthermore, Fodor (1983) is quite explicit that complex interactions may take place *within* a module. Thus, it is possible that a context word such as MONEY has a direct association to BANK within the lexicon, and somehow ensures that the module outputs only the relevant meaning of BANK. The critical question for the modularity hypothesis is whether the activation of meaning is affected when the context is constraining but not predictive—for example, *to* FLY versus *the* FLY (cf. Forster, Chapter 9, for example).

Connectionism

Connectionist (or "parallel distributed processing") models attempt to explain perceptual, cognitive, and behavioral phenomena in terms of neuronlike processing units and simple rules governing the connections between them. The connections can be excitatory or inhibitory and can vary in strength. Information processing activity occurs in the reciprocal interactions across a large set of such units. In connectionist models of learning, the connection strengths are typically increased or decreased depending on whether units become simultaneously active (analogous to classical conditioning) or whether the final state of the network is a desirable one (analogous to instrumental conditioning). The pattern of network activation in response to an input stimulus may then depend on the system's "experience."

A relatively simple example of the connectionist approach is the interactive-activation model of visual-word recognition proposed by McClelland and Rumelhart (1981). In this model, some processing units are activated by simple visual features. These feature detectors can in turn activate processing units representing letters. The letter detectors can then activate processing units corresponding to words. Thus, there are different "levels" of representation for features, letters, and words. The distinctive aspect of this model is that excitatory connections between levels are bidirectional: Activation of a word detector can in turn activate corresponding letter detectors, and letter detectors can activate corresponding feature detectors. Processing can therefore be as much "top down" as "bottom up." In addition, inhibitory connections exist between mutually inconsistent units within the same level. Thus, as the letter *T* becomes more highly activated, other letters become less so.

When a stimulus word is first presented, the pattern of network activation is likely to be highly unstable. The feature detectors activated by a letter will tend to activate detectors for other letters sharing similar features. Spuriously activated letter detectors in turn will tend to spuriously activate incorrect word detectors. However, it will usually be the case that the detectors for the correct features, letters, and words will be more active on the average than the incorrect ones at the same levels. The mutually reinforcing feedback connections between the correct detectors, and the increasing inhibition of incorrect detectors, will over time expand the differential of activation between the correct and incorrect detectors, until this differential reaches some maximum. When the system settles into this final state, the word (and the letters and the features) has been "recognized."

In the interactive-activation model, each processing unit corresponds to a particular conceptual object, such as a feature, letter, or word. However, in some connectionist models (e.g., McClelland & Rumelhart, 1985), the representation of a concept is distributed over a large number of processing units, and each processing unit may participate in the representation of many or all possible concepts. How concepts are represented has implications for the dynamics of the system: In a system where each concept is identified by a single processing unit, *N* processing units can represent *N* concepts, all of which can in principle be simultaneously active. At the other extreme, if all processing units participate in the representation of each concept, then many more concepts can be represented by the system

(2^N if each unit has two stable states, e.g., "on" and "off"); however, only one concept can then be active at a time.

The availability of top-down processing in connectionist models provides a direct account of context effects in word and letter recognition. For example, McClelland and Rumelhart (1981) apply their interactive-activation model to the word superiority effect (Reicher, 1969), in which tachistoscopic letter recognition is enhanced by embedding the letter in a word. It is assumed that letter detectors begin activating word detectors even before the letter detectors are sufficiently activated for a confident decision about letter identity. Feedback from the word detectors then enhances the activation of the letter detectors, increasing the likelihood that letter detector activation will reach a critical level in the brief period in which sensory input is available. In contrast, a single letter or a letter embedded in a nonword would not activate word detectors and so could not benefit from the reflexive feedback.

Context-dependent models of ambiguity resolution are clearly consistent with connectionist models. Even though OAK and PALM are not likely to be directly associated, for example, the presentation of OAK may activate a higher-level representation of *tree*, which then reflexively feeds back to a particular interpretation of PALM. Such a model might superficially seem to be at odds with experiments showing the availability of both meanings at a short delay but selectivity at longer delays (Swinney, 1979; Seidenberg, Tanenhaus, Leiman, & Bienkowski, 1982; Tanenhaus, Leiman, & Seidenberg, 1979). However, in computer simulations, McClelland (1987) shows that this effect is also predicted by the interactive-activation model. In essence, the early processing of an ambiguous stimulus may be determined primarily by the stimulus itself: As processing continues, the stimulus information interacts with contextual information, such that feedback and inhibition selectively increase the activation of the context-appropriate interpretation over time.

Historical Perspectives

The ideas of both modularity and connectionism can be traced to the writings of Plato and Aristotle. In the long history of psychology, they are in fact recurring themes. However, the issue of which of the two approaches (regarding them as mutually exclusive) must be correct has only become an issue in recent centuries. In the prior history of psychology, for example, you can find some individuals who contribute to both approaches.

The modularity theme is first clearly and systematically expressed in Plato's *Republic* (Book IV) with his triadic division of the soul. Aristotle divided the human soul into the vegetative, sensitive, and rational (*De Anima*, Books II, III in Barnes, 1984). Without question, *De Anima* was a central psychological text throughout medieval times and even well into the Renaissance (Schmitt & Skinner, 1988, p. 455).

From the time of Plato and Aristotle it has become almost commonplace to divide the mind or soul into separate functions. A high point, perhaps the most thoroughgoing of all modular statements, was reached in portions of the psychology propounded by St. Thomas Aquinas in the thirteenth century. St. Thomas divided the mind into a number of different "powers," following Aristotle and early Christian writings. Especially in his *Summa Theologiae*, a fully descriptive, exhaustive, faculty psychology was developed. It is also fully theological ". . . powers are not for the sake of organs, but organs for the sake of powers" (*Summa Theologae*, I,q.78,a.3).

In the seventeenth and eighteenth centuries, a number of individuals continued to propose divisions of various sorts. Among the most famous were Locke, Wolff, Reid, and Kant. Thus, for example, Locke (1894) wrote of "perception as it is the first faculty of the mind exercised about our ideas" (p. 183); and "the next faculty of the mind whereby it makes a further progress towards knowledge, is what I call retention . . ." (p. 192); and "another faculty we may take notice of is that of discerning and distinguishing between the several ideas it has (p. 202)."

By the nineteenth century there were significant new developments which considerably enriched and diversified the modular theme. Gall contributed the doctrine of systematic, organic localization of function corresponding to his psychological faculties:

> The moral and intellectual dispositions are innate; their manifestation depends on organization; the brain is exclusively the organ of the mind; the brain is composed of as many particular and independent organs, as there are fundamental powers of the mind;—these four incontestable principles form the basis of the whole physiology of the brain. (Cited in Herrnstein & Boring, 1965, p. 219)

The century wore on, the neurosciences were developing, and the localization-of-function doctrine seemed to receive more and more credibility. Certainly an early boost was from J. Muller's so-called law of specific nerve energies, which implied a sharp and inherent distinction between sensory domains: "Therefore, sensation is not the conduction of a quality or state of external bodies to consciousness, but the conduction of a quality or a state of our nerves to consciousness, excited by an external cause" (cited in Clarke & O'Malley, 1968, p. 206). Almost invariably, localization of function was paired with a faculty psychology.

Another significant development was in psychiatry, especially during the latter third of the century with the fascination for topics such as multiple personality, conscious and unconscious, hysteria, and hypnotism. Consideration of these topics led investigators to propose various divisions of personality (Ellenberger, 1970).

Another variation of the modular theme was in the area of mental testing, the first applied area of the new psychology. A striking example is Spearman's supposition of a number of test-specific separate abilities, as well as a general factor which participates in all intellectual acts (Spearman, 1904).

Still another manifestation of the modularity theme was in the area of motivation. Following Darwin, the topic of instincts became very popular; there is a chapter in the *Origin of Species* with the heading "instincts." Many became concerned with the question of the number and division of instincts. An excellent example, very famous at the time, was W. McDougall's *An Introduction to Social Psychology* (1860/1908). He enumerates a number of the "principle instincts" and their corresponding emotions (Chapter III). A few examples are the instinct of flight, the instinct of repulsion, and the instinct of curiosity. Debate has continued to the present day with regard to the number and division of needs, drives, motives, etc.

The connectionist theme, as has sometimes been pointed out, is first clearly enunciated in Aristotle's *Treatise on Memory*, and the idea of associations has become a commonplace idea in psychology. But its *central* importance in psychology was a claim not made until the development of British empiricism. This is perhaps natural, given the tendency of the empiricists to atomize the mind into separate and distinct ideas. Hume (1739–1740/1888), for one, makes this clear when he likens the force of association to the force of gravity. Writing about the cohesion of our ideas as a result of association, he remarks: "Here is a kind of attraction, which in the mental world will be found to have as extraordinary effects as in the natural, and to show itself in as many and as various forms" (pp. 12–13). It could be claimed that the theme culminated in James Mill's *Analysis of the Phenomena of the Human Mind*, which was a relentless application of association to the basic phenomena of psychology. His is perhaps the best example of "mental chemistry" as described by his son, J. S. Mill. An example of James Mill's approach is well illustrated in the following:

> Brick is one complex idea, mortar is another complex idea; these ideas, with ideas of position and quantity, compose my idea of a wall. My idea of a plank is a complex idea, my idea of a rafter is a complex idea, my idea of a nail is a complex idea. These, united with the same ideas of position and quantity, compose my duplex idea of a floor. In the same manner my complex idea of glass, and wood, and others, compose my duplex idea of a window; and these duplex ideas, united together, compose my idea of a house, which is made up of various duplex ideas. How many complex, or duplex ideas, are all united in the idea of furniture? How many more in the idea of merchandize? How many more in the idea called Every Thing? (Mill, 1829/1967, pp. 115–116)

This tradition was, of course, the one that was first brought within the reach of research by Ebbinghaus. Until the appearance of contemporary cognitive psychology, the Ebbinghaus research tradition would be in place, although somewhat modified by stimulus-response psychologies.

The connectionism theme underwent a revolutionary change with the early behavioral research on animals performed by Thorndike, Pavlov, and others. Instead of an association of ideas, which both Thorndike and Pavlov rejected, we have the "connection"—in Thorndike's jargon—between stimulus and response, or as he put it in his earliest writing when describing what his subject cat had learned:

> Starting, then, with its store of instinctive impulses, the cat hits upon the successful movement, and gradually associates it with the sense impression of the interior of the box until the connection is perfect, so that it performs the act as soon as confronted with the sense-impression. (Thorndike, 1898, p. 15)

With the advent of behaviorism, the connectionist tradition was strongly represented in the various learning theories. Tolman was, of course, the most famous exception to the nonmentalistic stimulus-response assumption in that he retained some of the flavor of the old association of ideas.

The associationists' answer to the localization-of-function concept would have to be some type of network model of neural functioning; and there have been numerous attempts to detail this approach. It is perhaps fair to say that until the very influential work of Hebb, *The Organization of Behavior*, was published in 1949, a satisfactory model, based on the twentieth-century neurosciences, was not developed.

By the late nineteenth century on to the present, the explicit issue of which theme, connectionism or modularity, is correct has been under considerable discussion. It is likely that this debate began with the questioning of the centrality and ubiquity of connections. By the later nineteenth century, critics abounded: W. James, H. Bergson, O. Kulpe, etc. The defenders, people like G. E. Muller and Titchner, replied.

Particularly instructive is W. James's treatment of associations in his monumental *Principles of Psychology* of 1890 (1950). He totally rejects the theory that associations between ideas operate within the mind. Instead he suggests that associations operate solely on the neural level "between processes in the brain" (James, 1950, p. 554), and what are associated are not ideas but objects. Thus, James (1890/1950) proposes a connectionist model of neural events while rejecting the traditional connectionism:

> The whole body of the associationist psychology remains standing after you have translated "ideas" into "objects," on the one hand, and "brain-processes" on the other; and the analysis of faculties and operations is as conclusive in these terms as in those traditionally used. (p. 604)

Comparisons of Modularity and Connectionism

Both modularity and connectionism are essentially "reflex" theories of behavior (hence the title of this chapter). Both approaches view cognition as ultimately stimulus-driven. That is, the system remains relatively static and unchanging until the introduction of a stimulus. A stimulus automatically triggers certain operations or associations, leading deterministically (or probabilistically) to a predictable response or change in state of the system. As such, these approaches contrast with views of the organism as continuously dynamic, exploring and actively acquiring information (e.g., Gibson, 1979). It is notable in this regard that Fodor (1983), in his dedication, credits a statement by Merrill Garrett as the inspiration for his work: "What you have to remember about parsing is that basically it's a reflex."

Both modularity and connectionist theories have mainly addressed "peripheral" processes (broadly defined), such as perception, pattern recognition, categorization, motor control, and, most ambitiously, grammatical syntax—as opposed to slower, more complex processes such as language comprehension, thinking, and problem solving. This restriction is explicit in modularity, since more complex processes are less likely to be modular and more likely to involve the unidentified central processes. For connectionism, this has been more a matter of programmatic convenience, tackling "simpler" problems first. Rumelhart and McClelland (1986) note that they focused initially on problems in which conventional symbol processing models have been least successful; they outline some new directions for future investigation, including sequential symbol processing and language processing. It should be noted, however, that in the same volume, Norman (1986) expresses some skepticism about such endeavors.

It is interesting that both modularity and connectionism make evolutionary claims to speed and efficiency of computation. Fodor (1983) argues that processing of certain information benefits from specialized computational procedures: Processing would be much slower if the same computational procedures were used for all kinds of information. In addition, the mandatoriness (automaticity) of modular processing ensures that important computations are carried out even though central processing resources are engaged elsewhere—as noted by one author, it is important to recognize a tiger even if one is not expecting it. In contrast, connectionists argue that the inherent slowness of neural processes is overcome by the massive parallelism and redundancy of representation. McClelland (1987, 1988) argues that feedback from higher levels and inhibition between incompatible representations act very rapidly to reduce noise at lower levels.

Both Fodor and McClelland acknowledge that computational efficiency is purchased at some cost to achieving veridical representation of the input. Fodor (1983, 1987) suggests that processing modules occasionally make errors because, by virtue of their "informational encapsulation," they cannot base their decisions on all possibly relevant information. So, for example, the Muller-Lyer illusion persists despite higher-level knowledge that the two lines are really equal. In the interactive-activation model, errors can occur because the system will be biased toward more familiar stimuli. The first letter of GAT may be easily misperceived as C, for example, because the features are sufficiently close to those of CAT that the activated word node provides strong contextual support for that interpretation. In short, both modular and connectionist systems are heuristic, as opposed to algorithmic.

Both modularity and connectionism make strong claims for "biological plausibility." Modularity makes this claim at a more macroscopic level, based on the apparent specialization of different areas of the brain for different functions. Connectionism makes the claim at a more microscopic level, in that the models are directly based on assumed properties of neurons. It is, of course, likely that neurons are highly interconnected within a brain module but not between brain modules. However, where modular theorists tend to emphasize "characteristic breakdown of function" as a consequence of brain damage, connectionists emphasize "graceful degradation of function." Because of the high degree of redundancy in connectionist networks, computer simulations generally show little deterioration of performance if a few connections are randomly eliminated; as progressively more connections are eliminated, performance deteriorates smoothly. Thus, whereas modularity emphasizes the discreteness of functional loss, connectionism emphasizes continuity and neural plasticity.

Connectionist models are generally much more concerned with learning than are modular models. Some connectionist models are directly concerned with how the strengths of connections change as a consequence of their history of activation and inhibition. In contrast, modular theories tend to emphasize properties of fully implemented modules which are not expected to change over time. This may reflect Fodor's (1983) argument that modules are innately specified and "hardwired." Of course, no one would argue that specific vocabulary or grammatical rules (like adding *s* for pluralization) are not learned. Rather, the specifics are considered to be trivial; interest is focused on the underlying logical structure and performance characteristics of the module (e.g., universal grammar).

Any modular theory can in principle be modeled by a connectionist network. As such, modularity and connectionism are not at all logically incompatible. Consider again the interactive-activation model of McClelland and Rumelhart, in which feature detectors activate (and are activated by) word detectors. The "upward" connection strengths could be adjusted independently of the "downward" connection strengths (a necessary degree of freedom to preserve the neural analogy, since the transmission of impulses by a neuron is generally unidirectional). If the downward strengths are simply set to zero, one has a purely bottom-up modular system. Fodorian modularity can be further enhanced by requiring activation at a given level to attain a maximum before influencing the activation at the next level (for example, by setting relatively high thresholds for activation).

Connectionist models do not have to have top-down connections at all. However, while modularity can thus be viewed as a trivial case, the absence of top-down activation would rob connectionism of one of its most distinguishing (and most controversial) processing capabilities. Indeed, most empirical research concerning modularity and connectionism has focused on just this issue. As noted previously with regard to ambiguity and context, this issue is very difficult to resolve. McClelland (1987) notes that "unidirectional and interactionist models can make identical predictions for a large number of experiments, if it is assumed that lower levels are free to pass on ambiguities they cannot resolve to higher levels" (p. 5). Context effects which may be explained by feedback from higher levels to lower levels can often be alternatively explained by decision biases at higher levels. For example, the word superiority effect discussed previously might be explainable as an inference based on the known spelling of a perceived word, rather than enhancement of letter perception per se. Fodor (1983) challenges interactionists to demonstrate that information at higher levels can actually affect what is represented at lower levels, and not merely the final results of such processing.

Elman and McClelland (1988) report experiments which may successfully meet Fodor's challenge. They demonstrated that lexically restored phonemes (e.g., perceived *s* at the end of Christma*, where * is an ambiguous *s/sh* stimulus) can shift the boundaries of subsequent phonemes as if the restored phoneme were actually presented. Since phoneme boundaries presumably exist at a relatively low level of speech perception, it appears that the higher-level word representation was able to influence activation at the lower level. Whether similar effects can be demonstrated for other types of stimuli remains to be seen.

Some Problems for Modularity

Fodor (1983) makes an explicit distinction between modular processes, which tend to be more peripheral (i.e., perceptual and motor processes), and "central" processes. Modular systems are characterized by domain specificity, mandatoriness, informational encapsulation, and speed; central systems do not have these characteristics. Fodor recommends that cognitive science should concentrate on the modular peripheral processes first, and only when they are relatively well understood should we attempt to study the complex, presumably interactive, central processes. However, one can make exactly the opposite argument: If the peripheral systems are really modular, then there is no need to understand how they work in order to investigate the central processes—all one needs to know is what information output by the modules is available for central processing. Of course, if the modularity hypothesis is wrong, exclusive focus on either peripheral or central processes has been a wild goose chase all along.

To deliberately ignore central processes is to exclude many important and well-studied phenomena—for example, attention, working memory, retrieval strategies, decision making, and problem solving. Fodor, in fact, acknowledges that nonmodular systems do carry a lot of the burden of information processing. To recognize the importance of central processes without specifying any of their properties may pose a threat to the testability of any modular theory. That is, the failure to confirm a prediction can always be attributed to the unknown central processes. Hence, it may not be possible to disconfirm the theory.

Another problem also concerns testability: The essence of the modularity hypothesis is that there should be no effect of higher-level information on the functioning of a lower-level module. Empirically, this is a null hypothesis, which can never be proved—it is always possible that there *is* such an effect, which simply was not detected. In a sense, this is a "good" problem, since the null hypothesis can be rejected by finding the unpredicted effect, which makes the model testable (unless, as discussed previously, one falls back on the excuse of unknown central processes). At any rate, this puts modularity in the uncomfortable position of having to rely more heavily on arguments of parsimony, rather than direct positive corroboration.

Modularity is implicitly a "late selection" theory of attention, akin to the theories of Deutsch and Deutsch (1963), Norman (1968), and Keele (1973), as opposed to "early selection" theories of Broadbent (1958) and Treisman (1964). There is indeed much evidence that early processing occurs automatically, i.e., without requiring attentional resources, consistent with the mandatoriness and autonomy of modules (see, for example, the review by Keele & Neill, 1978). However, there is also considerable evidence that allocation of attention can greatly speed the detection of even very simple stimuli (e.g., Posner, Snyder, & Davidson, 1980). Such effects of presumably central processing would appear to violate the assumption of "cognitive impenetrability" of modules.

Since processing is assumed to be unidirectional, any reversibility of cognitive operations is inconsistent with modularity. It can be argued, for example, that we can generate meaning from phonemic input, or we can generate phonemes to express meaning. In order to salvage modularity, it is necessary to postulate separate input and output phonemic modules. In this particular case, this may not be implausible. McCann and Besner (1987), for example, argue for separate input and output lexicons. However, if there are many such reversibilities, it would be markedly unparsimonious to rely repeatedly on multiple, informationally redundant modules.

The problem of reversibility also applies to the analogy of brain localization. Bidirectional communication between brain structures appears to be the general rule. For example, Broca's area and Wernicke's area seem to be ideal candidates for modules. However, damage to Broca's area impairs processing of grammar in comprehension as well as in production (Caramazza & Zurif, 1976; Geschwind, 1972). This would seem to imply that communication occurs in both directions. One might argue that Broca's area really consists of two separate modules, one for input and one for output. However, it would be necessary to account for their contiguous location; and in the absence of any physical evidence for bifurcation, the analogy of hypothetical modules to localized brain structures is still seriously undermined.

The claim to "biological plausibility" is also weakened by examples of functional plasticity in the brain. According to Fodor, modules are innate and "hardwired." It is certainly the case that localization is to a degree genetically determined. Even prior to birth, Broca's area and Wernicke's area in the left cerebral hemisphere are more highly developed than the corresponding areas in the right hemisphere (Chi, Dooling, & Giles, 1972; Wada, Clark, & Hamm, 1975). However, if the left hemisphere is damaged or removed at an early age, the right hemisphere can assume many functions of the left (Smith, 1966; Smith & Burkland, 1966).

Some Problems for Connectionism

A number of writers have criticized connectionism on the grounds that there are very few constraints on the possible models (e.g., Estes, 1988; Massaro, 1988; Phillips, 1988; Schneider, 1987). One problem concerns the freedom to organize the processing units any way one chooses. One does not then really know whether the emergent performance reflects connectionist principles per se, or instead the particular organization one has arbitrarily chosen. For example, the interactive-activation model of McClelland and Rumelhart incorporates the implicit assumption that word recognition is accomplished directly from the visual orthography, without phonetic recoding. While some evidence does support direct orthographic access (e.g., Baron, 1973), other evidence supports phonological recoding (Meyer, Schvaneveldt, & Ruddy, 1974; Rubenstein, Lewis, & Rubenstein, 1971). The performance of the model would undoubtedly be changed by the insertion of a phonemic level; this change, however, would have little or nothing to do with the connectionist principles.

Many connectionists in fact refer to "modules," which may confuse comparison to Fodor's concept of modularity. In connectionist modules, processing units are more highly interconnected within modules than between modules. This allows different parts of the network a degree of autonomy; there are, however, no necessary constraints on "shallowness" of output, directionality, or cognitive impenetrability. McClelland (1987) applauds the concept of "informational encapsulation," which in his model means that the processing units of one level are connected only to the immediately adjacent upper and lower levels. (In the interactive-activation model, feature detectors are not connected directly to word detectors.) Since top-down communication is still a central feature, this is clearly not in accord with Fodor's notions. Nor is it clear than this is a desirable constraint—there is good reason to believe that word recognition is accomplished through two parallel routes, directly from visual orthography and indirectly through phonological recording (Baron & Strawson, 1976; Meyer & Gutschera, 1975; Meyer & Ruddy, 1973). Fodor's modularity at least does not preclude a lower-level module from projecting upward to more than one higher level.

Another common criticism of connectionism is the problem of "hidden units." Minsky and Papert (1969) demonstrated that certain fairly simple categorizations cannot be solved by connectionist systems consisting of only two layers corresponding to input and output. As a simple example, imagine that there are four stimuli, a red circle, a red square, a green circle, and a green square, which must be mapped into two categories, "1" and "2." There are four "feature detectors," for red, green, circle, and square, which must connect to two output units corresponding to categories 1 and 2. It is trivial to design a system which outputs "1" for a red square or red circle, or "2" for a green square or green circle—simply have the red detector activate output "1," and the green detector activate output "2" (Figure 15.1a). It is even fairly simple to output "1" for just a red square and "2" for all else. (In Figure 15.1b, activation of category 2 by either green or circle inhibits activation of category 1.) However, suppose one wishes to output "1" for a red square or a green circle, and "2" for a red circle or a green square. Each feature detector must equally activate both category units; there is no way to build the system to categorize all four stimuli correctly. The solution is simple, however, if intermediate, "hidden" units are allowed, as shown in Figure 15.1c.

The problem with such hidden units is that they may allow unlimited computational power (Minsky & Papert, 1969). Massaro (1988) shows that such systems can generate not only observed patterns of performance, but with minor changes, patterns that do not occur at all. The problem of hidden units is illustrated by the simple example in Figure 15.1c: The hidden units actually represent each possible stimulus. It is a trivial matter to simply define units for each possible combination of features and map them into the desired output units. However, this strains credulity—where do all these units come from? The problem is only thinly disguised by having networks of hidden units such that there is no 1-to-1 relationship between stimuli and units.

Whereas Fodor's modularity declines to specify the properties of central control processes, most connectionist theories attempt to do away with them altogether: "Connectionist representations are truly active, in the sense that they give rise to further processing activity directly, without any need for a central processor or a production-matching-and-application mechanism that examines them and takes action on the basis of this examination" (McClelland, 1988, p. 109). Norman (1986), however, suggests that connectionist networks need to be augmented by some mechanism for conscious control of activation. Schneider and Detweiler (1987) make some progress in this direction by combining connectionist modules

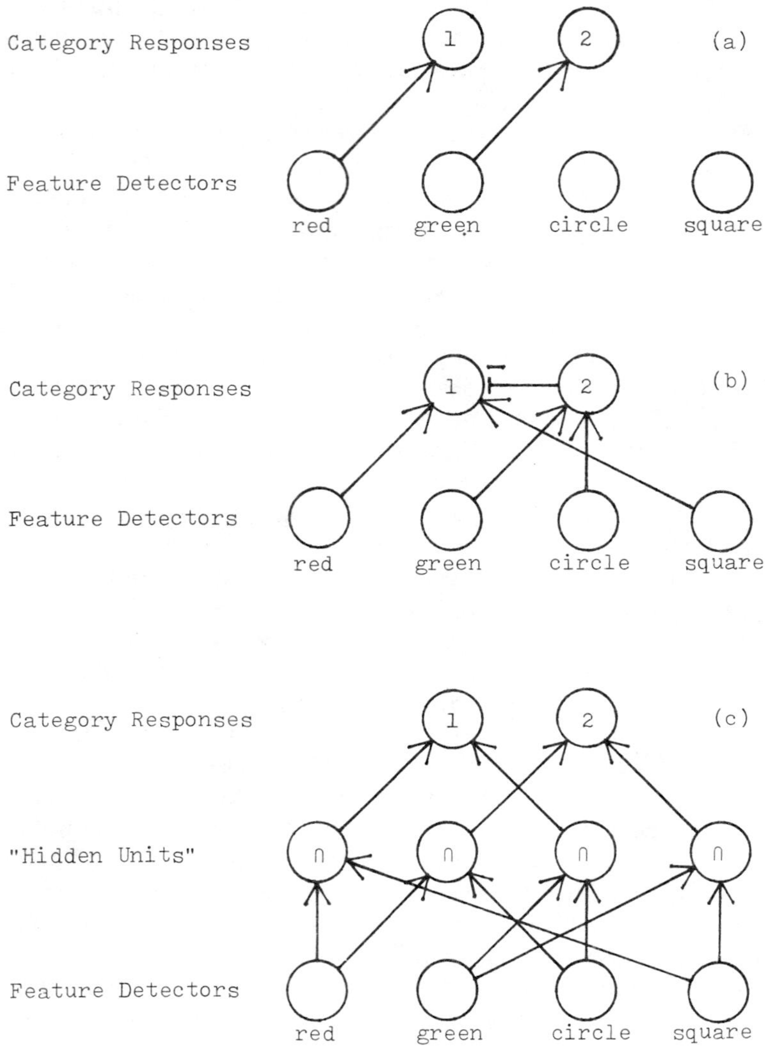

FIGURE 15.1. Simple connectionist models for categorization:
(a) Categorizes all red stimuli as "1" and all green stimuli as "2"; (b) categorizes a red square as "1," all else as "2." Note that any input into "2" results in inhibition of "1"; (c) Categorizes red square and green circle as "1" and red circle and green square as "2." Intersection (∩) indicates that both inputs are necessary to activate hidden units (i.e., "high threshold.") Alternatively, lateral inhibition between hidden units may prevent units with only one source of activation from activating category responses.

with a central architecture for working memory. It is not clear, however, whether the emergent behavior is due to connectionist principles or merely to the choice of modules and the design of the control architecture.

Connectionist models may also have difficulty with evidence that cognitive control appears to involve the direct selective inhibition of distracting information. In the Stroop effect (after Stroop, 1935), for example, the meaning of a word interferes with naming the color of ink in which it is written. This effect in itself is simple to model in a connectionist system. However, experiments have repeatedly shown that the response activated by the distractor word is selectively inhibited, with the consequence that it is actually less available on a subsequent trial (see, for example, Neill, Chapter 6). In connectionist models, the activation of a processing unit reflects the sum of excitatory and inhibitory influences on the unit. If the correct color-associated unit inhibits all incompatible units, the distractor-activated unit should remain more activated than other, less recently activated units. Connectionist systems do not provide for the selective inhibition of a more highly activated processing unit. The problem is solvable by postulating an inhibitory connection from a hidden unit for each possible stimulus to the response unit corresponding to the distractor. However, such a solution is not only blatantly ad hoc, but would have difficulty accommodating changes in task requirements, such as to name the word rather than the color.

In general, connectionist systems seem inadequate to model spontaneous changes in processing strategies. As an example, the nature of the previously discussed word superiority effect depends on subject expectations of relative stimulus frequencies. Hawkins, Reicher, Rogers, and Peterson (1976) found that homophones such as CENT versus SENT show a word superiority effect when homophones are expected, but not if they are unexpected. It appears that the word superiority effect can reflect either a phonemic or a higher (semantic?) level of processing, depending on expected utility. A pure connectionist system would probably require a large number of learning trials to shift the appropriate connection weights; if strategy shifts can be implemented rapidly, a more specialized symbol processing mechanism may be required.

Despite the direct modeling of neuronal activity, connectionist systems may still suffer from lack of "biological plausibility." As noted previously, learning requires readjustment of the connection strengths with experience. The presence of "hidden units" requires a "back-propagation" algorithm for this readjustment, which is conceded to have no known biological counterpart (Rumelhart, Hinton, & Williams, 1986). Also, connectionist systems are quite homogeneous in the organization and parameter settings of their component parts. Both Estes (1988) and Phillips (1988) note that neuronal organization at different brain loci has become more varied with evolution:

The evolution of the brain has not yielded a machine of uniform design like a digital computer but rather a melange of different evolutionary ages. There is scant reason to expect any single type of processor model to apply uniformly throughout the ensemble of neural systems that makes up the brain." (Estes, 1988, pp. 206–207)

Unfortunately, allowing still more degrees of freedom in the construction of a connectionist system would only further fuel the criticism of unlimited computational power.

Prognoses and Prescriptions

As noted in the introduction, both modularity and connectionism are attempts to answer fairly traditional questions about perception, memory, language, and cognition. At the same time, however, both approaches are reflective of the current trend toward an interdisciplinary "cognitive science," integrating work in biology, philosophy, linguistics, and artificial intelligence with cognitive psychology. This trend has been accompanied by an increasing reliance on computer simulation as a test of theory. Schneider (1987) notes, "Connectionism will produce some loss of the empirical tradition of psychology and perhaps promote an animosity toward other views" (p. 82). However, the methodology of simulation presupposes that we know the properties of the behavior we are attempting to model. Fodor (1983) is quite explicit in asserting that the properties of language are quite well understood, and the problem now is merely to design the architecture of a system which mirrors these properties. We suspect, however, that most psychologists (including those allied with either modularity or connectionism) would be reluctant to adopt such antiempirical *hubris* toward the phenomena they study. Connectionism and modularity will probably raise new questions about human behavior; conventional empirical investigation and the uncovering of new phenomena will continue for quite some time.

The biggest challenge for connectionism and modularity in the future will be to achieve some degree of consistency across models of different phenomena. Connectionist models have proliferated to the point of almost a new model for each behavioral simulation. Schneider (1987) notes:

> When a connectionist model fails, there are many interpretations or outs for why it failed. Connectionist models are sensitive to the initial state, structure, number of elements, specific problems, learning sequence, learning rule, and coding patterns of the initial model. (p. 81)

If the parameters have to be changed for every behavior, then connectionism fails in its attempt to generate general testable theories. Similarly, it is always possible to change one's assumptions about what constitutes a module in order to fit the data at hand. Modularity purports to "carve the mind at its joints" (cf. Garfield, 1987); those joints should not change with every behavior. A paramount goal for computer simulations should be to parsimoniously model multiple phenomena within the *same* program!

Modularity and connectionism both contain many ideas which seem plausible, biologically and psychologically. As argued in this chapter, other assumptions are likely to prove untenable or unproductive. The "truth" is likely to be some compromise between the two positions. Tanenhaus, Dell, and Carlson (1987) suggest one promising "connectionist approach to modularity" which acknowledges that there may be varying *degrees* of modularity, which may be distinguishable by their "activation history functions." Essentially, they propose that context effects can be described on a feedback-time continuum from no feedback or late feedback at the modular end, to early feedback, priming, and full preactivation at the nonmodular end. While Tanenhaus et al. propose this mainly as a conceptual framework, the actual examination of activation history functions may provide a new direction for empirical research.

Modularity and connectionism have both unquestionably sparked new questions, new controversies, and new perspectives in contemporary cognitive psychology. This is manifest in the ongoing intensity of interest and debate over their principles. Modularity is appreciated for its bold attempt to achieve simplicity and parsimony in understanding the mind, and for the potential testability of its strong assumptions. Connectionism is a boon to anyone who questions how particular functions *could* be embodied in a neural network such as the brain. And while it is true that computer simulation has grown in importance, traditional empirical investigation of human subjects still appears to be in a healthy state. So far, the ideas of modularity and connectionism have stimulated interesting experiments, and there is no reason to assume that they will not continue to do so.

References

Abbott, V., Black, J. B., & Smith, E. E. (1985). The representation of scripts in memory. *Journal of Memory and Language, 24,*179–199.

• Allen, J. F. (1987). *Natural language understanding.* Menlo Park, CA: Benjamin/Cummings.

Allport, D. A. (1977). On knowing the meaning of words we are unable to report. In S. Dornic (Ed.), *Attention and performance VI,* 505–533. Hillsdale, NJ: Erlbaum.

Allport, D. A., Tipper, S. P., & Chmiel, N. R. J. (1985). Perceptual integration and postcategorical filtering. In M. I. Posner & O. S. M. Marin (Eds.), *Attention and performance XI* (pp. 107–132). Hillsdale, NJ: Lawrence Erlbaum Associates.

Anderson, J. R. (1976). *Language, memory, and thought.* Hillsdale, NJ: Erlbaum.

Anderson, J. R. (1983). *The architecture of cognition.* Cambridge, MA: Harvard University Press.

Anderson, J. R. (1987). *A rational approach to memory.* Presented to the annual meeting of the Psychonomics Society, Seattle, WA.

Anderson, J. R., & Bower, G. H. (1973). *Human associative memory.* Hillsdale, NJ: Erlbaum.

• Anderson, R. C., & Ortony, A. (1975). On putting apples into bottles—A problem of polysemy. *Cognitive Psychology, 7,* 167–180.

Anderson, R. C., Pichert, J. W., Goetz, E. T., Schallert, D. L., Stevens, K. W., & Trollip, S. R. (1976). Instantiation of general terms. *Journal of Verbal Learning and Verbal Behavior, 15,* 667–679.

Aquinas, St. Thomas (1947–1948). *Summa Theologae.* New York: Benzinger.

• Armstrong, S. L., Gleitman, L. R., & Gleitman, H. (1983). On what some concepts might not be. *Cognition, 13,* 263–308.

• Averbach, E., & Coriell, A. S. (1961). Short-term memory in vision. *Bell System Technical Journal, 40,* 309–328.

Baddeley, A. D. (1986). *Working memory.* New York: Basic Books.

Baddeley, A. D., & Hitch, G. J. (1974). *Working memory.* In G. Bower (Ed.), *Recent advances in learning and motivation* (Vol. 8, pp. 67–89). New York: Academic Press.

Bahrick, H. (1987). Functional and cognitive memory theory: An overview of some key issues. In D. S. Gorfein & R. R. Hoffman (Eds.), *Memory and learning: The Ebbinghaus Centennial Conference* (pp. 387–395). Hillsdale, NJ: Erlbaum.

Baillargeon, R., Spelke, E. S., & Wasserman, S. (1985). Object permanence in five-month-old infants. *Cognition, 20,* 191–208.

Balota, D. A., & Chumbley, J. I. (1984). Are lexical decisions a good measure of lexical access? The role of word frequency in the neglected decision stage. *Journal of Experimental Psychology: Human Perception and Performance, 10,* 340–357.

Balota, D. A., & Chumbley, J. I. (1985). The locus of word-frequency effects in the pronunciation task: Lexical access and/or production? *Journal of Memory and Language, 24,* 89–106.

Balota, D. A., Pollatsek, A., & Rayner, K. (1985). The interaction of contextual constraints and parafoveal visual information in reading. *Cognitive Psychology, 17,* 364–390.

Barclay, J. R., Bransford, J. D., Franks, J. J., McCarrell, N. S., & Nitsch, K. E. (1974). Comprehension and semantic flexibility. *Journal of Verbal Learning and Verbal Behavior, 13,* 471–481.

Barnes, J. (Ed.) (1984). *The Complete Works of Aristotle* (Vol. I). Princeton, NJ: Princeton University Press.

Baron, J. (1973). Phonemic stage not necessary for reading. *Quarterly Journal of Experimental Psychology, 25,* 241–246.

Baron, J., & Strawson, C. (1976). Use of orthographic and word-specific knowledge in reading words aloud. *Journal of Experimental Psychology: Human Perception and Performance, 2,* 386–393.

Barsalou, L. W. (1982). Context-independent and context-dependent information in concepts. *Memory & Cognition, 10,* 82–93.

Barsalou, L. W. (1983). Ad hoc categories. *Memory & Cognition, 11,* 211–227.

Barsalou, L. W. (1985). Ideals, central tendency, and frequency of instantiation as determinants of graded structure in categories. *Journal of Experimental Psychology: Learning, Memory, and Cognition, 11,* 629–654.

Barsalou, L. W. (1987). The instability of graded structure: Implications for the nature of concepts. In U. Neisser (Ed.), *Concepts and conceptual development: Ecological and intellectual factors in categorization.* New York: Cambridge University Press.

Barsalou, L. W. (1988). The content and organization of autobiographical memories. In U. Neisser & E. Winograd (Eds.), *Remembering reconsidered: Ecological and traditional approaches to the study of memory.* New York: Cambridge University Press.

Barsalou, L. W. (1989). Intra-concept similarity and its implications for inter-concept similarity. In S. Vosniadou & A. Ortony (Eds.), *Similarity and analogical reasoning.* New York: Cambridge University Press.

Barsalou, L. W., & Bower, G. H. (1984). Discrimination nets as psychological models. *Cognitive Science, 8,* 1–26.

Barsalou, L. W., & Medin, D. L. (1986). Concepts: Fixed definitions or context-dependent representations? *Cahiers de Psychologie Cognitive, 6,* 187–202.

Barsalou, L. W., & Sewell, D. R. (1985). Contrasting the representation of scripts and categories. *Journal of Memory and Language, 24,* 646–665.

Barsalou, L. W., Spindler, J. L., Sewell, D. R., Ballato, S. M., & Gendel, E. M. (1987). *Assessing the stability of category representations with property generation.* Unpublished manuscript.

Bassili, J. N., & Smith, M. C. (1986). On the spontaneity of trait attribution:

Converging evidence for the role of cognitive strategy. *Journal of Personality and Social Psychology, 50,* 239–245.

Becker, C. A. (1980). Semantic context effects in visual word recognition: An analysis of semantic strategies. *Memory & Cognition, 6,* 644–652.

Bednall, E. S. (1978). *Frequency, semantic priming and ambiguity effects in word recognition.* Unpublished doctoral dissertation, Monash University.

Bernbach, H. (1970). A multiple-copy model for postperceptual memory. In D. A. Norman (Ed.), *Models of human memory.* New York: Academic Press.

Besner, D., & McCann, R. S. (1988). Word frequency and pattern distortion in visual word identification and production: An examination of four classes of models. In M. Colthart (Ed.), *Attention and performance XII: The psychology of reading.* Hillsdale, NJ: Erlbaum.

Biederman, I. (1987). Recognition-by-components: A theory of human image understanding. *Psychological Review, 94,* 115–147.

Billman, D. O. (1983). *Procedures for learning syntactic categories: A model and test with artificial grammars.* Doctoral dissertation, University of Michigan, Ann Arbor, MI: University Microfilm.

Billman, D. O. (1985). *Increasing efficiency in acquiring syntactic categories: An adaptive attentional procedure.* Paper in Symposium: On Deriving Language from Speech, presented at the Meeting of the Society for Research on Child Development, Toronto.

Billman, D. O., & Heit, E. (in press). Observational learning from internal feedback: A simulation of an adaptive learning method. *Cognitive Science.*

Billman, D. O., Heit, E., & Dorfman, J. (1987). Facilitation from clustered features: Using correlations in observational learning. In *Proceedings of the Ninth Annual Conference of the Cognitive Science Society.* Hillsdale, NJ: Erlbaum.

Billman, D. O., Richards, J., & Heit, E. (1988). *Abstraction of correlational rules in implicit concept learning tasks.* In review.

Bobrow, D. G., & Winograd, T. A. (1977). An overview of KRL, a knowledge representation language. *Cognitive Science, 1,* 3–46.

Bolinger, D. (1965). The atomization of meaning. *Language, 41,* 555–573.

Bower, G. H., Black, J. B., & Turner, T. J. (1979). Prototypes in person perception. In L. Berkowitz (Ed.), *Cognitive Psychology, 11,* 177–220.

Bowman, D. (1979). *Children's processing of lexical ambiguity in sentence contexts.* MA thesis, Department of Psychology, Tufts University, Medford, MA.

Brachman, R. J., & Levesque, H. J. (Eds.) (1985). *Readings in knowledge representation.* Los Altos, CA: Morgan Kaufmann.

Bransford, J. D., Franks, J., Vye, N., & Sherwood, R. (1988). New approaches to instruction because wisdom can't be told. In S. Vosniadou & A. Ortony (Eds.), *Similarity and analogical reasoning.* New York: Cambridge University Press.

Bransford, J. D., & Johnson, M. K. (1973). Consideration of some problems of comprehension. In W.G. Chase (Ed.), *Visual information processing.* New York: Academic Press.

Britton, B. K., Glynn, S. M., & Smith, J. W. (1985). Cognitive workbench model. In B. K. Britton & J. B. Black (Eds.), *Understanding expository text.* Hillsdale, NJ: Erlbaum.

Broadbent, D. E. (1958). *Perception and communication.* London: Pergamon Press.

Brooks, L. R. (1978). Non-analytic concept formation and memory for instances.

In E. H. Rosch & B. B. Lloyd (Eds.), *Cognition and categorization.* Hillsdale, NJ: Erlbaum.

Brooks, L. R. (1987). Decentralized control of categorization: The role of prior processing episodes. In U. Neisser & E. Winograd (Eds.), *Remembering reconsidered: Ecological and traditional approaches to the study of memory.* New York: Cambridge University Press.

Brown, A. S. (1979). Priming effects in semantic memory retrieval processes. *Journal of Experimental Psychology: Human Learning and Memory, 5,* 65–77.

Brunson, B. A. (1986). *Thematic argument structure.* Unpublished manuscript, Department of Linguistics, University of Toronto, May 1986.

Brunson, B. A. (1988). *A processing model of Walpiri syntax and implications for linguistic theory.* Technical report CSRI-208, Computer Systems Research Institute, University of Toronto, July 1988.

Bubka, A. (1988). *The self-terminating race model for lexical access in ambiguity processing.* Unpublished doctoral dissertation, Adelphi University, Garden City, NY.

Burgess, C., & Simpson, G. B. (1988a). Cerebral mechanisms in the retrieval of ambiguous word meanings. *Brain and Language, 33,* 86–103.

Burgess, C., & Simpson, G. B. (1988b). Neuropsychology of lexical ambiguity resolution: The contribution of divided visual field studies. In S. L. Small, G. W. Cottrell, & M. K. Tanenhaus (Eds.), *Lexical ambiguity resolution in the comprehension of human language.* Los Altos, CA: Morgan Kaufmann.

Burgess, C., Tanenhaus, M. K., & Seidenberg, M. S. (1988). *Context and lexical access: Implications of nonword interference for lexical ambiguity resolution.* Unpublished manuscript, Department of Psychology, Rochester University, Rochester, NY.

Cairns, H. S., & Kamerman, J. (1975). Lexical information processing during sentence comprehension. *Journal of Verbal Learning and Verbal Behavior, 14,* 170–179.

Calkins, M. W. (1896). Association. *Psychological Review Monograph Supplements, 1,* Number 2.

Cantor, N., & Mischel, W. (1979). Prototypes in person perception. In L. Berkowitz (Ed.), *Advances in experimental social psychology.* New York: Academic Press.

Caramazza, A., & Zurif, E. B. (1976). Dissociation of algorithmic and heuristic processes in language comprehension: Evidence from aphasia. *Brain and Language, 3,* 572–582.

Carey, S. (1985). *Conceptual change in childhood.* Cambridge, MA: MIT Press.

Carlson, G. N., & Tanenhaus, M. K. (1988). Thematical roles and language comprehension. In W. Wilkins (Ed.), *Syntax and semantics 21: Thematic relations.* Orlando, FL: Academic Press.

Carr, T. H., McCauley, C., & Sperber, R. D. (1982). Words, pictures, and priming: On semantic activation, conscious identification, and the automaticity of information processing. *Journal of Experimental Psychology: Human Perception and Performance, 8,* 757–777.

Carroll, J. B., Davies, P., Richman, B. (1971). *Word frequency book.* New York: Houghton-Mifflin.

Carroll, M., & Kirsner, K. (1982). Context and repetition effects in lexical decision and recognition memory. *Journal of Verbal Learning and Verbal Behavior, 21,* 55–69.

Catchpole, J. (1987). *The locus of the word frequency effect.* Unpublished honours thesis, Department of Psychology, Monash University.

Chafin, R., & Herrmann, D. J. (1987). Relation element theory: A new account of the representation and processing of semantic relations. In D. Gorfein & R. Hoffman (Eds.), *Memory and learning: The Ebbinghaus Centennial Conference.* Hillsdale, NJ: Erlbaum.

Chapman, L. J., & Chapman, J. P. (1969). Illusory correlation as an obstacle to the use of valid psychodiagnostic signs. *Journal of Abnormal Psychology, 74,* 272–280.

Charniak, E. (1981a, July). A common representation for problem-solving and language-comprehension information. *Artificial Intelligence, 16*(3), 225–255.

Charniak, E. (1981b, July–September). The case-slot identity theory. *Cognitive Science, 5*(3), 285–292.

Charniak, E., Gavin, M. K., & Hendler, J. A. (1983). *The Frail/NASL reference manual* (Tech. Rep. CS-83-06). Providence, RI: Brown University, Department of Computer Science.

Cheng, P. W., & Holyoak, K. J. (1985). Pragmatic reasoning schemas. *Cognitive Psychology, 17,* 391–416.

Chi, J., Dooling, E., & Giles, F. (1972). Left-right asymmetries of the temporal speech areas of the human fetus. *Archives of Neurology, 34,* 346–348.

Chiarello, C. (1985). Hemisphere dynamics in lexical access: Automatic and controlled priming. *Brain and Language, 26,* 146–172.

Chomsky, N. (1965). *Aspects of the theory of syntax.* Cambridge, MA: MIT Press.

Chomsky, N. (1980). *Rules and representations.* New York: Columbia University Press.

Chomsky, N. (1986). *Knowledge of language: Its nature, origin, and use.* New York: Praeger.

Clark, H. H., & Clark, E. V. (1977). *Psychology and language: An introduction to psycholinguistics.* New York: Harcourt.

Clark H. H., & Lucy, P. (1975). Understanding what is meant from what is said: Study in conversationally conveyed requests. *Journal of Verbal Learning and Verbal Behavior, 12,* 335–359.

Clarke, E., & O'Malley, C. D. (1968). *The human brain and spinal cord: A historical study illustrated by writings from antiquity to the 20th century.* Berkeley, CA: University of California Press.

Clarke, R., & Morton, J. (1983). Cross modality facilitation in tachistoscopic word recognition. *Quarterly Journal of Experimental Psychology, 35A,* 79–96.

Clifton, C., Jr., & Ferreira, F. (1987). Modularity in sentence comprehension. In J. L. Garfield (Ed.), *Modularity in knowledge representation and natural-language understanding.* Cambridge, MA: MIT Press.

Collins, A., Brown, J. S., & Larkin, K. M. (1980). Inference in text understanding. In R. J. Spiro, B. C. Bruce, & W. F. Brewer (Eds.), *Theoretical issues in reading comprehension.* Hillsdale, NJ: Erlbaum.

Collins, A. M., & Loftus, E. F. (1975). A spreading-activation theory of semantic processing. *Psychological Review, 82,* 407–428.

Collins, A. M., & Quillian, M. R. (1969). Retrieval time from semantic memory. *Journal of Verbal Learning and Verbal Behavior, 8,* 240–248.

Collins, J. L., & Williamson, M. M. (1984). Assigned rhetorical context and semantic abbreviation in writing. In R. Beach & L. S. Bridwell (Eds.), *New directions in composition research.* New York: Guilford Press.

Conrad, C. (1974). Context effects in sentence comprehension: A study of the subjective lexicon. *Memory & Cognition, 2,* 130–138.

Conrad, C. (1978). Some factors involved in the recognition of words. In J. W. Cotton & R. L. Klatzky (Ed.), *Semantic factors in cognition.* Hillsdale, NJ: Erlbaum.

Cooper, E. A., Gorfein, D. S., & Bubka, A. (1988, April). *Secondary meaning priming facilitates ambiguity decisions.* Presented at the annual meeting of the Eastern Psychological Association, Buffalo, NY.

Corriveau, J. P. (1987). On the role of time in reader-based text comprehension. *Proceedings of the 9th Annual Conference of the Cognitive Science Society,* 794–801.

Craik, F. I. M., & Lockhart, R. S. (1972). Levels of processing: A framework for memory research. *Journal of Verbal Learning and Verbal Behavior, 11,* 671–684.

Crain, S., & Steedman, M. (1985). On not being led up the garden path: The use of context by the psychological syntactic processor. In D. R. Dowty, L. J. Karttunen, & A. M. Zwicky (Eds.), *Natural language parsing: Psychological computational and theoretical perspectives* (Studies in natural language processing). New York: Cambridge University Press.

Cruse, D. A. (1977). The pragmatics of lexical specificity. *Journal of Linguistics, 13,* 153–164.

Cutler, A. & Norris, D. G. in W. E. Cooper & E. C. T. Walker (Eds.) (1979). *Sentence processing: Psycholinguistic studies presented to Merrill Garrett.* Hillsdale, NJ: Erlbaum.

Daneman, M., & Carpenter, P. A. (1980). Individual differences in working memory and reading. *Journal of Verbal Learning and Verbal Behavior, 19,* 450–466.

Daneman, M., & Green, I. (1986). Individual differences in comprehending and producing words in context. *Journal of Memory and Language, 25,* 1–18.

Dauite, C. A. (1984). Performance limits on writers. In R. Beach & L. S. Bridwell (Eds.), *New directions in composition research.* New York: Guilford.

de Groot, A. M. B. (1984). Primed lexical decisions: Combined effects of the proportion of related prime-target pairs and the stimulus-onset: Asynchrony of prime and target. *Quarterly Journal of Experimental Psychology, 36A,* 253–280.

den Heyer, K. (1986). Manipulating attention-induced priming in a lexical decision task by means of repeated prime-target presentations. *Journal of Memory and Language, 25,* 19–42.

den Heyer, K., Goring, A., & Dannenbring, G. L. (1985). Semantic priming and word repetition: The two effects are additive. *Journal of Memory and Language, 24,* 699–716.

Deutsch, J. A., & Deutsch, D. (1963). Attention: Some theoretical considerations. *Psychological Review, 70,* 80–90.

Donnellan, K. S. (1966). Reference and definite description. *Philosophical Review, 75,* 281–304.

Dosher, B. A., & Corbett, A. T. (1982). Instrument inferences and verb schemata. *Memory & Cognition, 10,* 531–539.

Duncan, J. (1985). Two techniques for investigating perception without awareness. *Perception and Psychophysics, 38,* 296–298.

Durgunoglu, A. Y., & Roediger, H. L. (1987). Test differences in accessing bilingual memory. *Journal of Memory and Language, 26*(4), 377–391.

Dyer, F. N. (1973). The Stroop phenomenon and its use in the study of perceptual, cognitive, and response processes. *Memory & Cognition, 1,* 106–120.

Ebbinghaus, H. (1885/1964). *On memory: A contribution to experimental psychology* (H. A. Ruger & C. E. Busenious, Trans.). New York: Dover Press.

Ellenberger, H. (1970). *The Discovery of the unconscious.* New York: Basic Books.

Ellis, A., & Marshall, J. (1978). Semantic errors or statistical flukes: A note on Allport's "On knowing the meaning of words we are unable to report." *Quarterly Journal of Experimental Psychology, 30,* 569–575.

Elman, J. L., & McClelland, J. L. (1988). Cognitive penetration of the mechanisms of perception: Compensation for coarticulation of lexically restored phonemes. *Journal of Memory and Language, 27,* 143–165.

Eriksen, C. W., & Hoffman, M. (1963). Form recognition at brief duration as a function of adapting field and interval between stimulations. *Journal of Experimental Psychology, 66,* 485–499.

Eriksen, C. W., & Schultz, D. W. (1978). Temporal factors in visual information processing: A tutorial review. In J. Requin (Ed.), *Attention and performance VII* (pp. 3–23). Hillsdale, NJ: Erlbaum.

Eriksen, C. W., & Schultz, D. W. (1979). Information processing in visual search: A continuous flow conception and experimental results. *Perception and Psychophysics, 25,* 249–263.

Estes, W. K. (1950). Towards a statistical theory of learning. *Psychological Review, 62,* 145–154.

Estes, W. K. (1986a). Array models for category learning. *Cognitive Psychology, 18,* 500–549.

Estes, W. K. (1986b). Memory storage and retrieval processes in category learning. *Journal of Experimental Psychology: General, 115,* 155–174.

Estes, W. K. (1988). Toward a framework for combining connectionist and symbol-processing models. *Journal of Memory and Language, 27,* 196–212.

Estill, R., & Kemper, S. (1982). Interpreting idioms. *Journal of Psycholinguistic Research, 9,* 559–568.

Evans, J. (1976). *Children's comprehension and processing of ambiguous words in sentences.* Ph.D. dissertation, Department of Psychology, University of Texas, Austin.

Faigley, L., & Miller, T. P. (1982). What we learn from writing on the job. *College English, 44,* 557–572.

Fawcett, B. L. (1985). *The representation of ambiguity in opaque constructs* (Tech. Rep. CSRI-178). Department of Computer Science, University of Toronto.

Fawcett, B. L., & Hirst, G. (1986, June). The detection and representation of ambiguities of intension and description. *Proceedings of the 24th Annual Meeting of the Association for Computational Linguistics* (pp. 192–199). New York.

Ferreira, F., & Clifton, C., Jr. (1986). The independence of syntactic processing. *Journal of Memory and Language, 25,* 348–368.

Fillmore, C. J. (1968). The case for case. In E. W. Bach & R. T. Harms (Eds.), *Universals in linguistic theory* (0–88). New York: Holt, Rinehart and Winston.

Fischler, I. (1977). Semantic facilitation without association in a lexical decision task. *Memory and Cognition, 5*(3), 335–339.

Fischler, I., & Bloom, P. (1979). Automatic and attentional processes in the effects of sentence contexts on word recognition. *Journal of Verbal Learning and Verbal Behavior, 18,* 1–20.

Fischler, I., & Bloom, P. (1980). Rapid processing of the meaning of sentences. *Memory & Cognition, 8,* 216–225.

Fiske, S. E., & Taylor, S. E. (1984). *Social cognition.* Reading, MA: Addison-Wesley.

Fodor, J. A. (1983). *The modularity of mind: An essay on faculty psychology.* Cambridge MA: MIT Press.

Fodor, J. A. (1987). Modules, frames, fridgeons, sleeping dogs, and the music of the spheres. In J. L. Garfield (Ed.), *Modularity in knowledge representation and natural-language understanding.* Cambridge, MA: MIT Press.

Fodor, J. A., & Pylyshyn, Z. W. (1981). How direct is visual perception? Some reflections on Gibson's "ecological approach." *Cognition, 9,* 139–196.

Fodor, J. A., & Pylyshyn, Z. W. (1988). Connectionism and cognitive architecture: A critical analysis. *Cognition, 28,* 3–71.

Fodor, J. D., & Frazier, L. (1980). Is the human sentence parsing mechanism an ATN? *Cognition, 8,* 417–459.

Fodor, K. I. (1979). Levels of processing and the structure of the language processor. In W. E. Cooper & E. C. T. Walker (Eds.), *Sentence processing: Psycholinguistic studies presented to Merrill Garrett.* Hillsdale, NJ: Erlbaum.

Forbach, G. B., Stanners, R. F., & Hochhaus, L. (1974). Repetition and practice effects in a lexical decision task. *Memory & Cognition, 2,* 337–339.

Ford, M., Bresnan, J. W., & Kaplan, R. M. (1982). *The mental representation of grammatical relations.* Cambridge, MA: MIT Press.

Forster, K. I. (1976). Accessing the mental lexicon. In R. J. Wales & E. Walker (Eds.), *New approaches to language mechanisms.* Amsterdam: North-Holland.

Forster, K. I. (1979). Levels of processing and the structure of the language processor. In W. E. Cooper & E. Walker (Eds.), *Sentence processing: Psycholinguistic studies presented to Merrill Garrett.* Hillsdale, NJ: Erlbaum.

Forster, K. I. (1981). Priming and the effects of sentence and lexical contexts on naming time: Evidence for autonomous lexical processing. *Quarterly Journal of Experimental Psychology, 33A,* 465–495.

Forster, K. I. (1985). Lexical acquisition and the modular lexicon. *Language and Cognitive Processes, 1,* 87–108.

Forster, K. I., & Bednall, E. S. (1976). Terminating and exhaustive search in lexical access. *Memory & Cognition, 4,* 53–61.

Forster, K. I., & Davis, C. (1984). Repetition priming and frequency attention in lexical access. *Journal of Experimental Psychology: Learning, Memory and Cognition, 10,* 680–698.

Foss, D. J. (1969). Decision processes during sentence comprehension: Effects of lexical item difficulty and position upon decision times. *Journal of Verbal Learning and Verbal Behavior, 8,* 457–462.

Foss, D. J. (1970). Some effects of ambiguity upon sentence comprehension. *Journal of Verbal Learning and Verbal Behavior, 9,* 699–706.

Foss, D. J. (1982). A discourse on semantic priming. *Cognitive Psychology, 14,* 590–607.

Foss, D. J., & Gernsbacher, M. (1983). Cracking the dual code: Toward a unitary model of phoneme identification. *Journal of Verbal Learning and Verbal Behavior, 22,* 609–632.

Foss, D. J., & Hakes, D. (1978). *Psycholinguistics: An introduction to the psychology of language.* Englewood Cliffs, NJ: Prentice-Hall.

Foss, D. J., & Jenkins, C. J. (1973). Some effects of context on the comprehension of ambiguous sentences. *Journal of Verbal Learning and Verbal Behavior, 12,* 577–589.

Foss, D. J., Starkey, P., & Bias, R. (1975). *Sentence comprehension in children.* Paper presented at the Midwestern Psychological Association, Chicago.

Fowler, C. A., Wolford, G., Slade, R., & Tassinary, L. (1981). Lexical access with and without awareness. *Journal of Experimental Psychology: General, 110,* 341–362.

Fox, M. (1987). *Constraint-directed search: A case study of job-shop scheduling.* Los Altos, CA: Morgan Kaufmann.

Frazier, L. (1987). Theories of sentence processing. In J. L. Garfield (Ed.), *Modularity in knowledge representation and natural-language understanding.* Cambridge, MA: MIT Press.

Frazier, L., & Fodor, J. D. (1978). The sausage machine: A new two-stage model of parsing. *Cognition, 6,* 291–325.

Fromkin, V., & Rodman, R. (1988). *An introduction to language* (4th ed.). New York: Holt, Rinehart and Winston.

Galambos, J. A., & Rips, L. J. (1982). Memory for routines. *Journal of Verbal Learning and Verbal Behavior, 21,* 260–281.

Garfield, J. L. (1987a). Introduction. In J. L. Garfield (Ed.), *Modularity in knowledge representation and natural-language understanding.* Cambridge, MA: MIT Press.

Garfield, J. L. (Ed.) (1987b). *Modularity in knowledge representation and natural-language understanding.* Cambridge, MA: MIT Press.

Garner, W. R. (1974). *The processing of information and structure.* Hillsdale, NJ: Erlbaum.

Garner, W. R., Hake, H. W., & Eriksen, C. W. (1956). Operationism and the concept of perception. *Psychological Review, 63,* 149–262.

Garnham, A. (1982). Testing psychological theories about inference making. *Memory & Cognition, 10,* 341–349.

Geis, M. F., & Winograd, E. (1974). Norms of semantic encoding and availability for fifty homographs. *Bulletin of the Psychonomic Society, 3,* 429–431.

Geis, M. F., & Winograd, E. (1975). Semantic encoding and judgments of background and situational frequency of homographs. *Journal of Experimental Psychology: Human Learning and Memory, 104,* 385–392.

Gelman, S. A. (1988). The development of induction with natural kind and artifact categories. *Cognitive Psychology, 20,* 65–95.

Gelman, S. A., & Markman, E. M. (1986). Categories and induction in young children. *Cognition, 23,* 183–209.

Gelman, S. A., & Markman, E. M. (1987). Young children's inductions from natural kinds: The role of categories and appearances. *Child Development, 58,* 1532–1541.

Gentner, D. (1981). Some interesting differences between nouns and verbs. *Cognition and Brain Theory, 4,* 161–178.

Gentner, D. (1983). Structure mapping: A theoretical framework for analogy. *Cognitive Science, 7,* 155–170.

Gentner, D. (1988). Mechanisms of analogical reasoning. In S. Vosniadou & A. Ortony (Eds.), *Similarity and analogical reasoning.* New York: Cambridge University Press.

Gentner, D., & France, I. M. (in press). The verb mutability effect: Studies of the combinatorial semantics of nouns and verbs. In S. L. Small, G. W. Cottrell, & M. K. Tanenhaus (Eds.), *Lexical ambiguity resolution.* Los Altos, CA: Morgan Kaufmann.

Gentner, D., & Stevens, A. (Eds.) (1983). *Mental models.* Hillsdale, NJ: Erlbaum.

Geschwind, N. (1972). Language and the brain. *Scientific American, 226,* 76–83.

Gibson, J. J. (1979). *The ecological approach to visual perception.* Boston: Houghton-Mifflin.

Gildea, P., & Glucksberg, S. (1983). On understanding metaphor: The role of context. *Journal of Verbal Learning and Verbal Behavior, 20,* 435–444.

Gildea, P., & Glucksberg, S. (1984). *Does context constrain lexical access for ambiguous words?* Paper presented to the Annual Meeting of the Psychonomics Society, San Antonio, TX.

Glanzer, M., & Nolan, S. D. (1986). Memory mechanisms in text comprehension. In G. H. Bower (Ed.), *The psychology of learning and motivation.* Orlando, FL: Academic Press.

Glass, A. L. (1983). The comprehension of idioms. *Journal of Psycholinguistic Research, 12,* 429–444.

Glucksberg, S. (1984). *How people use context to resolve ambiguity: Implications for an interactive model of language understanding.* Paper presented at the Annual Meeting of the Eastern Psychological Association, Baltimore.

Glucksberg, S., Kreuz, R. J., & Rho, S. H. (1986). Context can constrain lexical access: Implications for models of language comprehension. *Journal of Experimental Psychology: Learning, Memory, and Cognition, 12,* 323–335.

Goetz, E. T. (1979). Inferring from text: Some factors influencing which inferences will be made. *Discourse Processes, 2,* 179–195.

Goodman, G. O., McClelland, J. L., & Gibbs, R. W., Jr. (1981). The role of syntactic context in word recognition. *Memory & Cognition, 9,* 580–586.

Goodman, N. (1955). *Fact, fiction, and forecast.* Cambridge, MA: Harvard University Press.

Gorfein, D. S. (1983). *Memory availability and contextual constraint as a function of homograph dominance.* Presented to the Annual Meeting of the Psychonomics Society, San Diego, CA.

Gorfein, D. S. (1987). Explaining context effects in short-term memory. In D. S. Gorfein & R. R. Hoffman (Eds.), *Memory and Learning: The Ebbinghaus Centennial Conference.* Hillsdale, NJ: Erlbaum.

Gorfein, D. S., & Bubka, A. (1985). *Repeated homograph effects in lexical decision.* Paper presented at the Annual Meeting of the Psychonomics Society, Boston.

Gorfein, D. S., & Bubka, A. (1988, April). *What constitutes evidence for access to a homographs meaning.* Presented to the Conference on Semantic Ambiguity, Adelphi University, Garden City, NY.

Gorfein, D. S., & O'Brien, J. (1986). *The Adelphi norms for homophones.* Unpublished manuscript.

Gorfein, D. S., & Viviani, J. M. (1980). *There are no effects of retention interval.* Presented at the annual meeting of the Psychonomics Society, St. Louis, MO.

Gorfein, D. S., & Viviani, J. M. (1981). *What is PI release the release of?* Presented at the annual meeting of the Psychonomics Society, Philadelphia.

Gorfein, D. S., Viviani, J. M., & Leddo, J. (1982). Norms as a tool for the study of homography. *Memory & Cognition, 10,* 503–509.

Gough, P., Alford, J. A., & Holley-Wilcox, P. (1981). Words and context. In O. J. L. Tzeng & H. Singer (Eds.), *Perception of print.* Hillsdale, NJ: Erlbaum.

Gould, S. J. (1985). To be a platypus, *Natural History,* pp. 10–15.

Graesser, A. C., & Clark, L. F. (1985). *Structures and procedures of implicit knowledge.* Norwood, NJ: Ablex.

Green, D. M., & Swets, J. A. (1966). *Signal detection theory and psychophysics.* New York: Wiley.

Greenspan, S. L. (1986). Semantic flexibility and referential specificity of concrete nouns. *Journal of Memory and Language, 25,* 539–557.

Guthrie, E. R. (1935). *The psychology of learning.* New York: Harper.

Hall, R. A. (1972). Why a structural semantics is impossible. *Language Sciences, 21,* 1–6.

Hartley, D. (1749/1801). *Observations on man, his frame, his duty, and his expectations* (4th ed.). London: Johnson.

Hasher, L., & Zacks, R. T. (1979). Automatic and effortful processes in memory. *Journal of Experimental Psychology: General, 108,* 173–184.

Hawkins, H. L., Reicher, G. M., Rogers, M., & Peterson, L. (1976). Flexible coding in word recognition. *Journal of Experimental Psychology: Human Perception and Performance, 2,* 380–385.

Hayes, J. R., & Flower, L. S. (1980). Identifying the organization of the writing process. In L. W. Gregg & E. R. Steinberg (Eds.), *Cognitive processes in writing.* Hillsdale, NJ: Erlbaum.

Hayes, P. J. (1976). *A process to implement some word-sense disambiguations.* Working paper 23, Institut pour les etudes semantiques et cognitives, Universite de Geneve. Published as Tech. Rep. 6, Department of Computer Science, University of Rochester, Rochester, NY.

Hayes, P. J. (1977a). *Some association-based techniques for lexical disambiguation by machineu* (Tech. Rep. 25). Doctoral dissertation, Department of Computer Science, University of Rochester, Rochester, NY. Department de Mathematiques, Ecole polytechnique federale de Lausanne, Lausanne, Switzerland.

Hayes, P. J. (1977b). On semantic nets, frames and associations. *Proceedings of the 5th International Joint Conference on Artificial Intelligence* (pp. 99–107). Cambridge, MA.

Hebb, D. O. (1949). *The organization of behavior.* New York: Wiley.

Hekkanen, S. T. (1977). *Word recognition and the lexical decision task.* Unpublished master's thesis, University of South Florida, Tampa.

Hekkanen, S. T. (1981). The effects of context on the processing of ambiguous words (doctoral dissertation, University of South Florida). *Dissertation Abstracts International, 42,* 1646B.

Hendler, J. A. (1987). *Integrating marker-passing and problem-solving: A spreading activation approach to improved choice in planning.* Hillsdale, NJ: Erlbaum.

Henik, A., Friedrich, F. J., & Kellogg, W. A. (1983). The dependence of semantic relatedness effects upon prime processing. *Memory & Cognition, 11,* 366–373.

Herbart, J. F. (1816/1891). *A Textbook of Psychology* (M. K. Smith, Trans.). New York: Appleton.

Herrnstein, R. J., & Boring, E. G. (1965). *A source book in the history of psychology.* Cambridge, MA: Harvard University Press.

Hintzman, D. L. (1986). "Schema abstraction" in a multiple-trace memory model. *Psychological Review, 93,* 411–428.

Hintzman, D. L., Carre, F. A., Eskridge, V. L., Owens, A. M., Shaff, S. S., & Sparks, M. E. (1972). "Stroop" effect: Input or output phenomenon? *Journal of Experimental Psychology, 95,* 458–459.

Hirst, G. (1981). *Anaphora in natural language understanding: A survey.* New York: Springer-Verlag.

Hirst, G. (1983a, June). A foundation for semantic interpretation. *Proceedings of the 21st Annual Meeting for Association for Computational Linguistic* (64–73). Cambridge, MA

Hirst, G. (1983b). *Semantic interpretation against ambiguity.* Doctoral dissertation, Department of Computer Science, Brown University, Providence, RI.

Hirst, G. (1984a). A semantic process for syntactic disambiguation. *Proceedings, National Conference on Artificial Intelligence,* 148–152.

Hirst, G. (1984b). Jumping to conclusions: Psychological reality and unreality in a word disambiguation program. *Proceedings of the Sixtieth Annual Conference of the Cognitive Science Society,* 179–182. Boulder, CO.

Hirst, G. (1987). *Semantic interpretation and the resolution of ambiguity* (Studies in natural language processing). New York: Cambridge University Press.

Hirst, G. (1988). Resolving lexical ambiguity computationally with spreading activation and Polaroid Words. In S. L. Small, G. W. Cottrell, & M. K. Tanenhaus (Eds.), *Lexical ambiguity resolution.* Los Altos, CA: Morgan Kaufmann.

Hirst, G., & Charniak, E. (1982). Word sense and case slot disambiguation. *Proceedings, National Conference on Artificial Intelligence* (AAAI-82) (pp. 95–98). Pittsburgh, PA.

Hobbs, J. R. (1983). An improper treatment of quantification in ordinary English. *Proceedings 21st Annual Meeting, Association for Computational Linguistics* (pp. 57–63). Cambridge, MA.

Hobbs, J. R., & Shieber, S. M. (1987). An algorithm for generating quantified scopings. *Computational Linguistics, 13,* 47–63.

Hoffman, R. R. (1985). Some implications of metaphor for philosophy and psychology of science. In W. Paprotte & R. Dirven (Eds.), *The ubiquity of metaphor: Metaphor in language and thought* (pp. 327–380). Amsterdam: John Benjamins.

Hoffman, R. R., Cochran, E. L., & Nead, J. M. (1989). Cognitive metaphors in experimental psychology. In D. Leary (Ed.), *Metaphors in the history of psychology.* Cambridge: Cambridge University Press.

Hoffman, R. R., MacCormac, E. R., Lawler, J. M., & Carroll, J. M. (1989). *The metaphors of semantics and the semantics of metaphors: A case study in the logical representation of meaning.* Manuscript, Department of Psychology, Adelphi University, Garden City, NY.

Hoffman, R. R., & Nead, J. M. (1983). Generl contextualism, ecological science, and cognitive research. *Journal of Mind and Behavior, 4,* 507–560.

Hofstadter, D. R., Clossman, G. A., & Meredith, M. J. (1982, November). *"Shakespeare's plays weren't written by him, but by someone else of the same name." An essay on intensionality and frame-based knowledge representation.* Bloomington, IN: Indiana University Linguistics Club.

Hogaboam, T. W., & Perfetti, C. A. (1975). Lexical ambiguity and sentence comprehension. *Journal of Verbal Learning and Verbal Behavior, 14,* 265–274.

Holender, D. (1986). Semantic activation without conscious identification in dichotic listening, parafoveal vision, and visual masking: A survey and appraisal. *The Behavioral and Brain Sciences, 9,* 1–66.

Holley-Wilcox, P., & Blank, M. A. (1980). Evidence for multiple access in the processing of isolated words. *Journal of Experimental Psychology: Human Perception and Performance, 6,* 75–84.

Holmes, V. M. (1979). Accessing ambiguous words during sentence comprehension. *Quarterly Journal of Experimental Psychology, 44,* 13–35.

Honeck, R. P., Voegtle, K., Dorfmuller, M. A., & Hoffman, R. R. (1980). Proverbs, meaning, and group structure. In R. P. Honeck & R.R. Hoffman (Eds.), *Cognition and figurative language* (pp. 127–162). Hillsdale, NJ: Erlbaum.

Hubel, D. H., & Wiesel, T. N. (1962). Receptive fields, binocular interaction, and functional architecture in the cat's visual cortex. *Journal of Physiology, 166,* 106–154.

Hume, D. (1739/1896). *A treatise on human nature* (L. A. Selby-Bigge, Ed.). New York: Dover.

Hume, D. (1739–40/1888). *A treatise of human nature.* Oxford: University Press.

Jackendoff, R. (1983). *Semantics and cognition.* Cambridge, MA: MIT Press.

Jacoby, L. L. (1983). Remembering the data: Analyzing interactive processes in reading. *Journal of Verbal Learning and Verbal Behavior, 22,* 458–508.

Jacoby, L. L., & Brooks, L. R. (1984). Nonanalytic cognition: Memory, perception, and concept learning. In G. H. Bower (Ed.), *The psychology of learning and motivation: Advances in research and theory* (Vol. 18). New York: Academic Press.

Jacoby, L. L., & Dallas, M. (1981). On the relationship between autobiographical memory and perceptual learning. *Journal of Experimental Psychology: General, 10,* 306–340.

James, W. (1950). *The principles of psychology* (Vol. I). New York: Dover.

Janus, R. A., & Bever, T. G. (1985). Processing of metaphoric language: An investigation of the three-stage model of metaphor comprehension. *Journal of Psycholinguistic Research, 14,* 473–487.

Jastrzembski, J. E. (1981). Multiple meanings, number of related meanings, frequency of occurrence, and the lexicon. *Cognitive Psychology, 13,* 278–305.

Johnson-Laird, P. N. (1975). Meaning and the mental lexicon. In A. Kennedy & A. Wiles (Eds.), *Studies in long term memory.* London: Wiley.

Johnson-Laird, P. N. (1983). *Mental models.* Cambridge, MA: Harvard University Press.

Johnson-Laird, P. N. (1987). The mental representation of the meaning of words. *Cognition, 25,* 189–211.

Jolicoeur, P., Gluck, M., & Kosslyn, S. M. (1984). Pictures and names: Making the connection. *Cognitive Psychology, 16,* 243–275.

Just, M. A., & Carpenter, P. A. (1980). A theory of reading: From eye fixation to comprehension. *Psychological Review, 87,* 329–354.

Just, M. A., & Carpenter, P. A. (1987). *The psychology of reading and language comprehension.* Boston: Allyn and Bacon.

Kahneman, D. (1973). *Attention and effort,* Englewood Cliffs, NJ: Prentice-Hall.

Kahneman, D., & Miller, D. T. (1986). Norm theory: Comparing reality to its alternatives. *Psychological Review, 93,* 136–153.

Kahneman, D., Slovic, P., & Tversky, A. (Eds.) (1982). *Judgment under uncertainty: Heuristics and biases.* New York: Cambridge University Press.

Katz, J. J., & Fodor, J. A. (1963). The structure of a semantic theory. *Language, 39,* 170–210.

Keele, S. W. (1972). Attention demands of memory retrieval. *Journal of Experimental Psychology, 93,* 245–248.
Keele, S. W. (1973). *Attention and human performance,* Pacific Palisades, CA: Goodyear.
Keele, S. W., & Neill, W. T. (1978). Mechanisms of attention. In E. C. Carterette & M. P. Friedman (Eds.), *Handbook of perception* (Vol. 9, pp. 3–47). New York: Academic Press.
Keil, F. C. (1979). *Semantic and conceptual development: An ontological perspective.* Cambridge, MA: Harvard University Press.
Keil, F. C. (1981). Constraints on knowledge and cognitive development. *Psychological Review, 88,* 197–227.
Keil, F. C. (1987). Child-basic object categories and early development. In U. Neisser (Ed.), *Concepts and conceptual development: Ecological and intellectual factors in categorization.* New York: Cambridge University Press.
Kellas, G., Ferraro, F. R., & Simpson, G. B. (1988). Lexical ambiguity and the timecourse of attentional allocation in word recognition. *Journal of Experimental Psychology: Human Perception and Performance, 14,* 601–609.
Kellas, G., Simpson, G. B., & Ferraro, F. R. (in press). Aging and performance: A mental workload analysis. In P. Whitney & R. Ochsman (Eds.), *Psychology and productivity.* New York: Plenum Press.
Kellog, R. T. (1987). Effects of topic knowledge on the allocation of processing time and cognitive effort to the writing process. *Memory & Cognition, 15,* 256–266.
Kelly, E. F., & Stone, P. J. (1975). *Computer recognition of English word senses.* Amsterdam: North-Holland.
Kessel, F. S. (1970). The role of syntax in children's comprehension from ages six to twelve. *Society for Research in Child Development Monograph, 35,* 6. Chicago: University of Chicago Press.
Kieras, D. E. (1981). Component processes in the comprehension of simple prose. *Journal of Verbal Learning and Verbal Behavior, 20,* 1–23.
Kiger, J. I., & Glass, A. L. (1983). The facilitation of lexical decisions by a prime occurring after the target. *Memory & Cognition, 11,* 356–365.
Killion, T. H. (1979). Task effects in the processing of lexical ambiguity. Unpublished manuscript, University of Dayton Research Institute.
Kimble, G. A. (1961). *Hilgard and Marquis' conditioning and learning.* New York: Appleton Century Crofts.
Kintsch, W. (1988). The role of knowledge in discourse comprehension: A construction-integration model. *Psychological Review, 95,* 163–182.
Kintsch, W., & Mross, E. (1985). Context effects in word identification. *Journal of Memory and Language, 24,* 336–349.
Kintsch, W., & van Dijk, T. A. (1978). Toward a model of text comprehension and production. *Psychological Review, 85,* 363–394.
Kirsner, K., & Dunn, J. C. (1985). The perceptual record: A common factor in repetition priming and attribute retention. In M. I. Posner & O. S. M. Marin (Eds.), *Mechanisms of attention: Attention & performance XI.* Hillsdale, NJ: Erlbaum.
Kirsner, K., & Smith, M. C. (1974). Modality effects in word identification. *Memory & Cognition, 2,* 637–640.
Kirsner, K., Smith, M. C., Lockhart, R. S., King, M. L., & Jain, M. (1984). The

bilingual lexicon: Language specific units in an integrated network. *Journal of Verbal Learning and Verbal Behavior, 23,* 519–539.

Kleiman, G. M. (1980). Sentence frame contexts and lexical decisions: Sentence-acceptability and word-relatedness effects. *Memory & Cognition, 8,* 336–344.

Kolers, P. A. (1976). Reading a year later. *Journal of Experimental Psychology: Human Learning and Memory, 2,* 543–565.

Kolers, P. A. (1978). On the representations of experience. In D. Gerver & W. Snaido (Eds.), *Language interpretation and communication.* New York: Plenum.

Kolers, P. A. (1979). Reading and knowing. *Canadian Journal of Psychology, 33,* 106–117.

Koriat, A. (1981). Semantic facilitation in lexical decision as a function of prime-target association. *Memory & Cognition, 9,* 587–598.

Kovecses, Z. (1988). *The language of love.* Lewisburg, PA: Bucknell University Press.

Kroll, J. F., & Potter, M. C. (1984). Recognizing words, pictures and concepts: A comparison of lexical, object, and reality decisions. *Journal of Verbal Learning and Verbal Behavior, 23,* 39–66.

Kuhn, T. (1970). *The structure of scientific revolutions* (2nd ed.). Chicago: University of Chicago Press.

Kuhn, T. S. (1979). Metaphor in science. In A. Ortony (Ed.), *Metaphor and thought* (pp. 409–419). Cambridge: Cambridge University Press.

Kucera, J., & Francis, W. M. (1967). *Computational analysis of present-day American English.* Providence, RI: Brown University.

Lakoff, G. (1987). *Women, fire, and dangerous things: What categories tell us reveal about the mind.* Chicago: Chicago University Press.

Lakoff, G., & Johnson, M. (1980). *Metaphors we live by.* Chicago: University of Chicago Press.

Landauer, T. K. (1975). Memory without organization: Properties of a model with random storage and undirected retrieval. *Cognitive Psychology, 7,* 495–531.

Landauer, T. K., & Freedman, J. L. (1968). Information retrieval from long-term memory: Category size and recognition time. *Journal of Verbal Learning and Verbal Behavior, 7,* 291–295.

Leibniz, G. W. V. (1704/1898). Monadology. In *Leibniz—The monadology and other philosophical essays* (R. Latta, Trans.). Oxford: Oxford University Press.

Levy, B. A., & Kirsner, K. (1988). *Re-processing text: Priming word and message level processes.* Unpublished manuscript.

Liberman, A. M. (1970). The grammars of speech and language. *Cognitive Psychology, 1,* 301–323.

Lindsay, P. H., & Norman, D. A. (1977). *Human information processing.* New York: Academic Press.

Locke, J. (1670/1959). *An essay concerning human understanding* (A. C. Frasier, Ed.). New York: Dover Press.

Locke, J. (1690/1894). *Essay Concerning the Human Understanding.* (Vol. I), Oxford: University Press.

Loftus, E. F., & Cole, W. (1974). *Journal of Experimental Psychology, 102,* 1116–1122.

Lorch, R. F., Jr. (1982). Priming and search processes in semantic memory: A test of three models of spreading activation. *Journal of Verbal Learning and Verbal Behavior, 21,* 468–492.

Lorch, R. F., Jr., Balota, D. A., & Stamm, E. G. (1986). Locus of inhibition effects in the priming of lexical decisions: Pre- or postlexical access? *Memory and Cognition, 14,* 95–103.

Lowe, D. G. (1979). Strategies, context, and the mechanism of response inhibition. *Memory & Cognition, 7,* 382–389.

Lucas, M. (1987). Frequency effects on the processing of ambiguous words in sentence contexts. *Language and Speech, 30,* 25–46.

Luchins, A. (1942). Mechanization in problem solving. *Psychological Monographs, 54* (Whole Number, 248).

MacKay, D. G. (1966). To end ambiguous sentences. *Perception and Psychophysics, 1,* 426–436.

MacKintosh, N. J. (1975). A theory of attention: Variations in the associability of stimuli with reinforcement. *Psychological Review, 82,* 276–298.

MacLeod, C. Word context during initial exposure influences degree of priming in word fragment completion. *Journal of Experimental Psychology: Learning, Memory, and Cognition,* in press.

Malt, B., & Smith, E. E. (1984). Correlated properties in natural categories. *Journal of Verbal Learning and Verbal Behavior, 23,* 250–269.

Mandler, G. (1979). Organization and repetition: Organizational principles with special reference to rote learning. In L. G. Nilson (Ed.), *Perspectives in memory research.* Hillsdale, NJ: Erlbaum.

Mandler, J. M., & Murphy, C. M. (1983). Subjective estimates of script structure. *Journal of Experimental Psychology: Learning, Memory, and Cognition, 9,* 534–543.

Maratsos, M. P., & Chalkley, M. A. (1980). The internal language of children's syntax: The ontogenesis and representation of syntactic categories. In K. E. Nelson (Ed.), *Children's language.* New York: Gardner Press.

Marcel, A. J. (1980). Conscious and preconscious recognition of polysemous words: Locating the selective effects of prior verbal context. In R. S. Nickerson (Ed.), *Attention and performance VIII.* Hillsdale, NJ: Erlbaum.

Marcel, A. J. (1983a). Conscious and unconscious perception: An approach to the relations between phenomenal experience and perceptual processes. *Cognitive Psychology, 15,* 283–300.

Marcel, A. J. (1983b). Conscious and unconscious perception: Experiments on visual masking and word recognition. *Cognitive Psychology, 15,* 197–237.

Marcel, A. J., & Patterson, K. E. (1978). Word recognition and production: Reciprocity in clinical and normal studies. In J. Requin (Ed.), *Attention and performance VII* (pp. 209–226). Hillsdale, NJ: Erlbaum.

Marcus, M. P. (1977). *A theory of syntactic recognition for natural language.* Doctoral dissertation, Artificial Intelligence Laboratory, Massachusetts Institute of Technology, Cambridge, MA.

Marcus, M. P. (1980). *A theory of syntactic recognition for natural language.* Cambridge, MA: MIT Press.

Markman, E. M. (1979). Classes and collections: Conceptual organization and numerical abilities. *Cognitive Psychology, 11,* 395–411.

Markman, E. M., & Seibert, J. (1976). Classes and collections: Internal organization and resulting holistic properties. *Cognitive Psychology, 8,* 561–577.

Marshall, J. C., & Newcombe, F. (1973). Patterns of paralexia: A psycholinguistic approach. *Journal of Psycholinguistic Research, 2,* 175–199.

Marslen-Wilson, W. D. (1973). Linguistic structure and speech shadowing at very short latencies. *Nature, 244,* 522–523.

Marslen-Wilson, W. D., & Tyler, L. K. (1980). The temporal structure of spoken-language comprehension. *Cognition, 8,* 1–71.

Massaro, D. W. (1988). Some criticisms of connectionist models of human performance. *Journal of Memory and Language, 27,* 213–234.

Masson, M. E. J., & Miller, J. A. (1983). Working memory and individual differences in comprehension and memory of text. *Journal of Educational Psychology, 75,* 314–318.

McCann, R. S., & Besner, D. (1987). Reading pseudohomophones: Implications for models of pronunciation assembly and the locus of word-frequency effects in naming. *Journal of Experimental Psychology: Human Perception and Performance, 13,* 14–24.

McCauley, C., Parmalee, C. M., Sperber, R. D., & Carr, T. H. (1980). Early extraction of meaning of pictures and its relation to conscious identification. *Journal of Experimental Psychology: Human Perception and Performance, 6,* 265–276.

McCauley, R. (1987). The role of theories in a theory of concepts. In U. Neisser (Ed.), *Concepts and conceptual development: Ecological and intellectual factors in categorization.* New York: Cambridge University Press.

McClelland, J. L. (1987). The case for interactionism in language processing. In M. Coltheart (Ed.), *Attention and performance XII: The psychology of reading* (pp. 3–36). Hillsdale, NJ: Erlbaum.

McClelland, J. L. (1988). Connectionist models and psychological evidence. *Journal of Memory and Language, 27,* 107–123.

McClelland, J. L., & Rumelhart, D. E. (1981). An interactive activation model of context effects in letter perception: Part 1. An account of basic findings. *Psychological Review, 88,* 375–407.

McClelland, J. L., & Rumelhart, D. E. (1985). Distributed memory and the representation of general and specific information. *Journal of Experimental Psychology: General, 114,* 159–188.

McClelland, J. L., Rumelhart, D. E., & the PDP Research Group (1986). *Parallel distributed processing: Explorations in the microstructure of cognition. Vol. 2: Psychological and Biological Models.* Cambridge, MA: MIT Press.

McCormack, P. D. (1976). Language as an attribute of memory. *Canadian Journal of Psychology, 30*(4), 238–248.

McCormack, P. D. (1977). Bilingual linguistic memory: The independence-interdependence issue revisited. In P. Hornby (Ed.), *Bilingualism: Psychological, social and educational implications.* New York: Academic Press.

McDougall, W. (1860/1908). *Introduction to social psychology.* New York: Barnes & Noble.

McEvoy, C. L. (1982). Facilitation and suppression in the retrieval of pictorial labels (Doctoral dissertation, University of South Florida). *Dissertation Abstracts International, 43,* 2373B.

McKoon, G., & Ratcliff, R. (1981). The comprehension processes and memory structures involved in instrumental inferences. *Journal of Verbal Learning and Verbal Behavior, 20,* 671–682.

McRoy, S. W. (1987, October). *The influence of time and memory constraints on the resolution of structural ambiguity.* MSc thesis, Department of Computer Science, University of Toronto, October 1987. Published as technical report 209, Computer Systems Research Institute, University of Toronto.

McRoy, S. W., & Hirst, G. (1988). *Parsing as a race.* Manuscript 1988.

Medin, D. L., Altom, M. W., Edelson, S. M., & Freko, D. (1982). Correlated symptoms and simulated medical classification. *Journal of Experimental Psychology: Learning, Memory, and Cognition, 8,* 37–50.

Medin, D. L., & Schaffer, M. M. (1978). A context theory of classification learning. *Psychological Review, 85,* 207–238.

Medin, D. L., & Shoben, E. J. (1988). Context and structure in conceptual combination. *Cognitive Psychology, 20,* 158–190.

Medin, D. L., & Smith, E. E. (1984). Concepts and concept formation. *Annual Review of Psychology, 35,* 113–138.

Medin, D. L., Wattenmaker, W. D., & Hampson, S. E. (1987). Family resemblance, conceptual cohesiveness, and category construction. *Cognitive Psychology, 19,* 242–279.

Mehler, J., Segui, J., & Carey, P. (1978). Tails of words: Monitoring ambiguity. *Journal of Verbal Learning and Verbal Behavior, 17,* 29–35.

Merikle, P. M. (1982). Unconscious perception revisited. *Perception and Psychophysics, 31,* 298–301.

Merriam-Webster, Inc. (1984). *Webster's ninth new collegiate dictionary.* Springfield, MA: Merriam-Webster.

Merrill, E. C., Sperber, R. D., & McCauley, C. (1981). Differences in semantic encoding as a function of reading comprehension skill. *Memory & Cognition, 9,* 618–624.

Mervis, C. B. (1987). Child-basic object categories and early lexical development. In U. Neisser (Ed.), *Concepts and conceptual development: Ecological and intellectual factors in categorization.* New York: Cambridge University Press.

Mervis, C. B., & Rosch, E. (1981). Categorization of natural objects. *Annual Review of Psychology, 32,* 89–115.

Meyer, D. E., & Gutschera, K. D. (1975). *Orthographic versus phonemic processing of printed words.* Paper presented at the Meeting of the Psychonomic Society, Denver, CO.

Meyer, D. E., & Ruddy, M. G. (1973). *Lexical-memory retrieval based on graphemic and phonemic representations of printed words.* Paper presented at the Meeting of the Psychonomic Society, St. Louis, MO.

Meyer, D. E., & Ruddy, M. G. (1974). *Bilingual word-recognition: Organization and retrieval of alternative lexical codes.* Paper presented to the Eastern Psychological Association, Philadelphia.

Meyer, D. E., & Schvaneveldt, R. W. (1971). Facilitation in recognizing pairs of words: Evidence of a dependence between retrieval operations. *Journal of Experimental Psychology, 90,* 227–234.

Meyer, D. E., Schvaneveldt, R. W., & Ruddy, M. G. (1974). Functions of graphemic and phonemic codes in visual word-recognition. *Memory & Cognition, 2,* 309–321.

Meyer, D. M., Schvaneveldt, R. W., & Ruddy, M. G. (1975). Loci of contextual effects on visual word recognition. In P. M. A. Rabbitt & S. Dornic (Eds.), *Attention and performance V.* New York: Academic Press.

Michotte, A. (1963). *Perception of causality.* London: Methuen.
Mill, J. (1829/1967). *Analysis of the phenomena of the human mind* (2nd Ed.) New York: A. M. Kelley.
Mill, J. S. (1878). *Logic.* London: Longmans-Green.
Miller, G. A. (1956). The magical number seven, plus or minus two: Some limits on our capacity for processing information. *Psychological Review, 63,* 81–97.
Miller, G. A., & Johnson-Laird, P. N. (1976). *Language and perception.* Cambridge, MA: Harvard University Press.
Minsky, M. L. (1975). A framework for representing knowledge. In P. H. Winston (Ed.), *The psychology of computer vision.* New York: McGraw-Hill.
Minsky, M. L., & Papert, S. (1969). *Perceptrons.* Cambridge, MA: MIT Press.
Mish, F. C. (Ed.) (1984). *Webster's ninth new collegiate dictionary.* Springfield, MA: Merriam-Webster.
Montague, R. (1973). The proper treatment of quantification in ordinary English. In K. Hintikka, J. Jaakko, J. M. Moravcsik, & P. C. Suppes (Eds.), *Approaches to natural language: Proceedings of the 1970 Stanford Workshop on Grammar and Semantics.* Dordrecht: D. Reidel.
Morrow, D. G., Greenspan, S. L., & Bower, G. H. (1987). Accessibility and situational models in narrative comprehension. *Journal of Memory and Language, 26,* 165–187.
Morton, J. (1964). Interaction of information in word recognition. *Psychological Review, 76,* 165–178.
Morton, J. (1970). A functional model for memory. In D. A. Norman (Ed.), *Model for memory.* New York: Academic Press.
Morton, J., & Long, J. (1976). Effects of word transitional probability on phoneme identification. *Journal of Verbal Learning and Verbal Behavior, 15,* 43–52.
Morton, J., & Patterson, K. (1980). A new attempt at an interpretation, or an attempt at a new interpretation. In M. Coltheart, K. Patterson, & J. C. Marshall (Eds.), *Deep dyslexia.* London: Routledge & Kegan Paul.
Murphy, G. L. (in press). Comprehending complex concepts. *Cognitive Science.*
Murphy, G. L., & Brownell, H. H. (1985). Category differentiation in object recognition: Typicality constraints on the basic category advantage. *Journal of Experimental Psychology: Learning, Memory, and Cognition, 11,* 70–84.
Murphy, G. L., & Medin, D. L. (1985). The role of theories in conceptual coherence. *Psychological Review, 92,* 289–316.
Murphy, G. L., & Smith, E. E. (1982). Basic-level superiority in picture categorization. *Journal of Verbal Learning and Verbal Behavior, 21,* 1–20.
Nash, H. (1982). *How preschool children view mythological hybrid figures.* Washington, D.C.: University Press of America.
Neely, J. H. (1976). Semantic priming and retrieval from lexical memory: Evidence for facilitatory and inhibitory processes. *Memory & Cognition, 4,* 648–654.
Neely, J. H. (1977). Semantic priming and retrieval from semantic memory: Roles of inhibitionless spreading activation and limited-capacity attention. *Journal of Experimental Psychology: General, 106,* 227–234.
Neill, W. T. (1977). Inhibitory and facilitatory processes in attention. *Journal of Experimental Psychology: Human Perception and Performance, 3,* 444–450.
Neill, W. T. (1978). Decision processes in selective attention: Response priming in the Stroop color-word task. *Perception and Psychophysics, 23,* 80–84.

Neill, W. T. (1979). Switching attention within and between categories: Evidence for intra-category inhibition. *Memory & Cognition, 7,* 283–290.

Neill, W. T. (1982, March). *The suppression of distracting information in selective attention.* Paper presented at the Meeting of the Southeastern Psychological Association, New Orleans.

Neill, W. T. (1985). Levels of processing in disruptive effects of prior information. *Memory & Cognition, 13,* 477–484.

Neill, W. T. (1987). Selective attention and the suppression of cognitive noise. *Journal of Experimental Psychology: Learning, Memory, and Cognition, 13,* 327–334.

Neill, W. T., Hilliard, D. V., & Cooper, E. A. (1988). The detection of lexical ambiguity: Evidence for context-sensitive parallel access. *Journal of Memory and Language.*

Neill, W. T., & Lissner, L. S. (1988, April). *Attention and selective inhibition in alphanumeric character matching.* Paper presented at the Meeting of the Eastern Psychological Association, Buffalo, NY.

Neill, W. T., & Walling, J. R. (1981). Disruptive effects of prior information on tachistoscopic recognition. *Memory & Cognition, 9,* 217–224.

Neill, W. T., & Westberry, R. L. (1987). Selective attention and the suppression of cognitive noise. *Journal of Experimental Psychology: Learning, Memory, and Cognition, 13,* 327–334.

Neisser, U. (1976). *Cognition and reality.* San Francisco: Freeman.

Nelson, D. L., McEvoy, D. L., Walling, J. R., & Wheeler, J. W., Jr. (1980). The University of South Florida homograph norms. *Behavior Research Methods and Instrumentation, 12,* 16–37.

Nelson, K. (1974). Concept, word and sentence: Interrelations in acquisition and development. *Psychological Review, 81,* 267–285.

Nelson, K. (1978). Explorations in the development of a functional cognitive system. In W. Collins (Ed.), *Child psychology* (Vol. 12). Hillsdale, NJ: Erlbaum.

Nelson, K., Fivush, R., Hudson, J., & Lucariello, J. (1983). Scripts and the development of memory. In M. T. H. Chi (Ed.), *Contributions to human development: Trends in memory development research.* New York: Karger.

Nelson, K., & Gruendel, J. (1981). Generalized event representations: Basic building blocks of cognitive development. In M. E. Lamb & A. L. Brown (Eds.), *Advances in development psychology* (Vol. 1). Hillsdale, NJ: Erlbaum.

Newell, A. (1973). Production systems: Models of control structures. In W. G. Chase (Ed.), *Visual information processing* (pp. 463–526). New York: Academic Press.

Newman, J. E., & Dell, G. S. (1978). The phonological nature of phoneme monitoring: A critique of some ambiguity studies. *Journal of Verbal Learning and Verbal Behavior, 17,* 359–374.

Nickerson, R. S. (1986). *Using computers: The human factors of information systems.* Cambridge, MA: MIT Press.

Norman, D. A. (1968). Toward a theory of memory and attention. *Psychological Review, 75,* 522–536.

Norman, D. A. (1986). Reflections on cognition and parallel distributed processing. In J. L. McClelland, D. E. Rumelhart, & the PDP Research Group, *Parallel distributed processing. Vol. 2: Psychological and biological models.* Cambridge, MA: MIT Press.

Norman, D. A., & Bobrow, D. G. (1975). On Data-limited processes. *Cognitive Psychology, 7,* 44–64.

Nosofsky, R. M. (1984). Choice, similarity, and the context theory of classification. *Journal of Experimental Psychology: Learning, Memory, and Cognition, 10,* 104–114.

Nosofsky, R. M. (1986). Attention, similarity, and the identification-categorization relationship. *Journal of Experimental Psychology: General, 115,* 39–57.

Oakhill, J. V. (1982). Constructive processes in skilled and less skilled comprehenders' memory for sentences. *British Journal of Psychology, 73,* 13–20.

Oden, G. C. (1987). Concept, knowledge, thought. *Annual Review of Psychology, 38,* 203–227.

Oden, J. N., & Spira, J. L. (1983). Influence of context on the activation and selection of ambiguous word senses. *Quarterly Journal of Experimental Psychology, 35A,* 51–64.

O'Keefe, J., & Nadel, L. (1978). *The hippocampus as a cognitive map.* Oxford: Oxford University Press.

O'Keefe, J., & Nadel, L. (1979). The hippocampus as a cognitive map. *Behavioral and Brain Sciences, 2,* 487–533.

Olson, D. L., McEvoy, C. L., Walling, J. R., & Wheeler, J. W., Jr. (1980). The University of South Florida homograph norms. *Behavior Research Methods and Instrumentation, 12,* 16–37.

Olson, G. M., Duffy, S. A., & Mack, R. L. (1984). Thinking-out-loud as a method for studying real-time comprehension processes. In D. E. Kieras & M. Just (Eds.), *New methods in the study of immediate processes in comprehension.* Hillsdale, NJ: Erlbaum.

Onifer, W., & Swinney, D. A. (1981). Accessing lexical ambiguities during sentence comprehension: Effects of frequency of meaning and contextual bias. *Memory & Cognition, 9,* 225–236.

O'Seaghdha, P. G. (in press). The dependence of lexical relatedness effects on syntactic connectedness. *Journal of Experimental Psychology: Learning, Memory, and Cognition.*

Palmer, S. E. (1977). Hierarchical structure in perceptual representation. *Cognitive Psychology, 9,* 441–474.

Palmer, S. E. (1983). The psychology of perceptual organization: A transformational approach. In J. Beck, B. Hope, & A. Rosenfeld (Eds.), *Human and machine vision.* New York: Academic Press.

Panman, O. (1982). Homonymy and polysemy. *Lingua, 58,* 105–136.

Parker, P. (1982). The metaphorical plot. In D. Miall (Ed.), *Metaphor: Problems and perspectives* (pp. 138–158). Brighton, England: Harvester Press.

Partridge, E. (1966). *Origins: A short etymological dictionary of modern English.* New York: Macmillan.

Patterson, K. E., & Marcel, A. J. (1977). Aphasia, dyslexia and the phonological coding of written words. *Quarterly Journal of Experimental Psychology, 29,* 307–318.

Penfield, W., & Roberts, L. (1959). *Speech and brain mechanisms.* Princeton, NJ: Princeton University Press.

Perfetti, C. A., & Goodman, D. (1970). Semantic constraint on the decoding of ambiguous words. *Journal of Experimental Psychology, 86,* 420–427.

Perfetti, C. A., Lindsay, R., & Garson, B. (1971). *Association and uncertainty:*

Norms of association to ambiguous words (Learning Research & Development Center Tech. Ref. No. 17). Pittsburgh, PA: University of Pittsburgh.

Peterson, R. R. (1986). *The effects of backward priming on word recognition in single-word and sentence contexts.* Unpublished dissertation, University of Nebraska.

Peterson, R. R., & Simpson, G. B. (1987, April). The effect of backward priming on word recognition in single-word and sentence contexts. Paper presented at the Meeting of the Eastern Psychological Association, Washington, D.C.

Phillips, W. A. (1988). Brainy minds: A critical notice of *Parallel Distributed Processing. Quarterly Journal of Experimental Psychology, 40a,* 389–405.

Plato (1985). *The Republic.* New York: Norton.

Pompa, L. (Ed.), (1982). *Vico, selected writings.* Cambridge: Cambridge University Press.

Posner, M. I. (1969). Abstraction and the process of recognition. In G. H. Bower & J. T. Spence (Eds.), *Psychology of learning and motivation* (Vol. 3, pp. 43–100). New York: Academic Press.

Posner, M. I. (1978). *Chronometric explorations of mind.* Hillsdale, NJ: Erlbaum.

Posner, M. I. (1982). Cumulative development of attention theory. *American Psychologist, 37,* 168–179.

Posner, M. I., & Snyder, C. R. R. (1975a). Attention and cognitive control. In R. L. Solso (Ed.), *Information processing and cognition: The Loyola symposium,* Hillsdale, NJ: Erlbaum.

Posner, M. I., & Snyder, C. R. R. (1975b). Facilitation and inhibition in the processing of signals. In P. M. A. Rabbitt & S. Dornic (Eds.), *Attention and performance V,* 669–682.

Posner, M. I., Snyder, C. R. R., & Davidson, B. J. (1980). Attention and the detection of signals. *Journal of Experimental Psychology: General, 109,* 160–174.

Postman, L., & Keppel, G. (Eds.) (1970). *Norms of word association.* New York: Academic Press.

Potter, M. C., So, K-F, Von Eckardt, B., & Feldman, L. B. (1984). Lexical and conceptual representation in beginning and proficient bilinguals. *Journal of Verbal Learning and Verbal Behavior, 23,* 23–38.

Prather, P., Schmidt, M., & Marakovitz, S. (1988). *Time course of lexical access in school aged children.* Manuscript. Boston: V.A. Medical Center.

Prather, P., & Swinney, D. (1988). Lexical processing and ambiguity resolution: An autonomous process in an interactive box. In S. L. Small, G. W. Cottrell, & M. K. Tanenhaus (Eds.), *Lexical ambiguity resolution in the comprehension of human language.* Los Altos, CA: Morgan-Kaufmann.

Pribram, K. (1981). The brain, the telephone, the thermostat, the computer, and the hologram. *Cognition and Brain Theory, 4,* 105–119.

Putnam, H. (1977). Meaning and reference. In S. P. Schwartz (Ed.), *Naming, necessity, and natural kinds.* Ithaca, NY: Cornell University Press.

Quillian, M. R. (1962). A revised design for an understanding machine. *Mechanical translation, 7,* (1), 17–29.

Quillian, M. R. (1967). Word concepts: A theory and simulation of some basic semantic capabilities. *Behavioral Science, 12,* 410–430.

Quillian, M. R. (1968). Semantic memory. In M. L. Minsky (Ed.), *Semantic information processing* (pp. 227–270). Cambridge, MA: MIT Press.

Quillian, M. R. (1969). The teachable language comprehender: A simulation program and theory of language. *Communications of the ACM, 12,* 459–476.

Rasmussen, J. (1986). *Information processing and human-machine interaction: An approach to cognitive engineering.* New York: North-Holland.

Ratcliff, R., Hockley, W., & McKoon, G. (1985). Components of activation: Repetition and priming effects in lexical decision and recognition. *Journal of Experimental Psychology: General, 114,* 435–450.

Ratcliff, R., & McKoon, G. (1988). A retrieval theory of priming in memory. *Psychological Review, 95,* 385–408.

Reder, L. M. (1983). What kind of pitcher can a catcher fill? Effects of priming in sentence comprehension. *Journal of Verbal Learning and Verbal Behavior, 22*(2), 189–202.

Reicher, G. M. (1969). Perceptual recognition as a function of meaningfulness of stimulus material. *Journal of Experimental Psychology, 81,* 275–280.

Reiger, C. J., III (1975). Conceptual memory and inferences. In R. C. Schank (Ed.), *Conceptual information processing.* Amsterdam: North-Holland.

Reiser, B. J., & Black, J. B. (1982). Processing and structural models of comprehension. *Text, 2,* 225–252.

Rescorla, R. A., & Wagner, A. R. (1972). A theory of Pavlovian conditioning: Variations in the effectiveness of reinforcement and non-reinforcement. In A. H. Black & W. F. Prokasy (Eds.), *Classical conditioning II: Current research and theory.* New York: Appleton-Century-Crofts.

Rifkin, A. (1985). Evidence for a basic level in event taxonomies. *Memory & Cognition, 13,* 538–556.

Rips, L. J. (1988). Similarity, typicality, and categorization. In S. Vosniadou & A. Ortony (Eds.), *Similarity and analogical reasoning.* New York: Cambridge University Press.

Robinson, E. S. (1937). *Association theory today.* New York: Century.

Roediger, H. L. (1980). Memory metaphors in cognitive psychology. *Memory & Cognition, 8,* 231–246.

Roediger, H. L., & Blaxton, T. A. (1987). Retrieval modes produce dissociations in memory for surface information. In D. S. Gorfein & R. R. Hoffman (Eds.), *Memory and learning: The Ebbinghaus Centennial Conference.* Hillsdale, NJ: Erlbaum.

Roediger, H. L., & Neely, J. H. (1982). Retrieval blocks in episodic and semantic memory. *Canadian Journal of Psychology, 36,* 213–243.

Roediger, H. L., Neely, J. H., & Blaxton, T. A. (1983). Inhibition from related primes in semantic memory retrieval: A reappraisal of Brown's (1979) paradigm. *Journal of Experimental Psychology: Learning, Memory, and Cognition, 9,* 478–485.

Rosch, E. H. (1973). On the internal structure of perceptual and semantic categories. In T. M. Moore (Ed.), *Cognitive development and acquisition of language.* New York: Academic Press.

Rosch, E. H. (1978). Principles of categorization. In E. H. Rosch & B. B. Lloyd (Eds.), *Cognition and categorization.* Hillsdale, NJ: Erlbaum.

Rosch, E. H., & Mervis, C. B. (1975). Family resemblances: Studies in the internal structure of categories. *Cognitive Psychology, 7,* 573–605.

Rosch, E. H., Mervis, C. B., Gray, W. D., Johnson, D. M., & Boyes-Braem, P. (1976). Basic objects in natural categories. *Cognitive Psychology, 8,* 382–439.

Roth, E. M., & Shoben, E. J. (1983). The effect of context on the structure of categories. *Cognitive Psychology, 15,* 346–378.

Rubenstein, H., Garfield, L., & Millikan, J. A. (1970). Homographic entries in the internal lexicon. *Journal of Verbal Learning and Verbal Behavior, 9,* 487–494.

Rubenstein, H., Lewis, S. S., & Rubenstein, M. A. (1971). Evidence for phonemic recoding in visual word recognition. *Journal of Verbal Learning and Verbal Behavior, 10,* 645–657.

Rueckel, J. G., & Oden, G. C. (1986). The integration of contextual and featural information during word identification. *Journal of Memory and Language, 25,* 445–460.

Rumelhart, D. E., Hinton, G. E., & Williams, R. L. (1986). Learning internal representations by error propagation. In D. E. Rumelhart, J. L. McClelland, & the PDP Research Group, *Parallel distributed processing. Vol. I: Foundations.* Cambridge, MA: MIT Press.

Rumelhart, D. E., & McClelland, J. L. (1982). An interaction, activation model of context effects in letter perception: Part 2. *Psychological Review, 89,* 60–94.

Rumelhart, D. E., & McClelland, J. L., & the PDP Research Group (1986). *Parallel distributed processing: Explorations in the microstructure of cognition. Vol 1: Foundations.* Cambridge, MA: MIT Press.

Rumelhart, D. E., & Ortony, A. (1978). The representation of knowledge in memory. In R. C. Anderson, R. J. Spiro, & W. E. Montague (Eds.), *Schooling and the acquisition of knowledge.* Hillsdale, NJ: Erlbaum.

Savin, H. B. (1973). Meaning and concepts: A review of Jerrold & Katz's *Semantic Theory. Cognition, 2,* 213–128.

Scarborough, D. L., Cortese, C., & Scarborough, H. (1977). Frequency and repetition effects in lexical memory. *Journal of Experimental Psychology: Human Perception and Performance, 3,* 1–17.

Schachter, D. L. (1987). Implicit memory: History and current status. *Journal of Experimental Psychology: Learning, Memory, and Cognition, 12,* 432–444.

Schank, R. C. (Ed.) (1975). *Conceptual information processing.* Amsterdam: North-Holland.

Schank, R. C. (1982). *Dynamic memory: A theory of reminding and learning in computers and people.* New York: Cambridge University Press.

Schank, R. C., & Abelson, R. P. (1977). *Scipts, goals, plans, and understanding: An inquiry into human knowledge structures.* Hillsdale, NJ: Erlbaum.

Schank, R. C., Collins, G. C., & Hunter, L. E. (1986). Transcending inductive category formation in learning. *The Behavioral and Brain Sciences, 9,* 639–651.

Schmidt, R. A. (1975). A schema theory of discrete motor skill learning. *Psychological Review, 82,* 225–260.

Schmitt, C. B., & Skinner, Q. (Eds.) (1988). *The Cambridge history of renaissance philosophy.* Cambridge: University Press.

Schneider, W. (1987). Connectionism: Is it a paradigm shift for psychology? *Behavior Research Methods, Instruments, and Computers, 19,* 73–83.

Schneider, W., & Detweiler, M. (1987). A connectionist/control architecture for working memory. In G. H. Bower (Ed.), *The psychology of learning and motivation.* New York: Academic Press.

Schneider, W., & Shiffrin, R. M. (1977). Controlled and automatic human information processing. I. Detection, search and attention. *Psychological Review, 84,* 1–66.

Schubert, L. K. (1987, July). On parsing preferences. *Proceedings of Coling 84:*

10th International Conference on Computational Linguistics (pp. 247–250). Stanford, CA.

Schuberth, R. E., & Eimas, P. D. (1977). Effects of context in the classification of words and nonwords. *Journal of Experimental Psychology: Human Perception and Performance, 3,* 27–36.

Schuberth, R. E., Spoehr, K. T., & Lane, D. M. (1981). Effects of stimulus and contextual information on the lexical decision process. *Memory and Language, 9,* 68–77.

Schvaneveldt, R. W., & Meyer, D. E. (1973). Retrieval and comparison processes in semantic memory. In S. Kornblum (Ed.), *Attention and performance IV* (pp. 395–409). New York: Academic Press.

Schvaneveldt, R. W., Meyer, D. E., & Becker, C. A. (1976). Lexical ambiguity, semantic context and visual word recognition. *Journal of Experimental Psychology: Human Perception and Performance, 2,* 243–256.

Schwanenflugel, P. J., & LaCount, K. L. (1988). Semantic relatedness and the scope of facilitation for upcoming words in sentences. *Journal of Experimental Psychology: Learning, Memory, and Cognition, 14,* 344–354.

Schwanenflugel, P. J., & Shoben, E. J. (1985). The influence of sentence constraints on the scope of facilitation for upcoming words. *Journal of Memory and Language, 24,* 232–252.

Schwantes, F. M., Boesl, S. L., & Ritz, E. G. (1980). Children's use of context in word recognition: A psycholinguistic guessing game. *Child Development, 51,* 730–736.

Schwartz, S. P. (1979). Natural kind terms. *Cognition, 7,* 301–315.

Searle, J. (1972). Chomsky's revolution in linguistics. *The New York Review,* 16–24.

Seidenberg, M. S. (1985). The time course of information activation and utilization in visual word recognition. In D. Besner, T. Waller, & G. MacKinnon (Eds.), *Reading research: Advances in theory and practice* (Vol. 5). New York: Academic Press.

Seidenberg, M. S., & Tanenhaus, M. K. (1979). Orthographic effects on rhyme monitoring. *Journal of Experimental Psychology: Human Learning and Memory, 5,* 546–554.

Seidenberg, M. S., & Tanenhaus, M. K. (1986). Modularity and lexical access. In I. Gopnik (Ed.), *McGill studies in cognitive science.* Norwood, NJ: Ablex.

Seidenberg, M. S., Tanenhaus, M. K., Leiman, J. M., & Bienkowski, M. (1982). Automatic access of the meanings of ambiguous words in context: Some limitations of knowledge-based processing. *Cognitive Psychology, 14,* 489–537.

Seidenberg, M. S., Waters, G. S., Sanders, M., & Langer, P. (1984). Pre- and postlexical loci of contextual effects on word recognition. *Memory & Cognition, 12,* 315–328.

Shallice, T., & Warrington, E. K. (1975). Word recognition in a phonemic dyslexic patient. *Quarterly Journal of Experimental Psychology, 27,* 187–199.

Sharkey, N. E., & Sharkey, A. J. C. (1987). What is the point of integration? The loci of knowledge-based facilitation in sentence processing. *Journal of Memory and Language, 26,* 255–276.

Shiffrin, R. M., & Schneider, W. (1977). Controlled and automatic information processing. II. Perceptual learning, automatic attending, and a general theory. *Psychological Review, 84,* 127–190.

Shipley, E. F. (1988, June). *Two types of hierarchies: Class inclusion hierarchies and kind hierarchies.* Paper presented at the Annual Meeting of the Jean Piaget Society, Philadelphia.

Shoben, E. J. (1982). Semantic and lexical decision. In C. R. Puff (Ed.), *Handbook of research methods in human memory and cognition* (pp. 287–314). New York: Academic Press.

Shultz, T. R., & Pilon, R. (1973). Development of the ability to detect linguistic ambiguity. *Child Development, 44,* 728–733.

Sidner, C. L. (1979). *Towards a computational theory of definite anaphora comprehension in English discourse.* Doctoral dissertation, Department of Electrical Engineering and Computer Science, Massachusetts Institute of Technology. Published as Tech. Rep. 537, Artificial Intelligence Laboratory, Massachusetts Institute of Technology.

Simpson, G. B. (1981). Meaning dominance and semantic context in the processing of lexical ambiguity. *Journal of Verbal Learning and Verbal Behavior, 20,* 120–136.

Simpson, G. B. (1984). Lexical ambiguity and its role in models of word recognition. *Psychological Bulletin, 96,* 316–340.

Simpson, G. B., & Burgess, C. (1985). Activation and selection processes in the recognition of ambiguous words. *Journal of Experimental Psychology: Human Perception and Performance, 11,* 28–39.

Simpson, G. B., & Burgess, C. (1988). Implications of lexical ambiguity resolution for word recognition and comprehension. In S. L. Small, G. W. Cottrell, & M. K. Tanenhaus (Eds.), *Lexical ambiguity resolution in the comprehension of human language.* Los Altos, CA: Morgan Kaufmann.

Simpson, G. B., Burgess, C., & Peterson, R. R. (1988). Human comprehension processes and the indeterminacy of meaning. *Cognitive Systems, 2,* 213–232.

Simpson, G. B., & Foster, M. R. (1986). Lexical ambiguity and children's word recognition. *Developmental Psychology, 22,* 147–154.

Simpson, G. B., & Lorsbach, T. C. (1983). The development of automatic and conscious components of contextual facilitation. *Child Development, 54,* 760–772.

Simpson, G. B., Peterson, R. R., Casteel, M. A., & Burgess, C. (1989). Lexical and sentence context effects in word recognition. *Journal of Experimental Psychology: Learning, Memory, and Cognition, 15,* 88–97.

Slamecka, N. J. (1987). The law of frequency in D. S. Gorfein & R. R. Hoffman (Eds.), *Memory and learning: The Ebbinghaus Centennial Conference.* Hillsdale, NJ: Erlbaum.

Small, S. L. (1980). *Word expert parsing: A theory of distributed word-based natural language understanding.* Doctoral dissertation (published as Tech. Rep. 954), Department of Computer Science, University of Maryland.

Smith, A. (1966). Speech and other functions after left (dominant) hemispherectomy. *Journal of Neurology, Neurosurgery, and Psychiatry, 29,* 467–471.

Smith, A., & Burkland, C. W. (1966). Dominant hemispherectomy. *Science, 153,* 467–471.

Smith, E. E., Haviland, S. E., Reder, L. M., Brownell, H., & Adams, N. (1976). When preparation fails: Disruptive effects of prior information on perceptual recognition. *Journal of Experimental Psychology: Human Perception and Performance, 2,* 151–161.

Smith, E. E., & Medin, D. L. (1981). *Categories and concepts.* Cambridge, MA: Harvard University Press.

Smith, E. E., & Osherson, D. N. (1984). Conceptual combination with prototype concepts. *Cognitive Science, 8,* 337–362.

Smith, E. E., Osherson, D. N., Rips, L. J., & Keene, M. (in press). Combining prototypes: A selective modification model. *Cognitive Sciences.*

Smith, M. C., Theodor, L., & Franklin, P. E. (1983). The relationship between contextual facilitation and depth of processing. *Journal of Experimental Psychology: Learning, Memory, and Cognition, 9,* 697–712.

Somers, H. L. (1987). *Valency and case in computational linguistics* (Edinburgh information technology series 3). Edinburgh University Press.

Sommers, F. (1959). The ordinary language tree. *Mind, 68,* 160–185.

Sommers, F. (1963). Types and ontology. *Philosophical Review,* U72U, 327–363.

Spearman, C. E. (1904). General intelligence objectively determined and measured. *American Journal of Psychology, 15,* 201–293.

Spelke, E. S. (1982). Perceptual knowledge of objects in infancy. In J. Mehler, M. Garret, & E. Walker, *Perspectives on mental representation.* Hillsdale, NJ: Erlbaum.

Sperber, R. D., McCauley, C., Ragain, R. D., & Weil, C. (1979). Semantic priming effects on picture and word processing. *Memory & Cognition, 7,* 339–345.

Stanovich, K. E., & West, R. F. (1979). Mechanisms of sentence context effects in reading: Automatic activation and conscious attention. *Memory & Cognition, 7,* 77–85.

Stanovich, K. E., & West, R. F. (1981). The effect of sentence context on ongoing word recognition: Tests of a two-processes theory. *Journal of Experimental Psychology: Human Perception and Performance, 7,* 658–672.

Stanovich, K. E., & West, R. F. (1983). On priming by a sentence context. *Journal of Experimental Psychology: General, 112,* 1–36.

Stanovich, K. E., West, R. F., & Feeman, D. J. (1981). A longitudinal study of sentence context effects in second-grade children: Tests of an interactive-compensatory model. *Journal of Experimental Child Psychology, 32,* 185–199.

Stefik, M. (1981). Planning with constraints (MOLGEN: Part 1). *Artificial Intelligence, 16,* 111–140.

Sternberg, R. J., & Smith, E. E. (1988). *The psychology of human thought.* New York: Cambridge University Press.

Sternberg, R. J., Tourangeau, R., & Nigro, G. (1979). Metaphor, induction, and social policy. In A. Ortony (Ed.), *Metaphor and thought* (pp. 325–355). Cambridge: Cambridge University Press.

Stowe, L. A. (1988). Thematic structures and sentence comprehension. In G. N. Carlson & M. K. Tanenhaus (Eds.), *Linguistic structure in language processing.* Dordrecht: D. Reidel.

Stroop, J. R. (1935). Studies of interference in serial verbal reactions. *Journal of Experimental Psychology, 18,* 643–662.

Swinney, D. A. (1979). Lexical access during sentence comprehension: (Re)consideration of context effects. *Journal of Verbal Learning and Verbal Behavior, 18,* 645–659.

Swinney, D. A. (1984). Theoretical and methodological issues in cognitive science: A psycholinguistic perspective. In W. Kintsch, J. R. Miller, & P. G. Polson (Eds.), *Method and tactics in cognitive science* (pp. 217–233). Hillsdale, NJ: Erlbaum.

Swinney, D. A., & Hakes, D. T. (1976). Effects of prior context upon lexical access during sentence comprehension. *Journal of Verbal Learning and Verbal Behavior, 15,* 681–689.

Swinney, D. A., Onifer, W., Prather, P., & Hirshkowitz, M. (1979). Semantic facilitation across sensory modalities in the processing of individual words and sentences. *Memory & Cognition, 7,* 159–165.

Swinney, D. A., Zurif, E., & Nicol, J. (1989). The effects of focal brain damage on sentence processing: An examination of the neurological organization of a mental module. *Journal of Cognitive Neuropsychology, 1,* 25–37.

Tabossi, P. (1982). Sentential context and the interpretation of unambiguous words. *Quarterly Journal of Experimental Psychology, 34A,* 79–90.

Tabossi, P. (1987). *Context type determines whether lexical access is exhaustive or selective.* Paper presented at the Annual Meeting of the Psychonomic Society, Seattle, WA.

Tabossi, P. (1988a). Accessing lexical ambiguity in different types of sentential context. *Journal of Memory and Language, 27,* 324–340.

Tabossi, P. (1988b). Effects of context on the immediate interpretation of unambiguous nouns. *Journal of Experimental Psychology: Learning, Memory, and Cognition, 14,* 153–162.

Tabossi, P., Colombo, L., & Job, R. (1987). Accessing lexical ambiguity: Effects of context and dominance. *Psychological Research, 49,* 161–167.

Tabossi, P., & Johnson-Laird, P. N. (1980). Linguistic context and the priming of semantic information. *Quarterly Journal of Experimental Psychology, 32,* 595–603.

Tanenhaus, M. K., Burgess, C., D'Zmura, S. H., & Carlson, G. N. (1987). Thematic roles in language processing. *Proceedings of the 9th Annual Conference of the Cognitive Science Society* (pp. 587–596). Seattle, WA. Hillsdale, NJ: Erlbaum.

Tanenhaus, M. K., & Carlson, G. N. (1989). Lexical structure and language comprehension. In W. D. Marslen-Wilson (Ed.), *Lexical representation and process.* Cambridge, MA: MIT Press.

Tanenhaus, M. K., Dell, G. S., & Carlson, G. (1987). Context effects in lexical processing. A connectionist perspective on modularity. In J. Garfield (Ed.), *Modularity in knowledge representation and natural language understanding.* Cambridge, MA: MIT Press.

Tanenhaus, M. K., & Donnenwerth-Nolan, S. (1984). Syntactic context and lexical access. *Quarterly Journal of Experimental Psychology, 36,* 649–661.

Tanenhaus, M. K., Leiman, J. M., & Seidenberg, M. S. (1979). Evidence for multiple stages in the processing of ambiguous words in syntactic contexts. *Journal of Verbal Learning and Verbal Behavior, 18,* 427–440.

Taylor, B. H., & Rosenberg, R. S. (1975). A case-driven parser for natural language. *American Journal of Computational Linguistics* (4), microfiche 31.

Thibadeau, R., Just, M. A., & Carpenter, P. A. (1982). A model of the time course and content of reading. *Cognitive Science, 6,* 157–203.

Thompson, D. M., & Tulving, E. (1970). Associative encoding and retrieval: Weak and strong cues. *Journal of Experimental Psychology, 86,* 255–262.

Thorndike, E. L. (1898). Animal intelligence, an experimental study of the associative processes in animals. *Psychological Review.* Monograph Supplements, II, 4.

Thorndike, E. L., & Lorge, I. (1933). *The teacher's word book of 30,000 words.* New York: Bureau of Publications, Columbia University, Teachers College.

Thorp, G. R. (1986). *The categorization of natural and nominal kind terms.* Unpublished doctoral dissertation, Monash University.

Tipper, S. P. (1985). The negative priming effect: Inhibitory priming by ignored objects. *Quarterly Journal of Experimental Psychology, 37A,* 571–590.

Tipper, S. P., & Cranston, M. (1985). Selective attention and priming: Inhibitory and facilitatory effects of ignored primes. *Quarterly Journal of Experimental Psychology, 37A,* 591–611.

Tipper, S. P., & Driver, J. (1988). Negative priming between pictures and words in a selective attention task: Evidence for the semantic processing of ignored stimuli. *Memory & Cognition, 16,* 64–70.

Tipper, S. P., MacQueen, G. M., & Brehaut, J. C. (1988). Negative priming between response modalities: Evidence for the central locus of inhibition in selective attention. *Perception and Psychophysics, 43,* 45–52.

Titchener, E. B. (1915). *A beginner's psychology.* New York: Macmillan.

Trabasso, T., & Bower, G. H. (1968). *Attention in learning.* New York: Wiley.

Treisman, A. M. (1964). The effect of irrelevant material on the efficiency of selective attention. *American Journal of Psychology, 77,* 533–546.

Treisman, A., & Gelade, G. (1980). A feature-integration theory of attention. *Cognitive Psychology, 12,* 97–136.

Treisman, A., & Schmidt, H. (1982). Illusory conjunctions in the perception of objects. *Cognitive Psychology, 14,* 107–141.

Tulving, E. (1983). *Elements of episodic memory.* New York: Oxford University Press.

Tulving, E., Schacter, D. L., & Stark, H. S. (1982). Priming effects in word-fragment completion are independent of recognition memory. *Journal of Experimental Psychology: Learning, Memory, and Cognition, 8,* 336–342.

Tulving, E., & Thompson, D. M. (1973). Encoding specificity and retrieval processes in episodic memory. *Psychological Review, 80,* 353–373.

Turvey, M. T. (1973). On peripheral and central processes in vision: Inferences from an information-processing analysis of masking with patterned stimuli. *Psychological Review, 80,* 1–52.

Turvey, M. T., & Carello, C. (1981). Cognition: The view from ecological realism. *Cognition, 10,* 313–321.

Turvey, M. T., Shaw, R. E., Reed, E. S., & Mace, W. M. (1981). Ecological laws of perceiving and acting: In reply to Fodor & Pylyshyn (1981). *Cognition, 9,* 237–304.

Tversky, B., & Hemenway, K. (1983). Categories of environmental scenes. *Cognitive Psychology, 15,* 121–149.

Tversky, B., & Hemenway, K. (1985). Objects, parts, and categories. *Journal of Experimental Psychology: General, 113,* 169–193.

Tyler, L. K., & Wessels, J. (1983). Quantifying contextual contributions to word recognition processes. *Perception and Psychophysics, 34,* 409–420.

Ullman, S. (1980). Against direct perception. *The Behavioral and Brain Sciences, 3,* 373–415.

Underwood, G. (1980). Attention and the non-selective access of ambiguous words. *Canadian Journal of Psychology, 34,* 72–76.

Vanderwart, M. (1984). Priming by pictures in lexical decision. *Journal of Verbal Learning and Verbal Behavior, 23,* 67–83.

Van Petten, C., & Kutas, M. (1987). Ambiguous words in context: An event-related potential analysis of the time course of meaning activation. *Journal of Memory and Language, 26,* 188–208.

Vico, G. B. (1725/1970). *New Science* (T. G. Bergen & M. H. Fisch, Trans.). Ithaca, NY: Cornell University Press.

Wada, J. A., Clark, R., & Hamm, A. (1975). Cerebral hemispheric asymmetry in humans. *Archives of Neurology, 32,* 239–246.

Walls, W. F., & Siple, P. (1987). *Similarity effects on semantic activation by pictures and words.* Paper presented at the Annual Meeting of the Psychonomic Society, Seattle, WA.

Walters, M. F. (1988). *The priority effect in implicit memory.* Unpublished doctoral dissertation, Adelphi University, Garden City, NY.

Waltz, D. L., & Pollack, J. B. (1985). Massively parallel parsing: A strongly interactive model of natural language comprehension. *Cognitive Science, 9,* 51–74.

Wankoff, L., & Cairns, H. (1987). *Sentential ambiguity detection and its relation to conservation skill.* Paper presented at the Conference on Language of the Young Child: Frontiers of Research. Brooklyn College, CUNY, New York.

Wanner, E. (1980). The ATN and the Sausage Machine: Which one is baloney? *Cognition, 8,* 209–225.

Warren, R. E. (1972). Stimulus encoding and memory. *Journal of Experimental Psychology, 94,* 90–100.

Warren, R. E., & Warren, N. T. (1976). Dual semantic encoding of homographs and homophones embedded in context. *Memory & Cognition, 4,* 586–592.

Watkins, M. J., & Peynircioglu, Z. F. (1983). On the nature of word recall: Evidence for linguistic specificity. *Journal of Verbal Learning and Verbal Behavior, 22,* 385–394.

Wattenmaker, W. D., Dewey, G. I., Murphy, T. D., & Medin, D. L. (1986). Linear separability and concept learning: Context, relational properties, and concept naturalness. *Cognitive Psychology, 18,* 158–194.

Wellman, H. M., & Gelman, S. A. (1988). Children's understanding of the nonobvious. In R. J. Sternberg (Ed.), *Advances in the Psychology of Human Intelligence* (Vol. 4). Hillsdale, NJ: Erlbaum. 99–135.

West, R. F., & Stanovich, K. E. (1982). Source of inhibition in experiments on the effect of sentence context on word recognition. *Journal of Experimental Psychology: Learning, Memory, and Cognition, 8,* 385–399.

Westberry, R. L. (1983). *The nature of attentional control as a personality dimension.* Unpublished doctoral dissertation, University of South Florida, Tampa.

Westberry, R. L. (1984). The nature of attentional control as a personality dimension (doctoral dissertation, University of South Florida, 1983). *Dissertation Abstracts International, 45,* 1034B.

Whitlow, J. W., Jr., Smith, E. E., & Medin, D. L. (1982). Retrieval of correlated predicates. *Journal of Verbal Learning and Verbal Behavior, 21,* 381–402.

Whitney, P. (1986). Processing category terms in context: Instantiations as inferences. *Memory & Cognition, 14,* 39–48.

Whitney, P. (1987). Psychological theories of elaborative inferences: Implications for schema-theoretic views of comprehension. *Reading Research Quarterly, 22,* 299–310.

Whitney, P., & Kellas, G. (1984). Processing category terms in context: Instantiation and the structure of semantic categories. *Journal of Experimental Psychology: Learning, Memory, and Cognition, 10,* 95–103.

Whitney, P., McKay, T., Kellas, G., & Emerson, W. A., Jr. (1985). Semantic activation of noun concepts in context. *Journal of Experimental Psychology: Learning, Memory, and Cognition, 11,* 126–135.

Whitney, P., McKay, T., Kellas, G., & Emerson, W. A., Jr. (1985). Semantic activation of noun concepts in context. *Journal of Experimental Psychology: Learning, Memory, and Cognition, 11,* 126–135.

Whitney, P., & Williams-Whitney, D. L. (in press). Psycholinguistics at work in the information age. In P. Whitney & R. B. Ochsman (Eds.), *Psychology and productivity.* New York: Plenum Press.

Whitney, P., Williams-Whitney, D. L., & Hewitt, M. (in press). Toward a contextualist view of elaborative inferences. In A. C. Graesser & G. H. Bower (Eds.), *The psychology of learning and motivation.* New York: Academic Press.

Wilkins, A. J. (1971). Conjoint frequency, category size, and categorization time. *Journal of Verbal Learning and Verbal Behavior, 10,* 382–385.

Wilks, Y. A. (1973). Preference semantics. In E. L. Keenan, III (Ed.), *Formal semantics of natural language.* New York: Cambridge University Press, 329–348.

Winston, M. E., Chafin, R., & Herrmann, D. (1987). A taxonomy of part-whole relations. *Cognitive Science, 11,* 417–444.

Wong, D. (1981). *On the unification of language comprehension with problem solving.* Doctoral dissertation, Department of Computer Science, Brown University, Providence, RI.

Woods, W. A. (1975). What's in a link: Foundations for semantic networks. In D. G. Bobrow & A. Collins (Eds.), *Representation and understanding.* New York: Academic Press.

Woods, W. A. (1979). *Semantics for a question-answering system.* A volume in the series Outstanding Dissertations in the Computer Sciences. New York: Garland Publishing.

Woods, W. A. (1968). Procedural semantics for a question-answering machine. *AFIPS Conference Proceedings, 33* (Fall joint computer conference), 457–471.

Woods, W. A., Kaplan, R. M., & Nash-Webber, B. L. (1972, June). The Lunar Sciences Natural Language Information System: Final report (Report 2378). Cambridge, MA: Bolt, Beranek and Newman.

Woodworth, R. S. (1938). *Experimental psychology.* New York: Henry Holt.

Yates, J. (1985). The content of awareness is a model of the world. *Psychological Review, 92,* 249–284.

Zeaman, D., & House, B. J. (1963). The role of attention in retardate discrimination learning. In N. R. Ellis (Ed.), *Handbook of mental deficiency.* New York: McGraw-Hill.

Author Index

Subject Index